T0203349

Formal Methods Applied to Industrial Complex Systems

Dedicated to Mr Paul Caspi

Series Editor
Jean-Charles Pomerol

Formal Methods Applied to Industrial Complex Systems

Edited by

Jean-Louis Boulanger

WILEY

First published 2014 in Great Britain and the United States by ISTE Ltd and John Wiley & Sons, Inc.

ISTE Ltd
27-37 St George's Road
London SW19 4EU
UK

www.iste.co.uk

John Wiley & Sons, Inc.
111 River Street
Hoboken, NJ 07030
USA

www.wiley.com

Library of Congress Control Number: 2014936487

British Library Cataloguing-in-Publication Data
A CIP record for this book is available from the British Library
ISBN 978-1-84821-632-7

Printed and bound in Great Britain by CPI Group (UK) Ltd., Croydon, Surrey CR0 4YY

Contents

Introduction

I.1. Context

Although formal program analysis techniques have a long history (including work by Hoare [HOA 69] and Dijkstra [DIJ 75]), formal methods were only established in the 1980s. These techniques are used to analyze the behavior of software applications written using a programming language. The correctness of a program (correct behavior, program completion, etc.) is then demonstrated using a program proof based on the calculation of the weakest precondition [DIJ 76].

The formal method (Z [SPI 89], VDM [JON 90] and the B method [ABR 96, ARA 97]) for industrial applications and their suitability for use in industrial contexts dates back to the late 1990s. Formal specifications use mathematical notations to give a precise description of system requirements.

NOTE 1.– Z – A Z specification is made up of schematic diagrams and of sets used to specify a computer system. A specification is a set of schematic diagrams.

NOTE 2.– The Vienna development method (VDM) is a formal method based on a denotational and operational vision (programs are seen as mathematical functions), unlike Z or the B method, which are based on axiomatic set theory.

Introduction written by Jean-Louis BOULANGER.

One stumbling block is the possibility of implementation within the context of industrial applications (on a large scale, with cost and time constraints, etc.); this implementation requires tools to have attained a sufficient level of maturity and performance.

Note that for critical applications, at least two formal methods make use of recognized and widely available design environments covering part of the code specification process while implementing one or more verification processes: the B method [ABR 96], the LUSTRE language ([HAL 91, ARA 97]) and its graphic version SCADE[1] [DOR 08]. The B method and the SCADE environment have been used successfully in industrial tools.

To give an example, Atelier B, marketed and sold by CLEARSY[2], is a tool that covers the entire development cycle involved in the B method (specification, refining, code generation and proof). Note that Atelier B[3] has been freely downloadable since version 4.0.

Formal methods are based on a variety of formal verification techniques such as proof, model checking [BAI 08] and/or simulation.

Formal methods are now becoming increasingly widely used, but are still relatively marginal when viewed in terms of the number of lines of code involved. To date, far more lines of ADA ([ANS 83]), C ([ISO 99]) and C++ code have been produced manually than through the use of a formal process.

For this reason, other formal techniques have been implemented in order to verify the behavior of software applications written in languages such as C and ADA. The main technique, abstract program interpretation, is used to evaluate all the behaviors of a software application by static analysis. In

---

1 The SCADE development environment is marketed by ESTEREL-Technologies – see http://www.esterel-technologies.com/.

2 For more information on CLEARSY and Atelier B, see http://www.clearsy.com/.

3 Atelier B and the associated information may be obtained at http://www.atelierb.eu/.

recent years, this type of technique has been applied to a number of tools, including POLYSPACE[4], Caveat[5], Absint[6], FramaC[7] and ASTREE[8].

The effectiveness of these static program analysis techniques has been greatly improved with increases in the processing power of personal computers. Note that these techniques generally require the insertion of additional information, such as preconditions, invariants and/or postconditions, into the manual code.

SPARK Ada[9] is an approach in which the ADA language [ANS 83] has been extended [BAR 03] to include these additional tools and a suite of tailored tools has been created.

I.2. Aims of this book

[BOW 95] and [ARA 97] provided the first feedback from industrial actors concerning the use of formal techniques, notably the B method [ABR 96], the LUSTRE language [HAL 91, ARA 97] and SAO+, the precursor of SCADE[10] [DOR 08]. Other works, including [MON 00, MON 02] and [HAD 06], give an overview of formal methods from a more academic perspective.

Our aim in this book is to present real-world examples of the use of formal techniques in an industrial context.

For our purposes, the phrase "formal techniques" is taken to mean the different mathematically based approaches used to demonstrate that a software application respects a certain number of properties.

---

4 See http://www.mathworks.com/products/polyspace/ for further information concerning Polyspace.

5 See http://www-list.cea.fr/labos/fr/LSL/caveat/index.html for further information concerning Caveat.

6 See http://www.absint.com/ for further information concerning Absint.

7 Further details may be found at http://frama-c.com/.

8 See http://www.astree.ens.fr/ for further information concerning ASTREE.

9 http://www.altran-praxis.com/spark.aspx offers additional information concerning SPARK Ada technology.

10 Note that SCADE started out as a development environment using the LUSTRE language, before becoming a language in its own right from version 6 onwards (the code generator for version 6 uses a SCADE model instead of LUSTRE code as input).

Note that the standard use of formal techniques consists of producing specification and/or design models, but that formal techniques are increasingly seen as tools for verification (static code analysis, to demonstrate that properties are respected, to demonstrate good management of floating points, etc.).

This book is the fourth volume in a series covering different aspects:

– *Static Analysis of Software* [BOU 11] concerns examples of the industrial implementation of formal techniques based on static analysis, such as abstract interpretation, and includes examples of the use of ASTREE, CAVEAT, CODEPEER, FramaC and POLSYPACE.

– *Formal Methods: Industrial Use from Model to the Code* [BOU 12b] presents different formal modeling techniques used in the field of rail transport, such as the B method, SCADE, Simulink DV, GaTel and Control Build and other techniques.

– *Industrial Use of Formal Method, Formal Verification* [BOU 12a] presents different tools used in formal verification: SPARK ADA, MaTeLo, AltaRica, Polyspace, Escher and B-event.

– This volume gives examples of the industrial implementation of the B method [ABR 96], SCADE and verification using Prover Verifier. Note that this volume (which presents examples of application using the B method) constitutes a useful addition to university textbooks such as [LAN 96], [WOR 96] and [SCH 01].

I wish to thank all the industrial actors who have freely given their time to contribute such interesting and informative chapters for this book.

I.3. Bibliography

[ABR 96] ABRIAL J.R., *The B Book: Assigning Programs to Meanings*, Cambridge University Press, Cambridge, August 1996.

[ANS 83] ANSI, Norme ANSI/MIL-STD-1815A-1983, Langage de programmation Ada, 1983.

[ARA 97] ARAGO, "Applications des méthodes formelles au logiciel", *Observatoire Français des Techniques Avancées (OFTA)*, vol. 20, Masson, June 1997.

[BAI 08] BAIER C., KATOEN J.-P., *Principles of Model Checking*, MIT Press, 2008.

[BAR 03] BARNES J., *High Integrity Software: The SPARK Approach to Safety and Security*, Addison-Wesley, 2003.

[BOU 11] BOULANGER J.-L. (ed.), *Static Analysis of Software*, ISTE, London, & John Wiley & Sons, New York, 2011.

[BOU 12a] BOULANGER J.-L. (ed.), *Industrial Use of Formal Method, Formal Verification*, ISTE, London, & John Wiley & Sons, New York, 2012.

[BOU 12b] BOULANGER J.-L. (ed.), *Formal Methods: Industrial Use from Model to the Code*, ISTE, London, & John Wiley & Sons, New York, 2012.

[BOW 95] BOWEN J.P., HINCHEY M.G., *Applications of Formal Methods*, Prentice Hall, 1995.

[COU 00] COUSOT P., "Interprétation abstraite", *Technique et Science Informatique*, vol. 19, nos. 1–3, pp. 155–164, January 2000.

[DIJ 75] DIJKSTRA E.W., "Guarded commands, nondeterminacy and formal derivation of programs", *Communications of the ACM*, vol. 18 no. 8, pp. 453–457, August 1975.

[DIJ 76] DIJKSTRA E.W., *A Discipline of Programming*, Prentice Hall, 1976.

[DOR 08] DORMOY F.-X., "Scade 6 a model based solution for safety critical software development", *Embedded Real-Time Systems Conference*, 2008.

[HAD 06] HADDAD S., KORDON F., PETRUCCI L., (eds.), *Méthodes formelles pour les systèmes répartis et coopératifs*, Hermes, 2006.

[HAL 91] HALBWACHS N., CASPI P., RAYMOND P., *et al.*, "The synchronous dataflow programming language Lustre", *Proceedings of the IEEE*, vol. 79, no. 9, pp. 1305–1320, September 1991.

[HOA 69] HOARE C.A.R., "An axiomatic basis for computer programming", *Communications of the ACM*, vol. 12, no. 10, pp. 576–580, 583, 1969.

[ISO 99] ISO. ISO C standard 1999, Technical report, 1999. Available at http://www.open-std.org/jtc1/sc22/wg14/www/docs/n1124.pdf.

[JON 90] JONES C.B., *Systematic Software Development Using VDM*, 2nd ed., Prentice Hall International, 1990.

[LAN 96] LANO K., *The B Language and Method: A Guide to Practical Formal Development*, Springer Verlag London Ltd., 1996.

[MON 00] MONIN J.-F., *Introduction aux méthodes formelles*, Hermès, 2000.

[MON 02] MONIN J.-F., *Understanding Formal Methods*, HINCHEY M. (Trans. ed.), Springer Verlag, 2002.

[SCH 01] SCHNEIDER S., *The B-Method: An Introduction*, Palgrave, 2001.

[SPI 89] SPIVEY J.M., *The Z Notation: A Reference Manual*, Prentice Hall International, 1989.

[WOR 96] WORDSWORTH J., *Software Engineering with B*, Addison-Wesley, 1996.

Formal Description and Modeling of Risks

1.1. Introduction

Formal methods are currently used to design software aspects of systems. The "internal model verification" aspect of these methods is based on the hypothesis that the model contains requirements that must be respected by the program. To obtain a useful set of requirements, we recommend establishing a connection between risk analysis, specifications and formal models. This approach allows us to define one or more formal models for use at a system level. As we will see, the proposed system model combines risks, software and hardware requirements and usage procedures.

This approach requires us to modify certain practices. Risk analysis generally takes place during the system development cycle and during the development of associated application software. The system design processes include a feasibility analysis stage, where designers define the characteristics of the environment and identify the associated risks. In this chapter, we will show that system risk analysis can be carried out using a formal model. This formal model can be used as a reference point, as a tool to support reflection and as a tool for analyzing the impact of changes. Our aim in this book is to provide an approach for the formalization and monitoring of risks, taking account of the requirements of system components (software and hardware). The proposed methodology is based on the use of the formal method known as the "B method" [ABR 96].

Chapter written by Jean-Louis BOULANGER.

This methodology conforms to the requirements set out in the European Committee for Electrotechnical Standardization (CENELEC[1]) reference document for application to rail transport systems. This document consists of three standards: EN 50126 [CEN 99], EN 50129 [CEN 03] and EN 50128 [CEN 01, CEN 11]. These three standards recommend the implementation of a process based on the notion of requirements, with consideration given to operational safety throughout the whole system design cycle.

This chapter is divided into four sections. First, we will present the standard safety procedures used for rail transport systems. Then, we will establish a methodological context. Next, we will present a case study, analyzing the risk of collision between two trains. Finally, we will present a formal model and analysis. We will conclude by considering the methodology and its implementation.

1.2. Standard process

1.2.1. *Risks, undesirable events and accidents*

In the context of rail transport systems, we wish to avoid accidents. An accident (see definition 1.1) is a situation that may be associated with different types of damage (individual or collective).

DEFINITION 1.1.– (ACCIDENT – EN 50129).– *An accident is an unexpected event or a sequence of events leading to death, injury, loss of a system or service, or damage to the environment.*

With terrestrial transports, as indicated in [BAR 90], accidents may be categorized into different classes:

– *System-initiated accidents*: the users of the system are in a passive position and are victims of the damage, which can be attributed to failures on the part of the staff (maintenance, intervention, operation, etc.), to failures internal to the system or to anomalous circumstances in the environment.

– *User-initiated accidents*: this category refers to events surrounding one or several users (malaise, panic, suicide, etc.).

---

1 See http://www.cenelec.eu/Cenelec/Homepage.htm.

– Accidents initiated by a system–user interaction: as opposed to the previous category, in this case the user is active and interacts with the system. Incorrect use of the system lies at the root of this type of accident (e.g. non-compliance with the audio signal for door closure).

In aiming to avoid accidents, we must take account of the possibility of these accidents occurring when creating a system. The definition given above highlights the notion of an event, which may be refined by considering the notion of undesirable events (see definition 1.2).

DEFINITION 1.2.– (UNDESIRABLE EVENT).– *An undesirable event is an event that must be avoided, or that must have a very weak probability of occurring.*

We can distinguish between two types of damage: individual damage and collective damage.

A user-initiated accident is likely to provoke damage to individuals, whereas the remaining two categories can cause damage either to individuals or collectivities. Once the category is identified, the level of severity of the accident[2] can be determined: insignificant (minor), marginal (significant), critical and catastrophic.

In [HAD 98], which applies exclusively to the context of rail transport, the authors proposed an accident typology connecting categories of accidents, potential accidents, damage types, severity levels, types of danger and dangerous elements. This typology allows us to establish links between dangerous elements, such as a lightning strike, and system accidents, such as a train collision.

The "accident" situation is definitive; the concept of potential accidents is therefore a useful one. The notion of a potential accident refers to a known situation which may lead us to an accident.

For rail transport systems, the list of potential accidents (see definition 1.3) includes derailment, passengers falling, collision, dragging or trapping individual victims, electrocution, fire, explosions, flooding, etc.

---

2 We have chosen to focus on the rail transport domain [CEN 99]; however, we have indicated alternative terms in brackets whenever they are used in other sectors.

DEFINITION 1.3.– (POTENTIAL ACCIDENT).– *A potential accident is an unexpected event or a series of events that may lead to an accident following the occurrence of an additional event which is not mastered by the system.*

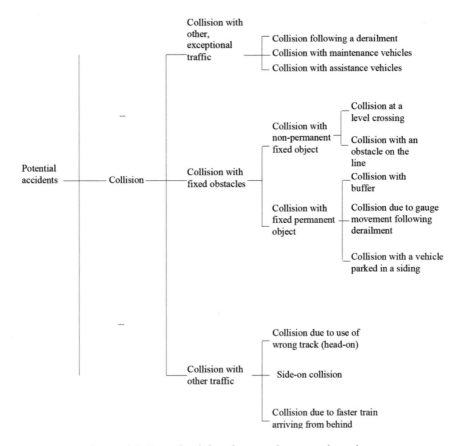

Figure 1.1. *Example of classification of a potential accident*

Figure 1.1 is taken from [HAB 95]. It shows an example of the classification of a potential accident, in this case a collision. The potential accident situation is linked to the notion of danger (see definition 1.4).

DEFINITION 1.4.– (DANGER – EN 50126).– *A danger is a condition which may give rise to a potential accident.*

A danger (see definition 1.4) is therefore a *dangerous situation*, the consequences of which may be damaging to human life (injury or death), to society (loss of production, financial loss, damage to image, etc.) or to the environment (damage to the natural and animal world, pollution, etc.). The terms "danger" and "threat" are used on the basis of whether the origin is random or voluntary (deterministic). The term "threat" is therefore used in the context of safety and/or security/confidentiality activities.

Dangers may be grouped into three categories: dangers created by the system or its equipment, dangers created by human activity (operator errors, maintenance errors, passenger actions, etc.) and dangers linked to unusual environmental circumstances (earthquakes, wind, fog, heat, humidity, etc.).

For a given system, dangerous situations are identified through systematic analysis, which consists of two complementary phases:

– an empirical phase, based on feedback (existing lists, accident analysis, etc.);

– a creative and/or predictive phase that may be based on brainstorming, forecasting studies, etc.

The notion of danger (dangerous situations) is directly linked to the notion of fault.

Figure 1.2 shows the pathway leading from an undesirable event to an accident. Note that the potential accident will only occur with the right operational context. For example, if a driver fails to follow a red light when moving onto a different line, the risk of an accident is much lower if this line is a small one with little traffic than if the train is joining a main line with high traffic levels. The passage from an undesirable event to a dangerous situation is linked to the technical context in a similar way.

Figure 1.3 shows the full sequence of events from a cause to a potential accident (see [BLA 08], for example, for further details). The notion of causes is used to bring in different types of faults which may affect the system, such as faults concerning one or more functions (a function may be associated with multiple parts of the internal equipment), equipment faults, human error or external factors (electromagnetic compatibility (EMC), etc.).

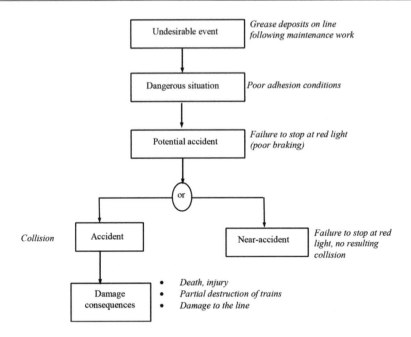

Figure 1.2. *Chain of events leading to an accident*

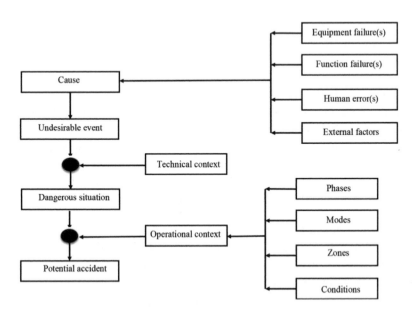

Figure 1.3. *Chain of events leading to a potential accident*

Figure 1.4 shows the combinatorics involved in a potential accident. Analysts must then identify representative scenarios (cause/undesirable event/dangerous situation/potential accident).

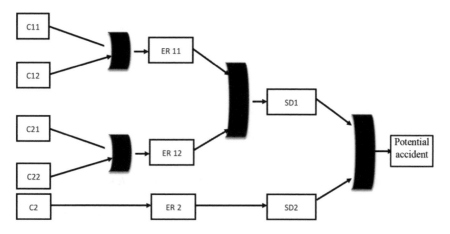

Figure 1.4. *Combinatorics of events leading up to a potential accident*

1.2.2. *Usual process*

In safety applications, safety demonstration [AUC 96] relies on two kinds of activities:

– Risk analysis is performed at the system specification level. Undesirable events are identified by safety engineers and the risk analysis checks that system specifications are robust enough to prevent these events from occurring. A system safety framework is used to describe the activities to be performed throughout the system lifecycle.

– Testing activities: dedicated system engineers specify a "safety oriented" testing strategy, and a specific team is responsible for the implementation of testing tasks.

Once the system-level specifications and basic implementation concepts are validated by risk analysts, development is organized as for any other project. The safety testing strategy is destructive; discontinuity occurs in the safety activity process, meaning that safety objectives cannot be easily traced. It is also difficult to test for completeness [BOU 97b] and to test system completion mechanisms.

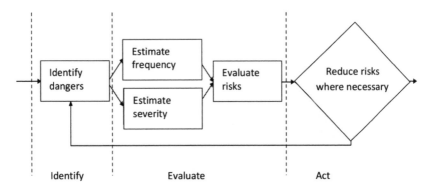

Figure 1.5. *Safety management*

1.2.3. *Formal software processes for safety-critical systems*

Using the software lifecycle shown in Figure 1.6, formal methods allow us to integrate validation and verification activities into the design and development process. Refinement and proof activities contribute to design and development steps. Consequently, safety properties become traceable if they have been included in the formal model. The "missing link" in this type of approach is located between system and risk analysis and formal modeling. There is no traceability between safety objectives at the system level and properties which are proved during the software lifecycle. This means that there is no traceability between proven properties and the safety testing strategy.

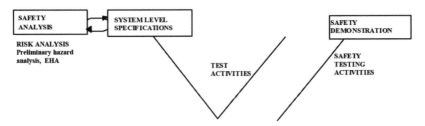

Figure 1.6. *Classic lifecycle*

In system modeling, a distinction is traditionally made between safety and liveness properties. A safety property stipulates that specific "bad things" will not happen during execution, while liveness properties stipulate that certain "good things" will (eventually) happen.

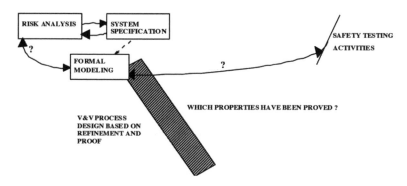

Figure 1.7. *Software formal process for safety critical system*

1.2.4. *Formal methods for safety-critical systems*

"A system may be proved if and only if it has been designed to be proved". In our opinion, formal methods (whether model checking methods or rewriting-based methods) are efficient for, and applicable to, large safety-critical systems if the system design makes the system provable [RUS 93]. The objective of this study is to define a system design process, including the demonstration that safety properties have been achieved. It is a constructive approach based on the safety kernel concept [RUS 89].

1.2.5. *Safety kernel*

In the field of safety, a safety kernel (see Figure 1.8) is a set of components, whose *correction properties* ensure that *safety properties* for the whole system are verified. In this section, we will demonstrate the applicability of this approach to safety-critical systems. Kernel-based architectures are characterized by a set of second-order properties: $\forall \; \alpha \in op^*$, $P(\alpha)$. Such properties state that whatever operations or events (op*) occur from the kernel environment, the system's properties will be verified.

This type of approach involves two main design features:

– The safety properties of the system must be formalized in terms of kernel functions and related correction properties.

– No assumption is made for the system components, which are not within the kernel.

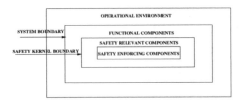

Figure 1.8. *Safety kernel*

1.3. Methodology

1.3.1. *Presentation*

In the context of our work, we wish to define a risk mastery process, which allows us to design a safe system rather than demonstrating the safety of a system at the end of the development process. In [BOU 97a], we presented the issues surrounding development based on the notion of properties. In this section, we will show how risk analysis may be integrated into the system (or subsystem) design phase.

The abstract system model must show and take account of all properties derived from risks. This abstract model is the starting point of the design process. The description of objects then becomes increasingly precise, design choices are made and the abstract model is refined or broken down in order to define an implementation. Different steps are validated by demonstrating that properties have been respected and by verifying the conservation of behavior of intermediate models.

1.3.2. *Risk mastery process*

Following an initial, informal requirement specification stage, which aims to give an understanding of the formal specification (specification of general principles of the rail transport system, expression of risks to cover and preliminary risk analysis, informal listing of general safety principles), our proposed risk-elimination procedure consists of five distinct steps:

1) Formalization of the evaluation target (as specified in ITSEC[3] [DEL 96] and [ITS 91, ITS 93]).

---

3 ITSEC: information technology security evaluation criteria. More information is available at www.itsec.org.

This involves the creation of a formal specification of the command system environment, the failure modes to consider and the safety objectives (formalization of risk coverage), with the aim of providing a precise, formal definition of the scope of the study.

2) Formal definition of the abstract command system and demonstration of risk coverage.

The abstract system is defined by the functions it fulfills and the properties of these functions that constitute safety principles. It should therefore be possible to demonstrate that these principles are sufficient to "fence in" the risk.

3) Projection of the abstract system onto subsystems and equipment. Introduction of the formal definition of the safety kernel of the command system.

This phase involves the specification of the system architecture, which is then used to refine the properties of the abstract command system as set out in step 2. Our definition of the notion of a safety kernel is set out in [RUS 89], as the set of material and software components which are required in order to cover risks and which, in terms of safety properties, are insensitive to normal or abnormal changes to the rest of the command system.

4) Demonstration of the properties of the safety kernel.

We must show that the safety properties of the kernel are invariant to all operations outside of the kernel (including the failure of elements outside the kernel, within the limits specified in point 1) and demonstrate that the properties of the kernel are sufficient to guarantee the properties of the abstract system.

5) Risk elimination.

In this step, we must show that the implementation of the kernel satisfies our safety properties. This activity involves a certain number of checks and requires us to provide a number of justifications over the course of the production cycle. Figure 1.8 shows possible errors for each stage in the development process along with the means of identifying anomalies.

The aim of this approach is to force system designers to clearly set out design principles which are essential for safety, to minimize the system subset which requires formal validation and, finally, to produce a traceable proof tree in which the "leaves" are closed by:

– validation of materials, either in terms of intrinsic safety or probabilities;

– analyzing the physical implementation (track plans, physical installation);

– properties of the usage principles of the system;

– proof or safety validation of programs.

In this context, we will limit our consideration to phases 1, 2 and 3.

Activity	Error/risk	Coverage
Identification of root properties	Edge errors Incomplete mission analysis Poor description of risks	Analysis of the requirement acquisition process Feedback analysis Preliminary risk analysis
Allocation of properties to subsystems and identification of the properties of interfaces between subsystems	Property incompleteness Incoherency between properties	Implementation of traceability Proof of root properties
Development of subsystems and validation with regard to properties	Design faults made during the development process	Risk analysis of the development process Proof of formal models Testing of non-formal components
Interfaces between formal/ non-formal components	Incoherency between interfaces (e.g. interfacing between generic program and data) Incompleteness of services	SEEA[4] Constraint identification Constraint testing
Generation of executable elements: – code generation – compilation – linkage	Code does not conform to the application Poor formal/non-formal integration Poor integration between generic program and data	Risk analysis of the code generation process. Certification/qualification of tools Test of correct operation
Executable elements	Analysis of installation procedures	Dynamic verification of the checksum of the executable element

Table 1.1. *Connections between activities and risks*

---

4 SEEA: software error effect analysis. The SEEA is a software analysis methodology based on failure modes, effects and criticality analysis (FMECA), where we examine the effect of an error on each entry in a piece of code. This approach is widely used in the domain of rail transport for critical software applications.

1.4. Case study

This section corresponds to phase 1. We will define the perimeters of the study by establishing environmental characteristics and a list of risks.

1.4.1. *Rail transport system*

The whole ground transportation system in its environment is composed of the following subsystems:

– *Rolling stock*: this subsystem performs functions according to dynamics and kinematics, and according to commands set by the control/monitoring system.

– *Control and communications*: this is divided into two functional subsystems: one is devoted to operations control (train description, communication with operators, etc.) and the other one is automatic train pilot (ATP). ATP is divided into ground ATP and on-board ATP. Finally, the ground functions of ATP are distributed across the topology, while the on-board functions are replicated on trains.

– *Vital signaling*: this subsystem monitors trackside equipment such as points, train detectors, track circuits and wayside signals. It interacts with ATP for route setting: routes are defined at ATP level and are set by the signaling system.

– *Civil engineering*: this subsystem defines the physical implantation of trackside equipment, the topology (distances, slopes, etc.) etc. It interacts with ATP subsystems through parameters known as "topological parameters".

1.4.2. *Presentation*

We will use an example to illustrate the proposed methodology, considering train collision problems. As we see in [CLE 01], trains represent a particularly safe mode of transport, and collision is the main type of accident which may arise. The movement of trains along a line must respect rules established in order to guarantee safe circulation. The risks associated with moving trains include collision, derailment and travel risks (access to dangerous zones, etc.).

The risk of collision may be classified into several types:

– collision from behind (with a rail transport vehicle);

– head-on collision (with a rail transport vehicle);

– side-on collision;

– collision with an object or another type of vehicle.

The analysis of different collision types is outside the scope of this book; in the following sections, we will focus on side-on collisions.

1.4.3. Description of the environment

A railway line (Figure 1.9) is made up of several tracks. Trains use tracks to move from one point to another. A track is made up of several track circuits (TCs). A track circuit is a physically defined portion of track, which detects the presence of trains by "shunting[5]".

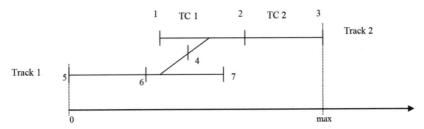

Figure 1.9. *Example of topology*

A basic track circuit (a branch) has the following characteristics:

– beginning and end;

– state (shunted, non-shunted);

– previous track circuit and next track circuit.

A single abscissa reference point is defined by deconstructing the line. Each position (track object or train) is characterized by a pair (track number

---

5 The track circuit has a power supply. When two wheels of the same axle of a train are in the zone delimited by the track circuit, a short circuit occurs, and the train is said to be shunting the track circuit. The main function of the track circuit is to detect shunting.

and abscissa). Passages from one track to another are carried out using switches. As we see in Figure 1.10, a switch is a three-branch track circuit, made up of a fixed component and a mobile component (the point). A point has three logical states: uncontrolled (operational fault detected), a straight position or a divergent position.

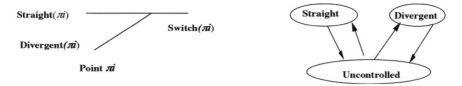

Figure 1.10. *Static and dynamic definitions of a switch*

A switch can therefore be seen as a track circuit, and has the following characteristics:

– Track circuit characteristics:

- point abscissa, divergent abscissa and direct abscissa,

- track circuit following point, TC following direct, TC following divergent;

- state: shunted and non-shunted.

– Switch characteristics,

- type: right and left,

- state: direct, divergent and uncontrolled.

We may define a certain number of operators which aim to manipulate the characteristics of a point.

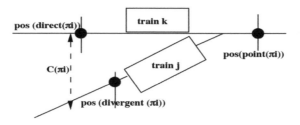

Figure 1.11. *Side-on collision*

1.4.4. *Definition of side-on collision*

The movement of trains on a switch creates a risk of side-on collision. This type of collision is due to the fact that a train moving on the switch may "catch" a stationary train in the point zone (see Figure 1.11). Figure 1.12 gives an example of a formalization of the side-on collision risk. This formalization takes account of time and the position of the two trains.

$$\forall\, t \in \text{TIME}, \forall\, k, j \in \text{Train},$$

$$\text{Side\_collision } (k,j,t) \Leftrightarrow$$

$$\exists\, \pi i \in \text{POINTS},$$

$$\text{pos\_2\_cdv(directe } (\pi i)) = \text{cdv\_support } (k,t)$$
$$\wedge \quad \text{pos\_2\_cdv(déviée } (\pi i)) = \text{cdv\_support } (j,t)$$
$$\wedge \quad \text{pos (directe } (\pi i)) \le a(k,t) \le \text{pos (pointe}(\pi i))$$
$$\wedge \quad \text{pos (déviée } (\pi i)) \le a(j,t) \le \text{pos (pointe}(\pi i))$$
$$\wedge \quad |\, a(k,t) - a(j,t)\,| \le C(\pi i) \qquad \text{(TRACK GAUGE)}$$

Figure 1.12. *Property associated with side-on collision*

This formalization is constructed using a number of position operators:

– The operator "pos_2_tc" gives us the support track circuit of a coordinate.

– The operator "tc_support" gives us the support track circuit of a train.

– "pos" gives us the abscissa of a coordinate.

– "a" is an operator giving the abscissa of a train.

Train spacing in manual drive mode is regulated by the implementation of lateral signaling. These signals have two characteristics:

– a position (track, abscissa);

– a state: permissive or restrictive.

Signals are associated with routes. Routes represent pathways that are accessible to trains, and are characterized by:

– start and end positions;

– an entry signal;

– a list of switches located on the pathway and their expected positions (divergent, direct);

– information characterizing the fact that the route is accessible, which corresponds to the state of lights and the position of points located on the pathway.

1.4.5. *Risk analysis*

We may analyze the risk of side-on collision using a fault tree analysis. Fault tree analysis is used to identify the causes of potential problems with a product, process or service. This analytical tool is generally used for reliability predictions or in analyzing design performance. Fault tree creation is a graphical methodology that enables systematic description of the impact of faults, which may occur during the lifetime of a system (see [IEC 90] for further details). This method takes account of both "material" faults (hardware) and human error. This technique gives us an overview of potential problems and their relationships, while requiring a detailed analysis permitting active intervention during the design phase. Figure 1.13 shows a reduced and simplified version of the fault tree associated with the risk of side-on collision.

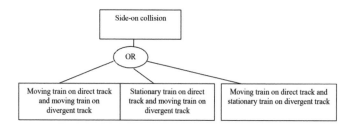

Figure 1.13. *Fault tree*

Figure 1.13 shows two types of cases of side-on collision: either both trains are moving or one of the trains may be stationary. For cases where both trains are moving (Figure 1.14), we may identify physical faults (absence of signals, faulty display or physical non-detection of the train), a behavioral fault (the driver does not respect the signal) and a control/command system failure.

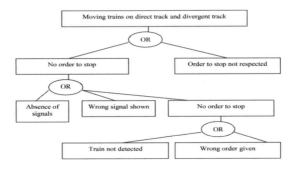

Figure 1.14. *Fault tree for the case of two moving trains*

Side-on collisions in cases where only one of the trains is moving (Figure 1.15) result from the fact that the stationary train is outside the safe position (the crossing point). This may occur if there has been a delay in responding to a signal, or if track objects are not in the correct positions.

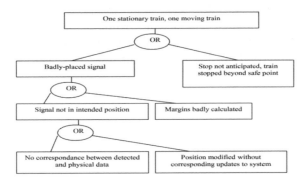

Figure 1.15. *Fault tree for the case of one moving and one stationary train*

1.5. Implementation

In this section, we will present the broad outlines of the B model and the connections between risk analysis and the proof of the model, corresponding to phase 2 of our proposed process.

1.5.1. *The B method*

The B method was developed by J.-R. Abrial [ABR 96]. It is a model-oriented formal model, such as Z [SPI 89] and VDM [JON 90], and allows incremental development from specification to coding using the notion of refining [MOR 90], using a single formalism, the abstract machine language. Proof obligations are generated at each stage of the B development in order to guarantee the validity of the refined version and the consistency of the abstract machine.

On reaching the final refinement (implementation), the level of modeling is sufficiently concrete to allow the use of a compatible automatic code generator (C, ADA and others). The B (sub-) language available at the implantation level is known as B0. The syntax and semantic restrictions placed on B0 allow the direct construction of the translator. The B method is currently used in the context of rail transport to develop safety software applications (for example, [DEH 94], [BEH 93] and [WAE 95]). Abrial has also proposed an extension known as "Event-B" [ABR 00, ABR 01], intended for use in analyzing system aspects.

1.5.2. *Implementation*

The initial component of our model represents the system aspect, and needs to include the basic functions and properties associated with the risks which must be covered. Subsystems, then components and their properties, are introduced iteratively by refinement and decomposition until we obtain the level of description introduced by the textual specification. The model must be traceable in relation to the textual specification, as presented in section 1.3, in terms of both functions and associated properties.

1.5.3. *Specification of the rail transport system and side-on collision*

The component *system_0* gives the initial behavior of the command control system of a rail transport system in the form of a safety property that must be demonstrated in order to cover the risks involved in this type of system. In this case study, the risk we wish to cover is the side-on collision risk, associated with switches, as shown by the property in Figure 1.13.

The implantation of the system takes the form of three subsystems:

– trains and their physical behaviors (wheel/rail interaction), via the machine *Physical_0*;

– signal control, via the machine *Vital_Signalling_System_0*;

– the train autopilot system via the machine *ATP_0* (TRACK, TRAIN).

The B model as a whole will not be presented in this chapter; instead, we will consider certain aspects of the formalization. Figure 1.16 shows a view of the associated structure of the B model.

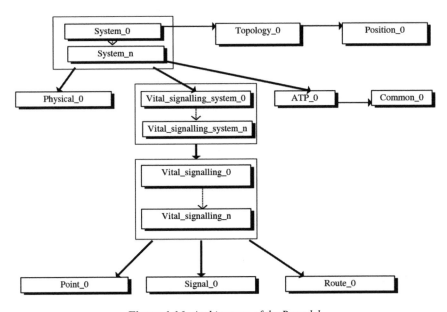

Figure 1.16. *Architecture of the B model*

A physical track is made up of track circuits, points and signals. The signals are related to routes which describe the authorized pathways that trains may take. These four object types are introduced as a set. The links between objects are described through mathematical functions which are used to describe properties. The set is located in the component "Topology_0".

$$
\begin{array}{llll}
& pos\_to\_track & \in POSITION & \to TRACK \\
\wedge & points\_gauge & \in POINTS & \to \text{NAT} \\
\wedge & track\_associate & \in POINTS & \to TRACK \\
\wedge & route\_def & \in ROUTE & \leftrightarrow TRACK \\
\wedge & route\_signal & \in ROUTE & \to SIGNAL \\
\wedge & f\_route & \in ROUTE & \to SIGNAL \times SIGNAL
\end{array}
$$

The fact that three signal lights are associated with each point is shown by the following properties:

$$\wedge \quad f\_point\_sig\_s \quad \in POINTS \quad \rightarrow SIGNAL$$
$$\wedge \quad f\_point\_sig\_n \quad \in POINTS \quad \rightarrow SIGNAL$$
$$\wedge \quad f\_point\_sig\_r \quad \in POINTS \quad \rightarrow SIGNAL$$

The set of track circuits may be seen as a graph, described by the variable "track_next", which has the following properties:

$$track\_next \quad \in TRACK <\!\!-\!\!> TRACK$$
$$\wedge \quad \forall track. \, (track \in TRACK) \Rightarrow (\text{card} \, (track\_next \, (track)) < 4) \quad //$$
maximum three connections.
$$\wedge \quad \forall track. \, (track \in TRACK) \Rightarrow (\text{card} \, (track\_next \, (track)) > 1) \quad //$$
minimum two connections.

The component "system_0" introduces essential properties of the system, notably properties associated with safety. The properties characterizing the physical behaviors of the system are also introduced at this point. The two properties below indicate that the track objects (points and track circuits) have intrinsic safety. The first property shows that points can only be controlled from one position. The second property shows that if a track circuit is free, then no train is present.

$$\forall \, po. \, (po \in POINTS) \quad \Rightarrow \neg \, (\, controlled\_normal \, (po) = TRUE \wedge$$
$$controlled\_reverse \, (po) = TRUE))$$
$$\wedge \quad \forall \, ta. \, (ta \in train) \quad \Rightarrow free\_track(pos\_to\_track(train\_pos(ta)))$$
$$= FALSE).$$

The property preventing side-on collision is included in the main machine "system_0" in the following form:

$$\wedge \quad \forall ta1. \, (ta1 \in train) \Rightarrow \forall ta2.(ta2 \in train) \Rightarrow \forall po.(po \in POINTS) \Rightarrow$$
$$\neg \, side\_collision\_ \, (ta2, ta1, po).$$

Figure 1.17. gives a simplified representation of the proof.

The B model introduces the physical properties needed to produce a proof, but these need to be validated using trade procedures (e.g. drivers must respect signals) and specific demonstrations (components such as signals and track circuits must possess intrinsic safety).

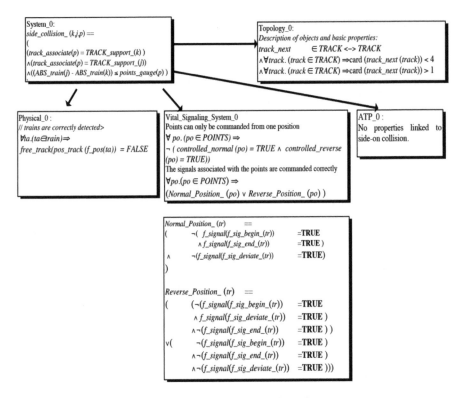

Figure 1.17. *Structure of proof*

1.6. Conclusion

In this chapter, we have shown how the implementation of safety analysis (using a fault tree or FMECA, for example) during system design allows us to increase trust levels. This approach is particularly recommended for "safety" applications.

The aim of the suggested approach is to compel system designers to specify the design principles (intrinsic safety, usage procedures, maintenance processes, etc.) required for system safety, to minimize the subset of the system requiring formal validation, and, finally, to produce a traceable proof procedure. The notion of safety kernels aims to limit the size of elements involved in safety and to highlight the faults that must be taken into account in the design process.

In this chapter, we have used the B method as a support language; other languages may be used, but it is essential to formalize and trace the principles used in order to facilitate the demonstration of system safety.

1.7. Glossary

ATC: automatic train control

ATP: automatic train protection

CENELEC: Comité Européen de Normalisation Electrotechnique (European Committee for Electrotechnical Standardization)

FMECA: failure modes, effects and criticality analysis

FTA: fault tree analysis

ITSEC: information technology security evaluation criteria

1.8. Bibliography

[ABR 96] ABRIAL J.-R., *The B Book: Assigning Programs to Meanings*, Cambridge University Press, August 1996.

[ABR 00] ABRIAL J.-R., Event driven circuit construction, MATISSE project, August 2000.

[ABR 01] ABRIAL J.-R. Event driven distributed program construction, MATISSE project, August 2001.

[AUC 96] AUCLAIR J.P., BARANOWSKI F., CASPI P., *et al.*, "Principes d'organisation pour la réalisation de logiciels critiques", AFCET, 1996.

[BAR 90] BARANOWSKI F., Définition des objectifs de sécurité dans les transports terrestres, Technical Report 133, INRETS-ESTAS, 1990.

[BEH 93] BEHM P., "Application d'une méthode formelle aux logiciels sécuritaires ferroviaires", *Ateliers Logiciel Temps Reel – 6èmes Journées Internationales du Génie Logiciel,* Part 5.1, 17–19 November 1993.

[BLA 08] BLAS A., BOULANGER J.-L., "Comment améliorer les méthodes d'analyse de risques et l'allocation des THR, SIL et autres objectifs de sécurité", *LambdaMu 16, 16ème Congrès de Maîtrise des Risques et de Sûreté de Fonctionnement*, Avignon, 6–10 October 2008.

[BOU 97a] BOULANGER J.-L., DELEBARRE V., NATKIN S., *et al.*, "Deriving safety properties of critical software from the system risk analysis, application to ground transportation systems", *HASE'97*, Maryland, MD, 11–12 August 1997.

[BOU 97b] BOULANGER J.-L., DELEBARRE V., NATKIN S., Validation des spécifications et génération de tests de sécurité s'appuyant sur un modèle formel d'un système de transport ferroviaire, CEDRIC Research Report No 97-17, December 1997.

[CEN 99] CENELEC, EN 50126., Railways application – the specification and demonstration of reliability, availability, maintainability and safety (RAMS), 1999.

[CEN 01] CENELEC, EN 50128., Railways application – communication, signaling and processing systems – software for railway control and protection systems, 2001.

[CEN 11] CENELEC, EN 50128., Railways application – communication, signaling and processing systems – software for railway control and protection systems, 2011.

[CEN 03] CENELEC, EN 50129., Railways application – safety related electronic systems for signaling, 2003.

[CLE 01] CLÉON L.-M., LECUSSAN R., "L'apport des études d'accidentologie", *Revue Générale des Chemins de fer*, pp. 17–22, February 2001.

[DEH 94] DEHBONEI B., MEJIA F., "Formal development of software in railways safety critical systems", in MURTHY B.T.K.S., MELLITT C., BREBBIA G., *et al.*, (eds.), *Railway Operations*, COMPRAIL '94, vol. 2, Computational Mechanics Publications, pp. 213–219, 1994.

[DEL 96] DELEBARRE V., NATKIN S., "Conception et évaluation de logiciels critiques: de la sécurité logique à la sécurité physique", *Congrès sur l'application des méthodes formelles*, ENSIMAG, Grenoble, January 1996.

[HAB 95] HABIB H.-M., "La maitrise des risques dans le domaine des automatismes des systèmes de transport guidés: le problème de l'évaluation des analyses préliminaires de risques", *Revue Recherche Transports Sécurité*, vol. 49, pp. 101–112, December 1995.

[HAD 98] HADJ-MABROUCK H., STUPARU A., BIED-CHARRETON D., "Exemple de typologie d'accidents dans le domaine des transports guides", *Revue Générale des Chemins de Fers*, 1998.

[IEC 90] INTERNATIONAL ELECTROTECHNICAL COMMISSION (IEC), Fault tree analysis (FTA), International standard IEC 61025, International Electrotechnical Commission, Geneva, Switzerland, 1990.

[ITS 91] ITSEC, Information technology security evaluation criteria, Technical report, June 1991.

[ITS 93] ITSEM, Information Technology Security Evaluation Manual, CEC Publication, September 1993.

[JON 90] JONES C.B., *Systematic Software Development Using VDM*, 2nd ed., Prentice Hall International, 1990.

[MOR 90] MORGAN C., *Deriving Programs from Specifications*, Prentice Hall International, 1990.

[RUS 89] RUSHBY J., "Kernel for safety", *Safe and Secure Computing Systems*, Blackwell Scientific Publications, London, 1989.

[RUS 93] RUSHBY J., Formal methods and the certification of critical systems, SRI Research report, November 1993.

[SPI 89] SPIVEY J.M., *The Z Notation: A Reference Manual*, Prentice Hall International, 1989.

[WAE 95] WAESELYNCK H., BOULANGER J.-L., "The role of testing in the B formal development process", *ISSRE 95*, Toulouse, October 1995.

An Innovative Approach and an Adventure in Rail Safety

2.1. Introduction

In the context of a project with high stakes for success and limited room for maneuver, the decision to use formal proof to demonstrate the safety of critical software may seem daring. This choice was made possible by the presence of teams with a strong belief in this technique at each stage of the development process and their intuition, drive and will to succeed were essential to the success of the project.

When compared with testing methods, formal proof requires skill sets which are harder to find; the tools involved use highly precise algorithms, and the method as a whole is more difficult to master. When used well, however, this approach produces significant gains, both in economic terms and with regards to the safety assurances given by the results.

Formal proof limits the number of iterations in software development, as programs are consolidated early in the development cycle. Furthermore, it results in higher trust levels than those obtained by testing when demonstrating system safety, through exhaustive exploration of the satisfaction of safety requirements by system behaviors.

In the 1980s, the RATP (*Régie Autonome des Transports Parisiens*, Autonomous Operator of Parisian Transports) was involved in launching critical systems including the first control-command programs for rail

Chapter written by Sylvain FIORONI.

transport across its network, and needed to ensure that the safety levels of the developed systems were at least equivalent to those of existing systems, based on the physical principles of "intrinsic safety[1]". In this context, careful consideration was given to formal proof, and the potential of this technique quickly became apparent. The "classic" software development process (structured method, testing, verification and analysis) produces high-quality programs, but trust levels in safety terms (based essentially on a percentage of coverage) remain questionable when compared with intrinsic safety methods, which allow us to demonstrate that given safety levels have been attained.

Formal proof therefore had much to offer, and the safety level of a program would no longer be based on the classic software development process alone. The RATP decided to use this method to evaluate the safety levels of the critical programs of the SACEM[2] [OFT 97] by retro-engineering. The lack of viable tools on an industrial scale meant that the RATP was obliged to implement studies of formal evaluation techniques for safety programs. This approach proved fruitful, highlighting around 20 faults which had not been picked up during testing, and led to the creation of the techniques used in the formal B method [ABR 96] (developed by Jean-Raymond Abrial, who was involved in the study process).

RATP management were convinced of the interest presented by the approach, and the B method was used in the 1990s to develop the critical programs used in SAET-METEOR[3] [CHA 96, MAT 98] for the fully-automatic line 14 of the Paris metro. This decision led to the creation of a partnership and the provision of resources for the industrialization of formal proof tools for the B method [ABR 96].

---

1 The method which uses the known physical properties of components related to their behavior in the case of breakdown or disturbances, ensuring that the state of the system remains safe even when faults arise.

2 *Système d'Aide à la Conduite, à l'Exploitation et à la Maintenance* (Driving, Use and Maintenance Support System), implemented for the central section of the RER. A line in 1989 aimed at increasing transport capacity by increasing train frequency, from every 2.5 min to every 2 min.

3 *Système d'Automatisation de l'Exploitation des Trains – METro Est Ouest Rapide* (SAET-METEOR) Automatic Train Exploitation System went into service in October 1998. For further details, see [BOU 12] – Chapter 2.

The combination of the B method for software design, producing programs which are intrinsically safe by construction, and an ASA+[4] modeling of the specification with property verification [BOU 06] based on model-checking [BAI 08] to consolidate the textual specification [BOU 00] led to the detection of a number of faults. The combination of the two approaches was a great success, and, since their implementation in 1998, the programs in question have never needed to be modified for safety reasons.

In addition to the assurance proof provides in relation to safety requirements, these first applications of formal techniques clearly show that the formalization of a system and of requirements plays a significant role in consolidating system functionality and in safety demonstration, as the approach requires rigorous identification of a context and the elimination of indeterminism and uncertainties.

The RATP has continued to use critical systems, including rail transport control-command programs, with safety software designed using tool-based formal methods (the B method, Petri networks, etc.). Furthermore, the RATP also uses formal modeling for the verification of system aspects (Event-B, AADL, etc.). The use of formal techniques concerns all automatisms used by the RATP with high and very high levels of safety integrity[5] to varying extents [GLE 09]. Recent innovations made by the organization in the context of major modernization work on the Paris metro, which will be presented later in this chapter, have employed *a posteriori* proof techniques applied to finished programs. This has been made possible by increases in processor computing power and the introduction of design tools using formal languages, such as SCADE®.

From a project management perspective, the utility of these contributions is determined by their capacity to add value. A satisfactory response must be provided to each constraint – cost, delay, technical constraints and regulatory conditions – to reduce overall project risks. In order for an approach to be acceptable, particularly in regulatory terms, we must be able to guarantee the veracity of results established by these tools.

---

4 ASA+™ (Automata and Structured Analysis) is a method based on SADT and state machines developed by the Verilog company.
5 i.e. SSIL levels 3 and 4, as set out in the CENELEC standards [CEN 01].

2.2. Open Control of Train Interchangeable and Integrated System[6]

The Open Control of Train Interchangeable and Integrated System (OCTYS) project presented significant risks, as the proof technology involved had never been used in an industrial context and no feedback from equivalent projects was available. Moreover, the approach needed to be qualified in order to integrate proof results in the regulatory approach for system approval.

Three groups were involved in successfully integrating proof into demonstrations of the safety of the Sol OCTYS Line 3 program: Ansaldo STS[7], Prover Technology[8] and the RATP[9].

In this context, the RATP continued to promote advanced methods for the development of safety software (a policy which began in the 1990s with the choice of the formal B model), with the conviction that formal models provide the highest system safety levels while also reducing costs.

Ansaldo STS's presentation of their software validation approach based on the use of proof with Prover Technology's ProverVerifier™ tool in 2007 rapidly solved the issue of qualifying the results of proof produced by tools. This qualification, essential for safety demonstrations to be considered acceptable from a regulatory perspective, posed certain technical problems; more importantly, it required significant financial backing, and this requirement hindered the production of proofs. After extensive reflection, the RATP agreed to cover these technical and financial aspects, convinced that their investment would bring worthwhile results, and provided Ansaldo STS with a complement to the existing proof engine, allowing the demonstration report produced by this existing engine to be certified.

Along with the validation activities carried out by Ansaldo STS for OCTYS, the RATP asked Prover Technology to develop tools associated with the proof engine to guarantee that the SCADE® model would not be altered when translated into the language of the proof engine and to verify

---

6 Further information is given in Chapter 5 of this book, which describes the OCTYS project for line 3 of the Paris metro.

7 See www.ansaldo-sts.com for more information on Ansaldo STS.

8 Further details of Prover Technology and their products are available at http://www.prover.com/.

9 See http://www.ratp.fr/ for more information.

the generated proof; they then qualified the whole chain, known as the "Prover Certifier™".

In order to reach a safety level compatible with rail transport requirements (SSIL[10] level 4, as set out in the CENELEC EN 50128 [CEN 01, CEN 11] standard), the solution uses two representations of a system as input, the SCADE®[11] model and the source code generated using the SCADE® model (in C or Ada), and formally establishes the equivalence of these two representations. This process also allows us to check for errors in the source code generation process. The engine attempts to establish proof that the safety requirements have been satisfied using one of these representations. Based on the outcome of the proof, the tool produces either a counter-example (failure) or a plot of the proof (success). This plot, known as the "proof certificate", is made up of a pre-defined set of inference and rewriting rules, to be verified by a tool known as a "proof certifier".

The RATP also took charge of the adaptations and additions required to transpose the proof activity carried out by Ansaldo STS for the certified chain. The formal proof of equivalence between the SCADE® model and the target code was a particularly sensitive point requiring attention.

Once the question of certification had been resolved, new initiatives were launched as part of an agreement between Ansaldo STS and the RATP to remove the project risks associated with failure to attain a suitable level of safety requirement coverage using proof by the time of implementation. This was done using a mixed methodology with proof of full functionality and tests of other functions, and by incremental scheduling using markers, based on the time needed to move from validating the unproven functions of the proof to a test-based approach.

The final remaining issue concerned the capacity of proof tools to process a program representing the real configuration of a line within an acceptable execution period. Tests carried out in 2008 by Ansaldo STS and Prover Technology on the Sol OCTYS Line 3 program using the full line topology resulted in an explosion in the amount of memory required by the proof engine. Ansaldo STS put forward a solution to this problem in 2007, which

10 SSIL: Software Safety Integrity Level. The standard [CEN 01] identifies five safety levels, from 0 (the lowest) to 4 (the highest).
11 Ansaldo STS developed the Sol program using the SCADE® modeling tool, supplied by Esterel Technologies.

was adopted to allow OCTYS to be brought into service in 2009: proof was carried out for "test" configurations which had been shown, by Ansaldo STS, to cover all of the real configurations of line 3. In the course of 2010, a study carried out by Prover Technology in partnership with Ansaldo STS and the RATP succeeded in removing these technical difficulties, and it is now possible to carry out proof at the whole-line level.

The validation of the requirements of the Sol OCTYS Line 3 program represents a successful example of the use of formal proof. The enterprise was a daring one, but, due to the deep-seated convictions of those involved, it was successfully completed, with early consideration of all of the risks involved in the activity and progressive removal of the difficulties which were encountered. The gains generated by this process exceeded initial expectations (the bulk of the safety requirements were proved, with reduced costs and easy implementation of modified versions of the software, etc.). The "Prover Certifier™" certified solution has been accepted by the relevant regulatory bodies.

This experience resulted in the creation of an industrially-viable technological approach focusing on the proof of safety requirements for a program modeled using SCADE®. This approach has breathed new life into the use of formal proof, at a time when SCADE® is widely used in industrial contexts.

2.3. Computerized interlocking systems[12]

The computerized interlocking systems (PMI) operation at the RATP was the driving force behind the use of advanced model-checking techniques during the validation phase to establish safety demonstrations for existing critical programs.

The specificity of PMI[13] is that it provides generic equipment for real-time interpretation of interlocking graphs, which display the operations of the interlocking system. The graphs are developed within a proprietary design suite using a two-step process. The first stage involves implementation of the behavior of the elementary functions of the system in

12 More information on the PMI project and the use of formal methods is given in Chapter 4.
13 For more details on PMI, particularly its architectural aspects, readers may wish to consult the relevant chapter in [BOU 11].

the form of a set of generic graphs. The second stage consists of parameterizing these graphs to produce a site configuration. The design suite then instantiates the graphs in the form of a database loaded into the equipment.

The configuration of a PMI was previously validated through testing using a platform made up of a piece of target equipment in a simulated environment. Aiming to optimize verification and validation costs, the RATP wished to replace safety testing activities with proofs of interlocking graphs, instantiated for the configuration of the systems under consideration. To this end, the organization commissioned a PMI proof suite, known as Prover iLock PMI. The long-term goal of this project was to generate automatic safety validation of systems, whatever the configuration used.

Development of the Prover iLock PMI proof suite was based on a PREDIT[14] research project known as PROOFER, bringing together the RATP, THALES RSS, responsible for the supply and development of PMIs, Prover Technology, who developed the proof suite, and VERIMAG, who validated the mathematical principles used in the proof. The chosen pathway involved constructing a "conservative" abstraction of the execution of instantiated interlocking graphs, which was then used for proof.

The research project involved a feasibility study, which confirmed the efficiency and safety of the proof validation method proposed by Prover Technology. Industrialization of the proof suite began in September 2006 and ended in November 2008 with its qualification by the RATP. The suite includes the proof itself and a certification mode, producing a safety level of SSIL4 as set out in the CENELEC EN 50128 standards [CEN 01].

The graph design suite may be used to model the generic rules of safety properties which must be respected by the interlocking graphs in the form of state automata, and instantiate these rules for the configuration of the system to validate.

From 2008 to 2011, this method was successfully applied in demonstrating the safety of 11 PMI systems across three metro lines, producing the expected benefits: reduced costs when compared to test-based methods, semi-automatic proof of new configurations by reusing the generic

---

14 http://www.predit.prd.fr/predit3.

rule database, identification of unsafe situations which would have been difficult to identify through testing, etc.

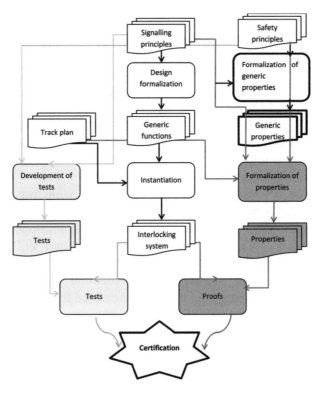

Figure 2.1. *Proof suite*

2.4. Conclusion

Formal proof has attracted the interest of the rail transport community with the first rail safety control-command programs. The successful use of formal proof in large-scale projects has, on several occasions, confirmed its status as an efficient and economically viable basis for safety in automated systems.

The OCTYS and PMI projects discussed in this chapter highlight the superiority of proof compared to test-based methods in demonstrating safety, particularly in identifying unsafe situations, and through its capacity to verify high level requirements, which are difficult, if not impossible, to verify through testing[15].

The decision to use formal proof is a daring one. In order to succeed, it requires a tailored project response, taking account of all of the technical difficulties and risks involved in the relevant activity from the earliest stages of the project. The challenge presented by this approach, alongside the conviction and collaborative working practices required from those involved, leads to the development of close working relationships. Those involved in projects of this type are generally more than satisfied with their choice.

With the resources currently available, a wide variety of developments are possible, for example use of the B method or proof during the validation of software designed using a formal language such as SCADE®. The generalization of formal proof in the development of critical systems may not be far off.

2.5. Glossary

CENELEC[16]: *Comité Européen de Normalisation ELECtrotechnique*, European Committee for Electrotechnical Standardization

OCTYS: Open Control of Train Interchangeable and Integrated System

PMI: *Poste de Manœuvre Informatisé*, Computerized Interlocking Systems

RATP[17]: *Régie Autonome des Transports Parisiens*, Autonomous operator of Parisian Transports

SAET: *Système d'Automatisation de l'Exploitation des Trains*, Automatic system for Train Operations

SIL: Safety Integrity Level

SSIL: Software SIL

---

15 For example the non-occurrence of a dangerous situation.
16 See http://www.cenelec.eu/Cenelec/Homepage.htm.
17 See http://www.ratp.fr.

2.6. Bibliography

[ABR 96] ABRIAL J.R., *The B-Book*, Cambridge University Press, 1996.

[OFT 97] OFTA Observatoire Français des Techniques Avancées, Application des techniques formelles au logiciel (Arago20), June 1997.

[BAI 08] BAIER C., KATOEN J.-P., *Principles of Model Checking*, The MIT Press, 2008.

[BOU 00] BOULANGER J.-L., GALLARDO M., Processus de validation basée sur la notion de propriété, in Lambda Mu 12 à Montpellier, 27–30 March 2000.

[BOU 06] BOULANGER J.-L., Expression et validation des propriétés de sécurité logique et physique pour les systèmes informatiques critiques, Thesis, Université de Technologie de Compiègne, 2006.

[BOU 11] Boulanger J.-L., *Sécurisation des architectures informatiques industrielles*, HERMES-Lavoisier, 2011.

[BOU 12] Boulanger J.-L., *Formal method, Industrial Use from Model to the Code*, ISTE, London, John Wiley & Sons, New York, 2012.

[CEN 01] CENELEC, Software for railway control and protection systems, Technical Report EN50128, Comité Européen de Normalisation Electrotechnique, 2001.

[CEN 11] CENELEC, Software for railway control and protection systems, Technical Report EN50128, Comité Européen de Normalisation Electrotechnique, 2011.

[CHA 96] CHAUMETTE A-M., LE FEVRE L., "Système d'automatisation de l'exploitation des trains de la ligne METEOR", *REE*, 8 September 1996.

[GLE 09] Gledel V., "Formal techniques in CBTC software development", *Scade User Group Conference*, October 2009.

[ISO 08] ISO, ISO 9001:2008, Systèmes de management de la qualité – Exigence, December 2000

[MAT 98] MATRA and RATP, "Naissance d'un Métro. Sur la nouvelle ligne 14, les rames METEOR entrent en scène, PARIS découvre son premier métro automatique", Numéro 1076 -Hors-Série, *La vie du Rail & des transports*, October 1998.

Use of Formal Proof for CBTC (OCTYS)

3.1. Introduction

Ansaldo STS[1] is an international company and a leader in the rail and urban transport markets. The company is a subsidiary of the Finmeccanica group and is present in 30 countries, with 4,300 employees and an annual turnover of around €1.9 billion in 2010.

With over 150 years of history and a number of major success stories to its name – including the Copenhagen metro and high speed train networks in France, Italy and Korea – Ansaldo STS offers reliable, tailored solutions for projects of varying size and complexity.

As suppliers of signaling systems and all-inclusive integrated transport systems, Ansaldo STS offers a wide range of systems and services, from standard signaling equipment to sophisticated automatic train control systems, new-generation electronic interlocking systems and centralized traffic management, maintenance and usage systems.

Ansaldo STS were pioneers in the introduction and use of innovative technologies such as High Speed systems, the European Railway Transportation Management System (ERTMS), PCC, Communications

Chapter written by Christophe TREMBLIN, Pierre LESOILLE and Omar REZZOUG.
1 See www.ansaldo-sts.com for more details.

Based Train Control[2] (CBTC) and driverless subway systems, with a permanent focus on safety, reliability, interoperability and performance.

The desire for continuous improvement with regards to these criteria led Ansaldo STS to implement and evaluate formal proof techniques for software, with the aim of using these procedures on an industrial scale if they proved successful.

A laboratory was set up to look into these considerations as part of the Ouragan/OCTYS project, carried out by Ansaldo STS for the RATP[3].

This chapter concerns the implementation of these techniques over the course of the project, the pathways which were explored, the difficulties which had to be overcome and the feedback which led Ansaldo STS to extend the experiment to other projects and broaden the field of application of these formal methods.

3.2. Presentation of the Open Control of Train Interchangeable and Integrated System CBTC

3.2.1. *Open Control of Train Interchangeable and Integrated System*

The Open Control of Train Interchangeable and Integrated System (OCTYS) program was a renovation contract for lines 3, 5, 9, 10 and 12 of the Paris metro, involving the installation of a CBTC speed control and train autopilot system.

The OCTYS contract was split into five lots, and lot [2] was assigned to Ansaldo STS in March 2004:

1) radio and network communications for all lines;

2) ground control for lines 3, 10 and 12;

3) onboard equipment for trains on lines 3, 10 and 12;

---

2 Communication Based Train Control: a system for the use, direction and safety management of train and subway systems. CBTC is a system made up of on-board equipment and on-ground equipment in constant communication, generally by radio. It has been subjected to standardization [IEE 04].

3 See http://www.ratp.fr/.

4) ground control for lines 5 and 9;

5) onboard equipment for trains on lines 5 and 9.

OCTYS is "interchangeable", i.e. the equipment involved is not limited to a specific line but may be installed on any of the lines in question. The interchangeability principle means that equipment of the same or different types provided by different suppliers can be mixed (for example, a line may be managed using ground equipment from lot [2] and lot [4], controlling trains with onboard equipment from lot [3] or [5]).

The first phase in the project was the creation of an interchangeability specification by the industrial actors responsible for each lot. This reference document defined the role of each piece of system equipment used on OCTYS-enabled lines, along with the interfaces for each element.

During the second phase of the project, each group developed their assigned equipment in accordance with the interchangeability specification.

The OCTYS system was brought into service on line 3 of the Paris metro on 29th March 2010. Line 3 includes 23 stations spread over 11.7 km and is used by 45 MF67 type trains.

3.2.2. Purpose of CBTC

CBTC is a train control system based on continuous bidirectional communication between ground and onboard equipment.

The system is designed for managing subway lines (either as part of renovations on existing lines or in equipping new lines or extensions of lines). The main aims of the system are as follows:

– to ensure train safety through continuous control of the speed of the vehicle in relation to the speeds authorized at different points along the line and in relation to different static (points, bumpers) and dynamic obstacles (e.g. other trains);

– to participate in ensuring the safety of passenger transfers (i.e. embarkation and disembarkation at stations) through management of safe opening and closure of train and platform doors;

– to contribute to the safety of personnel during track maintenance and in case of incidents.

In addition to these safety objectives, CTBC allows operators to:

– optimize the journey time of each train through automatic direction;

– optimize the time gap between two trains by enabling vehicles to follow each other more closely, independent of the existing lateral signaling system;

– ensure high line availability levels.

3.2.3. *CBTC architectures*

As we see from Figure 3.1, the CBTC system is distributed across a range of pieces of equipment; each device is partly or wholly responsible for CBTC functions.

CBTC equipment includes:

– onboard equipment carried by trains;

– ground equipment used by all or part of the track.

The CBTC equipment used on trains consists of an onboard autopilot. Each train must be equipped with one of these devices in order to derive maximum profit from the capacities of the CBTC system. However, CBTC systems are also able to operate with mixed traffic, i.e. traffic which includes non-CBTC equipped or non-communicating trains. This property means that the system is robust during transitional phases (before all trains have been equipped) and in cases where equipped trains are unavailable.

The central function of the onboard autopilot is to determine the position of the train on the line. This localization is absolute, i.e. the autopilot provides localization details in relation to the whole of the line. To establish localization data, the autopilot uses markers located along the track and onboard odometric sensors. The markers are used for initialization and for precise recalibration of the position of the train where necessary (notably at stations in order to ensure that the doors open safely). The autopilot continuously transmits localization data (along with other information) to CBTC ground equipment via a radio network.

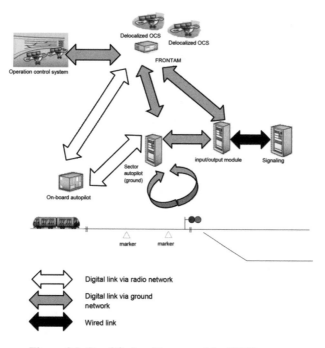

Figure 3.1. *Simplified architecture of the CBTC system*

The autopilot is also responsible for continuous calculation and control of the maximum speed authorized for the train. This speed depends on both static information (permanent speed limits for given points on the line) and dynamic information (movement authority). The autopilot interfaces with rolling stock, and is able to stop the train if necessary. This interface is also used to transmit direction orders contained in the autopilot when the train driver selects "Automatic" mode.

The autopilot is also involved in ensuring the safety of passenger exchanges.

The second type of equipment used in CBTC is the zone controller or sector autopilot. The sector autopilot centralizes train localization information for a given sector. It combines this localization data with information received from the interlocking system (state of signals, track circuits, points etc.) to obtain a track mapping, before issuing movement authority limits for each train. These limits are points beyond which the train must not, under any circumstances, pass.

The sector autopilot is also responsible for centralizing alarm systems and must protect the zones affected by these alarms. The sector autopilot is involved in managing these alarms via an interface with the central command post.

The interface between the interlocking system and the sector autopilot may be digital (via a wired network), if the interlocking system is equipped to perform this function, or use an additional device known as the input/output module. This module is directly connected to the interlocking system and converts wired "input/output module" information into digital information which is then sent over the network to the sector autopilot.

The interface with the central command system takes place using a dedicated device, the FRONTAM. This equipment receives commands from the control post to be transmitted to elements of the CBTC system, and sends back the supervision information required for use of the line.

The FRONTAM is also responsible for gathering and transmitting the information required for CBTC equipment maintenance to operators.

3.3. Zone control equipment

3.3.1. *Presentation*

As a type of safety equipment, zone control equipment must conform to SIL[4] level 4 as set out in the CENELEC standards (EN 50216 [CEN 00], EN 50128 [CEN 01], EN 50129 [CEN 03]).

The zone control equipment is supported by a safety platform[5] (2 out of 3) produced by Ansaldo STS. This platform is able to host different software applications requiring safe execution and high availability levels.

The functions required for the zone controller are defined by the functional specification of the equipment, which forms part of the interchangeability specification.

During the creation of their assigned aspects of the OCTYS system, teams from Ansaldo STS refined this document to produce a detailed

---

4 SIL: Safety Integrity Level.

5 See [BOU 10] Chapter 3 for more information on the CSD architecture.

functional specification. It was then used as the basis for software modeling using the SCADE® tool[6], supplied by Esterel Technologies. The functional specification of the equipment and the detailed functional specification took the form of system requirements. Each requirement was identified using a unique reference and classified according to its safety level (vital or non-vital). Each requirement in the functional equipment specification was followed up by one or more requirements in the detailed functional specification.

The application developed by Ansaldo STS is made up of two main components:

– a SCADE® model providing the main functions of the sector autopilot.

– an "out of SCADE®" layer which manages incoming and outgoing messages (including safety protocols) and prepares data for functional processing by the SCADE® model. This preparatory stage allows us to move from the reference frame used for data exchange between interchangeable equipment to the reference frame established by Ansaldo STS for software modeling of the sector autopilot using SCADE®.

The zone controller, as safety equipment, is subject to CENELEC standards (50126, 50129, 50128). These standards define the level of technical and hierarchical independence required for each team involved in the development, verification and validation of the equipment.

The CENELEC standards cover the whole of the equipment development cycle, from specification to implementation, and define the level of qualification required for each tool used in the whole cycle.

3.3.2. SCADE[7] model

3.3.2.1. The generic model

Ansaldo STS used the SCADE® program during the OCTYS project to develop the sector autopilot subsystem for their attributed CBTC system. SCADE is a graphical specification modeling tool, associated with an

---

6 For more information see Chapter 6 [BOU 12].
7 SCADE is distributed by ESTEREL-TECHNOLOGIES: see http://www.esterel-technologies.com .

automatic code generator, which notably enables execution and evaluation of all or part of the created model.

The OCTYS SCADE® model of the sector autopilot is broken down into 18 main functions. The execution of these 18 functions leads to the creation of over 300 SCADE® nodes, organized in a partition. Each part of the partition corresponds to a function.

The SCADE® model developed by Ansaldo STS is a cyclically executed sequential model.

Each individual SCADE® node is considered as a terminal requirement. Each of these nodes explicitly refers to the requirement or requirements in the detailed functional specification for which it guarantees partial or full implementation.

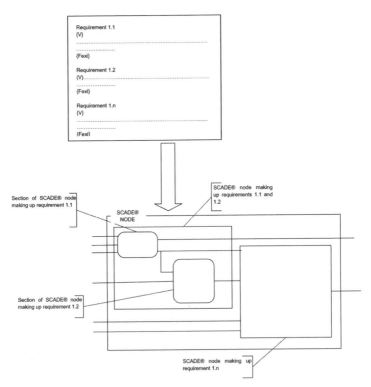

Figure 3.2. *Traceability between the detailed functional specification and the SCADE® model*

3.3.2.2. *The instantiated model*

The SCADE® model is a generic model, i.e. one which was developed independent of the topological properties of a given line. An "instantiated" model, however, results from the application of a generic model to a given track topology.

The instantiated model was obtained using an automatic generation tool using the track topology and the generic SCADE® model as input in accordance with instantiation rules supplied by the person in charge of modeling at the same time as the generic SCADE® model.

The size of the instantiated model is directly linked to the complexity of the line (in terms of the number of elements included in its topology). Moreover, as the SCADE® model interacts with a variety of equipment (onboard autopilots, adjacent sector autopilots, interlocking systems, etc.), the number of inputs/outputs for the model increases rapidly as the complexity of the line increases.

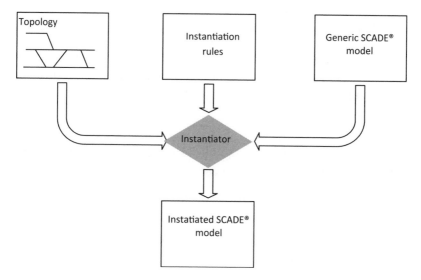

Figure 3.3. *Instantiation process for the SCADE® model*

For the SCADE® model to be validated, we must ensure that each requirement is correctly implemented. This validation is usually carried out by manual analysis of each requirement, leading to the creation of different scenarios covering nominal and boundary cases. The increasing complexity of these systems has made this process increasingly difficult, costly and time-consuming.

This complexity was apparent from the outset in the development of the SCADE® model, and, from the beginning of the project, Ansaldo STS launched a study into the possibility of using a proof engine to optimize validation activities.

3.4. Implementation of the solution

One advantage of software modeling using a tool such as SCADE® is the relative ease with which it can be combined with a proof engine, allowing formal verification of properties. A formal verification module is included in the development environment of the SCADE® suite.

The use of formal techniques is recommended by standard CENELEC EN 50128 [CEN 01], and Ansaldo STS decided to evaluate the use of formal proof techniques applied to the sector autopilot as part of the OCTYS project.

The aim of this evaluation was to demonstrate the applicability and the interest of this technique in the context of rail transport, with the following three objectives:

– detect as many model anomaly imperfections as possible earlier in the design phase, while identifying high-level requirements in order to reduce the number of repetitions of the V cycle;

– simplify the demonstration of safety criteria applicable to safety programs for rail transport;

– increase the trust level obtained at the end of the validation process for the onboard software in the sector autopilot. Formal demonstration of a property gives an exhaustive result, unlike conventional testing methods, where it is difficult, if not impossible, to cover all possible combinations.

This investigation was carried out in collaboration with Prover Technology in order to benefit from their expertise in the field of formal proof.

The investigation consisted of:

– verifying the capacity of Prover Technology's Prover iLock Verifier™ engine to interpret a SCADE® sector autopilot model, such as the prototype supplied by Ansaldo STS;

– defining, then modeling, the safety properties applicable to the sector autopilot and verifying the capacity of the proof engine to produce useful results;

– automating the interpretation of a generic sector autopilot model applied to a test topology, with the ability to change over time, by the proof engine.

This phase demonstrated that, for a simplified topology, the proof engine could either validate the safety properties applicable to the sector autopilot, or produce counter-examples which could then be used by the engineers at Ansaldo STS.

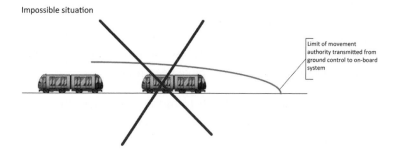

Figure 3.4. *The movement authority limits for a train must never contain another train*

For example, during this phase, the following properties were shown to be respected by the instantiated SCADE® model of the sector autopilot:

– the space between a train and its movement authority limit, as supplied by the sector autopilot, could not contain another train (Figure 3.4);

– movement authority limits never overlap (Figure 3.5).

The results of this study showed that the Prover Technology proof engine constituted a reasonable alternative, or addition, to traditional hosted testing methods in the specification and modeling context established by Ansaldo STS.

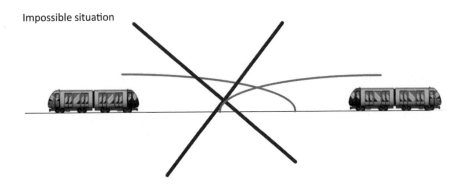

Figure 3.5. *Movement authority limits never overlap*

As an additional advantage, the Prover Technology solution is also able to verify that all treatments used in demonstrating each property conform to the requirements of the CENELEC standard for a SSIL[8] 4.

The certified solution, Prover Certifier™, established by Prover Technology in partnership with the RATP, works by generating a proof certificate (of several gigabytes in size). This proof certificate is then analyzed in conjunction with the model by an independent tool, which then issues a safety certificate if no errors have been found.

However, the absence of feedback from the use of activities of this type at the operational level meant that it was not possible to provide sufficient guarantees that the implementation of this activity would remain compatible with the objectives involved in implementing OCTYS on metro line 3.

The activity was therefore carried out in two stages, each identified by a marker. In order to pass a marker, a certain percentage of the safety requirements of the detailed functional specification had to be verified. If the system failed to meet the marker targets, the team would fall back on traditional testing solutions. This approach was selected after consultation with the RATP.

---

8 SSIL for Software Safety Integrity Level. The SSIL4 is the highest level of software safety for rail applications.

3.5. Technical solution and implementation

3.5.1. *Property definition*

The SCADE® model was based on the detailed functional specification, set out as a list of requirements. The purpose of each defined property was to cover as many requirements as possible, and each requirement had to be covered exhaustively. A complex requirement might be covered by multiple properties.

A function is said to be covered by properties if all of the requirements of the function are covered in full. If one or more requirements of a function are not covered, the classic test-based coverage procedure is applied. The global methodology must take account of this distribution of function coverage across traditional methods and property-based approaches.

To avoid dependency problems (particularly specification interpretation errors), those responsible for modeling and for property definition need to work independently, using the detailed functional specification in isolation in order to carry out their tasks.

As requirements are generic, the defined properties are also generic. However, except in certain specific cases, properties are generally validated using an instantiated model containing all functions. In this way, property correctness is verified in a real instantiated context and not in absolute terms.

The passage from requirements to properties is a critical methodological point. This phase is based on intellectual and purely manual activity, and the safety levels required for the activity must be respected during this stage.

A property definition framework (see Figure 3.6) may be used to direct this activity and facilitate property checking by third parties. For each established property, this model requires users to identify the covered requirement, and to explain the property in cases where the connection between the requirement and the property is not self-evident. In this way, we ensure that the property will be sufficiently detailed, enabling third parties to verify their completeness in relation to the target requirements.

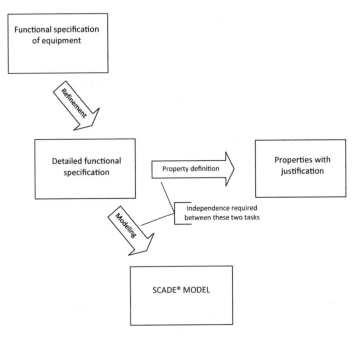

Figure 3.6. *Property definition principle*

3.5.2. *Two basic principles of property definition*

3.5.2.1. *Safety first*

When expressing a property, we focus on the safety aspect of the requirement. We do not, therefore, wish to demonstrate that a concession (i.e. a permissive state of a safety variable, for example) will be made for all situations which should permit this concession; instead, we wish to show that the concession is made only in cases where all required safety conditions are met.

This approach means that the person responsible for property definition must have sufficient knowledge of the system to allow clear understanding of the safety aspect of the functions of the model.

A sector autopilot, for example, should not be able to extend a movement authority limit unless a certain number of conditions are met. Based on this principle, the chosen properties must verify that all of these conditions are met when a movement authority limit is extended. These properties will not, however, verify the fact that the movement authority limit will be extended every time these conditions are present.

Focusing on the safety aspect of requirements means that verification of the functional availability of the system is not carried out at the property level: correct operation scenarios are defined in parallel. These scenarios are created and played out using a classic software development and validation process.

No technical obstacles to the use of properties in verifying the functional availability of the system were identified; however, it seemed too ambitious and risky to verify both availability and safety during the first use of this development mode. It was considered wiser to focus on the safety aspect of requirements, obtaining maximum coverage, while limiting the technical and planning risks associated with the first use of formal proof in an industrial and operational context.

3.5.2.2. *Conservation of modularity*

When a requirement uses a data flow produced by an earlier requirement, this intermediate flow is used directly without referring back to the initial input flow of the SCADE® model.

Movement authority limits, for example, are calculated in part based on the results of the mapping function (which aims to provide a precise, correct and up-to-date image of the positions of trains on the line). This creates a dependency relationship between the relevant requirements in the specification.

This means that the obtained properties are less complex, from a syntactic perspective, and allows easier verification of their adequacy in relation to requirements.

EXAMPLE.– Let us consider a requirement which defines the behavior of a flow (flow1) as a function of inputs i1 and i2.

Another requirement defines the behavior of a second flow (flow 2) as a function of flow 1 and a third input into the model, i3.

The property covering the second requirement is expressed directly using flow 1, and not as a function of i1 and i2.

"Flow2 permissive →(f(flow1,e3)=true)" and not "Flow2 permissive → (f(f'(e1,e2),e3)=true)".

When establishing properties, the SCADE® model is considered as a "gray" box (neither a totally opaque black box nor a completely transparent white box, see Figure 3.7). All of the intermediate flows used in the requirements must therefore be accessible for use when treating properties. Using the example given above, the internal flow, flow1, must be accessible even if, in functional terms, it does not need to leave the SCADE® model.

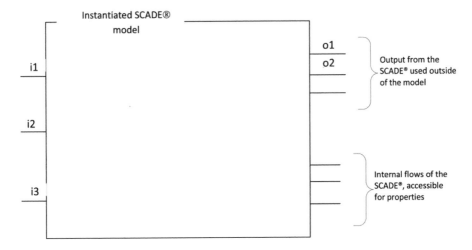

Figure 3.7. *Accessible input/output*

3.5.3. *Test topologies*

The establishment of test topologies allows us to verify the SCADE® model as soon as it becomes available, without needing to wait for the data needed to instantiate a real line.

This test basis is established manually, taking account of:

– the topology of the OCTYS test basis;

– topologies from the real line (line 3);

– topological cases induced by functional requirements and not covered by the two categories above.

A manual analysis methodology has been established to verify that all topological cases for an existing line are covered by the test topologies.

The use of test topologies also facilitates control of the size of the instances under study.

3.5.4. *Initial analyses*

These first analyses highlight problems associated with the size of the analyzed models and with environmental constraints.

3.5.4.1. *Model size*

The larger the analyzed model, the longer the analysis takes, and the harder it becomes for the proof engine to reach a conclusion. The first tests on the test topology showed that the time required to analyze certain properties was too long (more than a day, in certain cases) for the intended, repeated use.

The models therefore needed to be broken down into simpler models until the properties were simple enough to pass in an acceptable period of time.

Memory limitations and the exponential relationship between model size and complexity mean that it takes much less time to analyze two smaller models than to analyze a single model combining the two components.

As we see in Figure 3.8, the test topology was made up of two disconnected sets, and the first transformation involved separating these sets into two different topologies.

This transformation enabled faster production of results.

As properties are generic, it would theoretically be possible to verify them using a real line topology; however, the instantiated SCADE® models for a real line are larger than those for the first test topology, and the machine capacity required by the proof engine to treat these instantiated models proved to be too great.

Prover Technology also worked on a formal analysis engine and on the parameterization of analysis strategies to produce sufficiently high performances for problems of this type.

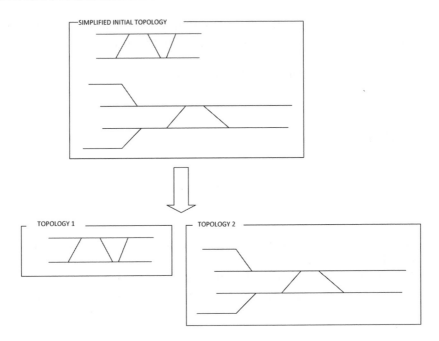

Figure 3.8. *Partition of the test basis*

The response times currently obtained for analyzed properties allow full validation of the largest topologies in around 24 h.

Work continued after the implementation of OCTYS on line 3 involving Prover Technology, the RATP and Ansaldo STS, and a representative section of properties were demonstrated using the topology of a zone controller taken from line 3. The time taken to implement this process still needs to be optimized.

3.5.4.2. *Environment management*

The first analyses also produced counter-examples, but after inspection, these were seen to apply to impossible situations.

As we have already seen, the SCADE® model of the sector autopilot receives information from different sources:

– on the ground: information from signals (point positions, etc.) or other subsystems (e.g. the power status of the line);

– orders from the line command system;

– trains: train localization messages, direction of traffic on the tracks, – CBTC controls, etc.

– other sector autopilots.

The proof engine considers that inputs into an analyzed SCADE® model are able to vary freely and independently. This leads the proof engine to create situations which are impossible in the real-world, for one of two reasons:

– Physical constraints (the same train cannot be present at different, non-neighboring parts of the line).

– External properties, guaranteed by the external equipment producing the data flows.

The most obvious reaction to these impossible cases is to eliminate different sets of impossible input to avoid producing false counter-examples. To do this, we must specify and create an environment model limiting the behavior of certain inputs into the SCADE® model, allowing us to remove impossible input sets.

However, the creation of an environment model adds complexity to the system which must be analyzed by the proof engine. We must therefore ensure that this model remains as simple as possible and that it does not give false success readings for properties.

For each set of "impossible" input data we discover, we need to determine whether it might be better to modify the model to make it resistant to this input. This approach is only meaningful if the modification of the SCADE® model does not add complexity.

The purpose of the environment model is not to specify the full behavior of the different inputs into the SCADE® model, but simply to eliminate impossible cases which have the ability to create problems. The environment model for the OCTYS system was therefore developed iteratively (see Figure 3.9) based on the study of each generated counter-example.

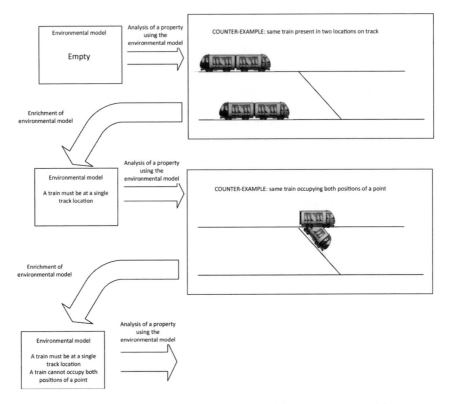

Figure 3.9. *Iterative process of enrichment of the environment model*

Each behavior introduced into the environment model is the subject of a requirement describing the behavior. Each requirement must be justified, either by a requirement contained in the specification documents of external equipment, or by a physical reality. This methodology produces an environment model which does not impose excessive limitations on the model. An environment model which wrongly eliminates data sets (e.g. which forces a train to always occupy the same position on a point) will give erroneous property results. The same care is needed when creating this environment model as when describing properties.

As in the case of the SCADE® model, the environment model is generic, and therefore needs to be instantiated using the topology requiring verification.

3.5.5. *The property treatment process*

The property treatment process involves two main stages:

– a search for counter-examples;

– property validation.

This corresponds to two different usage modes in the proof engine (see Figure 3.10).

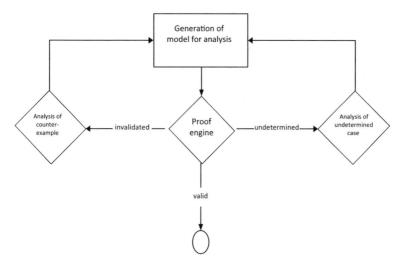

Figure 3.10. *Overview of the property treatment process*

During the first stage, the proof engine seeks counter-examples to disprove a property, starting from the initial state of the system with iterations for the following states, or application cycles. This step validates (or invalidates) the fact that the system respects a property from initialization up to a given cycle number. For as long as this is not verified, the proof engine cannot give a positive conclusion concerning the validity of the property. Counter-examples produced by the engine are used directly to determine the cause of invalidation. The successful application of this stage maximizes the chance of obtaining positive results during the second stage.

Note that if a property is valid, this signifies that the proof engine has been unable to find counter-examples. The search for counter-examples therefore needs to be stopped after a certain number of cycles. The problem lies in determining how many cycles are needed in order to search for counter-examples to be considered meaningful.

For instance, a property might be established to validate the following requirement: "when delay "T" is exceeded, then variable "s" must be restrictive". In order to search for counter-examples to be meaningful, the number of cycles studied must be sufficient for delay T to be exceeded.

The chosen number of cycles is also limited by technical considerations: the higher the number, the more time and machine space will be used in searching for counter-examples.

In cases where the proof engine is able to produce a counter-example, this counter-example must be analyzed in order to correct the issue. This step is repeated until no further counter-examples can be found.

In the second stage, the proof engine is required to validate the property. The proof engine uses different strategies for validation, and the most suitable strategy may vary depending on the properties requiring proof.

Ansaldo STS mostly used the induction strategy, based on the mathematical principle of recurrence. In cases where the engine is unable to produce a conclusion, this strategy presents the advantage of producing a counter-example by induction. This counter-example can then be used to identify and remove the cause of non-determination and to make the property converge or correct the SCADE® model.

3.5.5.1. *Counter-example analysis*

When a property is invalidated, the associated counter-example must be analyzed. This analysis may result in:

– enrichment of the environment model;

– modification of the property;

– modification of the input requirement and of the property;

– modification of the SCADE® model.

Counter-example analysis is a cooperative process, involving the person responsible for the property and the person responsible for the specification document and for modeling. The person responsible for the property considers the SCADE® model as a gray box, and is not, therefore, able to complete analysis of the counter-example when working alone.

Several stages are involved in analyzing a counter-example (see Figure 3.11). The first stage is carried out by the person responsible for property definition, in order to check that:

– the invalidation is not due to an impossible input set;

– the property is truly suitable for the requirement and for all topological cases.

This stage may lead to modification of the property.

The second stage consists of providing the person responsible for creating the specification document with enough elements to carry out their own analysis. To facilitate this stage, the counter-example is transformed into a scenario suitable for direct use with the tools available to the specification team.

These tools enable step-by-step replay of the scenario in a graphical environment representing the topology of the track, the trains using the line and significant output from the SCADE® model. This graphical interface allows faster analysis of the counter-example.

There are two possible conclusions to this analysis:

– The behavior of the model is normal, and the problem therefore lies in the passage from requirements to properties. This error may be due to a faulty or incomplete understanding of the requirement, which should be re-written by the person responsible for the specification document in order to remove ambiguities and assist those responsible for defining properties to cover this requirement;

– The behavior of the model is abnormal, and the SCADE® model needs to be corrected.

The engine provides a single counter-example, so it is important to note that multiple problems may be present. In cases where the analysis of a counter-example leads to modification of the SCADE® model, the verification process needs to be restarted for the new model.

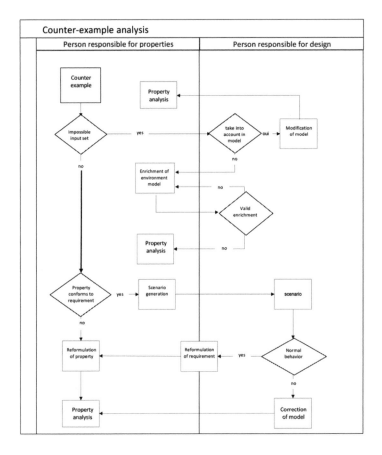

Figure 3.11. *Counter-example analysis*

The time required to modify and re-instantiate the SCADE® model varies according to the complexity of the identified problem, so it may be worthwhile to artificially model the property to try and determine if the encountered problem is unique.

Several techniques may be used to do this:

– exclusion of the topology from which, the problem originated;

– elimination of the set of input data which produced the counter-example;

– transformation of the property to remove the invalid part of the model. For example, if the property takes the form S1=true ≥ C1 and C2, and the counter-example shows that the implementation of condition C1 is incorrect, we may use the property S1=true ≥ C2 to check if the implementation of C2 is correct.

These modifications are obviously temporary and must be removed before the next full analysis of the modified model.

3.5.5.2. *Analyzing a counter-example produced by induction*

Unlike counter-examples produced by the invalidation of a property, an induction-based counter-example cannot be played out using the usual simulation process. These counter-examples are therefore more difficult to study.

An induction-based counter-example provides a system state where the property is valid, but ceases to be valid for the next cycle.

The first step in studying an induction-based counter-example (see Figure 3.12) is to determine whether the "randomly selected" set of input data given by the counter-example represents a genuinely attainable system state.

If the set of input data is attainable, the induced counter-example is used to manually create a scenario for direct use with the tools available to the specification team. From this point onwards, the counter-example is treated in the usual way.

If the set of input data is impossible, this implies incoherency between input values. Coherency is usually guaranteed by past events, but this notion is lost when using an induction strategy.

For instance, if two intermediate flows in a system show strong correlation (for example is flow1 is permissive then flow2 cannot be zero) and these two flows are memorized for use in the following cycle, coherency between the two flows needs to be maintained.

This coherency may be ensured:

– by introducing a lemma (in this case, flow1= true → flow2 <> 0). The lemma is used to limit the model so that the induction strategy can only take account of input data sets which are realistic for the system;

– using pre-existing properties of intermediate flows, which can then act as constraints on the input flows.

In both cases, the application of constraints using a lemma or one or more properties is only methodologically permissible if the lemma or properties in question are themselves valid.

In cases where specific lemmas are created, these lemmas must therefore be proved by the proof engine in the same way as the other properties of the system. Unlike the constraints introduced by an environment model, third-party verification of the lemma is not required.

In cases where lemmas or properties are used as constraints, we must take care to avoid creating circular references (i.e. using property px to prove py, py to prove pz and pz to prove px).

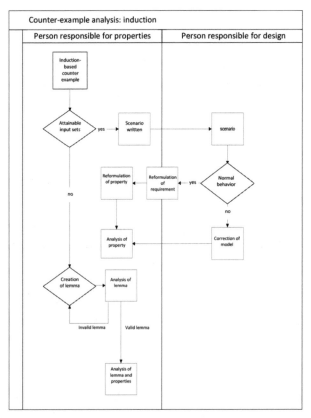

Figure 3.12. *Analysis of a counter-example obtained through induction*

3.5.5.3. *Partitioning a property*

For certain particularly complex requirements, properties may be divided into smaller units in order to reduce the complexity of the problem and optimize the response time of the proof engine.

The use of this technique may lead to the creation of additional observables in the SCADE® model. These observables are needed to validate properties covering only a subset of the requirement; evidently, the full set of properties must cover the whole requirement.

For example, let us consider the following requirement: "s1 is permissive if, and only if, all of the following conditions are met:

– Fx.s1 is permissive;

– E2 is greater than the value of Fy.s4 calculated during the previous cycle minus Fy.s4;

– Fz.s3 has been different to zero for a cycle time of at least t1".

The last two conditions are complex in their own right (involving arithmetic calculations and temporal aspects). To increase efficiency, it may be useful to have access to C2 and C3, where:

– C2 is true if and only if E2 is greater than the value of Fy.s4 calculated during the previous cycle minus Fy.s4;

– C3 is true if and only if Fz.s3 has been different to zero for a cycle time of at least t1.

The requirement is then covered by three properties:

– first property, which verifies the conjunction of the three conditions;

– second property, which verifies condition C2 according to its definition;

– third property, which verifies condition C3 according to its definition.

3.5.6. *Non-regression*

The SCADE® model may evolve over time following changes to the input specification.

Modification of the SCADE® model naturally entails modifications to the associated properties. The lifecycle of each modified/created property must therefore be reapplied.

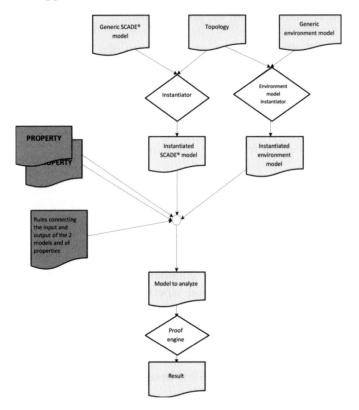

Figure 3.13. *Non-regression*

These property modifications are treated in delta in relation to the modifications identified in the requirements. However, this work in delta is not sufficient, as the SCADE® model is analyzed as a whole. Modification of a function Fx may prevent convergence of the properties of a second function, Fy, if certain output values from Fx are used as the input by Fy.

We therefore need to be able to carry out non-regression analysis of the set of properties in an acceptable length of time for each delivery of a modified SCADE® model. This is made simpler by carrying out as many tasks as possible automatically.

The first task consists of constructing the instantiated SCADE® model according to the analyzed topology and an instantiated environment model using the same topology. Once these two models have been created, they are concatenated with the properties and the names of the instantiated input/output variables produced by the SCADE® model, the environment model and the set of properties.

The model obtained in this way is then analyzed by the proof engine.

The proof engine analyzes the different properties sequentially or in groups, and the results are plotted in a file which is used to produce the proof report for the SCADE® model.

The available tools allow us to obtain a result for this non-regression process within a week of machine time.

3.6. Results

In the context of the OCTYS SOL project, formal proof techniques were used to cover a significant part of the safety requirements of the SCADE® model.

The objectives established at the outset were largely exceeded, and technical difficulties (property definition response time, property convergence) were solved by cooperative working involving the teams at Ansaldo STS and Prover Technology.

The implementation of a formal proof validation method for the OCTYS project was therefore successful.

This approach also proved fruitful for Ansaldo STS in two respects:

– One of the main difficulties involved in this methodology lies in the passage from requirements to properties, and is essentially related to the quality of requirement definition. This activity forms an important element in the "virtuous circle" of clarification and removal of ambiguity in a specification. The first phase of property definition may therefore be extremely time-consuming.

– The model was subject to functional evolutions in response to evolution requests. Property validation was therefore carried out several times on models which had not ceased to evolve. The technique of updating corresponding properties proved more efficient than the use of a traditional test strategy: property updates are limited to a syntactic expression, and the new behaviors induced by the modification are essentially covered by the use of a proof engine. Using a test-based approach, however, modification of a requirement may affect a significant number of scenarios, requiring manual verification of the sufficiency of existing scenarios to cover the requirement. The new approach therefore generated gains in terms of productivity and reduced the costs generated by evolution requests.

Another factor which adds complexity is the difficulty in obtaining the convergence of certain properties. This difficulty can be due to the intrinsic complexity of a requirement, or to production/modeling choices (for example the inability to produce intermediate observables for establishing lemmas). The decision to use a proof engine must therefore be made as early as possible in order to establish modeling rules for use by those responsible for modeling, making it easier to use the proof engine later on.

3.7. Possible improvements

Optimization activities are currently underway to build on this initial experience in using properties in the development cycle.

The first aim is to maintain the levels of coverage obtained through the use of a proof engine. Different clients may require different functions, leading to modifications to the detailed specification of the SCADE® model. If these modifications affect a function treated by the proof engine, every effort is made to update the associated properties at the same time. More generally, the development of any new function in the SCADE® model must be verified using the proof engine, with the long-term objective of obtaining complete coverage of the SCADE® model via the proof engine.

A second objective is to convert all of the properties for a real instantiation of the line. The aim in this case is to avoid having to verify the completeness of test bases for future projects. Property conversion is an automated process, whereas the verification of test base completeness involves manual verification aspects. The removal of this stage would simplify the validation cycle for the SCADE® model for a given line.

The obstacles to achieving this aim are essentially related to the size of the model to analyze, which makes it difficult to obtain responses from a proof engine within a time period which would be compatible with an industrial process. However, the intermediate results obtained with assistance from Prover Technology are promising and have not highlighted any particular difficulties.

3.8. Conclusion

The objectives established at the outset when introducing the use of formal proof methods were met in full.

The use of formal proof was seen to:

– be fully compatible with the methodologies generally used in developing safety programs;

– save time (both in design and validation terms) during system updates. The number of versions was also reduced as verifications were made earlier than when using standard methods;

– be based on technologies which are sufficiently mature for use in an industrial context and are not limited to theoretical use;

– increase trust levels compared with a traditional test-based approach. The use of a proof engine guarantees mastery of all possible combinations, something which is difficult to attain using a traditional approach.

Other benefits, not directly related to the initial objectives, were obtained through the use of formal methods.

In addition to the expected gains in terms of time, trust, quality and, consequently, safety, the use of formal proof improves the quality of the specification, with earlier removal of ambiguity and imprecision from the specification document. Fewer updates needed to be made to the specification documents based on remarks from those involved in the later stages of the development cycle; benefits were also noted in terms of maintenance, impact analysis following modifications, and the reusability of specification documents.

On-site integration and operational testing of equipment in real situations (using a test basis and/or a real line) were more than satisfactory and few anomalies were encountered. The implementation of formal techniques allows us to produce programs which are reliable from an early point in the cycle, to test these programs in limit situations, and, consequently, to reduce the number of iterations of the development cycle.

In order to derive full benefit from these positive results, we now need to increase the proportion of formally-proved properties, and begin to use formal techniques in demonstrating the functional availability of the system.

3.9. Glossary

CBTC: Communications Based Train Control

CENELEC[9]: *Comité Européen de Normalisation ELECtrotechnique*, European Committee for Electrotechnical Standardization

ERTMS: European Rail Traffic Management System

MES: *module d'Entrée/Sortie*, input/output module

OCTYS: Open Control of Train Interchangeable and Integrated Systems

OURAGAN: *Offre Urbaine Renouvelée et Améliorée, Gérée par un Automatisme Nouveau*, Revised and Improved Urban Offer with New Automatic Management

PAE: *Pilote automatique embarqué*, Onboard autopilot

PAS: *Pilote Automatique Secteur*, Sector autopilot

PCC: *Poste de Commande Centralisé*, Central command system

SIL: Safety Integrity Level

SSIL: Software SIL

TOR: *Tout ou Rien*, All or Nothing, hit-or-miss

---

9 See http://www.cenelec.eu/Cenelec/Homepage.htm

3.10. Bibliography

[BOU 12] BOULANGER J.-L. (ed.), *Formal Methods Industrial Use from Model to the Code*, ISTE, London, & John Wiley & Sons, New York, 2012.

[BOU 10] BOULANGER J.-L. (ed.), *Safety of Computer Architectures*, ISTE, London, & John Wiley & Sons, New York, 2010.

[CEN 00] CENELEC – EN 50126, Railway applications – the specification and demonstration of reliability, availability, maintainability and safety, January 2000.

[CEN 01] CENELEC – EN 50128, Railway applications. Communications, signalling and processing systems, Software for Railway Control and Protection Systems, May 2001.

[CEN 03] CENELEC, NF EN 50129, Railway applications – communication, signalling and processing systems – safety-related communication in transmission systems, European Standard, 2003.

[IEE 04] IEEE, 1474.1, IEEE Standard for Communications-Based Train Control (CBTC) Performance and Functional Requirements, 2004.

Safety Demonstration for a Rail Signaling Application in Nominal and Degraded Modes using Formal Proof

4.1. Introduction

Amongst other products, Thales[1] produces rail signaling systems for both subway and standard railway lines. The purpose of a signaling system is to manage light signals and switches in order to ensure train safety. Signal systems constitute a key element for rail transport safety.

Rail signaling systems are critical systems, and must be subject to a rigorous verification process, showing that they will not lead to safety hazards (collision between trains, derailment, injury to personnel, etc.), before they can be used. This verification is generally obtained through testing. Whilst this technique has been shown to be effective, it is also extremely expensive.

The development of formal methods offers other verification techniques like formal proof. As an alternative to testing, this technique allows us to prove mathematically that a critical system will never engender dangerous situations.

Chapter written by Jean-Marc MOTA, Evguenia DMITRIEVA, Amel MAMMAR, Paul CASPI, Salimeh BEHNIA, Nicolas BRETON and Pascal RAYMOND.
1 See http://www.thalesgroup.com/ for more details.

Formal proof is mainly used in two ways:

– To demonstrate that a program is intrinsically safe by construction, and may therefore be used for any real-world configuration. This kind of approach, promoted by a number of authors [JON 90, ABR 96], is known as theorem proving. Notable instances of the successful application of this approach include automatic metro driving systems [BDM 98, BOU 06].

– To demonstrate the safety of a specific (as opposed to generic) system. This approach can only be applied to systems with a finite states space, and is known as model-checking [QUS 82, CES 86, BAI 08]. Model-checking was used for the SAET-METEOR[2] project [BOU 00].

These two approaches both have their pros and cons. Theorem proving produces generic proofs which can then be reused; however, it requires high levels of mathematical ability and significant initial investment.

Model-checking techniques have a narrower field of application and are limited by the number of states which need to be covered. These techniques are subject to the combinatorial explosion phenomenon; even if they require a lower level of mathematical expertise, they need to be carried out for each individual system.

In the context of a renovation plan for the signaling system on some lines of the Paris metro, Thales and the RATP[3] implemented a formal proof methodology based on model-checking techniques to demonstrate that the Thales signaling system would not create dangerous situations.

The basis for this methodology was defined as part of the PREDIT PROOFER project [BMM 08], with the participation of Thales, RATP and Prover Technology[4] [SHS 00] for the development of proof tools. The Verimag[5] laboratory also provided expertise in formal methods to ensure the correctness of the proof process.

---

2 See Chapter 3 for more information on the use of formal methods in relation to SAET-METEOR.

3 See http://www.ratp.fr/.

4 Further information on Prover Technology and their products is available at http://www.prover.com/.

5 For more information on the Verimag laboratory and their work, see www.verimag.imag.fr/.

4.1.1. *Context*

The use of rail transport systems involves critical real-time systems in interaction with a non-deterministic environment. This environment notably includes a human component, with qualified employees applying operating rules.

The overall safety of a transport system is therefore based on:

– the correctness and adequacy of the operating rules;

– the absence of safety hazards in the real-time subsystems (local automatisms and the control center) involved in the system.

The correctness and adequacy of the operating rules must cover:

– new technologies used to design real-time systems;

– degraded modes of the automatisms;

– human errors made by operators.

The absence of safety hazards in real-time systems has already been demonstrated by formal proofs on a number of real-life systems (SAET-METEOR, interlocking systems) [BFG 96, BOU 00, BOU 06, RLR 98, BDM 98, FS 05, BAN 05].

The aim of our approach [BMM 08] was to extend these safety demonstration techniques using formal proof to the system as a whole, including automated elements, the operating rules and operators. This approach has to take two major elements into account:

– The environment represented by a set of elements interacting with the computerized interlocking system. It includes materials: trains, circuit tracks, swichtes, sensors and actuators, but also human operatives (drivers, control operator, field employees etc.), and the behavior of these operators also needs to be modeled.

– The environment model is a critical element for the correctness of the verifications. If the environment model is biased, then the obtained proofs may not be correct. The correctness of proofs critically depends on the correctness of the environment model. Unlike the program, which is a solution to the automatism problem that can be proved, the environment model constitutes an input element of the problem and therefore cannot be proved. The environment model in this case was sent to railway experts at Thales and RATP for validation to ensure that the modeled hypotheses conformed to reality.

In this chapter, we shall present the proof process used by Thales and RATP to demonstrate the safety of the signaling systems used for the RATP network in Paris. We shall begin by introducing the rail application concerned by our proof activities, the Thales system used for the metro. We shall then present the models used in the formal proof process, before describing the proof suite designed by Prover Technology.

The results of application of the proof process to the Thales signaling system for RATP line 1 will be described and discussed in detail, before considering a number of potential improvements.

4.2. Case description

The Thales rail signaling application chosen as the subject of a formal proof process was a computerized interlocking system called, in French, *poste de manœuvre à enclenchement informatique* (PMI[6]). This application was selected by the RATP for use in local maneuvering systems as part of a renovation and modernization program [GAL 07].

Two PMIs were brought into service at the Porte des Lilas and Mairie des Lilas locations on line 11 and at Porte des Lilas and Gambetta on line 3B [GAL 08] of the Paris metro without using a formal proof process. The first two "formally proved" PMIs were deployed on line 1 at the end of 2009/beginning of 2010. Since then formal verification has been systematically and successfully applied for installation of new PMI systems or upgrade of existing ones on four different metro lines.

In section 4.2.1, we shall give a brief overview of the architecture of the PMI system. Section 4.2.2 is about the computerized interlocking module (CIM) subsystem, which constitutes the operational core of the signaling system. In section 4.2.3, we shall present the proof-based verification process; the perimeter of this verification will be discussed in section 4.2.4.

---

6 For more information on the architecture of the PMI, see Chapter 8 of [BOU 11].

4.2.1 *Operational architecture of the PMI system*

Figure 4.1 shows the functional architecture of the PMI system. This system is made up of the following modules:

– The MMM (Movement Management Module), the local control and supervision subsystem which is mainly in charge of the signalmen dialogs and the communication with the centralised traffic control system. The system is backed up by an active standby system to ensure availability.

– The MSS (Maintenance Support System), the operator maintenance support module. This subsystem allows maintenance teams to locate faulty equipment and analyze faults.

– The COMS (Communication System), the communications system of the PMI, which is responsible for communications between all operational modules and centralized usage support systems, where these systems exist. The system is backed up by an active standby system to ensure availability.

– The CIM (Computerized Interlocking Module) subsystem, responsible for ensuring the safe circulation of trains by controlling and managing switches and the corresponding signals. This module is also responsible for interfacing with field equipment (track circuits, switches, signals, movement authorization units, etc.). Again, the system is backed up by an active standby system to ensure availability.

In the context of our formal proof activities, we shall focus on the CIM module, which provides signaling functions and is responsible for safe management of ground equipment.

The MMM subsystem responsible for managing the user interface (HCI) and the COMS subsystem responsible for transmitting information between the MMM and the CIM are not directly responsible for the signaling function as such, but must ensure that commands and operator controls are transmitted to the CIM. The MMS subsystem assists maintenance personnel in identifying the reasons for faults, and as such is not responsible for any safety functions.

These conclusions are based on safety analyses carried out by Thales and RATP. During this process, different functions of the PMI system were studied and each associated with safety levels in order to guarantee the attainment of system-level safety objectives.

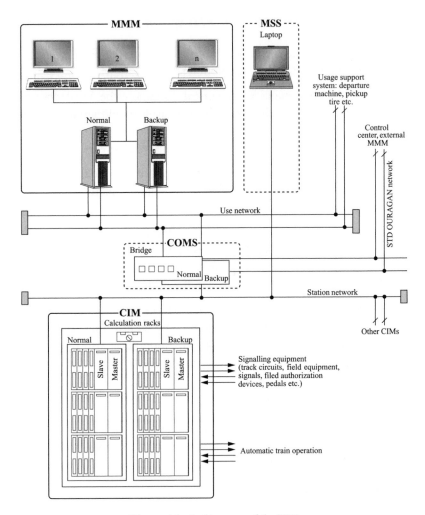

Figure 4.1. *Architecture of the PMI*

4.2.2. *CIM subsystem*

As we have seen, the CIM subsystem is made up of two modules covering the same function, providing active backup to ensure system availability. The two modules are identical in terms of both hardware and software.

Each module of the CIM is itself part of a dual redundancy system[7] to guarantee safety and damage prevention in the system and to enable the system to cope with hardware faults. These doubled units are referred to as master and slave units. From a hardware perspective, the two units are identical. From a software perspective, the units operate in the same way, but with a time delay: when the master unit carries out functional processing, the slave unit carries out auto-testing, and vice-versa. This means that a random fault will not have the same consequences on the treatments carried out by the two units, and the fault will then be detected using voting logic.

A two-out-of-two voting logic is used: the two units must produce the same output. Otherwise, the module will go into "safe" mode (all output will be restrictive). The voting logic operates at software level, where each unit compares its output by taking into account the output calculated by the other unit. If the comparison is successful, the unit orders output; in case of failure, the module goes into "safe" mode, as described above.

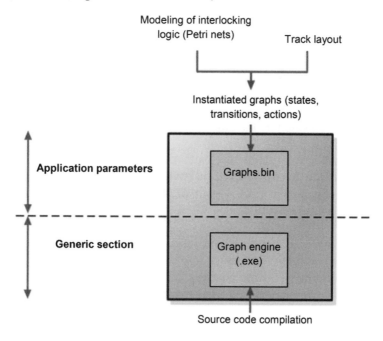

Figure 4.2. *Program architecture of a CIM module*

---

7 The safety principles established for the PIPC and reused for the PMI are presented in Chapter 5 of [BOU 09].

The software used in each unit, or, for the sake of simplicity, the CIM program, is made up of an executable program and application parameters (see Figure 4.2). The executable file is generic for all interlocking units: each time an interlocking unit is installed on an RATP line, only the application parameters are modified. The executable program is responsible for managing material resources, auto-testing, comparing results from the two processing units, acquiring input and producing output, and interpreting application parameters.

Application parameters are produced by modeling the operational aspect of a rail signaling application. The main feautures of an interlocking unit, i.e. the management, creation and removal of routes, interlocking management, management of degraded modes (cancellation procedures), switch and signal management, are modeled using formalism similar to a Petri net [PN 13].

This modeling is generic and does not apply to any specific unit. To construct a given unit, generic models are instantiated using a tool, ASIFER in the case of Thales, for graph modeling and instantiation.

Graph instantiation consists in identifying which objects remain abstract. The generic graph modeling switch management, for example, is instantiated for each switch controlled by the unit. Each switch has a unique ID. The generic graph modeling the route formation is also instantiated for each possible route managed by the unit.

These instantiated graphs are known as applied graphs, and are more numerous than the generic graphs. Instantiation is carried out using technical plans which contain the track layout of the interlocking unit and describe each route and its operation modes.

Applied graphs are saved as text format in files with the extension .gap. They are then compiled into binary format using ASIFER, resulting in a file labeled "graphs.bin". This file contains the specific application parameters of each unit and is interpreted by the executable program.

4.2.3. *CIM program verification with and without proof*

Two activities are involved in verifying the CIM program described above:

– Verification of the generic part, i.e. the executable file. This program is developed using a classic V cycle. Verification is carried out through unit testing, integration and validation, following the usual procedure for critical software. The aim of these testing activities is to cover the requirements set out in the specification and design documents: each requirement must be covered by one or more test scenarios, and testing stops when 100% coverage has been reached. These test cases are supplemented by safety analyses throughout the course of the development cycle.

– Verification of the signaling function, involving the specific instaciated graphs for each unit. This verification aims at checking that the functional specifications of the interlocking logic, modeled as Petri nets, will not contribute to the occurrence of an undesirable event. Undesirable events are identified through hazard analysis and described in the relevant documentation, based on known undesirable events from the domain of rail transport, notably derailment and collision.

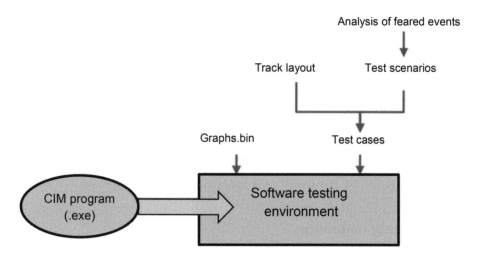

Figure 4.3. *Test-based verification process for signaling functions*

This second verification process also involves testing. In this case, the aim of the test cases is to cover all of the signaling principles used to prevent an undesirable event from occurring using one or more test scenarios.

Generic scenarios are developed to cover signaling principles, as shown in Figure 4.3.

Our goal is to use proof techniques to replace, or at least, as a starting point, to reduce the number of these test cases. The purpose of the verification process remains unchanged: to verify that the instantiated graphs, as modeled and executed by the CIM, do not lead to the creation of dangerous situations. In this approach, undesirable events and signaling principles are analyzed to obtain a set of properties for verification. These properties are then instantiated for the track layout for a given unit, and are used as proof obligations, which are then proved using a proof engine. This verification process is illustrated in Figure 4.4.

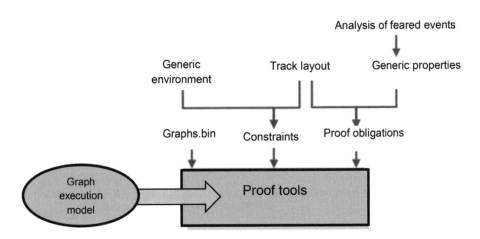

Figure 4.4. *Proof-based verification process for signaling functions*

4.2.4. *Scope of verification*

In the previous sections, we identified the part of the CIM program covered by the proof activity. This is the part of the program which is responsible for the interlocking logic: the safety critical core of the system. Note that the dependable architecture is not covered by the formal proof activity. Our analytical approach considers that the program, by commanding switch points and signals, reacts to train movements, and, if signaling rules are not respected, these train movements may have disastrous consequences that may lead to loss of human life. This is shown in Figure 4.5.

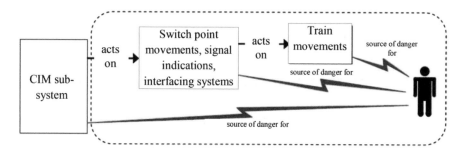

Figure 4.5. *Analytical perspective*

Using this approach, the instantiated graphs, produced by the instantiation of generic graphs for a given unit, are verified by proof. To ensure the correctness of the carried out proofs, we presume implicitly that all of the other components of the PMI system, constituting the interface between these instantiated graphs and the physical environment (trains, field equipments and human operatives), have been verified and comply with the relevant safety requirements. We therefore use the following hypotheses:

HYPOTHESIS 4.1.– All information used by or produced by the instantiated graphs is delivered by equipments and over connections which comply with the relevant safety requirements.

HYPOTHESIS 4.2.– The geographical location of field equipments is presumed to be in accordance with technical plans (track layout).

Note that, by considering accident scenarios as consequences of faults, we are able to cover different possible causes of accidents (system failure due to a fault in the graphs, operative errors, environmental disturbances, etc.).

4.3. Modeling the whole system

Three elements need to be present to enable proof activities. The first one is the *application model*, which denotes an abstraction of only the PMI safety kernel, the CIM. The second element is a set of properties to demonstrate. The third and last element is the *environment model*, i.e. a modeling of the different elements in interaction with the PMI (track circuits, switch, operating agents, etc.).

We shall now discuss the techniques and approaches used in the formal modeling of these three elements.

4.3.1. *Application model*

As we saw in the previous section, the CIM is made up of two aspects. The first aspect corresponds to a set of graphs. The second part is the graph engine, which is responsible for scheduling the different graphs.

To model the CIM, we therefore need to obtain a formal model of the graphs and the graph engine. The different approaches and techniques developed by Prover Technology to carry out this translation are presented in section 4.4.

The main steps involved in designing this formal model are shown in Figure 4.6. This figure highlights the development chain involved in graph creation. Firstly, the system specification is used to develop a detailed specification. Next, a set of generic graphs is created, showing the behavior of different system functions.

The generic graphs are then instantiated using signaling data available in the track layout. For a given metro line, for example, the graph qualifying the movement instruction for a switch will be instantiated for all switches of the line. Once all of the instantiated graphs have been created, they are translated into a formal model. Note that the input of the translator does not include a model of the graph engine, which is directly implemented in the translator itself.

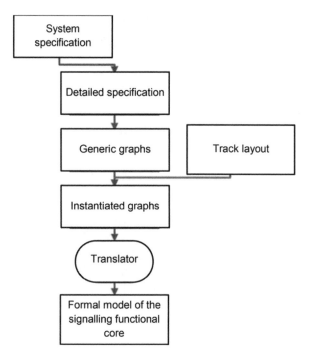

Figure 4.6. *Construction of the application model.*

4.3.2. *Safety properties*

4.3.2.1. *Scenario trees: refinement of undesirable events*

To define the safety properties which the PMI needs to satisfy, Thales began by using safety hazards identified through safety analyses produced by their railway safety experts and confirmed by the RATP: derailment, collisions between two trains, etc. (see Figure 4.7). These safety hazards were then refined to produce safety properties. This was achieved by studying the different possible scenarios using a specific formalism established by railway engineers.

This formalism, in tree form, allows us to describe the different scenarios associated with a safety hazard. The scenarios are then used to model systems from the perspective of accidents to avoid, using a hierarchical representation of the events which may lead to an accident. While the form of this notation is different to that used for FMECA [VIL 97] for operational safety, the aims of the two approaches are identical.

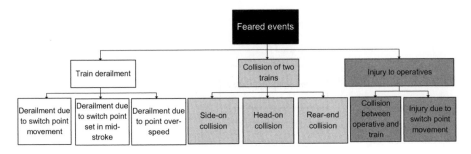

Figure 4.7. *Undesirable events*

Some of the described scenarios are considered to lead a risk, while others do not. Only risk scenarios are retained for use in defining safety properties. Figure 4.8 shows an example of a tree for an event related to derailment of a train due to a switch point movement. A dotted box shows an absence of hazard. A gray box represents a hazard scenario.

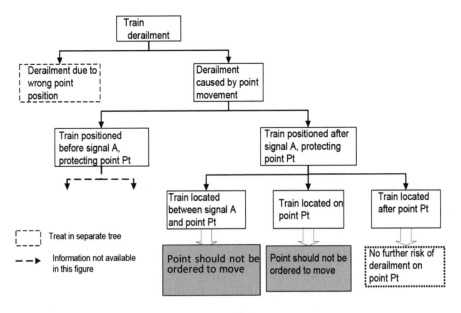

Figure 4.8. *Thales scenario tree*

4.3.2.2. *Fault trees*

A fault tree is used for each safety hazard to synthesize dangerous scenarios and characterize the risk (see Figure 4.9). The formalism associated with the fault trees is based on one defined in [VIL 97], which allows the use of logical operators (AND, OR, XOR, etc.).

In this way, we begin the formalization of the risk, i.e. the negation of safety properties. This does not yet constitute a formal description, since elements in natural language are used to describe the field configuration. These configurations are subject to formal modeling later on as part of the environment model, described in section 4.3.3.

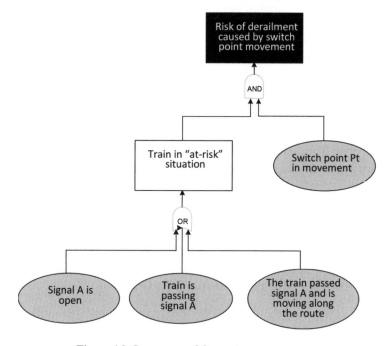

Figure 4.9. *Property modeling using an automaton*

4.3.2.3. *Generic automaton modeling*

Thales used the same graph formalism used by railway engineers to model safety properties. The form of the property graphs follows the example shown in Figure 4.10.

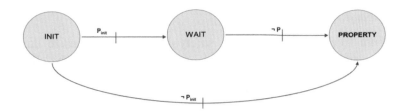

Figure 4.10. *Property modeling using an automaton*

The automaton is made up of three state kinds:

– *Init*. This state corresponds to the initial state upon initialization of the CIM

– *Wait*. This state is accessible if the safety property has been verified at initialization, at which point the CIM must be in a state where it cannot issue switch commands or open signals. This is verified at initialization by the property labeled P_{init} in Figure 4.10. Moreover, when P_{init} is verified, then safety property P is also verified. The automaton remains in the Wait state for as long as safety property P is verified.

– *Property*. This state is a looping error state showing the existence of a dangerous situation, i.e. violation of a safety property.

Reuse of the signaling formalism allows us to describe properties in a generic manner. For each rail signaling unit, the property is instantiated as many times as necessary for each track configuration. As in the case of the application model, a translator is used to transform instantiated proof graphs, in this case the graphs describing safety properties, into a formal language useable by the Prover Technology proof tools [SHS 00].

4.3.3. *Environment Model*

4.3.3.1. *General Points*

From an abstract perspective, the systems we wish to verify are discrete controllers. These controllers behave in the following manner:

– environment sampling to obtain input, i.e. an *external message;*

– calculation of the appropriate reaction for this input;

– production of corresponding output, typically actuator orders.

The main goal of the project was to verify the safety of the control system. Safety, notably the absence of derailments, depends on a number of factors, which may be *functional* (the controller produces the correct commands) or non-functional (the controller reacts at sufficient speed). In this chapter, we shall focus on safety properties, i.e. on the absence of safety hazards generated by design anomalies in the controller.

Interactions between the controller and the environment mean that some functional properties can only be validated in the presence of well-defined environmental hypotheses. Once again, these are functional hypotheses, i.e. they have an influence on what the controller is calculating.

For example, the hypothesis that the environment reacts "slowly" in relation to the calculation time of the controller is a non-functional hypotheses. The assumption that switch points only move when commanded to do so is a functional hypothesis. Non-functional hypotheses are essential to system safety: they should therefore be clearly identified as postulates required for the correctness of the verification.

4.3.3.2. *Logical reaction time*

The calculation aspect of the CIM is relatively sophisticated, carried out by a set of simultaneous agents (the graphs) which exchange and process internal messages until a stable state is reached. This iterative procedure poses problems relating to the predictability of response time, but we shall not go into the issue here.

Verifications are therefore only valid based on the (non-functional) hypothesis that the treatment of external messages always converges in a limited time. Once this postulate has been established, we wish to verify high-level properties from the perspective of a hypothetical external user. For this hypothetical observer, the only perceptible events are those which concern program input/output. As input and output take place sequentially, it is almost possible to observe a time delay between the emission of output and the acquisition of the next input value.

However, for the sake of simplicity, we shall use the hypothesis that this delay is negligible, and consider that the following actions occur at exactly the same time:

– the emission of output corresponding to the previous external message;

– acquisition of the next external message.

This combined event is known as a *reaction*, and the reaction sequence is used to define a discrete time notion known as the controller clock.

Note that, from a functional perspective, the output of the nth reaction depends on the input acquired during the $(n-1)^{th}$ reaction. To avoid confusion, we shall distinguish between:

– the sequence of input read during the nth reaction *RI*;

– the sequence of input processed during the nth reaction *PI*, i.e. the input on which the nth output is functionally dependent: $S_{[n]} = CIM(RI_{[n]})$; the relationship between these two sequences is $PI_{[n]} = RI_{[n-1]}$.

We shall now show that the logical time induced by the sequence of reactions is sufficient to date not only the properties expected of the controller, but also the environmental hypotheses.

4.3.3.3. *Environment model*

In general terms, a controller is not intended to operate correctly in a "chaotic" environment, and this consideration naturally leads us to express environmental hypotheses. Typically, in the considered domain, a controller will not be able to prevent derailments if switch are able to move in a random manner; proofs must therefore take account of environmental hypotheses such as the fact that switches will only move if ordered to do so by the controller.

The conjunction of these necessary hypotheses is known as the environment model: the term "model" should be taken to mean a mathematical abstraction of reality.

4.3.3.3.1. Discrete time vs. continuous time

The environment of the controller is (at least partly) constituted by the physical world. So-called "realistic" models of the physical world are time-continuous.

Precise reasoning concerning the interactions between a discrete controller and a continuous environment is possible (in these cases, we speak of hybrid systems), but of no great interest in this case, as the controller only handles logical output. We therefore employ the principle that the environment is a dynamic system operating through discrete changes (a light may go out, a switch may move to the left position, etc.).

4.3.3.3.2. Logical time vs. real time

From the perspective of an external observer, we therefore have two notions of discrete time:

– the notion of time induced by the input/output sequence of the controller;

– the notion of time linked to the sequence of discrete changes in the environment.

A new postulate is required: the controller will not be able to operate correctly if changes in the environment occur "too quickly". In computer science, this is known as the real-time aspect; evidently, this aspect is of great importance in safety terms, but is completely orthogonal to the function aspect. To summarize, a controller must:

– calculate sufficiently quickly (real time aspect);

– calculate correctly (functional aspect).

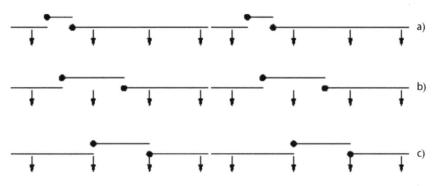

Figure 4.11. *Top to bottom: a) non real-time system, b) real-time and c) synchronous system*

In our approach, we are only concerned with functional verification; we shall therefore presume that the controller is quicker than the environment. In concrete terms, this means that an environmental variable may change once, at most, between two controller samplings. This principle is illustrated in Figure 4.11:

– in the top example, an environmental variable moves from low to high then from high to low between samplings: the system is not operating in real time;

– in the second example, the variable changes once, at most, between two samplings, and all changes are perceived by the controller: the system operates in real time.

Let us suppose that the system is operating in real time, and a discrete change takes place in the environment between two successive samplings. It is clear that the precise moment at which the change occurs has no effect on the operation of the controller: in functional terms, it is as if the environmental change took place at the exact instant of sampling by the controller. A synchronous system of this type is shown in the third example in Figure 4.11.

4.3.3.4. *Modeling causality: parallel play*

The reasoning set out in the previous sections justifies the decision to consider the environment as a reactive system, evolving at the same logical instants as the controller. Like the controller, the environment is therefore a reactive system which receives inputs, i.e. controller outputs and which produces outputs, i.e. inputs for the controller. Unlike the controller, the environment is not deterministic, i.e. the inputs produced by the environment is not exactly determined by the output of the controller: at most, we may consider that a relationship exists between orders and inputs.

Let us now look more closely at the causality relationships between these input and output variables:

– During the nth reaction, the environment "reads" the outputs produced by the controller, noted $S_{[n]}$.

– These outputs S_n is a function of the inputs read by the controller during the previous reaction (*i.e.* $S_{[n]} = CIM(RI_{[n-1]})$).

– The outputs produced by the environment during the nth reaction is read by the controller, i.e. $RI_{[n]}$.

When modeling the environment, we express properties using the environment, i.e. we express the relationships between commands and sensors. Stating that the inputs produced at instant n (i.e. the $RI_{[n]}$) may depend on the outputs received at the same instant ($S_{[n]}$) implies that the environment is *infinitely fast*, something which is contrary to the initial postulate: $RI_{[n]}$ cannot be causally dependent on $S_{[n]}$. At most, $RI_{[n]}$ may be caused by the previous actions of the controller, i.e. at most, $S_{[n-1]}$.

This may be seen as a *parallel play* principle: the environment and controller evolve through successive, perfectly simultaneous "turns":

– they read their respective inputs at the same time: $RI_{[n]}$ for the controller, $S_{[n]}$ for the environment;

– they then "calculate" the next decisions;

– they produce their respective reactions at the same time: $S_{[n+1]}$ (dependent on $RI_{[n]}$) for the controller and $RI_{[n+1]}$ (dependent on $S_{[n]}$) for the environment.

Note that this notion of delay by the environment in taking account of commands is entirely logical, and simply reflects the causality principle, without taking account of potential delays in reaction. In other words, effects occur at least one logical instant after their causes; given the dynamics of the environment, the real delay may be longer. If this is the case, and if it will have an effect on the expected properties, then the "real" delay must be taken into account in the functional hypotheses.

4.3.3.5. *Example of hypothesis expression*

An important hypothesis for some properties is that the switch will only move if ordered to do so.

For ease of reading, we shall use simplified notation compared to that used by the "real" CIM: we thus have a command *Cmd_L* to order movement to the left and *Cmd_R* to order movement to the right. The current position of the switch point is given by the sensors *Pt_L* and *Pt_R*.

As a first approximation, the hypothesis stipulates that *Pt_L* cannot go from being false to being true unless command *Cmd_L* has been issued (with a similar stipulation for the right-hand position). However, a command is only effective on the ground for a period of time, counted by a timer. Once this time has elapsed, the switch point will not move, even if the logical command *Cmd_L* (respectively *Cmd_R*) is still true. For this, we need to define a new variable *Cmd_Lcu* (*Cmd_Rcu* respectively) which indicates whether a left command is current from an environment perspective:

$$Cmd\_Lcu_{[n]} = Cmd\_L_{[n-1]} \land \lnot end\_timer_{[n-1]}$$

Once variable *Cmd_Lcu* has been defined, the hypothesis above is expressed by:

$$(Pt\_L[n] \land \lnot Pt\_L[n-1]) \Rightarrow Cmd\_Lcu[n-1]$$

4.3.3.6. *Counter-example guided modeling*

4.3.3.6.1. The environment

Environment modeling consists in defining new variables and/or new properties in the CIM corresponding to the field equipments, such as switches and track circuits, and procedures, such as the interlocking cancellation procedure. The difficulty lies in obtaining a suitable environment model.

A suitable environment model must not be:

– Excessively limiting. If behaviors leading to safety hazards are not taken into consideration in the environment model, then the proof process will not detect the risk of accidents occurring.

– Overly permissive, including non-realistic behaviors which would lead to risk situations. In this situation, certain properties would be falsely violated.

A "suitable" model may be obtained through proof, and notably by searching for counter-examples. The process used is incremental and iterative (see Figure 4.12). Once a property has been modeled, we search for counter-examples using a Bounded Model-checker (BMC) [BCC 99, BCC 03] developed by Prover Technology. When the BMC finds a counter-example, it produces a plot leading to a state which falsifies the property being demonstrated. Once this plot has been analyzed, one or more constraints are added to the formal environment model. As the name indicates, a constraint limits the number of possible states of the model. Thus, following our approach, this constraint qualifies a behavior of the environment in relation to the system, or, in other words, allows us to eliminate some behaviors which cannot occur in real life, according to the defined hypotheses. Once the environment model has been enriched using these new constraints, we repeat the search for counter-examples. The process is reiterated until the BMC is unable to find further counter-examples. Experience has shown that in cases where the BMC has not found a counter-example after a given number of iterations, the property will always be correct. However, this principle needs to be demonstrated, and the proof process will be presented in the following section.

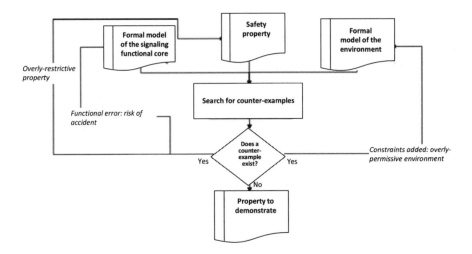

Figure 4.12. *Use of counter-example searches for modeling*

As an illustration, let us take the example of the switch modeling. A switch may be in one of three states: right, left or open. The CIM uses two sensors to obtain the position of a switch point on the track (one for the left position and one for the right position). There may be a difference between the real position of a switch point on the ground and the position reported to the CIM by the sensors if a sensor is faulty. When modeling a switch, we must therefore define environmental variables relating to the real position of the switch point and the state of the sensors.

The model of the real behavior of the switches is formalized using a set of constraints, established following the counter-example analysis procedure.

These constraints may be translated into natural language as follows:

– A switch point may not be in both left and right positions at the same time.

– A switch point will not change position without a movement order.

– A switch point cannot move from one position to the opposite position in a single cycle.

As we have seen, the environment also affects operating rules. As an example, let us consider the interlocking cancellation process for switch positions. The cancellation of interlocking for the left and right switch positions respectively aims at allowing opening of the starting signal of a route in case of a material breakdown leading to an absence of state information, "switch ordered and controlled on left (right)", although the switch may already be in the position required for the route.

Manual interlocking procedures cancel the effects of the automatic interlocking. Such procedures are designed to override safety functions of the CIM and allow control operator to manage manually routes in case of faulty equipments. For switch point position interlocking, the operator command "cancel interlocking of switch position" is common for both the left and right switch position. The reception of the cancellation command by the CIM must be confirmed by the field employee using field authorization device within a given period of time; if not, the command is lost.

Evidently, we need to model this procedure for proof purposes. However, by seeking counter-examples, this modeling can be limited to a strict minimum, i.e. to writing the constraint stipulating that the movement agent can only deliver the ground authorization if the switch is in a position compatible with the intended route. This constraint implies the respect of the operating rules by the field employee.

As we saw in section 4.1.1, the environment model was subject to multiple peer reviews at Thales and the RATP to ensure that the modeled hypotheses corresponded to the real environment. These verification activities are crucial, as a biased environment model could produce incorrect proofs.

4.3.3.6.2. Safety properties

The BMC is also useful in establishing safety properties. Counter-example analysis can highlight problems at the property level, rather than deficiencies at the environment or CIM level. Two sorts of problem may be encountered:

– The property is poorly expressed: either the logical expression of the safety property is not a faithful transcription of the informal property, or it does not express the designer's wishes. In that case, the BMC can be used as a tool for property debugging rather than for modeling.

– The property is too restrictive: counter-example analysis may show that the property sanctions a behavior by the CIM or the environment which does not generate safety hazards. The property must therefore be modified. This type of counter-example highlights specific cases linked to unusual track configurations which may not have been anticipated during the design phase.

4.3.3.6.3. The signaling function

In some cases, neither the environment model nor the safety properties are responsible for the production of a counter-example. In these cases, the source of the counter-example must lie in the signaling function, meaning that a potential accident risk has been detected. We therefore need to modify the signaling function to prevent this hazard scenario from occurring. In that case, the BMC may be seen as a design aid for the signaling function.

4.3.3.7. *Demonstrating safety properties*

As we have seen, the BMC is not intended to produce formal proofs, as such; it is used as a tool for modeling assistance and in correcting various models. However, it is also used in the demonstration process, where it acts as a filter. When no further counter-examples can be found, we consider that a property is demonstrable. The probability that the property will be false is weak as, as we stated in section 4.3.3.6.1, above a given exploration threshold, properties analyzed by the BMC have never proven to be false. However weak the probability may be, it is not null; nevertheless, experience has shown that the BMC approach filters out a maximum number of false properties, meaning that time need not be spent attempting to demonstrate these properties.

For the proof itself, we use a satisfiability (SAT)-solver developed by Prover Technology which will be discussed in greater detail in section 4.4.2. The SAT-solver gives one of three responses when presented with a safety property to demonstrate, an environment model and an interlocking system:

– The property is true, and has been proved automatically by the proof engine.

– The property is false: this response is theoretically possible, but it is never encountered as the properties have already successfully passed through the BMC filter, i.e. no counter-examples have been found.

– The property is considered to be indeterminate.

To obtain a proof, we therefore need to remove this indeterminate aspect. To do this, we add properties (lemmas) at a lower level in order to assist the proof engine in the demonstration process. Once these lemmas have been demonstrated, they may be used to remove states which the proof engine considers as valid but which are not reachable by the signaling system.

As an illustration, let us consider two variables A and B initialized to *True* and *False* respectively, and such that the value of each changes to the opposite value for each subsequent cycle. Represented in the form of a flow, this gives us:

$A:= True, False, True, False, True, ...$

$B:= False, True, False, True, False, ...$

In TECLA, the language used by the proof engine, variables A and B are defined as follows: $A:=True, \neg A$ and $B:= False, \neg B$. Let us consider the following property: $\neg(A \wedge B)$. The proof engine will not be able to demonstrate this property on its own; it will consider, wrongly, that the state where variables A and B are both *False* (or *True*) is a possible state. By adding and demonstrating the lemma $\neg(A \leftrightarrow B)$, we prevent the proof engine from considering states where A and B have the same values, and it will then be able to prove the property $\neg(A \wedge B)$ for all possible system states.

4.4. Formal proof suite

The proof suite used by Thales for formal analysis of PMI systems was developed by Prover Technology. The core of the suite is the Prover SL proof engine, which uses various SAT-based model checking techniques to analyze and prove safety properties.

The suite also includes a non-certified chain, which allows us to:

– obtain a system modeling using a formalism which can be understood by the proof engine;

– establish an environment model and the safety properties;

– prove safety properties and analyze counter-examples.

The use of a software solution as the only means of verifying SSIL4[8] safety systems [CEN 01] such as PMI systems will only be acceptable if this solution itself conforms to the SSIL4 safety requirements.

To respond to this requirement, the "certified chain", part of the suite, guarantees the validity of the proof results obtained using the uncertified chain through the use of *a posteriori* proof verification techniques. The components of the certified chain were developed in accordance with the SSIL4 requirements and the whole set of tools was qualified by the RATP.

4.4.1. *Modeling the system*

Before a system can be subjected to formal analysis, it must first be modeled, then translated into a formalism which can be understood by the analysis tool. Such a model must respond to two key requirements: firstly, it must constitute a correct abstraction of the real system, so that the proof of a safety property for the model will also be valid for the real system. Secondly, the level of abstraction used in the model must be sufficient to allow the analysis tool to prove the necessary properties.

A PMI system is made up of a set of automata (the *instantiated graphs*) and Boolean state variables, which are interpreted by a generic program (the Computerized Interlocking Module, CIM). The semantics of these automata

8 SSIL: Software Safety Integrity Level. Standard [CEN 01] identifies five safety levels, from 0 (the lowest) to 4 (the highest).

is completely defined by the way in which they are executed by the CIM. The first task involved in obtaining a system model is the formal definition of this operational semantics; this was carried out with assistance from the

designers at Thales and RATP experts, using the source code of the CIM. The semantics was defined by Prover Technology and sent to other members involved in the project for approval.

4.4.2. *Non-certified analysis chain*

Prover Technology has developed tools for day-to-day activities not requiring certified analysis, for use in establishing and correcting properties and seeking errors in PMI systems. These tools needed to be able to implement safety property analysis for a PMI system and to present the results of these activities to the user, indicating whether or not a property had been proved and, where necessary, describing the counter-example scenario which falsified the property.

Firstly, an initial implementation of the modeling principles described in section 4.4.1 was established. The translator was written in Python and implemented the full algorithm, including automatic generation of possible lemmas, iteration up to a fixed point mixing symbolic simulations and lemma analysis, and a final phase involving the simplification of results and a full reconstruction of the model in TECLA, Prover Technology's own formal language. The translator was used to obtain the set of valid lemmas and a model of the system, used to update safety properties and the PMI system in question.

Next, Prover Technology developed the TECLA Command Line Interpreter, or TCLI, a general interpreter used to load models expressed using TECLA, to add, remove or modify elements of the model, and to launch the analytical process using the Prover SL proof engine.

At the end of the analysis, results (counter-examples or proofs) can be retrieved and processed in the interpreter. This tool can be extended in Python and permits the use of parameterizable scripts.

Prover Technology then created a set of TCLI scripts, used to initialize a variety of types of analysis (counter-example searches, searches for counter-examples using induction, proof searches) along with a script for counter-examples, used for re-loading, replay in a simulated CIM and to create files describing counter-examples in a way which can then be used by the engineers involved in the verification process.

4.4.3. *The certified analysis chain*

Since PMI systems must conform to SSIL4 safety levels, the system safety verification chain must itself conform to SSIL4 [CEN 01]. Two main components require particular attention for certification: the translation process and safety property analysis.

The translation of a PMI system must conform to the SSIL4 safety criteria. For this reason, the correctness proof of the model was carried out on paper, and the proof was verified by the Verimag laboratory. A diversificative implementation was selected by the members of the project as a means of attaining the required SIL4 level. Thus, two different implementations were used, designed by different teams and using different languages (C and Ocaml), based on a specification document for translation principles.

The two translators use different input formats to describe the automata of the same PMI system: one is a common text file, the other is a binary file format. The translators were developed within a framework giving an SSIL2 certification. The two translators do not implement the full fixed point search algorithm, but simply a single symbolic simulation with pruning of the transition tree, starting from the set of lemmas (presumed to be valid) obtained by the translator used in the non-certified chain (see section 4.4.2).

For each external message, each of the translators produces a file containing the transition function of the external cycle for the message and a file containing the set of formulae representing the proof obligations of the pruning decisions made during the translation of the message (if the formulae are found to be true for the transition function, then all of the pruning decisions must be correct). The formulae contained in the files are expressed in a high level language, or HLL, a restricted variant of TECLA.

Once the two alternative models of a PMI system have been obtained, we use the analysis engine to verify the following considerations for each external message of the system:

– The formulae for the pruning decisions must be valid for the transition function (to ensure that no decision has been made wrongly).

– The lemmas must be valid for the transition function (to ensure that the fixed point has been reached).

– The transition functions produced by the two translators must be sequentially equivalent, i.e. if a same input is used, they should produce a same output (to ensure that the two translators have carried out the same translation, avoiding implementation errors).

For analysis certification, whether to analyze the verification of translation correctness or for safety property analysis, the concept of *a posteriori* proof verification is used to avoid the need to certify the proof engine itself. When the proof engine concludes that a property is valid, it does not simply declare the validity of the result; it also provides a demonstration of the property, known as a prooflog, in the form of a file with a sequence of simple logical inference rules representing the proof of the property. A separate proof checker then performs the mundane task of checking that each step in the prooflog is the result of a valid application of one of the permitted inference rules.In summary, for a given PMI system, we use two different translators to obtain two alternative models. We then use the proof engine to analyze the formulae of clearance decisions, the lemmas and the safety properties. If the proof engine and the proof checker produce a positive result for all of these analyses, this means that:

– The translations obey the principles set out in the specification documents.

– The fixed point has been reached.

– The safety properties are correct at the end of the CIM cycle.

4.4.4. *Assessment of the proof suite*

The specific architecture of the certified chain described in section 4.4.1 and the development process conforming to the SSIL4 requirements (SSIL2 for the diversified tools) should ensure that the proof suite conforms to SSIL4 safety requirements.

Evaluation of the conformity of these tools to the SSIL4 requirements was carried out by the RATP. This evaluation included industrial process checks, involving the acceptance of plans and verification of their application, and the functional safety verification of the V cycle for software development, using specification, design, coding and test phases.

Particular efforts were made to verify that the graph execution semantics used by the translators constituted a correct abstraction of the semantics implemented in the code of the generic CIM program. This verification was repeated with each evolution of the generic CIM program affecting the graph execution engine.

4.5. Application

The proof method described above was implemented as part of the RATP PMI line 1 project. Line 1 is the oldest line in the network, and is also the busiest line in the Paris metro system. It covers 16.6 km and serves 25 stations.

The PMI was not applied to the whole line, but only to its end-points. The zones of influence (represented by the boxes in Figure 4.13) were:

– North: from La Défense to Argentine.

– South: from Château de Vincennes to Porte de Vincennes.

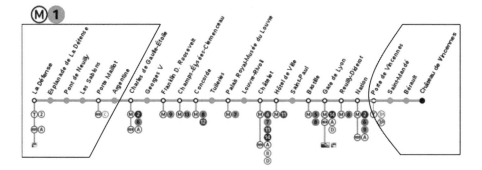

Figure 4.13. *Zones of action of the PMI on line 1*

Each end point is managed by a PMI, and each of these PMIs is made up of two CIMs. Each CIM is labeled with the name of a station or point on the line: "Défense", "Maillot", "Vincennes Terminus" and "Vincennes Garage". Signaling for the sections of line 1 outside the scope of the PMIs is managed by electromechanical systems.

Note that automation work was carried out for the trains on line 1, under the direction of SIEMENS. The Thales signaling system therefore needs to communicate with the SIEMENS automatic train system. The first shuttle (driverless train) has been put into service on 3rd November 2011. Driven and driverless trains have been circulated together for a period of 14 months. On 22nd December 2012 the oldest line in the Paris metro became completely automatic.

A two-phase approach has been selected to facilitate the implementation:

– The first phase concerns a specific signaling system for driven trains. The results of this phase are presented below. In parallel, functions required by the driverless trains have been installed to assist tests for the SIEMENS system. This phase was completed in February 2010, when the four CIMs were placed into service.

– Phase two consists in producing a signaling system for both driven and driverless trains.

In this chapter, we shall only consider phase 1. 26 generic properties were defined in order to demonstrate the absence of safety hazards caused by dysfunctions in one of the CIMs, each of which is the subject of a generic graph. 24 generic graphs were designed to model elements interacting with the PMI. These elements were instantiated as many times as necessary for each unit.

The Défense and Terminus units present similar complexity levels; Maillot is more complex, involves more track configuration variations (track crossovers, stabling sidings etc.), and is larger (contains more elements). Amongst other considerations, this means that there are more proof obligations to process and the calculation time required is greater. In table 4.1, the units are shown in processing order.

Unit name	Time taken to translate SIG data	Time taken to translate proof data	No. of demonstrated proof obligations	Duration of certified solution	No. of lemmas
Défense	4h12m 15s	5m20s	210	29h41m	1645
Maillot	21h13m11s	23m41s	564	11d	10066
Terminus	9h12s	2h9m46s	334	4.5d	14689
Garage	–	–	–	–	–

Table 4.1. *Statistics from the proof activity involved in the PMI RATP L1 project, phase 1*

In order to prove safety properties, we need to add lower-level properties, known as lemmas (see section 4.3.3.7) which assist the proof engine in the demonstration process. The average level of automatic proof for a given post is around 50%; for the remaining 50% of proof obligations, lemmas need to be supplied.

The number of lemmas used to demonstrate the safety properties of a unit does not necessarily constitute a good indicator of the difficulty inherent in producing (see Table 4.1). 10066 lemmas were needed to demonstrate the 564 safety properties for the Maillot unit, whereas for Terminus, 14689 lemmas were used to demonstrate 334 safety properties. This is due to the sequential treatment of the units.

When demonstrating the safety properties for the Maillot unit, we were able to reuse the lemmas identified for the Défense unit, with some modifications. The lemmas for Maillot were reused for Terminus in a similar way. As new units were processed, new cases were identified and added to the generic lemma database. Thus, for some safety properties, we had too many lemmas; however, by directly appplying the lemma database, we obtained a proof rate of over 80%. The specificities of each unit mean that new lemmas are required to enrich the database in order to process the remaining 20% of cases.

Note that the lack of data in the table for the Garage CIM is not due to an omission on our part, since it was not possible to obtain proof for this CIM; more specifically, it was not possible to generate a formal model of the interlocking system. Model-checking techniques are sensitive to the combinatorial explosion phenomenon, and the Garage unit was too large to handle using the available Pentium dual core 2 to 3 GHz processors with 8 Gb of RAM. The machines currently in use have i7 975 × 3.33 GHz cores with 24 Gb of RAM, plus a 64 Gb SSD disk for swap memory. Clearly, the increase in processing power raises the threshold at which the combinatorial explosion phenomenon becomes problematic.

Important modifications have been made to reduce the combinatorial explosion at its source, i.e. in the graph engine. After analysis, the Prover Technology team was able to identify and implement improvements to the Thales graph engine by modifying the algorithm. The proof tools were also modified in a similar way. The ProofLogChecker was also optimized, and the new release is, on average, twice as fast as the version used to produce the statistics in Table 4.1. As one can see in Table 4.1, the certified solution could take some days of calculus. With the early versions of the proof suite, if the proof check process was unintentionally interrupted, even on the last proof obligation (PO), it should be started from the beginning. Such a weakness could have jeopardized a commissioning deadline. To mitigate risks and delays, an improvement was implemented which permits to resume proof check from the last non verified PO without starting all over again.

Also an attention was focused on the use of distributed computing for the certified aspect. The difficulty does not lie in providing a technical solution, but rather in ensuring that the complexity of this solution remains low enough to enable assessment activities, i.e. verification that the proof tool design conforms to the CENELEC standards. Prover Technology implemented a technical solution, and the RATP applied the assessment process.

Other potential improvements are currently under investigation, such as the definition of design criteria to reduce the combinatorial explosion in signaling graphs.

The proof activity presented in the previous sections has been applied by Thales on:

– Two CIMs for line 12 (on the south end of the line). The proof established for this line is fairly close to that used for line 1 phase 1. The main difference between the two projects lies in the presence of degraded modes for line 12, i.e. the possibility of canceling interlocking orders.

– Four units for line 1 phase 2. As we have already stated, CIMs allow the safe circulation of both driven and driverless trains. Degraded modes need to be taken into consideration in this case; these modes are different to those found on line 12, notably due to the presence of driverless trains on line 1. Note that the optimization activities make it possible to obtain formal proof for the "Vincennes Garage" unit using "non-certified chain" in 2012. Distributed computing helped to obtain formal proof with "certified chain" for "Vincennes Garage" during the last upgrade of PMIs on line 1 on October 2013.

– Three units for line 8. For this project the proof process activites were not carried out by Thales alone, but as joint operations involving Thales and RATP. At the request of RATP, skills transfer through a program of training has been put in place. Since then, RATP can perform all of the formal safety demonstration activities.

– Two units for line 4 and two units for line 12 (on the north end of the line). The whole proof activities was performed by RATP on its own without any particular support from Thales.

– Since a number of upgrades were made by RATP in order to fix some minor problems or implement new signaling functions. Both development (modifications of generic and/or instantiated graphs) and validation (formal proof) activities were carried out by RATP. This phase of project confirmed the enormous existing potential of the presented approach as RATP were able to carry the whole validation process in a very limited time.

4.6. Results of our experience

In this section, we shall consider the experience gained from the activities described above and from current ongoing developments.

4.6.1. *Environment modeling*

The formalization of the environment of the interlocking system highlighted constraints which must be verified by the environment in order for the interlocking system to offer certain safety guarantees. We touched upon some of these constraints in section 4.3.3.6, and we shall discuss two in greater detail below.

One of our initial postulates for environment modeling is that the CIM must respect real-time constraints, i.e. calculate "sufficiently quickly" in relation to its environment. Constraints expressed in relation to environment changes, added to enable proof, have contributed to a more precise expression of this requirement.

Concerning the switch movements, we need to express the constraint stipulating that a switch point cannot pass from the left position to the right position in a single CIM cycle, i.e. the CIM cycle must be sufficiently short to enable us to observe that the switch point is neither in the left position or the right position, before observing that the switch point has reached one of these positions over the next cycles. Without this constraint, it would not be possible to demonstrate some safety properties. A similar constraint is required in relation to train movements. This movement is modeled through the occupation of track circuits, used as input data by the CIM.

We need to express the constraint that a train occupying track circuit A and heading towards the contiguous track circuit B cannot free up track circuit A and occupy track circuit B in a single CIM cycle. In other words, the CIM cycle must be short enough to observe that track circuits A and B are both occupied, before observing, during the next cycles, that track circuit A is now free and track circuit B is occupied. This constraint expresses the fact that trains do not "jump", and is relatively evident, given the speed and length of trains

We should also consider the case of manual interlocking. As stated in section 4.3.3.6, the cancellation of automatic interlocking occurs when the starting signal for a formed route cannot be opened as the CIM does not have the necessary input information concerning the switch point position. This may be due, for example, to a fault in the switch point position sensor. Interlocking cancellation allows the control operator to take over and, by confirming that the switch point is in the required position for the route in question, to oblige the CIM to allow the signal to open.

In that case, the responsibility for safety falls to the control operator. The manual interlocking for switch positions is covered by operating rules. These rules require the cancellation of automatic interlocking to be triggered (respecting certain conditions) by the control operator through a command sent to the CIM and confirmed by a field employee, who confirms that the switch is in a position which is compatible with the route (ground authorization) using authorization device near the switch.

Proof activities have highlighted the importance of field authorizations delivered by operatives. This authorization allows the CIM to proceed with signal opening. It is therefore crucial for the field employee to know what switch position is required for the planned route. In case of error, the interlocking cancellation may take place in unsafe conditions. Proof activities also allow us to identify the conditions required for the interlocking cancellation to be safely requested by an operator, and these conditions have been reviewed in conjunction with the operating rules.

Thus, the formal proof process highlighted both explicit and implicit hypotheses relating to the system environment, and showed the exact contribution of human operatives to the safe operation of the system.

4.6.2. Proof vs. testing

The combinatory nature of graphs means that a considerable number of test cases are required in order to reach sufficient levels of coverage. Proof allows us to verify a property for all possible states, and therefore gives 100% coverage, even if the term "coverage" is not, strictly speaking, appropriate in the context of proof. For this reason, the use of a formal proof approach considerably reduced the workload involved in validation activities carried out by Thales and RATP.

Our method and tools allow us to demonstrate the safety of a signaling system as a whole. Moreover, the proof methods permit the identification of risk scenarios. These scenarios may be linked to:

– Borderline behaviors (reinitialization of the CIM, management of degraded modes: interlocking cancellation, etc.). Note that the identified scenarios are either too complicated to be anticipated by a human operator, or use specific aspects of the functional apparatus in non-envisaged contexts.

– The implementation of new functions. When a proof is carried out alongside the design process for a new function, the counter-examples identified during proof, while not necessarily identifying hazard scenarios, may provide elements for reflection by the designer, lead to improvements in the quality of the implementation and reduce the number of iterations of the design cycle.

It is not unusual for a user to notice shortcomings in the days or weeks following the commissioning of a PMI which may lead to difficulties when using the line. In that case, improvements to the signal functions are required, and we need to ensure that these modifications do not create regressions and that the system remains safe.

Since these modifications are purely functional, they have no effect on the safety properties. This is not always the case for validation, which may lead to the modification of test cases. A first assessment of system safety can generally be obtained in a few hours using non-certified proof tools. The reactive nature of exhaustive proof-based approaches is an advantage when compared with test-based approaches.

4.6.3. *Limitations*

As noted in section 4.5, model-checking is sensitive to combinatorial explosion phenomena, and not all systems can be verified using this technique. For example, it is not currently possible to treat depots handling hundreds of routes; these cases occur on mainline train routes. The formal proof techniques are therefore not universally applicable.

Increases in computer processing power have resulted in these limits being pushed back, and the technology used by SAT solvers continues to evolve. Moreover, far-reaching action has been taken by modifying the graph engine algorithm, enabling its use for formal proof.

The next stage is to define design rules to directly limit combinatorial explosion in the graphs, and not only in the way in which the graphs are used. It is, however, necessary to maintain classic (test-based) validation processes for use when a proof approach cannot be implemented.

4.7. Conclusion and prospects

In this chapter, we have presented the PMI system, with a particular focus on the CIM subsystem which, by managing interlocking and commanding track equipment, can create potentially catastrophic situations presenting a risk to human life. The CIM program is made up of two distinct parts: an executable program (the graph engine) and a set of instantiated graphs.

The executable program is generic for all PMIs, and executes the instantiated graphs. These graphs are specific to each unit, and result from a modeling of the interlocking logic applied to the track layout of the unit. The instantiated graphs constitute the functional aspect of the CIM system and are subject to proof. The aim of the proof process is therefore to verify that the signaling functions, as implemented by the instantiated graphs, do not create dangerous situations.

The proof approach presented in this chapter is a key element in the safety files for the implementation of a PMI. The establishment of the method and associated tools was not without difficulties, but the benefits repay the investment. The formal proof approach allows us to:

– Clearly specify the hypotheses on which the safety demonstration is based. This activity required close collaboration between RATP and Thales teams to ensure the validity of the selected hypotheses.

– Express properties of a higher level than those which may be expressed through test-based activity.

– Assist the graph designer in implementing new functions.

– Identify risk scenarios which a test engineer would be unable to find, given the difficulty of the task.

Further work is needed to increase the productivity of the proof activities. A graphical representation of the counter-examples produced by proof tools, for example, would be of considerable benefit for the analytical process and would reduce processing time. Greater synergy between the design and proof teams is needed to define criteria for the correct establishment of a proof graph; in other words, we need to define a set of recommendations for graph design in a way which subsequently facilitates the proof activity. The skills and expertise of a wide range of partners will be essential in achieving this goal.

More generally, the use of proof allows us to do away with certain verification activities and removes the need for coverage calculations, reducing the validation workload for Thales and RATP. Detailed analysis of the results of the proof process and of validation activities has shown that there is still room for improvement in this respect.

We must continue to push the boundaries of combinatorial explosion by identifying and mastering the factors which contribute to this phenomenon. Following these planned improvements, if our tools are still not able to treat all of the units used by RATP, other ideas should be envisaged, such as the use of the formal specification to generate test cases; this would allow us to reuse at least some of the results of the proof process.

4.8. Glossary

CENELEC[9]: *Comité Européen de Normalisation ELECtrotechnique*, European Committee for Electrotechnical Standardization

FMECA: Failure Modes, Effects and Criticality Analysis

HCI :   Human-Computer Interface

LLL: Low Level Language

LFD: Logical Foundation Document

MEI: *Module d'Enclenchements Informatiques*, Computerized interlocking module

MMM: Movement Management Module

CC: Control Center

PIPC: *Poste Informatique à technologie PC*, System using PC technology

PMI :   *Poste de Manœuvre à enclenchement Informatisé*, Computerized interlocking system

RATP[10]:   *Régie Autonome des Transports Parisiens*, Autonomous Operator of Parisian Transports

SAT: Satisfiability

SAET: *Système d'Automatisation de l'Exploitation des Trains*, Automation system of train operations

---

9 See http://www.cenelec.eu/Cenelec/Homepage.htm.
10 See http://www.ratp.fr.

MSS: *Système d'Aide à la Maintenance*, Maintenance Support
System

COMS: *Système de Communication*, Communications System

SIL: Safety Integrity Level

SSIL :   Software Safety Integrity Level

TCLI: TECLA Command Line Interpreter

4.9. Bibliography

[ABR 96] ABRIAL J.R., *The B-Book*, Cambridge University Press, 1996.

[BAI 08] BAIER C., KATOEN J.-P., *Principles of Model Checking*, The MIT Press, 2008.

[BAN 05] BANCI, M., "Geographical versus functional modelling by statecharts of interlocking systems", *International Workshop on Formal Methods for Industrial Critical Systems (FMICS '04)*, Electronic Notes in Theoretical Computer Science, vol. 133, 2005.

[BEH 98] BEHM P., DESFORGES P., MEYNADIER J., "Meteor: an industrial success in formal development, B '98: recent advances", in BERT D. (ed.), *The Development and Use of the B Method*, Lecture Notes in Computer Science, vol. 1393, Springer, 1998.

[BEH 08] BEHNIA S., MAMMAR A., MOTA J.-M., *et al.*, "Industrialising a proof-based verification approach of computerised interlocking systems", *11th International Conference on Computer System Design and Operation in the Railway and Other Transit Systems, (Comprail '08)*, Toledo, Spain, 2008.

[BER 96] BERNARDESCHI C., FANTECHI A., GNESI S., *et al.*, "Proving safety properties for embedded control systems", *EDCC-2: 2nd European Dependable Computing Conference*, Lecture Notes in Computer Science, vol. 1150, 1996.

[BIE 99] BIERE A., CIMATTI A., CLARKE E., *et al.*, "Symbolic model checking without BDDS", *Proceedings of the 5th International Conference on Tools and Algorithms for Construction and Analysis of Systems (TACAS '99)*, LNCS, Springer Verlag, London, UK, pp. 193–207, 1999.

[BIE 03] BIERE A., CIMATTI A., CLARKE E., *et al.*, "Bounded model checking", *Advances in Computers*, vol. 58, pp. 117–148, 2003.

[BOU 00] BOULANGER J.-L., GALLARDO M., "Processus de validation basée sur la notion de propriété", *Lambda Mu 12 a*, Montpellier, 27–30 March 2000.

[BOU 06] BOULANGER J.-L., Expression et validation des propriétés de sécurité logique et physique pour les systèmes informatiques critiques, Thesis, University of Technology of Compiègne, 2006.

[BOU 10] BOULANGER J.-L. (ed.), *Safety of Computer Architectures*, ISTE, London, & John Wiley & Sons, New York, 2010.

[BOU 12] BOULANGER J.-L. (ed.), *Formal Methods Industrial Use from Model to the Code*, ISTE, London, & John Wiley & Sons, New York, 2012.

[CEN 00] CENELEC, EN 50126, "Railway applications – the specification and demonstration of reliability, availability, maintainability and safety", *European Committee for Electrotechnical Standardization*, January 2000.

[CEN 01] CENELEC, "Software for railway control and protection systems", *European Committee for Electrotechnical Standardization*, 2001.

[CEN 03] CENELEC, NF EN 50129, "Railway applications – communication, signalling and processing systems – safety-related communication in transmission systems", *European Committee for Electrotechnical Standardization*, 2003.

[CHO 06] CHOQUET-GENIET A., *Les Réseaux de Petri – Un outil de modélisation*, Dunod, 2006.

[CLA 86] CLARKE E., EMERSON E., SISTLA A., "Automatic verification of finite-state concurrent systems using temporal logic specifications", *TOPLAS*, vol. 8, no. 2, pp. 244–263, 1986.

[COL 13] COLOM J.M., DESEL J., (eds.), "Applications and Theory of Petri Nets", *34th International Conference on Applications and Theory of Petri Nets (Petri Nets 2013)*, Milan, Italy, June 2013.

[FER 05] FERREIRA N.G., SILVA P.S.M., "Automatic verification of safety rules for a subway control software", *International Workshop on Formal Methods For Industrial Critical Systems (FMICS '05)*, Electronic Notes in Theoretical Computer Science, vol. 130, 2005.

[GAL 07] GALLARDO M., "Poste de manoeuvre à enclenchement informatique (PMI)", no. 167, pp. 29–38, December 2007.

[GAL 08] GALLARDO M., BOULANGER J.-L., "Poste de manoeuvre à enclenchement informatique : Démonstration de la sécurité", *Conférence Internationale Francophone D'automatique (Cifa)*, Bucharest, Romania, November 2008.

[JON 90] JONES C.B., *Systematic Software Development using Vdm*, Prentice Hall International, 1990.

[QUE 82] QUEILLE J., SIFAKIS J., "Specification and verification of concurrent systems in CESAR", *International Symposium on Programming*, Lecture Notes in Computer Science, Springer Verlag, vol. 137, pp. 337–351, 1982.

[ROA 98] ROANES-LOZANO E., LAITA L.M., ROANES-MACAS E., "An application of an AI methodology to railway interlocking systems using computer algebra, *Tasks and Methods in Applied Artificial Intelligence: 11th International Conference on Industrial and Engineering Applications of Artificial Intelligence and Expert Systems*, vol. 1416, 1998.

[SHE 00] SHEERAN M., STAALMARCK G., "A tutorial on Staalmarck's proof procedure for propositional logic", *Formal Methods in System Design*, vol. 16, no. 1, pp. 23–58, 2000.

[VIL 97] VILLEMEUR A., *Sûreté de fonctionnement des systèmes industriels: fiabilité – facteurs humains – informatisation,* Eyrolles, 1997.

Formal Verification of Data for Parameterized Systems

5.1. Introduction

5.1.1. *Systerel*

Systerel[1] is an SME specializing in the development of safety-critical real-time systems.

Systerel's expansion strategy uses specific business capabilities and strong technical and methodological skills to offer customers real value-added services. The company's main achievements relate to:

– embedded systems with hard real-time or safety requirements;

– safety-related tools (data preparation and system maintenance, etc.);

– formal specification of complex industrial systems.

Systerel has progressively expanded outside of its traditional area of activity in rail transports and the company is currently involved in large-scale projects in the rail, aeronautical, energy and information systems sectors.

These activities have led Systerel to consider data verification issues relating to the configuration of parameterized systems.

Chapter written by Mathieu CLABAUT.
1 For more details, see http://www.systerel.fr/.

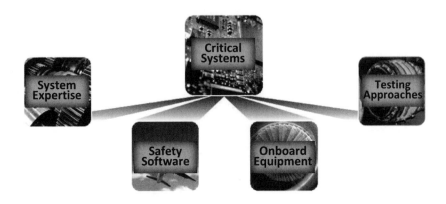

Figure 5.1. *Activities of Systerel*

5.1.2. *Data verification*

The question of data verification is related to efforts to reduce the development costs of safe2, software-based complex systems.

The costs involved in developing systems of this kind are very high, and industrial actors attempt to reduce the effort required by developing generic products, then adapting them for the specific requirements of a particular installation by modifying configuration data.

In the field of rail transport, this issue may be illustrated by the case of interlocking units. The purpose of these units is to safely form routes for use by trains. Before computers were widely used, interlocking units used specific mechanical or electromechanical solutions for each track zone, according to general signaling principles.

The use of computers allows us to separate the implementation of these signaling principles from their configuration using track data (topology, routes and signals, etc.).

In this way, a significant part of the functional aspect of the software is described by the configuration data, which therefore needs to be subject to a

2 In accordance with rail transport, CENELEC EN 50128 ([CEN 01] and [CEN 11]) and aeronautical standards, DO-178 [ARI 92].

development and verification process at least as strict as the processes applied to the program; in extreme cases, the software code itself may be considered as configuration data for a non-complex software sequencer.

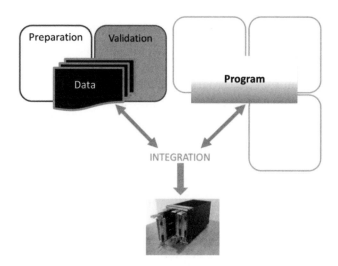

Figure 5.2. *Parameterized system*

In the following sections, we will consider the requirements and solutions associated with the verification of configuration data.

5.1.3. *Parameterized systems*

Before going further, let us establish a clear definition of parameterized systems.

5.1.3.1. *Systems*

The CENELEC EN 50128 [CEN 01] standard for rail transport provides a description of parameterized systems:

"A characteristic feature of railway control and protection systems is the need to design each installation to meet the individual requirements for a specific application. A system configured by application data allows type-approved generic software to be used, with the individual requirements for each installation defined as data (application specific data). This data is normally in the form of tabular information or an application specific language which is interpreted by the generic program."

5.1.3.2. Parameters

The parameter data for programs of this type is considered as a set of constants for system configuration. This may include:

– physical constants;

– parametric constraints used to define a command law;

– mission-specific constants (which may be downloaded);

– parametric constants related to design choices;

– validation and test data;

– constants produced during the definition of configuration data (authors, creation date, version and integrity, etc.).

The possible values for this data are constrained by specific properties contributing to system safety.

These properties may associate different types of data, and exist *independently of the system activity state*.

=> Properties define invariants in the system.

5.2. Data in the development cycle

The classic system specification and design cycle using subsystems, subsequently refined into material and software components, potentially over the course of multiple iterations, involves a number of functional and non-functional requirements. The specification and design of parameterized systems involves the definition of requirements, which are specific to the configuration data.

This data is then defined (valued) during a data preparation phase, which is specific to each installation.

The different phases of data treatment are discussed in detail below. These include:

– data and property identification;

– data and property modeling;

– property validation;

– production of configuration data for an installation;

– verification of configuration data;

– integration of data for initialization of an installation.

5.2.1. *Data and property identification*

The identification of parameter data and the associated properties is a key stage in developing safe parameterized systems. Our experience has shown that this is often a weak point in the process, particularly for developments where the highest level of safety is not required.

The properties involved during different phases of the development cycle are often specified using natural language. However, in certain contexts, where a development cycle using formal methods is already in place, a formal description may be produced at this stage.

5.2.2. *Modeling*

The quantity of configuration data for complex systems, for example a CBTC[3] system, may be considerable. This consideration has led industrial actors to establish data production and management processes based around a data model.

---

3 CBTC: *Communication Based Train Control.* CBTC is a system comprising onboard equipment on trains and fixed ground equipment in constant communication (generally over a radio link). It has been standardized [IEE 04].

5.2.3. *Property validation*

Unless properties are to be verified manually, they must be translated into formalisms suitable for use with the tools selected for verification.

We therefore need to ensure that properties are represented in a way which conforms to their specification. This is usually carried out using a combination of activities (independent critical checks, tool-based verification using test sets which do or do not validate the property being tested, etc.).

This verification should ideally be carried out by a domain expert with training in the formalism used to represent the properties in question.

5.2.4. *Data production*

This phase involves the collection of data relating to the domain context, product or specific installation, and its integration into a database which will be used to produce the final configuration embedded within the application software.

The configuration data is generally checked against real data before integration into the target applications, for example to check that the data conforms not only to plans but also to measurements obtained in practice.

5.2.5. *Property verification using data*

During this phase, we check that the configuration data verifies the required properties, either manually or using tools. This verification is carried out offline, i.e. before the data has been made available to the application.

The whole process may be reiterated following modifications to data or to properties until the full set of properties has been verified.

5.2.6. *Data integration*

Data may be integrated in the following different ways.

5.2.6.1. *Compilation*

Configuration data is converted into one or more source files in the target language. These files are then compiled and linked to the parameterizable program in order to produce the final application, which will be deployed onto the target after validation.

5.2.6.2. *Data-led software integration*

Software data-flow oriented designs lead to the definition of a family of generic software modules associated with concrete elements of the system. For an interlocking system, for example, a software module may be defined for each elementary unit of track.

The production of the instantiated application for a given track involves assembling different sets of elementary blocks with the correct parameters and connections. The integration of different instances of basic modules is therefore guided by the configuration data.

5.2.6.3. *Loading on initialization*

This widespread technique consists of supplying data during application initialization. The application is therefore responsible for verifying data coherence before completing the initialization phase, for example by verifying the conformity of presented and expected versions, ensuring data integrity using checksums, etc.

Data may be made available to a target application in different ways:

– Use of a flash memory card and the associated readers in the target processor.

– Use of an upload mechanism before initialization, etc.

5.2.6.4. *Online loading*

Certain systems, for example in the aerospace domain, are not physically accessible and therefore cannot be shut down for reconfiguration. These systems need to permit online reconfiguration of all or part of their onboard application.

In all cases, efforts are made to guarantee the integrity of configuration data, not only on initialization, but throughout the period of execution of the application.

5.3. Data verification

Once data with known properties has been produced, the next stage is to verify the conformity of the data with the identified properties. In this section, we will describe the different methods used for this purpose.

5.3.1. *Manual verification*

Manual analysis of data and properties may be used to verify configuration data. Two independent verifications are generally used with an aim of attaining target safety levels.

Evidently, this technique is time-consuming, costly and relatively inefficient. For certain data sets, up to 15% of properties have been found to be erroneous following a manual verification process.

Moreover, any changes to properties or data require considerable efforts to be made for re-verification.

5.3.2. *Algorithmic verification*

In most industrial contexts, a tool-based solution is used, with development of an *ad hoc* verification program, implementing a specific algorithm for each property to verify data conformity.

This method presents clear advantages in terms of productivity and verification quality when compared with manual verification techniques, but is not without its drawbacks:

– Property coding (see Table 5.1) is left to the developer, who may not have sufficient domain knowledge to ensure correct interpretation of properties.

– The property verifier must understand and master the subtleties of the programming language used to code the algorithmic verification.

– The verification program must be changed each time a property is modified or added.

When sequencing an I/O operation, the described ports and devices must be connected.

```
private static Boolean test_connected(int portId, int devId,
    List<Operation> seqs, Boolean[][] connectStatus) {
  for (int i = 0; i < seqs.size(); i++) {
    final Operation op = seqs.get(i);
    final int sPortId = op.getPort();
    final int sDevId = op.getDevice();
    if (connectStatus[sDevId][sPortId] == false) {
      System.out.println("Port and devices not connected...");
      return false;
    }
  }
  return true;
}
```

Table 5.1. *Example of algorithmic coding of property verification*

5.3.3. *Formal verification*

Formal verification, as promoted by Systerel, constitutes a third approach, which has recently been implemented for data verification.

5.3.3.1. *Why use a formal approach?*

Analysis of the difficulties involved in algorithmic verification highlights the problems inherent in connecting an informal specification, written in natural language, with a specification that can be understood and executed by a machine.

Formal language (see Figure 5.3) therefore represents the best compromise between a language used for property expression, which can be understood by human operators, and a language allowing these properties to be verified by a machine.

The selected formal language is a subset of B[4], a first-order predicate language based on set theory, which essentially uses standard mathematical notation ($\cap$, ϵ, $\exists$, $\forall$, $\subset$, $\neg$, $\Rightarrow$); this notation is clearly understood by the majority of engineers.

---

4 http://wiki.event-b.org/index.php/Event-B_Mathematical_Language.

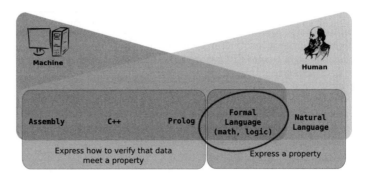

Figure 5.3. *Formal language: the best compromise between humans and machines*

The example in Table 5.1 is therefore written as follows:

When sequencing an I/O operation, the described ports and devices must be connected.

$\forall$(p,a) . p$\mapsto$a $\in$ dom(Sequences)
    $\Rightarrow$ (p$\mapsto$a) $\in$ dom(Connected)
    $\wedge$ Connected(p$\mapsto$a) = ON
// For any port p *and for any device likely to be involved in an I/O operation,* p *and* a *are connected.*

Table 5.2. *Formal expression of a property*

5.3.3.2. *The process*

Once properties have been identified and data have been produced, formal data verification (see Figure 5.4) can take place. This involves:

– formalization of the properties and the data model by a modeling expert;

– validation of the property formalization by a domain expert;

– adaptation of verification tools to the specific constraints of the project, where necessary (data extraction, specific development of the prover, etc.);

– data verification using the verification tools. In cases where properties are shown to be false, these are analyzed and the associated data or properties will be corrected.

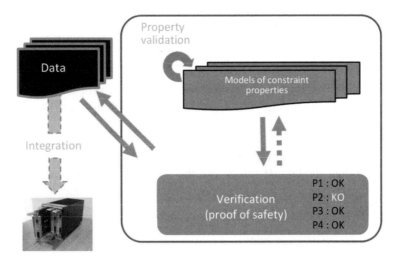

Figure 5.4. *Formal data verification process*

5.3.3.3. *Advantages*

The formal validation approach for configuration data has led to a certain number of improvements in terms of industrial processes. In this section, we will discuss the advantages of the method.

Property capitalization

The properties used may be grouped into different categories (see section 5.1.3), which may then be used in different ways.

Domain specific properties: These properties are specific to an industrial domain, and can generally be reused for all systems of the same type – for example the characterization of incompatible routes for interlocking systems, etc.

Product properties: These properties apply to a specific product line and may be reused for all instances of the product – for example in the case of interlocking systems, a property concerning the availability of crossing information from the ground system.

Installation properties: These properties are dependent on the final installation. Their reuse depends on the specific characteristics of different installations.

Systematic property classification during the identification phase allows us to organize the capitalization of formalized properties for different levels of reuse.

This is possible due to the formal specification of properties, and would be difficult to attain in the context of algorithmic verification (see section 5.3.2).

However, this reuse requires us to use an industrial process to standardize the chosen data models. If this is not the case, the need to modify the data extraction tools used to provide input for the proof core may outweigh the potential advantages.

Better validation of properties

The use of a formal language and associated tools allows us to carry out a number of verifications using the predicates describing properties. This allows early detection of problems associated with typing or poor definition resulting either from a poor formalization or from a poor formulation in natural language.

Maintenance and evolutions

The formal verification process for data allows us to dissociate the development and maintenance of verification tools from the maintenance of properties and data. This represents a considerable advantage in terms of flexibility, reusability and durability.

The core of the verification tools is, moreover, reusable from project to project. Maintenance is made easier by the reduction in the number of installation-specific tools, which can be reused transversally for any number of projects.

Furthermore, the use of Event-B for modeling presents advantages in terms of modularity, grouping modeling artifacts by component. This allows us to separate the data model from the property model, and to segregate properties according to their origin (business context, product line and installation, etc.).

Separation of roles

The formal verification process allows us to identify a certain number of roles with clearly defined, separate activities:

– Domain experts: identify and formulate properties using natural language, participating in the validation of formalized properties.

– Modeling experts: model data and properties in formal (mathematical) language.

– Verifiers: use tools to verify that the set of properties is respected by the set of configuration data. analyzing erroneous properties.

– Developers: adapt tools, notably data capture modules, which are specific to the data formats used to configure an application.

This separation of roles is not found in algorithmic verification, where the developer is also responsible for modeling and the domain expert needs to have a certain level of knowledge of software development.

Involvement of domain experts

The activities involved in modeling properties and other associated tasks, including the verification of the type and definition of formulations, generate interactions between modelers and domain experts. These interactions often lead to higher levels of precision in property specification, or even changes to these properties.

Interaction between modelers and domain experts, reinforced by the requirements of formalization, generally occurs early in the system development cycle, and represents a major advantage of the formal approach.

Detection of counter-examples

The use of formal property descriptions allows us:

– to obtain counter-example data sets at the end of the verification process in cases where properties have been found to be false. These data sets are used in error analysis;

– where appropriate, to use model-checking or constraint satisfaction methods to ensure property coherence, from the modeling stage onwards.

Temporal decoupling of tasks

The formal verification process allows complete dissociation of development tasks from data and property identification and modeling activities. This temporal decoupling (see Figure 5.5) reduces the workload involved in developing parameterized systems.

Note, also, that the reuse of the core of verification tools and certain data extraction modules considerably reduces the time required for tool development in subsequent projects. This also applies to the modeling phase, in that the majority of domain properties may be reused in future projects without needing to be modified.

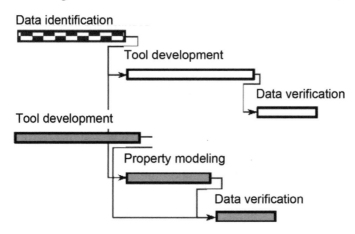

Figure 5.5. *Temporal decoupling of activities permits planning gains when compared to algorithmic verification (shown in white)*

5.3.3.4. *Tools*

The tools used for property verification are based around a proof core taken from the Rodin platform[5], and use data extraction modules to produce a shared representation of the data for verification, even if this data comes from a number of different sources of varying natures: relational databases, source files, Excel spreadsheets and binary files, etc.

Work is also underway to develop alternative tools for data verification using the same formalism.

---

5 http://wiki.event-b.org.

Proof core

The chosen proof core is a module of the Rodin platform, which is able to process formulas written in mathematical language, and allows us to verify predicates in relation to the referenced data.

Figure 5.6. *Screen capture from the RODIN platform*

Data extraction

Data must be extracted from the technical reference documents of the installation in order to be used by the proof core.

In a verification approach, it is important to analyze data as close as possible to its context of use in the final installation. This may be done either by direct analysis of the configuration files, which will be used by the final application, or by analyzing the system database and using a safe production chain for the final configuration data.

Extractors have been developed to obtain data from:

– relational databases;

– tabulated text files;

– spreadsheet calculation sheets;

– source code written in ADA, B or C;

– binary files in ELF format, etc.

5.4. Example of implementation

We will now discuss an implementation of formal data verification in the domain of space flight software.

5.4.1. *Presentation*

The application in question is a system responsible for managing the payload of a satellite (GPMU). The program is based on a hypervisor[6] providing a partitioned infrastructure (see Figure 5.6).

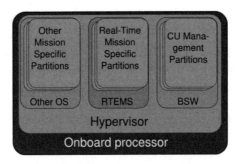

Figure 5.7. *Architecture of the GPMU*

The parameter data of an application of this type are used to configure both the different programs used in the partitions managed by the hypervisor and the hypervisor itself (see Figure 5.7). This data concern aspects such as the definition of partitions, their sizes, inter-partition communication ports, etc.

---

6 A hypervisor is a virtualization platform enabling multiple operating systems to work on a physical machine at the same time. Here, we have used Xtratum: http://www.xtratum.org.

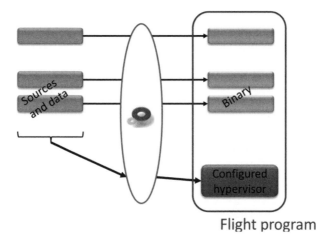

Flight program

Figure 5.8. *Use of configuration data*

5.4.2. *Property modeling*

The use of Event-B for property modeling allows us to structure properties using a modular model (see Figure 5.8). This modularity then contributes to improvements in model maintenance and reusability.

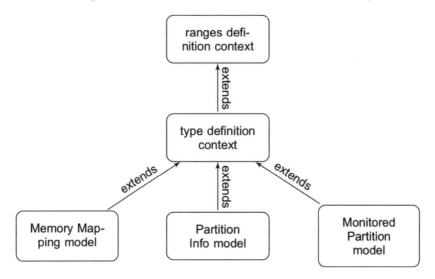

Figure 5.9. *Architecture of the data and property model*

```
// Context defining the memory mapping table
// of the configuration table of the MMDL partition
CONTEXT
    MMDL_CFT_MM_Ctx.buc EXTENDS    MMDL_CFT_Ctx

CONSTANTS
    MmdlBinaryTypes
    MmdlMemoryTypes
    StartAddress
    Length
    PartitionID
    BinaryType
    MemoryType
    MEMORY_TYPE_FLASH
    MEMORY_TYPE_RAM
    BINARY_TYPE_PARTITION_CODE
    BINARY_TYPE_CONFIG_TABLE
    BINARY_TYPE_CUSTOM_TABLE
    BINARY_TYPE_COMPAT_TABLE
    BINARY_TYPE_NONE

AXIOMS
    axm1  : BINARY_TYPE_PARTITION_CODE ∈ ℕ
    axm2  : BINARY_TYPE_CONFIG_TABLE ∈ ℕ
    axm3  : BINARY_TYPE_CUSTOM_TABLE ∈ ℕ
    axm4  : BINARY_TYPE_COMPAT_TABLE ∈ ℕ
    axm5  : BINARY_TYPE_NONE ∈ ℕ
    axm6  : MEMORY_TYPE_FLASH ∈ ℕ
    axm7  : MEMORY_TYPE_RAM ∈ ℕ
    axm8  : MmdlMemoryTypes ∈ ℙ(ℕ)
    axm9  : MmdlBinaryTypes ∈ ℙ(ℕ)
    axm10 : StartAddress ∈ 0‥sMmdlMemoryMappingTableSize-1 → ℕ // First field of an
MmdlSMemoryArea
    axm11 : Length ∈ 0‥sMmdlMemoryMappingTableSize-1 → ℕ // Second field of an MmdlSMemoryArea
    axm12 : PartitionID ∈ 0‥sMmdlMemoryMappingTableSize-1 → ℕ // Third field of an
MmdlSMemoryArea
    axm13 : BinaryType ∈ 0‥sMmdlMemoryMappingTableSize-1 → MmdlBinaryTypes // Fourth field of
an MmdlSMemoryArea
    axm14 : MemoryType ∈ 0‥sMmdlMemoryMappingTableSize-1 → MmdlMemoryTypes // Cinquième Fifth
field of an MmdlSMemoryArea

// For any given mapping field with a partition ID,
// all memory spaces are disconnected
    axm15 : ∀ i,j·  i ∈ dom(StartAddress) ∧ j ∈ dom(StartAddress)∧
            i ∈ dom(Length) ∧ j ∈ dom(Length)∧
            i ∈ dom(PartitionID) ∧ j ∈ dom(PartitionID) ∧
            i ≠ j ∧ PartitionID(i) = PartitionID(j)
      ⇒
            StartAddress(i)‥StartAddress(i)+Length(i)-1 ∩
        StartAddress(j)‥StartAddress(j)+Length(j)-1 = ∅
```

Figure 5.10. *Extract from a property model in Event-B*

5.4.3. *Data extraction*

The verified data was extracted as close as possible to the location of use by analyzing ELF format files produced by the compilation of source files written in C. The type and size of the data was obtained by source analysis.

The extraction process results in the production of an XML file which can then be used directly by the prover.

5.4.4. *Tools*

In addition to the data extraction module, two tools were created in the context of our experiments in proving data correctness for the aerospace domain.

The first of these tools is an autonomous command line tool, which produces a property verification report based on extracted data.

The second is a model for the integration of proof activities into the Rodin platform. This integration offers access to current and future functions of the platform, including an interactive prover, proof tree display to highlight problematic data entries, counter-example searches, etc.

Note that although the scope of our activity was small (500 lines of code, 70 pieces of data and 100 properties) the methodology and tools involved are suitable for use on a larger scale.

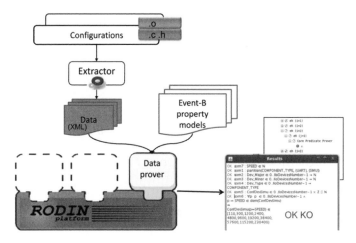

Figure 5.11. *Integration of the data prover into the Rodin platform, showing the data extraction and proof process*

5.5. SSIL4 process

The formal data verification process presented in this chapter cannot respond to the highest level of software safety required by the applicable standards on its own; formal verification tools with the required safety levels have yet to be developed.

A higher software safety level may be obtained by establishing a parallel verification process (formal or otherwise) or by increasing the safety level of verification tools.

5.6. Conclusion

While the main difficulty associated with data verification lies in the identification of properties during the different specification and design phases, our experience has shown that the implementation of formal data verification for a parameterized system presents considerable advantages.

It provides a significant contribution to improving the quality of verifications of the associated process.

5.7. Glossary

AQL: *atelier de qualification logiciel*, software qualification suite

BART: B automatic refinement tool

CBTC: communication based train control

CENELEC[7]: *Comité Européen de Normalisation Electrotechnique*, European committee for electrotechnical standardization

RATP[8]: *Régie Autonome des Transports Parisiens,* autonomous operator of Parisian transports

SSIL: software safety integrity level

5.8. Bibliography

[ABR 96] ABRIAL J.R., *The B-Book*, Cambridge University Press, 1996.

[ARI 92] ARINC, *Software Considerations in Airborne Systems and Equipment Certification*, Ed. B, no. ED12, DO-178B and EUROCAE, 1992.

---

7 See http://www.cenelec.eu/Cenelec/Homepage.htm.
8 See http://www.ratp.fr.

[CEN 01] CENELEC – EN 50128, "Railway applications. Communications, signalling and processing systems", *Software for Railway Control and Protection Systems*, May 2001.

[CEN 11] CENELEC – EN 50128, "Railway applications. Communications, signalling and processing systems", *Software for Railway Control and Protection Systems*, May 2011.

[IEE 04] IEEE, 1474.1, IEEE Standard for Communications-Based Train Control (CBTC), Performance and Functional Requirements, 2004.

ERTMS Modeling using EFS

6.1. The context

The European Railway Traffic Management System (ERTMS) defines the standard for interoperability between the onboard train protection systems (ETCS) and the railway infrastructure. This standard is decomposed into several documents (called subsets) focusing on specific parts of the system.

The ERTMS Formal Specs (EFS) is a project that focuses on modeling the requirements expressed in [SUB 11a] – System Requirements Specification related to the trainborne equipment, and applying the tests specified in [SUB 11b] – test cases on the model.

This modeling effort is aimed at generating code according to the customer's target language and providing the required artifacts to prove the match between the generated code and the ERA requirements, as presented in Figure 6.1. The customer can also use the model without code generation. In that case, EFS provides artifacts that can be used to verify the match between the model and the ERA requirements.

The modeling effort requires us to tackle the following issues:

– Natural language: requirements in [SUB 11a] are expressed in plain English. This may lead to misinterpretations inherent to natural languages.

Chapter written by Laurent FERIER, Svitlana LUKICHEVA and Stanislas PINTE.

Figure 6.1. *The EFS structure*

– Structure: [SUB 11a] organization follows the structure associated with requirements. This structure is not suited to model these requirements in a formal system, such as a computer program.

– Size: the size of the [SUB 11a] (500 pages – 39 messages – 47 packets – 176 variables) makes the work of checking the match between implementation and requirements extremely difficult. This work must nevertheless be performed for certification purposes.

– Completeness: while extreme care has been taken in specifying [SUB 11a], several requirements may still have been overlooked by the engineer. A formalization of these requirements, supported by automated tools, allows identification of the holes in the specification.

– Consistency: the amount and complexity of requirements prevents the use of only pair reviews to guarantee inconsistencies between the requirements. This consistency check must be supported by automated tools.

– Releases: the ERA specifications are in constant evolution to match new challenges. We must be able to update the model according to the new requirement releases.

The following sections will demonstrate how the EFS addresses the issues mentioned above.

6.2. EFS description

The EFS product is made up of two components.

– The *model* includes the requirements expressed in [SUB 11a], the complete data description, subsystem decomposition and business logic of a European vital computer (EVC), specified in union industry of signalling (UNISIG) [SUB 11a] specifications, expressed in the EFS language, and two kinds of tests: model unit tests verifying that a specific requirement has been correctly modelled, and integration tests from [SUB 11b].

– The *workbench* is a graphical tool designed to develop, maintain, and document model-based development for [SUB 11a]. It is a desktop application, running on the Microsoft .NET platform.

The *EFS language* is a domain specific language, developed by ERTMS Solutions for the sole purpose of modeling the ERTMS specifications. It is thus not weighed down by a history of irrelevant application domains, nor by universal features that are commonly included in general purpose formalizations. This language design is driven by two opposite constraints:

– Constraint 1: to be as close as possible to the artifacts used in the UNISIG [SUB 11a] specifications (e.g. plain English, state diagrams, tables) to demonstrate the equivalence between specification and implementation.

– Constraint 2: to be formal to allow interpretation, inferences and deduce system properties.

6.2.1. *Characteristics*

The following design principles used in EFS set it apart from other general-purpose formal methods: to be traceable, to be understandable, to allow support for automated reasoning and to be testable. The following sections present each design principle and show how they are applied in EFS.

6.2.1.1. *Traceability*

When considering railway transportation systems, traceability is an essential property, since such systems must satisfy the norm [CEN 01]. This norm requires complete and demonstrated traceability between all development cycle phases.

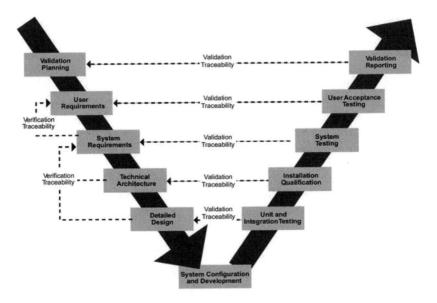

Figure 6.2. *V-cycle processes*

It supports traceability between requirements, the corresponding model, and the tests used to verify the model. This information allows the Workbench to enforce several structural constraints:

– each model element must be related to at least one requirement;

– each test must be related to at least one requirement;

– each requirement must be related to at least one model element and one test.

It is the responsibility of the modeling engineer, supported by the modeling process (see section 6.2.2), to ensure that both model and tests comply with the related requirements.

This trace information is used to perform impact analysis when changes occur in the model. When a requirement changes, impact analysis helps determine the parts of the model that are affected by this requirement, and should be reviewed.

Impact analysis is also used to select the tests that should be run again according to changes of part of the model. Note that this information is only of interest when performing integration tests, which require hardware mobilization, engineers etc. As we will see in section 6.2.1.4 that the tests performed on the model itself are quick and easy to execute.

Traceability is also used to measure the [SUB 11a] coverage both in terms of modeling and tests.

– Modeling is complete when all requirements related to the onboard unit can be traced to (at least) one model element.

– Testing is complete when all requirements related to the onboard units can be traced to (at least) one test. Note that this condition is not sufficient since tests should also cover all execution branches of the model.

6.2.1.2. *Understandability*

The EFS language has been specifically designed to be understandable by domain experts. A flaw of general-purpose formal language is that such languages can only be understood by formal language specialists[1]. This makes the formalization of the system unverifiable by the real users, the domain experts.

To overcome this, the EFS model is split into two layers:

– The complete behavior of the EVC system is specified using a *rule based layer*, a restricted formal language described in section 6.2.1.3. This is the only interpretation/translation artifact used in EFS.

– The *higher layers*, translations of the rule layer, display the model using artifacts commonly used in the UNISIG [SUB 11a] specifications (such as state diagrams, tables and flowcharts). The requirements that are expressed in plain English, cannot, in the general case, be translated into high level diagrams. In that case, the rules are translated in pseudo-code to be easily reviewed by the domain specialist.

These higher layers allow the domain expert to trace back the model to the specifications. Model animation, as we will see in section 6.2.1.4.2, is performed using the rule based layer, but is displayed to the user using higher layer views.

---

1 For instance, see [WOO 09] underlining that *the [SACEM] project team reported a difficulty in communication between the verifiers and the signaling engineers, who were not familiar with the B-method.*

Figure 6.3 shows that, even if the complete state machine is expressed in terms of rules (low level layer), the Workbench displays this information using state diagrams which correspond to the state diagrams as expressed in [SUB 11a], easing the model verification process.

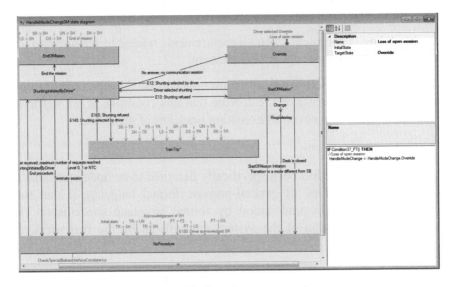

Figure 6.3. *State diagram example*

This allows us to identify and display two kinds of transitions: *explicit* transitions, which are explicitly described in the state diagrams of [SUB 11a], and the *implicit* transitions, which are described outside state diagrams. For instance, Figure 6.3 shows two kinds of transitions:

– black transition are explicitly defined in the state machines Start Of Mission, Shunting Initiated by Driver, ...

– Light grey transitions are described in other sections of [SUB 11a]. For instance, the transition Loss of Open Session leads to state Override. It has been modeled by requirement 5.11.4.2. This requirement specifically indicates that this situation has not been taken into account for the design of the flowchart.

Modeling this kind of transition is interesting to understand, during a test scenario, the reason why one reaches a specific state – even when no transition has been explicitly described in [SUB 11a].

Another example, illustrated by Figure 6.4, displays the [SUB 11a] English requirement in the left part of the description tab whereas the corresponding pseudo-code, based on the underlying model, is provided in the right part of the description tab. Using this artifact, the system engineer can easily verify that the implementation matches the related requirement.

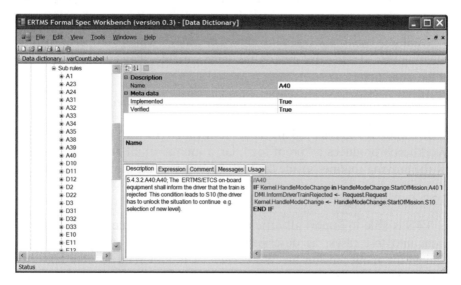

Figure 6.4. *Plain text requirement check against pseudo-code*

6.2.1.3. *Reasoning about the model*

The behaviour of the EFS model is expressed as simple rule applications. These rules are composed of two parts:

– *Preconditions*: a set of conditions that should all be evaluated to true in order to apply the rule.

– *Actions*: actions express the variable updates to be applied when the rule is activated. Each action consists of a single variable modification, where the variable's new value is the value of a single expression.

Rules can be organized in a hierarchical way to structure them together. This also allows optimizing the model interpretation by factorising common preconditions: when the preconditions of a rule are not valid, none of the sub-rules must be evaluated.

This formal model allows us to perform automated *simple proofs* such as *syntax checks* which ensure for instance that expressions are correct, that all variables used are defined, and allow us to perform type checks. Furthermore, automated *advanced proofs* can also be performed on the model, which include:

– enforce *structural constraints* to ensure model consistency, for instance, that types are not recursively defined;

– enforce *non-contradiction* between rules, which is performed by ensuring that, if two rules modify the same variable, they cannot be activated at the same time;

– ensure that all states of a state machine can be *reached.*

In order to enable independent verification of the formal proof, the Workbench produces a "proof log", i.e. a journal of all computations made by the proving routines inside the tool, executed on the model.

6.2.1.4. *Testability*

EFS is able to import all official [SUB 11b] test sequences and translate them into test cases, as described in section 6.2.1.4.1 which can be run against the model inside the Workbench. It is important to note that these [SUB 11b] test sequences are the same tests that are performed inside the ERTMS Reference Laboratories[2], on the final EVCs subsystems. Having the same tests performed on the formal model of the EVC and on the actual EVC hardware provides strong evidence of the compliance of requirements throughout the whole V-cycle.

6.2.1.4.1. Test definition

The Workbench enables the modeling of tests in the same way that tests are specified in [SUB 11b]. Tests are specified by a sequence of test cases, each test case being a sequence of steps. One step consists of:

– altering input values in the model, which corresponds to changes induced by *input observables*;

– checking output values from the model, which correspond to the *output observable* expected values.

---

2 CEDEX, DLR and Multitel as of 1st of January 2011.

This test formalization allows 100% of the model to be run inside the Workbench.

Added to the test formalization, the EFS stores the textual representation of the test, as expected in [SUB 11b]. This allows the domain expert to review the tests and ensure that they correspond to the expected system behavior.

Traditionally, the link between the Software Requirement Test Specification (SRTS) and the Software Requirements Specification (SRS) is manually established, i.e. a human lists all SRS elements tested by a given test of the SRTS, and manually assess if the tests are really testing the requirements. This corresponds to the feature concept defined for tests in [SUB 11b]. The EFS workbench allows us to automatically perform coverage analysis, based on the feature concept, and to identify the requirements that have not been verified by a test.

Moreover, due to model interpretation as presented in section 6.2.1.4.2, the Workbench can be used to cross-check the traceability information provided by features: the Workbench identifies the rules activated during a specific test and traces back the requirements involved in a specific test.

6.2.1.4.2. Interpretation

According to the fact that structure constraints are respected, the model can be interpreted in a unambiguous way to perform simulations and tests. The Workbench can execute tests against the model using the rule interpreter. During test execution, a timeline displays all events that occurred, providing a visual way to analyze and verify system behaviour. This diagram displays:

– the rules that are activated at a specific time;

– the variables changes;

– the observable values expected by the test currently run.

For instance, the screenshot presented in Figure 6.5 displays a model execution where the value of an observable does not correspond to the expected value (First expectation at column 12, displayed in red in the tool). This indicates that the test is not successful.

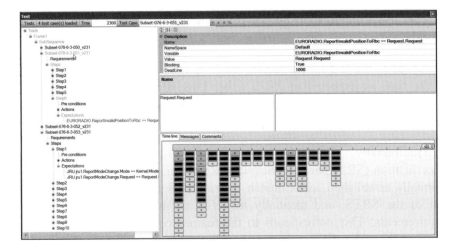

Figure 6.5. *Test execution*

A test can be executed as a whole, or step by step to trace the system evolution. During execution of a test, the test engineer can modify variables on the fly, to perform "what if" investigations on the model.

During a step by step test execution, the high level diagrams are updated according to the system current state, as presented for State diagrams in Figure 6.6, which allows the system engineer to easily review the model evolution.

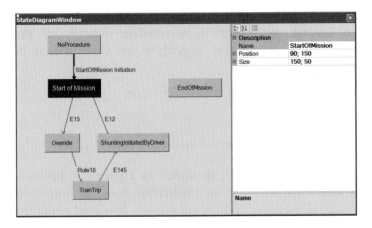

Figure 6.6. *Model evolution displayed in a state diagram*

6.2.1.4.3. Test results

Based on the results gathered during test execution, the Workbench issues a test result report indicating if the test is successful, and if not, the output observable values that were not satisfied. A detailed test log is available for each test, showing how the model has been simulated.

The Workbench also issues a rule coverage report, illustrating which rule is exercised for each test, with a granularity of a single rule and of a single test step. This test report can be used to univocally identify untested rules.

6.2.1.5. *Openness*

The complete model is stored by the Workbench in several fully documented XML files. This allows third party software to perform additional work based on the formalization effort performed by ERTMS Solutions. For instance, a third party team can use this information to perform some model testing on the model using ad hoc tools.

6.2.2. *Modeling process*

The modeling process is performed according to the following phases:

1) Review the requirements: the requirements have been manually encoded in the tool and need to be reviewed against the textual requirement as presented in [SUB 11a] to ensure that no error occurred during this phase. This phase is also used to split or group requirements according to the needs related to the modeling phase and to uniquely identify tables specified in [SUB 11a].

2) Update the model: update the model according to the requirement to be modeled, and create the relation between the model and the requirement. At the end of the modeling phase, the engineer indicates that the requirement has been implemented.

3) Review the model: when modeling is complete, another engineer must review the newly created model against the requirements it implements. When the review is complete, the engineer indicates that the model has been verified.

6.2.2.1. *Test creation*

A parallel work consists of creating tests which will ensure that the model corresponds to the expected behavior. The modeling process and the test creation is an iterative process, until both model and tests agree with the expected behavior.

Each test must identify the requirement it verifies. As soon as both model and tests are created, the test engineer can use the test environment of the Workbench to ensure that the model is behaving correctly and create a test report. Since test execution is based on an in-memory test interpreter, it is cheap to execute them. Therefore, it is easy to always rerun all tests and ensure non-regression on the entire model.

6.2.2.2. *Historical data*

Each action applied on to the system (review a requirement, modify a model element, verify a model...) is tracked with the following information: the person that performed the action, the action performed and a timestamp.

6.2.2.3. *Support modeling process*

The Workbench provides all the required tools to support the modeling process. It allows us to identify the requirements that had not yet been reviewed, or that are not completely implemented, to identify the model element which implementation is not complete, or which needs to be reviewed. It also identifies the requirements which are not covered by a test, or the rules which were never activated during testing.

6.2.3. *Interpretation or code generation*

The formal model is interesting *per se* since it provides a way to disambiguate the requirements expressed in natural language. It can also be used to detect gaps in the requirements or to determine the inconsistencies between them if any.

Due to its clean structure, the formal model can also be used to generate code to be embedded on the target platform. Target languages may vary from C, Ada to Scade or Simulink environments. Code generation plugins are created on a project basis, according to customers needs. The model can also be used as such by the customer, thus implying that the customer develops a SIL4 model interpreter.

Either in the context of code generation or in the context of interpretation, tests can be used to ensure that the behavior of the generated code is the same as the behavior of the interpreted model.

6.3. Braking curves modeling

Computation of braking curves, as specified in Chapter 3 of [SUB 11a], is a good example of the match between the EFS language and the domain it models.

6.3.1. *Computing braking curves*

Computing train braking curves requires considering the train characteristics and the trackside conditions that the train must satisfy, as depicted in Figure 6.7, which are:

– the location principles, train position and train orientation;

– the concept of Movement Authority (MA);

– determination of the most restrictive speed profile (MRSP) according to static speed restrictions, such as static speed profile, axle load speed profile, temporary speed restrictions, speed restrictions related to signaling, mode, train, level crossing;

– computation of the deceleration and brake build up time, according to the brake configuration of the train;

– acceleration or deceleration due to gradients;

– according to the MA, MRSP, deceleration factors related to the train brakes and the gradient, determination of the targets and brake deceleration curves;

– supervision limits such as ceiling supervision limits which allow us to define the Emergency Brake Intervention (EBI) curve, Service Brake Intervention (SBI) and Warning (W) based on the Permitted speed and target supervision limits;

– according to these limits, [SUB 11a] describes the speed and distance monitoring algorithms which allow the onboard application to generate braking commands, traction cut-off commands and display relevant information to the driver.

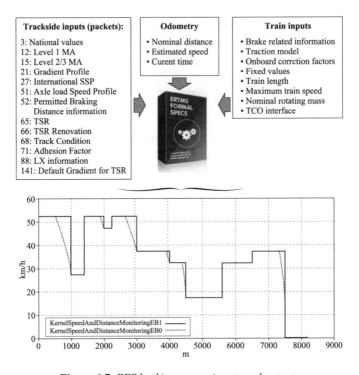

Figure 6.7. *EFS braking curves inputs and outputs*

The train characteristics and the trackside conditions are dependent on the odometry data:

– *Nominal distance*: as soon as a point of interest has been reached by the train, the corresponding speed restriction is removed from the computation of the maximum permitted speed.

– *Estimated speed*: several speed restrictions are dependent on the current speed.

– *Current time*: to evaluate the timers associated to an MA.

The output of the computation is a set of deceleration curves (EBD, SBD and GUI), expressed as a sequence of parabolic curves which never exceed the maximum permitted speed. These curves will be used by the onboard equipment in order to generate braking commands described in [SUB 11a] section 3.13.10. This formalization can be used as a reference implementation.

The following sections present the artifacts required to compute the braking curves, namely:

– the *Permitted speed* and associated speed limitation curves;

– the *Deceleration factors* according to gradients and train brakes;

– the *Deceleration curves* according to the permitted speed and deceleration factors;

– the Target supervision limits.

6.3.2. *Permitted speed and speed limitation curves*

The *permitted speed* (P), as defined in [SUB 11a] section 3.13.9.2, is the base function which provides the train permitted speed, in terms of a distance:

P (Distance) : Speed   [6.1]

It is a discontinuous step function which can be described as a sequence of constant speed values. An example is shown in Figure 6.8, providing the Permitted speed step function on the Y axis based on the train location, distance expressed on the X axis. This diagram is provided by the EFS Workbench. It is used as a visual validation tool of the computed curves.

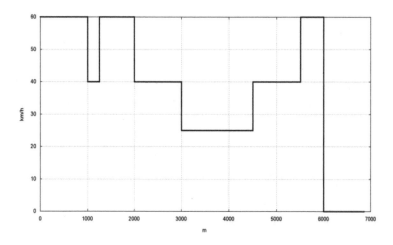

Figure 6.8. *Permitted speed*

6.3.2.1. *Single elements of the permitted speed*

The computation of the *permitted speed* (P) is based on the MA and the current MRSP, which in turn is computed in terms of static speed restrictions, such as SSP, TSRs, LXs, ... [SUB 11a] describes the messages used to configure each element which composes P (for instance, Packet 65: Temporary Speed Restriction is described in section 7.4.2.17) and the interpretation to be given to such packets (for instance, Temporary Speed Restrictions are described in section 3.11.5).

Each of the static speed restrictions has been modeled with another step function:

Speed Restriction (Distance): Speed   [6.2]

For instance, the speed restriction function related to a single TSR has been modeled in EFS language as follows:

```
FUNCTION TSRSpeedRestriction(
aTSR: TemporarySpeedRestriction
Distance: BaseTypes.Distance
) RETURNS BaseTypes.Speed

// During TSR
  aTSR.Location <= Distance AND
  Distance < aTSR.Location + TSRLength (aTSR) =>
aTSR.Speed

// Outside TSR
 => BaseTypes.Speed.MaxSpeed
```

The function *TSRSpeedRestriction()* is straightforward. It indicates that, when the parameter *distance* lies between the boundaries of the TSR, the maximum speed must correspond to the speed defined in that TSR, whereas everywhere outside those boundaries, the corresponding speed is not limited. It uses the function *TSRLength()* which provides the length of the TSR according to data from Packet 65, as described in [SUB 11a] section 7.4.2.17 (see Figure 6.9).

While computing braking curves, the EFS interpreter analyzes this function and creates the corresponding step function, with its graphical representation in the same way it does for the *P* function in Figure 6.8.

7.4.2.17   Packet Number 65: Temporary Speed Restriction

Description	Transmission of temporary speed restriction.		
Transmitted by	Any		
Content	Variable	Length	Comment
	NID_PACKET	8	
	Q_DIR	2	
	L_PACKET	13	
	Q_SCALE	2	
	NID_TSR	8	
	D_TSR	15	
	L_TSR	15	
	Q_FRONT	1	
	V_TSR	7	

Figure 6.9. *Packet 65: temporary speed restriction*

6.3.2.2. *Combining all compounds elements*

Since more than one TSR can be configured at a time in the system, the EFS interpreter combines all the temporary speed restrictions by minimizing them, according to [SUB 11a] in section 3.11.5.4:

3.11.5.4   When two or more temporary speed restrictions overlap, the most restrictive speed of the overlapping temporary speed restrictions shall be used in the area of overlap.

This is formally defined by:

```
FUNCTION SpeedRestrictions(Distance: BaseTypes.Distance)
 RETURNS BaseTypes.Speed
=> (REDUCE TSRs USING
 MIN(First => FUNCTION d : BaseTypes.Distance =>
            TSRSpeedRestriction(aTSR => X, Distance => d),
     Second => RESULT)
 INITIAL_VALUE BaseTypes.MaxSpeedFunction)(Distance)
```

where the REDUCE operator iterates over TSRs, the collection of active TSR, and applies the MIN function between the current TSR and what has already been computed. Initially (when no TSR has been considered), there is no speed restriction, hence, the result is equal to the maximum speed.

This function is used by the EFS interpreter to create the speed restriction related to all TSRs step functions as displayed in Figure 6.10. In this case, there are two TSRs: one with the speed limit of 40 km/h between 2,000 m and 5,500 m and another one with the speed limit of 25 km/h between 3,000 m and 4,500 m.

It is an interesting function because it displays the fact that the EFS language is a higher order language: it allows to handle and combine functions as if they we simple objects, such as a speed or a distance.

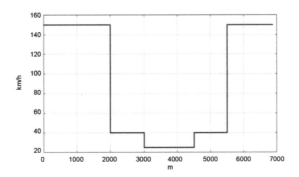

Figure 6.10. *Combined TSRs*

The same process is applied to compute the MRSP step function, as defined by [SUB 11a] in section 3.13.7.2:

> 3.13.7.2   The Most Restrictive Speed Profile shall be computed from all speed restrictions (see 3.13.2.2.13 & 3.13.2.3.2) by selecting the most restrictive parts of each element, some elements being compensated by the train length if requested by trackside (see 3.11.3.1.3 for SSP, 3.11.4.6 for ASP and 3.11.5.3 for TSR).

Since the train length is already taken into account for SSP, ASP and TSR, the MRSP is simply computed by minimizing the static speed restrictions from which it is composed. An example of MRSP is shown, by the dotted line, in Figure 6.11.

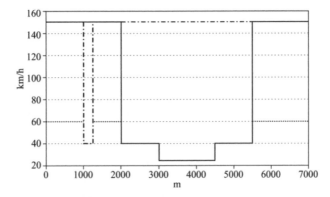

Figure 6.11. *MRSP, Level crossing and TSRs*

6.3.2.3. *Computing the permitted speed*

The permitted speed is defined in [SUB 11a] section 3.11.1.1:

> 3.11.1.1   The permitted speed at which the train is allowed to travel shall be limited to different kinds of Static Speed Restrictions and considering the End of Authority/Limit Of Authority.

The different kinds of static restrictions are defined by the MRSP whereas the End Of Authority/Limit Of Authority relates to the MA. Hence, the permitted speed is computed by minimizing those two speed restrictions, as displayed graphically in Figure 6.8.

6.3.2.4. *Traceability and understanding*

This approach allows to easily check that the model corresponds to the specification for two reasons:

– The model is traced to the corresponding requirements from [SUB 11a], as already stated in section 6.2.1.1. This allows us to easily understand where a requirement has been considered.

– The model is written in a functional language, so there is no need to analyze complex algorithms, nor to consider any side effects.

Moreover, the step functions can be used to understand the reasons why the speed, at a given location, is limited to given value. For instance, this traceability information is shown in Figure 6.11. The MRSP corresponds to the minimum of the speed restrictions constraining the train movement. It can be explained by displaying its constituting speed restrictions. The first consists of a speed restriction related to a level crossing whereas the second is a combination of speed restrictions related to TSRs as already displayed in Figure 6.10. Thanks to this graph, we can easily understand why the MRSP is limited to 40 km/h at 1,000 m (due to a level crossing) and limited to 25 km/h between 3,000 m and 4,500 m (due to a TSR).

6.3.3. *Deceleration factors*

The *deceleration functions* used in the deceleration curve computation (such as A_safe, A_expected and A_normal_service) as defined in [SUB 11a] by section 3.13.6 are functions which provide the train deceleration based on the train speed and distance:

A_safe(Distance, Speed): Acceleration

A_expected(Distance, Speed): Acceleration   [6.3]

A_normal_service(Distance, Speed): Acceleration

These functions are defined based on the acceleration/deceleration due to the gradient and the deceleration due to the several brakes configuration. The EFS interpreter can determine the deceleration step surfaces, a step function based on two parameters, the same way the most restrictive speed step functions were determined, as described in section 6.3.2.

For instance, Figure 6.12 presents the speed deceleration surface of A_brake_emergency computed for a specific train configuration and based on a gradient profile received from trackside. Each box in the graph represents a specific deceleration based on the train position (represented on the X axis) and a train speed.

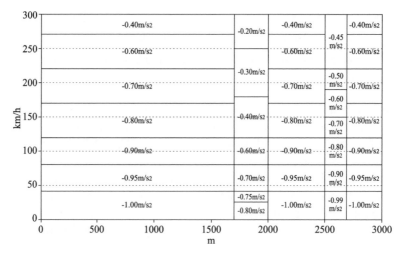

Figure 6.12. *A_brake_emergency (Distance, speed) deceleration surface*

6.3.4. *Deceleration curves*

The deceleration curves are computed based on the *permitted speed* P, on which ceiling speed limits have been applied (section 3.13.9.2), by respectively adding dV_ebi, dV_sbi and dV_warning, a function which gives a delta Speed based on a distance. For instance, dV_ebi is described in [SUB 11a] section 3.13.9.2.3:

3.13.9.2.3 For dv_ebi, the following formula shall be applied:

when $V_{MRSP} > V_{ebi\,min}$:

$$dV_{ebi} = \min\{dV_{ebi\,min} + C_{ebi} \cdot (V_{MRSP} - V_{ebi\,min}), dV_{ebi\,max}\}$$

with $C_{ebi} = \dfrac{(dV_{ebi\,max} - dV_{ebi\,min})}{(V_{ebi\,max} - V_{ebi\,min})}$

when $V_{MRSP} \le V_{ebi\,min} : dV_{ebi} = dV_{ebi\,min}$

which is in turn modeled by:

```
FUNCTION dv_ebi(V: BaseTypes.Speed)
 RETURNS BaseTypes.Speed
// V > V_ebi_min
 V > V_ebi_min =>
  MinSpeed(dV_ebi_min + C_ebi() * (V - V_ebi_min), dV_ebi_max)
// V <= V_ebi_min
 => dV_ebi_min

// C_ebi
FUNCTION C_ebi() RETURNS  BaseTypes.Speed
 => (dV_ebi_max - dV_ebi_min) / (V_ebi_max - V_ebi_min)
```

We can easily ensure that this model corresponds to its requirement. Based on this function, the function EBI, as described in section 3.13.9.2.2:

3.13.9.2.2 From an MRSP element or from the LOA, the Permitted speed, Warning, Service brake intervention and Emergency brake intervention supervision limits are defined (see Figure 43).

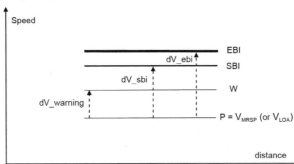

Figure 43: Ceiling supervision limits

is modeled by

```
FUNCTION EBI(distance : BaseTypes.Distance)
 RETURNS BaseTypes.Speed
// Permitted speed is not zero
 P ( distance ) > 0.0 =>
  AddIncrement(
    Function => P,
    Increment => CeilingSupervision.dv_ebi)(distance)

// Otherwise
 => 0
```

This gives the following EBI function shown by the dashed line based on the permitted speed showed by the dotted line in Figure 6.13. This figure easily shows that the EBI effectively corresponds to its requirements.

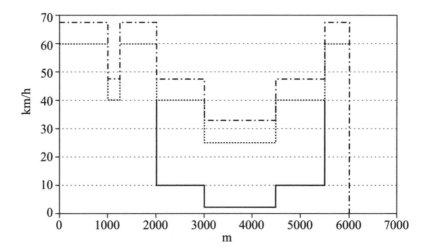

Figure 6.13. *EBI based on permitted speed (P)*

The EFS interpreter computes, based on a maximum speed function and a deceleration factor, the deceleration curve as requested in [SUB 11a] section 3.13.8.1.3. It then determines the supervised targets and computes the interconnected arcs of parabola according to these targets and the deceleration factors encountered as noted in [SUB 11a] section 3.13.6.2.1.9 (see Figure 6.14).

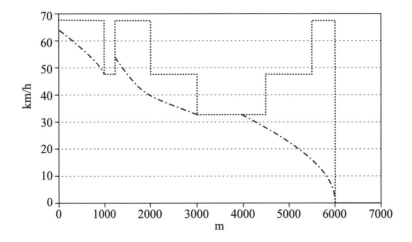

Figure 6.14. *Emergency brake deceleration based on EBI*

6.3.5. *Target supervision limits*

The *target supervision limits* are computed by considering the first distance for which a specific speed is encountered on a deceleration curve. For instance, dSBI1, as defined in [SUB 11a] section 3.13.9.3.3.1, is modeled by

```
FUNCTION d_SBI1(Vest : Default.BaseTypes.Speed)
 RETURNS  Default.BaseTypes.Distance
=> DistanceForSpeed(Function => SBD, Speed => Vest) + Vest * Tbs1
```

where DistanceForSpeed (SBD, Vest) provides the first distance where the curve SBD reaches the speed Vest.

6.3.6. *Symbolic computation*

A unique feature provided by EFS consists of the fact that braking curve computations are performed in a symbolical way, as opposed to computing such curves numerically, which induces approximations at each step of the numerical process.

To achieve this, for each function related to the train maximum speed (MRSP, MA, TSR, ...), EFS associates a symbolic representation of these step functions as a continuous sequence of constant functions, represented by the constant c and the bounds for which that step function is valid (see Figure 6.8).

$$maxSpeed\ (d) = c \hspace{4cm} [6.4]$$

Similarly, for each function related to the train deceleration factors (due to brakes capabilities, gradients, …) EFS associates a symbolic representation of such surfaces, as a continuous (both in terms of distance and speed) sequence of constant functions, represented by the constant c and the bounds of the surface (see Figure 6.12)

$$A\ (d,\ s) = c \hspace{4cm} [6.5]$$

Last, the deceleration curves (EBD, SBD and GUI) are represented as a sequence of parabolic curves according to the formula below. These curves are represented by the constants v_0, a and d_0 and the bounds for which this function is valid (see Figure 6.14)

$$EBD(d) = \sqrt{v_0^2 + a(d_0 - d)} \hspace{3cm} [6.6]$$

6.3.7. *Braking curves verification*

The EFS workbench allows us to verify the modeled braking curves due to the graphical display of such curves, this provides an insight into the correctness of the curve, but cannot be used as a formal verification tool. Non-regression tests can also be used to ensure – through a second modeling of the braking curve – that the behavior corresponds to the expected one, as described in section 6.2.1.4.

The ERA provides braking curves simulation tool [ERA], implemented using Excel sheets, which define a set of parameters on which the computation of braking curves depends, and provides as output the distance values for the braking curves. We created several scenarios (sets of parameters) and we automatically imported them, as non-regression tests, in the EFS model.

This allowed us to show that our results were similar to the ones provided by the ERA tool. The small differences we have observed are due to the fact that computations in the Excel tool are performed on a discrete set of speed values: the Excel sheet inverts the EBD curve by providing, for a discrete range of speed values v, separated by 0.1 km/h, the distance d where EBD(d) = v. However, the resulting value depends on the region of A_safe in which is situated the EBD curve (see Figure 6.9). And if between two successive speed values the region of A_safe changes, only one of the regions is taken into account and the resulting distance value may be erroneous. That error is then propagated for the following values.

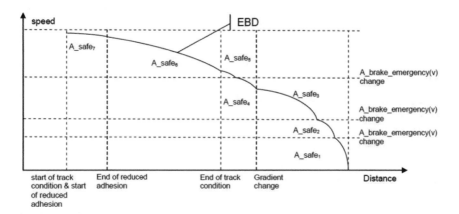

Figure 6.15. *EBD depending on A_safe*

Since these computations are continuous in EFS, this error and its propagation does not occur. One must note that the maximum observed error was of 0.25 m stopping distance, for a train launched at 140 km/h, which seems to be acceptable.

6.4. Conclusion

In this chapter, we have described that formalizing [SUB 11a] addresses several issues such as the fact that the specification is written in natural language and is intrinsically ambiguous. Furthermore, pair review is not sufficient to ensure that the specification is complete and consistent. Lastly, keeping pace with the successive releases of the document causes issues when the corresponding implementation has been performed using standard implementation techniques.

To handle these issues, we proposed to formalize the requirements expressed in [SUB 11a] and formalize the tests expressed in [SUB 11b]. The resulting model has the advantage of having an unambiguous interpretation. Tools can be used based on this model: interpretation of the model to animate it, test execution to ensure that the model behaves as defined in [SUB 11a] and [SUB 11b], automatic model walkthrough to statically prove properties about the model.

The formalization work is also focused on traceability issues: all model elements are traced back to their requirements, all tests are traced to the requirements they verify, as required by [CEN 01]. This information is used to perform coverage analysis, such as determining the requirements that are not modeled, or those that are not tested. Cross-checks between model traceability tables and test traceability tables are performed using information gathered during testing, and can be used to improve the tests.

The model can be used to generate code to be run on the target platform. Tests defined on the model are in that case used to ensure the correspondence between the model and the generated code.

We have also shown how the EFS environment has been used to compute braking curves as specified in document [SUB 11a]. We have shown that the language is perfectly suited to describe the requirements and close enough to them to allow a domain expert to assess that the model is correctly implemented. Moreover, the way we modeled the several speed restrictions allows a domain expert to understand, for a specific situation, the reason why a specific speed restriction applies. We have shown that the computed results match the expected results, as defined by the ERA. We have also shown that the symbolic computations used to compute braking curves allow being more precise than when using a numeric approach; but the difference between ERA's approach and EFS's are negligible.

6.5. Further works

We will model the speed and distance monitoring commands to generate braking commands, traction cut-off commands and relevant information to the driver using the state machines available in the EFS environment.

6.6. Bibliography

[CEN 01] CENELEC, "Software for Railway Control and Protection Systems, Technical Report EN50128", *Comité Européen de Normalisation Electrotechnique*, 2001.

[SUB 11a] SUBSET-026, Version 3.2.0, Baseline 3 second consolidation, Technical document, *ERTMS*, 11 January 2011.

[SUB 11b] SUBSET-076, Version 1.0.2, Scape of the test specifications, Mandatory Specification, *ERTMS*, 11 January 2011.

[ERA] ERASimulator Tool available at http://www.era.europa.eu/Core-Activities/ERTMS/Pages/Braking-Curves-Simulation-Tool.aspx.

[WOO 09] WOODCOK T., GORM LARSEN P., *et al.*, "Formal methods practice and experience", *ACM Comput. Surv.*, vol. 41, no. 4, available at http://deploy-eprints.ecs.soton.ac.uk/161/2/fmsurvey%5B1%5D.pdf.

7

The Use of a "Model-based Design" Approach on an ERTMS Level 2 Ground System

The ETCS/ERTMS has led to a new distribution of functions between the rolling stock and infrastructure for the lateral and cabin signaling systems already present on the national rail network. It uses concepts such as movement authorities, target points and speed controls, as well as exchange of information between the infrastructure and the train.

Through the SRS and the different subsets, the specifications of the ETCS/ERTMS define the European standard. For some functions, this offers possible optional interfaces with existing systems, i.e. national signaling systems.

Due to the industrial and standards context in which the systems are in operation, the reuse of pre-existing systems is preferable because of the substantial development costs and functional complexity necessary for the development of new systems. The adaptation of existing systems to meet national requirements necessitates modifications which may eventually compromise the project, if incorrect assumptions or inaccuracies lead to major non-conformities.

If we wish to make it possible to supply this type of modified system, we must be able to provide one single and common means of specification,

Chapter written by Stéphane CALLET, Saïd EL FASSI, Hervé FEDELER, Damien LEDOUX and Thierry NAVARRO.

which is unambiguous and independent of any particular application, and which defines what can be expected. These specifications by models serve as a common basis for all those involved and should be a means of exchanging information throughout the project.

This chapter presents the aims of modeling and the procedure that we have implemented to achieve it. For this, we based our work on a "model-based design" approach, which is widely used in the automotive and aeronautical sectors.

7.1. Introduction

To allow trains to run safely, it is essential to have systems which control speed and crossing. In Europe, more than 20 different systems have been installed, generally at a national level. So, in order to cross national borders, trains need to be equipped with at least one system of protection. This lack of standardization can explain the fragmentation of the European railway network (see the Figure 7.1). This fragmentation makes the on-board systems more complex, which leads to additional cost and breakdown risk, and makes them more complicated for the drivers to operate. Designed to alleviate these issues, the implementation of the ERTMS1 should standardize the railway signaling system throughout Europe.

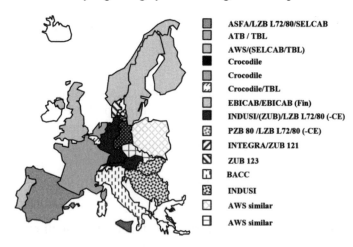

■	ASFA/LZB L72/80/SELCAB
■	ATB / TBL
■	AWS/(SELCAB/TBL)
■	Crocodile
■	Crocodile
▨	Crocodile/TBL
■	EBICAB/EBICAB (Fin)
■	INDUSI/(ZUB)/LZB L72/80 (-CE)
▧	PZB 80 /LZB L72/80 (-CE)
▨	INTEGRA/ZUB 121
◨	ZUB 123
▥	BACC
▨	INDUSI
□	AWS similar
⊟	AWS similar

Figure 7.1. *Extract of the report related to the model*

1 European rail traffic management system.

There are three ERTMS levels, and it is basically made up of two subsystems:

1) The ETCS[2] is the control system for the train. It transmits information about authorized speed and movement authorities to the driver, and it checks for compliance with these instructions.

2) The GSM-R[3] is the radio communication system used to exchange data between the train and the network. The system is based on the mobile phone standard GSM.

While opening up its high-speed network and increasing its capacity, RFF[4] aims to equip high-speed lines with ERTMS Level 2. To achieve this, SNCF and RFF are together investigating the possibility of using models to avoid the ambiguities that might result from a literal specification. These models could be used to support communication between those involved in infrastructure manufacture, operation and management. The ERTMS system carries out the functions of controlling spacing between trains and train speed, but does not include the "interlocking" part, which is handled by other equipment and is highly dependent on individual requirements in different countries. European frames of reference specify the exchanges between the train and network components of the ERTMS with precision; however, they do not define how the messages to the train should be built by the radio block center in line with the data provided from the interlocking system.

The SNCF, which is carrying out this modeling, has ERTMS experts who are highly experienced in the roll-out of these systems and who have an in-depth knowledge of the operation of national systems. The SNCF's goal is to combine national and European reference frameworks in one single model.

The modeling by SNCF is relevant to ERTMS Level 2, which features a regular transfer of information using the GSM-R link. ERTMS Level 2 comprises (see Figure 7.2):

– a "Eurobalise" group which, among other functions, notifies the train of its location;

---

2 European train control system.
3 GSM for railways.
4 RFF: Réseau ferré de France is the main railway infrastructure management organization in France.

– an onboard subsystem (EVC[5]) which, among other functions, allows the train to calculate speed curves and to control speed. These curves are calculated as a function of the movement authorities provided by the trackside subsystem (RBC[6]). In addition, the EVC communicates with the RBC to inform it of its location, of its movement authority requests, etc.;

– a trackside subsystem (RBC) which provides movement authorities to the train in line with the state of the track. It communicates directly with an interlocking (IXL[7]);

– an interlocking (IXL) which provides data to RBC on the current state of the track (e.g. position of switches, occupation of track circuits, and activated protective measures).

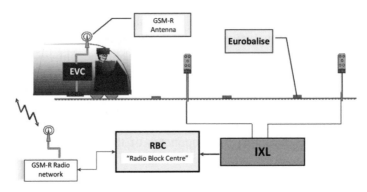

Figure 7.2. *Architecture of ERTMS Level 2*

7.2. Modeling an ERTMS Level 2 RBC

The RBC modeling by the SNCF must be fit for use on existing and future high-speed lines. To achieve this, the model must be able to cope with all of the characteristics of each of the lines, and to interface with all types of interlocking on them. In particular, the RBC must be able to interface with PRS[8], PRCI[9] and SEI[10] type interlockings. The range of technologies for the

---

5 European vital computer.
6 Radio block center.
7 Interlocking.
8 Completely relay based interlocking.
9 Modular relay based interlocking.
10 Computer based interlocking.

interlockings, all used for similar ranges of functions, show how equipment has evolved between the construction of different LGV (high speed) lines.

The architecture required for our modeling is summarized in Figure 7.3.

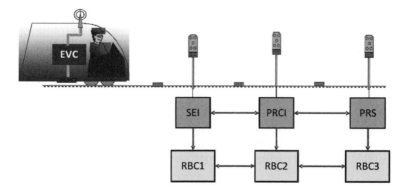

Figure 7.3. *Architecture of ERTMS Level 2 required for the model*

Before beginning, we had to select a modeling tool that could help us in all aspects of our work (modeling, simulation, testing and proving, etc.). We compared what was available on the market, using a ranked list of our pre-requisites. The following were our main requirements:

– a user-friendly interface, which makes it easier to handle and maintain the model;

– creation of state machine automatons, which is commonly practiced in railways and particularly at the SNCF;

– creation of a testing environment, which we could use to test our model.

– the capacity to easily create a graphic interface so we could observe the behavior of our model, to allow us to teach others about the ERTMS;

– the presence of a module to carry out proof activities;

– the possibility of generating a group of reports automatically.

We chose MATLAB/Simulink[11], which was best suited to these needs. Another useful feature of MATLAB/Simulink is the extensive online help

---

11 Produced by Mathworks: http://www.mathworks.com/.

and the large community of users, which could provide support during our modeling process.

Once we had chosen the tool, the next step was to establish the overall architecture of our model, as explained below.

7.2.1. *Overall architecture of the model*

As previously stated, we wished to be able to interface the RBC with several types of interlockings (SEI, PRCI and PRS). To achieve this, we decided that the RBC would be broken down in the following way:

– An interface for each interlocking with which the RBC might be linked. This would allow us to convert information from an interlocking into generic expressions which could be used by a generic module (see below).

– A generic core which would take generic expressions as input, which synthesize track information from interlocking, train messages and track configuration, and would then calculate e.g. the movement authorities for the train.

More concretely, on the basis of Figure 7.3, RBC1, RBC2 and RBC3s have the same generic core. However, the three RBC each have a unique interface module, because they are relayed to different types of interlockings. This is shown for the RBC1 and RBC2 in Figures 7.4 and 7.5.

In the case of the final application by those involved in manufacturing, they will have the choice of whether to internalize the interface box inside the RBC component, or to leave it as an external box.

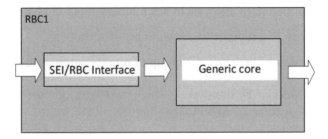

Figure 7.4. *Architecture of an RBC interfacing with an SEI*

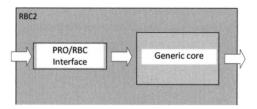

Figure 7.5. *Architecture of an RBC interfacing with a PRCI*

We will see in what follows that the two modules were modeled entirely under Simulink so as to be compatible with the library "Simulink Design Verifier", which we use for our proof activities.

7.2.2. *Functional separation*

In this section, we will present the methodology we used to achieve the functional separation of the RBC. We will also present the principle of refinement that we followed to obtain a modular model that was as understandable as possible. We will show how we worked by providing extracts from the Simulink block that we used to create our model.

7.2.2.1. *Interface between an interlocking and the RBC*

The interface enables synthesis of data from an interlocking. It was separated mainly in line with the requirements of the generic core. Ease of understanding for the generic part was important to us. For example, as the diagram below, which serves as a reminder of the global architecture of the interface model, shows (see Figure 7.6), the information "Etat des protections (state of protections)" tells us whether a portion of track is protected, without knowing which particular protections have been activated in the IXL.

Remember that the pieces of information calculated by the interface module are totally independent from each other, and have each been obtained through the same method. That is to say, each of them is encapsulated in a "subsystem" block (see Figure 7.7), which makes it possible to obtain information that has been synthesized and organized according to the movement direction. Following this, the information is assembled in a single flow so that its use is totally transparent in the generic part of the model.

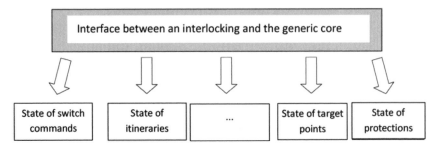

Figure 7.6. *Architecture of the interface module*

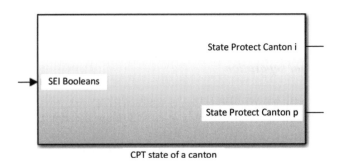

CPT state of a canton

Figure 7.7. *Definition of the function of the "state of protections" interface*

Each of the "subsystem" blocks has been refined (see Figure 7.8) into two branches (for each of the directions), made up of a first "EML[12]" block, which synthesizes information from the interlocking. This is followed by another "EML" block, which strongly types the module's outputs so as to curb flows as much as possible and lessen the combinatory explosion, to help the proof engine rapidly converge.

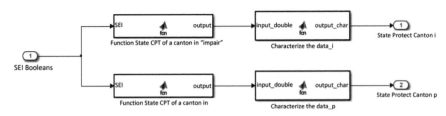

Figure 7.8. *Implementation of the function of the "state of protections" interface*

_____

12 Embedded MATLAB.

The "EML" blocks that synthesize the data from the interlocking are currently automatically translated from the dynamic part of the configurations. We will discuss this in more detail later (see section 7.3.3).

7.2.2.2. Generic core

The generic core is the "intelligent" part of the RBC. It allows us to supervise the trains that are communicating with the RBC, and, most importantly, to deliver movement authorities to the train. This module has been created on the basis of a functional approach, and using French signaling concepts as much as possible. Figure 7.9 provides a synthesis of the high-level separation that we have put in place. Concretely, the model is made up of functions such as "Gestion de la localisation", "Gestion des connexions", "Gestion des AU[13]" and "Gestion du MA[14]", etc.

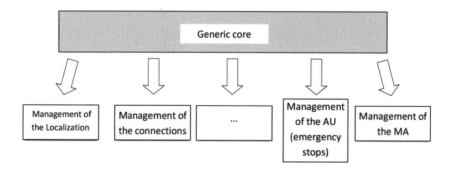

Figure 7.9. *Global architecture of the generic core*

The main difficulty is in making these functions concrete so that we have a model that can be read, maintained, simulated, tested and proved. Simulink offers a range of libraries and blocks so large that it can be hard to manage the selection. However, after several tests, we put a refinement strategy in place, which we then applied to the whole model. First, we decided to enact a functional separation by a series of refinements. This allowed us to obtain an implementation that was as simple as possible. This process involves the separation of a module into sub-modules, and so on, as is shown

---

13 Arrêt d'urgence – emergency stop.
14 Movement authority.

in Figure 7.10. The final model is made up of approximately 350 "Subsystem" blocks, and on average 4 successive levels of refinement (maximum of 10).

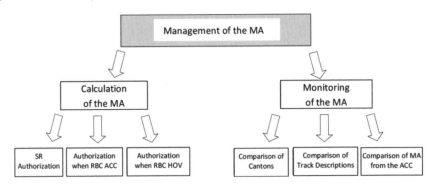

Figure 7.10. *Principle for refinement of the management function for MA*

This separation enabled us to have a more abstract view of the modules/functions and to obtain a structuring that clearly shows the functional separation. Following this, an implementation phase needed to take place. The functional separation is solely through the "Subsystem" blocks, as previously with the interface module. However, the functional implementation of the sub-modules is by logical operators, state graphs, truth tables, "Switch" blocks, memorizations and "EML" blocks when a loop was present etc. Below is an extract of the model where we use different types of blocks (see Figure 7.11).

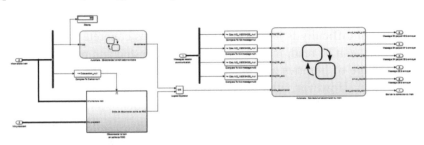

Figure 7.11. *Extract from a plate of the RBC model*

We also used "Goto/From" blocks, which improved the readability of the Simulink model by avoiding intermingled flows. However, these blocks are always used on the same plate. Simulink makes it possible to use these blocks between several levels; but in this case we lose the readability of the model, and it is more difficult to maintain.

We have summarized the methodology defined for the creation of the RBC model. The next state is the testing of the model. To do this, we first need to carry out the necessary configuration to the description of the track plan on which the RBC will be instanced.

7.3. Generation of the configuration

Because each railway line is complex and unique, it is not possible to define a typical system which can exhaustively manage all track configurations. For study and working purposes, a railway system such as the RBC is always linked to the topology of the track. This is why it is essential to create a refined configuration that takes all the unique features into account. In this section, in order to achieve this, we will illustrate the working method used to generate a configuration, which is required to test the model. First, we created a track plan which compiled, in one place, a large number of features known to the SNCF. The second stage is the transcription of the configuration into an Excel file. Finally, the Excel file is used to translate the configuration which will be used by MATLAB/Simulink.

7.3.1. *Development of a track plan*

This stage is largely based on the expertise of signalers. It aims to obtain a track layout (see Figure 7.12) that represents reality and includes as many unique features as possible without the data becoming too heavy for use in proof activities. If the configuration of the track contains too much data, there is a risk that combinatory explosion problems might be encountered, and that the proof activity would become difficult, indeed perhaps impossible. We managed to restrict ourselves to three track configurations, which grouped together as a set of features, and served as a working basis on which we could test our model. Limiting the number of track plans also reduces the work involved in describing the configuration, and simplifies the writing of test scenarios useful to the validation of the model.

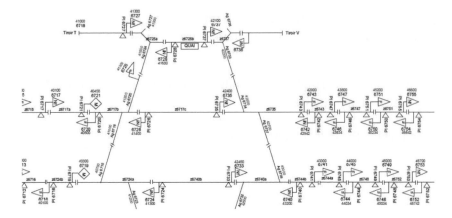

Figure 7.12. *Extract from a track plan*

tableau_pb_type	tableau_pb_DBC	tableau_pk_joint	tableau_pk_pt_auc	tableau_pk_pb	pb_etat_rv_aval_p	pb_etat_dbc_p	pb_etat_franch_p
Nf	DBC_null	6975	6994	7000	1	0	0
Nf	DBC_null	8975	8994	9000	1	0	0
F	DBC_null	14817	14836	14834	RV6607b	0	1
F	DBC_null	16217	16236	16234	RV6611	0	1
F	DBC_null	17383	17402	17400	RV6615a	0	1
Nf	DBC_null	19717	19736	19742	RV6619b	0	KIT6622
F	DBC_null	21017	21036	21034	RV6623b	0	1
F	DBC_null	22617	22636	22634	RV6627	0	1
Nf	DBC_null	0	0	0	1	0	0
Jalon	DBC_null	23375	23394	23400	RV6631a	0	CM6638 & CAG6640_G
Nf	DBC_null	24425	24444	24450	RV6631b	0	KIT6642
Nf	DBC_null	0	0	0	1	0	0
Jalon	DBC_null	25375	25394	25400	RV6643a	0	CM6648 & CAG6642_G
Nf	DBC_null	25875	25894	25900	RV6643b	0	KIT6652
F	DBC_null	28017	28036	28034	RV6657a	0	1
F	DBC_null	29517	29536	29534	RV6657b	0	1
F	DBC_null	31017	31036	31034	RV6661	0	1
Nf	DBC_null	12075	12094	12100	1	0	0
Nf	DBC_null	13575	13594	13600	1	0	0
F	DBC_null	14717	14736	14734	RV6608a	0	1
F	DBC_null	16317	16336	16334	RV6612	0	1
F	DBC_null	17717	17736	17734	RV6616	0	1
Nf	DBC_null	19217	19236	19242	RV6620a	0	KIT6620
F	DBC_null	20917	20936	20934	RV6624a	0	1
F	DBC_null	22725	22744	22742	RV6628	0	1
Nf	DBC_null	0	0	0	1	0	0
Jalon	DBC_null	23575	23594	23600	RV6636	0	CM6636 & CAG6641_D

Figure 7.13. *Example of a configuration in Excel format*

7.3.2. *Writing the configuration*

Using a track layout, we manually transcribed the configuration into a file in Excel format (see Figure 7.13). This file contains all the data required by the RBC (the interface module and the generic core). The interface module will use all the dynamic information (which transforms information from interlockings into more refined and summarized data) and the generic core will use the static information from the track. A static configuration usually lists features, such as the signals and their position, the type of signals and the position of the track circuit joints, etc. A dynamic configuration indicates, for example, whether it is possible to access a portion of the track in function of variable conditions such as the state of track relays and protections, etc.

7.3.3. *Translation of the configurations to the MATLAB/Simulink format*

We now need to translate the configuration from Excel format into a format that Simulink can use. To do this, we need a translator in MATLAB which can read a configuration file in Excel format and generate data that can be used by the Simulink model. Figure 7.14 summarizes our process of configuration generation. The Excel file contains both the static configuration[15] and the dynamic configuration[16] of the track. This is translated into two separate formats:

1) A MATLAB structure which contains all the static configurations that will be an input into the generic core.

2) A set of equations which allow the transformation of data from the interlocking to the information required by the generic core, as mentioned in section 7.2.1.

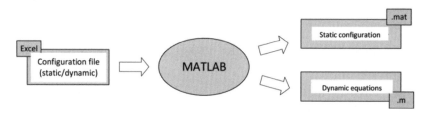

Figure 7.14. *Process of generating the configuration*

7.4. Validating the model

In the sections above, we have shown our process for modeling the RBC and generating the configuration. In this section, we will demonstrate the

---

15 A configuration that corresponds to the static track information (list of signals, position of signals, position of target points and switches, etc.).
16 Configuration which corresponds to the calculations carried out in the interface between the interlocking and the RBC core. These calculations use data from the interlocking. As a result, they need to be calculated at each model cycle.

approach that we used to validate our model. Our processes were as follows: first, we defined a language that would make it easy for signaling experts to write or check scenarios. Then, we wrote system-level scenarios and associated verifications for validating our RBC model to them.

The validation of the model was based on the instanced model, and involved applying test scenarios to it. This enabled us to verify that its behavior matched expectations. This included both the nominal modes and degraded modes of the environment.

7.4.1. *Development of a language in which to write the scenarios*

Our first step was to put primitives in a place that would enable us to write scenarios. To do this, we created a library for ourselves that would allow us to manipulate the set of all the model inputs. These primitives include the data from the interlocking, the messages from the train defined in the SRS (subset-26), and the messages from adjacent RBCs, also defined in the SRS (subset-39).

For example, here are some of the primitives we created:

– scn_modifier_valeur: this makes it possible to change the value of a piece of information from the interlocking;

– scn_envoyer_message_155: this makes it possible to send a message 155 to the RBC;

– scn_envoyer_message_129: this makes it possible to send a message 129 to the RBC;

– scn_envoyer_message_129_pq0: this makes it possible to complete sending of a message 129 by the packet 0.

7.4.2. *Writing the scenarios*

After we created the library of primitives, we wrote scenarios, particularly system scenarios. Our aim was to verify the expected function of the RBC in its operating environment. To do this, we manipulated the information from the subsystems which interface with the RBC.

As an example, we will find in Figure 7.15, the commands from a scenario that enable the modification of the "CAG_G"[17] information (respectively, "CAG_D"[18]) of the switch 6642 at cycle 2 at the value "false" (respectively, "true").

```
% positionnement des aiguilles
scn_modifier_valeur('simin66_CAG_G',2, scn_find(Conf_voie_66_scn.tableau_id_CAG_G,'6642'),false);
scn_modifier_valeur('simin66_CAG_D',2, scn_find(Conf_voie_66_scn.tableau_id_CAG_D,'6642'),true);
```

Figure 7.15. *"6642" switch commands*

We can send messages from the train to the RBC in the same way (see Figure 7.16). In this example, we send a message 129 from the train to the RBC at cycle 6. Then we supplement this message 129 with a packet 0 and a packet 11.

```
% Données train validées
scn_envoyer_message_129('simin66_Message_129',6,{'NID_ENGINE',1});
scn_envoyer_message_129_pq0('simin66_Message_129',6,{'NID_LRBG',6645, ...
                                        'D_LRBG',20, ...
                                        'L_DOUBTOVER', 10, ...
                                        'L_DOUBTUNDER', 10, ...
                                        'Q_DIRLRBG',enum_direction.Reverse, ...
                                        'Q_DLRBG',enum_direction.Reverse, ...
                                        'Q_DIRTRAIN',enum_direction.Reverse, ...
                                        'M_MODE',enum_mode.SN, ...
                                        'M_LEVEL',enum_level.Level_stm, ...
                                        'V_TRAIN',1, ...
                                        'Q_SCALE',enum_scale.scale_1_m});
scn_envoyer_message_129_pq11('simin66_Message_129',6,{'L_TRAIN',250});
```

Figure 7.16. *Sending a 129 message with packets 0 and 11*

All these primitives allow us to write the scenarios simply, and to avoid handling any strange variables. They are all in accordance with the European points of reference. As a result, we can use the same language with all the parties who are involved in the ERTMS.

7.4.3. *Verification of the scenarios*

To verify our model and then easily carry out replays in order to conduct non-regression tests, we need to add an automatic verification part to our

---

17 Information from the interlocking indicating that the switch is set to the left.
18 Information from the interlocking indicating that the switch is set to the right.

scenarios. To achieve this, we created a primitive to facilitate these tests. This was the primitive "scn_verifier_valeur" which can be used to verify a value calculated by the model against the one that would be expected. For example, in the extract below (see Figure 7.17), we verify that the variable "D_MAMODE", in the packet 80 of message 3 at cycle 15 is equal to 0. If it is not, the error message "Error OS" is displayed. Likewise, at cycle 15, we verify that the variable "L_ENDSECTION", found at packet 15, message 3 is equal to 1413.

```
erreur = scn_verifier_valeur(erreur, RBC_id, 15, 'T_M3_P80_D_MAMODE', 0, 'Erreur OS');
erreur = scn_verifier_valeur(erreur, RBC_id, 15, 'T_M3_P15_L_ENDSECTION', 1413, 'Erreur longueur MA');
```

Figure 7.17. *Verification of information in message 3*

All the scenarios have a verification part, which verifies that none of the evolutions denatures the rest of the model.

7.4.4. *Animation of the model*

At this stage, we had a Simulink model (that could include several RBC instances), a configuration (of one or several RBC), and scenarios and their associated verifications. All that remained was the simulation of the model to trace its execution, in order to use this information to verify our scenarios. This is summarized in Figure 7.18.

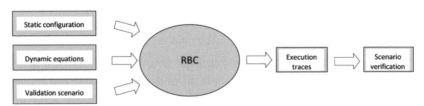

Figure 7.18. *RBC execution process*

The main difficulty is the analysis of execution traces. This is because the RBC produces a very large volume of information, and it is not easy to synthesize all the data to understand the context and analyze the results. For example, the RBC calculates localization information that is stored in a structure (see Figure 7.19), and then each item of information is organized according to its execution cycle (see Figure 7.20).

LRBG	<1x1 int32 timeseries>	0	14
RP_valide	<1x1 logical timeseries>		
Pk_MinSFE	<1x1 int32 timeseries>	0	17805
Sens_train	<1x1 struct>		
Canton_MinSFE	<1x1 int32 timeseries>	0	7
Canton_MinSRE	<1x1 int32 timeseries>	0	5
Canton_MaxSFE	<1x1 int32 timeseries>	0	7
Canton_LRBG	<1x1 int32 timeseries>	0	5
Pk_MaxSFE	<1x1 int32 timeseries>	0	17825
Pk_PE	<1x1 int32 timeseries>	0	17815
Pk_MinSRE	<1x1 int32 timeseries>	0	17330
Vitesse	<1x1 int32 timeseries>	0	5
Mode	<1x1 enum_mode timeseries>		
Niveau	<1x1 enum_level timeseries>		

Figure 7.19. *Trace produced by the RBC of the localization function*

Time series name: LRBG

Time	Data:1
1	0
2	0
3	0
4	14
5	14
6	14
7	14
8	14
9	14
10	14
11	14
12	14
13	14

Figure 7.20. *Value of the "LRBG" at each cycle*

As we can see, all this intertwining makes it difficult to use the results. In order to perform the analysis, we decided to create a graphic interface in MATLAB to display information which seemed important to us. With this interface (see Figures 7.21 and 7.22), we can easily observe for each cycle, the position of the train, the position of the switches, the movement authorities sent by the RBC and the state of the signals, etc. This graphic interface is automatically generated from a static configuration file.

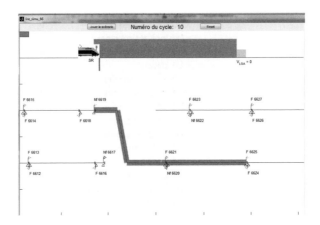

Figure 7.21. *Example of an "OS"-type MA*

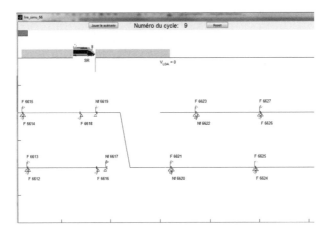

Figure 7.22. *Example of an "FS"-type MA*

The interface allows for two view-points, with the aim of having a system vision. The first (above) is that of the train, i.e. the way the train sees its movement authorities. The second (below) is that of the RBC, i.e. what the RBC sees at this moment. In Figure 7.21, we see that the train has a current movement authority in view (rectangle), while the RBC is no longer calculating this movement authority from its side. The following cycle (see Figure 7.22) shows that the RBC has now calculated a nominal movement authority (rectangle), which has been transmitted to the train and taken into account by it.

7.4.5. *Addition of coherence properties for the scenarios*

During validation, we soon noticed that we were introducing coherence errors between the data (e.g. the position of the points and the state of a route) when the scenarios were being written. This led to unexpected results and consequently time lost on analyses that were not useful. To improve the coherence of the scenarios, we added properties for the coherence of messages and for coherent information from the interlocking. These properties were automatically verified for each scenario and correspond to the model's constraints. As a result, these properties need to be verified by the equipment that interfaces with the RBC (e.g. the train, the interlockings).

By way of example, we will verify the rule below:

	For all the signals from the route, if a white crossing light is active, the route should be established.
R1	$$\forall \left(\begin{array}{l} \left(s \in \{Signaux \cup \mathrm{Re}\, p\grave{e}res \cup Jalons\} \wedge Origine\_itin\acute{e}raire(s) \right) \\ \rightarrow \\ \left(CM(s) \rightarrow KIT(s) \right) \end{array} \right)$$
	where: CM: state of the white light command associated with a signal/marker/reference point of the route. KIT: state of the establishment of the route associated with a signal. Origine_route: information which shows that a signal is from the route.

All these rules are expressed literally and more formally in order to remove all ambiguities of interpretation. They were modeled directly in MATLAB scripts, because it is not necessary to prove them. They made it possible to improve the quality of the scenarios. As a result of this, analysis was more efficient, because unreal scenarios were detected as soon as they were written (i.e. before simulation).

7.4.6. *Coverage of the model*

As previously mentioned, the type of scenario that we write is most frequently a system scenario. This type of scenario does not provide total coverage for the model. Therefore, in order to improve confidence in the modeling, we also investigated test coverage so we could observe the parts of the model that would not be tested. This gave us an indication of the relevance of our scenarios. For example, after running 40 scenarios, we obtain a level of coverage of 78% in decision, 66% in condition and 53% in MC/DC (see Figure 7.23) for the function "Calcul du MA", which calculates the train's movement authorities.

Controler mouvement train	713	81%	71%	57%
.... Calcul du MA	491	78%	66%	53%
.... Automate : Premier MA acquitte ?	8	100%	100%	100%
.... SF: Automate : Premier MA acquitte ?	7	100%	100%	100%

Figure 7.23. *Extract of a coverage report for the tests*

To obtain these results automatically, we use the module "Simulink verification and validation", which allows us to obtain a complete report on the model coverage. This report led us to conceptualize other scenarios to make our system scenarios more complete, and to improve confidence in the model. In addition, this also helped us to detect the parts of the model, which would never be accessible (dead code).

7.5. Proof of the model

We saw above how our model was tested at a system level by the writing of the scenarios. We would like to go further in the verification of our model. In particular, it seems important to us to be able to express the safety properties on the model and to prove them with the "Simulink design verifier" module. To do this, we carried out an activity that allowed us to identify the properties, which we considered important. Once identified, we needed to express them, and then prove them.

7.5.1. *Expressing the properties*

To express the properties, we used a pre-existing PHA[19] as a basis. We are interested solely in safety properties. Properties linked to availability cannot be expressed because SLDV[20] does not allow the expression of properties in temporal logic. In addition, we used blocks provided by SLDV to implement the properties. For example, in Figure 7.24, we expressed the following property:

19 Preliminary hazard analysis.
20 Simulink design verifier.

P1	If the train is located, then the LRBG belongs to the set of balises managed by the RBC.

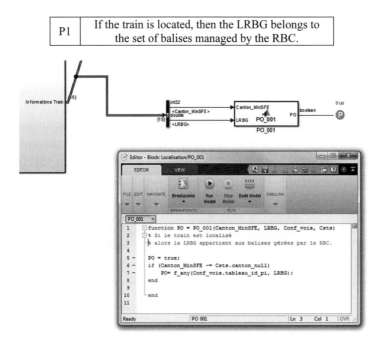

Figure 7.24. *Example of a proof property*

Note that the LRBG is the last balise read by the train. This makes it possible to guarantee that the RBC will not provide movement authorization to a train, which is on a portion of track not managed by the RBC.

The main difficulty is in expressing a property in the formal Simulink using information from the model. For example, we chose to characterize the notion of "train is located" by "the head of the train is located on the track". Similarly, we added set operators (e.g. belonging to a set) to make it easier to express properties and thus also more refined properties. The property P1 under Simulink is expressed in the following way:

P1	PO = true if (Canton_MinSFE ~= null) PO = f_any(Conf_voie.tableau_id_pi, LRBG) end where: Canton_MinSFE: the signaling block in which the train head is located. Conf_voie.tableau_id_pi : list of signals managed by the RBC. f_any(L,x): function which returns true if x belongs to L, false if not.

7.5.2. *Proof of the properties*

Before proving properties, we start the SLDV in "search for counter-example" mode so that it will provide an opening item, which transgresses the property. If this is the case, and before continuing with proving, we need to analyze the counter-example. Its presence means that there is an anomaly in the configuration, the modeling or the expression of the property. Once the anomaly has been corrected, we start the proof so that the SLDV can validate the properties. Figure 7.25 is a diagram that summarizes the proof process that we have applied.

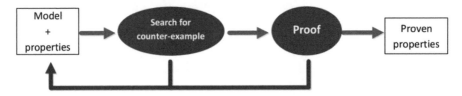

Figure 7.25. *Proof activity process*

The upper arrows represent the nominal process (i.e. when the proof is carried out without errors). The lower arrow represents the process when an error is present at one stage in the process. As we can see, an error during "search for counter-example" or during "proof" leads us to modify either the model or the properties.

7.6. Report generation

The aim of this step is that we should be able to work together with those involved in manufacturing for future high-speed lines, so as to ensure that the product matches the specifications throughout the entire development cycle. Therefore, in order to make communication effective, we need a documented model. This will help everyone to better understand the model, without having to go into the finer details. In addition, this will make it possible to understand our model without knowledge of the Simulink language. To achieve this, we document the model using the module "Simulink report generator". Using this method, we can automatically generate a report of the model in Word format, based on comments added in advance. An advantage of this method is that it guarantees documentation that is consistent with any developments, which have been implemented.

7.6.1. *Documentation of the model*

Using Simulink, it is possible to document the model through a dialog box (see Figure 7.26). We can, for each Simulink object, comment, and then extract the commentary automatically to take advantage of this function, we decided to comment on all the "subsystem" modules, as well as the inputs and outputs for each of the plates. This level of granularity is most relevant in order to obtain an overall understanding of the model. In fact, it allows us to obtain the description associated with each elaboration of our model, without extracting the implementation part. In addition, with MATLAB/Simulink, it is possible to generate the model in HTML format, so that we can navigate using simple mouse clicks. This format allows us to directly access the implementation, which is found in state charts, "EML" blocks, etc.

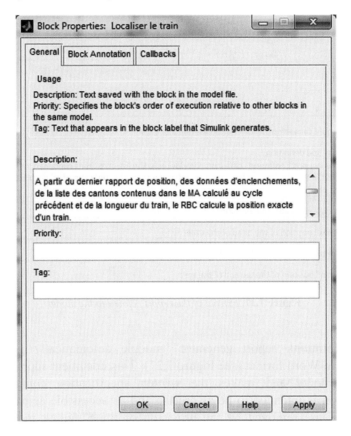

Figure 7.26. *Window where we can add comments*

7.6.2. *Automatic generation of the report*

Once the model has been documented, we generate a report automatically. To do this, we have configured the generator to have:

1) a screen copy of the model that we are describing;

2) a description of the module;

3) a description of the parameters used;

4) and a description of inputs and outputs.

Localize the train

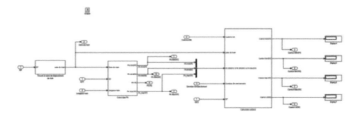

Role
The module calculates the localization elements of a train.
Principles and definitions From the last position report, data from interlockings, the list of cantons contained in the MA calculated in the previous cycle and the length of the train, the RBC calculates the exact position of the train.
This module calculates the localization of:
- the "max" position of the head of the train;
- the "min" position of the head of the train;
- the "min" position of the tail end of the train

Figure 7.27. *Extract of the report related to the model*

The "Simulink report generator" module automatically generates a document in Word format (see Figure 7.27). This document supplements the Simulink model and makes the written specification complete. This specification is intended to be as precise and as accessible as possible. All ambiguities are removed by the provision of the Simulink model, which describes the nominal and degraded functioning of the RBC. It is also easy to understand due to the literal documentation, which is provided alongside it. Finally, it should be remarked that this document makes it easier for a person to take over and handle the model. It would not be essential for them to understand all the blocks to obtain a general idea of how the model works.

7.7. Principal modeling choices

During our activities, we made some choices on the modeling, on the temporal aspects, which have an impact on simulation and the activities linked to it. In general, we decided to avoid all of the complexity linked to the communication protocol. Our aim was to express the functioning of an RBC. As a result, we allow the messages to come in an ordered manner, and the treatment is applied upstream. In addition, the model only manages one communicating train. This is because the architecture of ERTMS Level 2 implies that the treatment of the RBC on each train is operated only on the basis of information from the interlockings (i.e. independent of the position of other trains).

The timeouts manipulated by the RBC will all be configured, and expressed in the software application cycle. This means that we do not have to export a constraint on the time of the final cycle of the RBC. It also allows us to write scenarios independently of execution time. Furthermore, as we will notice, the final model is generic. Therefore, we are able to simulate several RBCs in the same environment and to test the system functions between two RBCs. The communication time between these two RBC was reduced to two cycles, so it would be possible to cross two messages sent at the same time by the two RBCs. We also introduced the notion of breakdown in communication. This allowed us to simulate the loss of communication between the two RBCs. Note that simulation with only one RBC does not allow any particular time constraint. This means that all imaginable degraded modes can be implemented.

Finally, the model was written in order to be as playful as possible. The aim was not to model the final application. To that end, we set aside, insofar as possible, the execution time of the model, and avoided adding optimizations, which would have contaminated our final understanding of the RBC. Additionally, our model needed to be compatible with the "Simulink design verifier" module. As a result, we held back in our use of certain Simulink blocks.

7.8. Conclusion

This modeling made it possible to confirm that the construction of a model is of capital importance in the development of a rail system as complex as this one. It helps us to clarify the interfaces between the equipment, to define the requirements of subsystems, the configuration rules and data. It also allows us to avoid all the ambiguities of the usual literal specification, to gain a global view of the system, and to master the equipment at a functional level. That the model may be dynamically animated makes it possible to create a reference of expected behavior for the system. This is always very difficult to describe in a literal specification. Moreover, this modeling provided gains in the capabilities of the "model-based design" approach, through introducing a working methodology to it, which could be applied to other projects in the future. Finally, the contribution of and the use of MATLAB/Simulink was invaluable to the implementation of our model. Because of its formalism, experts in rail signaling can use the model for their own purposes: this is a definite advantage for internal communication, or for communication with the signaling system manufacturers. This model will provide a common basis for all those involved in future high-speed lines equipped with ERTMS Level 2.

8

Applying Abstract Interpretation to Demonstrate Functional Safety

Contemporary safety standards require us to identify potential functional and non-functional hazards, and to demonstrate that the software does not violate the relevant safety goals. Examples of safety-relevant non-functional program properties are resource usage, especially worst-case execution time and stack usage, and absence of run-time errors. Classical software validation methods like code review and testing with measurements cannot really guarantee the absence of errors. For some non-functional program properties, this problem is solved by abstract interpretation-based static analysis techniques, which provide full control and data coverage and yield provably correct results. In this chapter, we will give an overview of abstract interpretation and its application to worst-case execution time analysis, worst-case stack usage analysis and run-time error analysis. We will discuss the requirements of contemporary safety standards with respect to the non-functional safety properties, and address the topic of tool qualification. We will illustrate the integration of abstract interpretation-based static analysis tools in the development process and report on practical experience.

8.1. Introduction

In automotive, railway, avionics and healthcare industries more and more functionality is implemented by embedded software. A failure of

Chapter written by Daniel KÄSTNER.

safety-critical software may cause high costs or even endanger human beings. Also for applications which are not highly safety-critical, a software failure may necessitate expensive updates. Therefore, utmost carefulness and state-of-the-art techniques for verifying software safety requirements have to be applied to make sure that an application is working properly.

Contemporary safety standards   including DO-178B, DO-178C, IEC-61508, ISO-26262, and EN-50128   require us to identify potential functional and non-functional hazards and to demonstrate that the software does not violate the relevant safety goals. For ensuring functional program properties, automatic testing and model-based testing are becoming more and more widely used. At the modeling level, formal techniques like model checking or theorem proving can be applied to mathematically prove or disprove functional properties.

Examples of safety-relevant non-functional program properties are resource usage, especially worst-case execution time and stack usage, and absence of run-time errors (e.g. division by zero, invalid pointer accesses and arithmetic overflows). For these program properties, identifying a safe end-of-test criterion is a difficult problem since failures usually occur in corner cases and full test coverage cannot be achieved. As a result, the required test effort is high, the tests require access to the physical hardware and the results are incomplete. In contrast, static analyses can be run by software developers from their workstation computer, they can be integrated in the development process, e.g. in model-based code generators, and allow developers to detect run-time errors as well as timing and space bugs in early product stages.

Abstract interpretation is a formal methodology for static program analysis, which is well suited to analyze non-functional software properties. It provides full control and data coverage and allows conclusions to be drawn that are valid for all program runs with all inputs. Such conclusions may be that no timing or space constraints are violated, or that run-time errors are absent: the absence of errors can be guaranteed. Nowadays, abstract interpretation-based static analyzers that can detect stack overflows and violations of timing constraints [SOU 05b] and that can prove the absence of run-time errors [DEL 07], are widely used in industry. From a methodological point of view, abstract interpretation-based static analyses can be seen as equivalent to testing with full coverage. For validating non-functional program properties they define the state-of-the-art technology [KAS 11].

In this chapter, we will give a brief overview of the theory of abstract interpretation and its application to worst-case execution time analysis, stack usage analysis, and run-time error analysis. We will discuss the role of non-functional software properties in contemporary safety standards, address the topic of tool qualification and illustrate the integration of abstract interpretation based static analysis tools in the development process. The chapter concludes with a summary of experimental results and practical experience.

8.2. Abstract interpretation

The theory of abstract interpretation [COU 77] is a mathematically rigorous formalism providing a semantics-based methodology for static program analysis. The semantics of a programming language is a formal description of the behavior of programs. The most precise semantics is the so-called concrete semantics, closely describing the actual execution of the program. Yet in general, concrete semantics are not computable. Even under the assumption that the program terminates, it is too detailed to allow for efficient computations. The solution is to introduce abstract semantics that approximate the concrete semantics of the program and are efficiently computable. The abstract semantics can be chosen as the basis for a static analysis. Compared to an analysis of the concrete semantics, the analysis result may be less precise but the computation may be significantly faster. By skillful definition of the abstract semantics, a suitable trade-off between precision and efficiency can be obtained.

Abstract interpretation supports formal correctness proofs: it can be proven that an analysis will terminate and that it computes an over-approximation of the concrete semantics, i.e. that the analysis results are *sound*. An analysis is called sound when the results hold for every possible program execution and every possible input scenario. In particular, a sound analysis never omits signaling an error that can appear in some execution environment.

This chapter focuses on applications of abstract interpretation, not the formal foundations. There are a variety of publications about the theory of abstract interpretation [COU 77, COU 79, COU 81, COU 92, COU 00a, COU 00c, COU 00b], and its practical applications [BLA 02, BLA 03, KAS 11, SOU 05c, THE 03]. Abstract interpretation, like model checking and theorem proving, is recognized as a formal verification method and recommended by the DO-178C and other safety standards (see Formal Methods Supplement [RAD 11a] to DO-178C [RAD 11b]).

8.3. Non-functional correctness

In general, an embedded system is called safety-critical when a malfunctioning of the system can result in physical injury or in damage to the health of people. Often, not only direct damage is considered, but also indirect damage, i.e. damage to property or to the environment. The *functional safety* of the system depends on the correct operation of the system in response to its inputs, including the safe management of likely operator errors, hardware failures and environmental changes. The goal of safety standards like DO-178B or ISO-26262 is to define criteria for demonstrating freedom from the unacceptable risk of such critical damage occuring. To that end, potential hazards have to be identified and it has to be demonstrated that the system does not violate the relevant safety goals. Both hardware and software have to be taken into account.

To demonstrate the correct behavior of the software, the functional correctness with respect to the specified requirements has to be shown. In addition to that, so-called *non-functional* aspects also have to be taken into account. The critical non-functional safety-relevant software characteristics are essentially implementation-level properties, e.g. whether real-time requirements can be met, whether stack overflows can occur, and whether there can be run-time errors like invalid pointer accesses, or divisions by zero. All current safety standards list these non-functional requirements among the verification goals (see section 8.6). The term "non-functional" is misleading: in fact, satisfying non-functional requirements is an essential part of functional safety. In the following we will briefly discuss the three main non-functional correctness properties: availability of sufficient stack space, satisfaction of real-time requirements and absence of run-time errors.

8.3.1. *Stack usage*

In embedded systems, the compiler stack is typically the only dynamically allocated memory. It is a memory area reserved for program execution where procedure frames are stored including local variables, function return values and intermediate values while evaluating expressions. Its size depends on the number of local variables as functions, the call stack and the executed program paths, among others. Typically, the required stack space for each task has to be allocated at configuration time, i.e. the maximal stack usage of the task must be statically known. Overestimating the maximum stack usage means wasting memory resources, whereas underestimation leads to stack overflows. Stack overflows are typically hard to diagnose and hard to reproduce; they can cause the program to behave in the wrong way, or to crash altogether and hence are a potential cause of catastrophic failure. The accidents caused by the unintended acceleration of the 2005 Toyota Camry illustrate the potential consequences of stack overflows: the expert witness' report commissioned by the Oklahoma court in 2013 identifies a stack overflow as the most probable cause of the unintended acceleration [DUN 13].

8.3.2. *Worst-case execution time*

Demonstrating timing correctness requires us to show that all real-time tasks meet their deadlines, or that deadline violations do not compromise the safety of the system. To demonstrate deadline adherence the worst-case response times (WCRT) of the real-time tasks in the system have to be determined. The WCRT of a task is based on its worst-case execution time (WCET) and takes additional overhead caused, e.g. by taking task pre-emptions and task blocking into account. Deadline or timing monitoring can be used to detect missed deadline and to trigger mitigating actions. Since error mitigation comes at the expense of degraded availability it should not be triggered by systematic software faults, but rather be confined to sporadic or transient faults.

Due to the characteristics of modern hardware and software architectures, determining the WCET of a task has become a challenge. Embedded control software tends to be large and complex. The software in a single electronic control unit typically has to provide different kinds of functionalities. It is usually developed by several people, several groups or even several different providers. Code generator tools are widely used. They usually hide implementation details from the developers and make understanding of the timing behavior of the code more difficult. The code is typically combined with third-party software such as real-time operating systems and/or communication libraries.

Concerning hardware, there is typically a large gap between the cycle times of modern microprocessors and the access times of main memory.

Caches and branch target buffers are used to overcome this gap in virtually all performance-oriented processors (including high-performance micro-controllers and DSPs). Pipelines enable acceleration by overlapping the executions of different instructions. Consequently, the execution behavior of the instructions depends on the execution history and can vary significantly. Cache memories usually work very well, but under some circumstances minimal changes in the program code or program input may lead to dramatic changes in cache behavior. For (hard) real-time systems, this is undesirable and possibly even hazardous. Making the safe, yet for the most part unrealistic, assumption that all memory references lead to cache misses results in the execution time being overestimated by several hundred percent. Software monitoring, dual-loop benchmarks and instrumentation-based tracing modify the code, which in turn changes the cache behavior. Hardware simulation, emulation, or direct measurement with logic analyzers can only determine the execution time for some fixed inputs. They cannot be used to infer the execution times for all possible inputs in general.

8.3.3. *Run-time errors*

Basically, run-time errors are errors that occur during the run-time of software. More specifically, we will focus on run-time errors, which correspond to undefined or unspecified behavior with respect to the semantics of the programming language. This class of errors is of particular interest for the programming language C, since it includes many common problems that cannot be detected by the compiler or prevented during the run-time. Examples are arithmetic exceptions (e.g. divide by zero), overflow, validity of addresses for pointers or array bound errors [MOT 14]. The C standard provides a list of unspecified and undefined behaviors in section J of [ISO 99].

The first category of run-time errors is related to conditions in which the source semantics are undefined. After such a run-time error, the actual execution will do something unknown. Examples are invalid array or pointer accesses, which might corrupt memory and destroy the data integrity of the program. It can even happen that the program code is dynamically modified resulting in erratic behavior, or that the program crashes with segmentation faults or bus errors. Further examples of errors from that class are integer division by zero, floating-point overflows, NaN or invalid operations without mathematical meaning that might cause the program to be stopped by an interrupt.

The second category of run-time errors is due to unspecified but implementation-defined behavior, what will happen after the error has occurred is unpredictable. Examples are integer overflows or invalid shifts for which the actual computations are quite different from the expected mathematical meaning.

8.4. Why testing is not enough

Testing and measuring is an integral part of the cognitive scientific process. However, applied to computer science problems, there are limits to testing: "Program testing can be a very effective way to show the presence of bugs, but is hopelessly inadequate for showing their absence" [DIJ 72]. A general limitation of testing methods is their incompleteness: for complex E/E systems exhaustive testing usually is not possible. Consequently, according to the DO-178 B/C, standards for verification testing alone is not enough.

This methodological limitation is particularly significant for non-functional program properties. First, it is not possible to specify dedicated test cases for non-functional requirements. Observing the reaction of the system to one specific stimulus to determine whether the reaction is correct is not sufficient, since the absence of errors has to be shown for all possible stimuli. A simple example: let us assume the program contains a computation $1/(S_1 - S_2)$ where S_1 and S_2 are volatile sensor inputs and there is no 0-check guarding the division statement. Then the behavior of the program is correct, only except in the case of both sensors returning identical values. As potential run-time errors are unknown – unless a dedicated program analysis has been performed – in order to find all such cases by testing the program has to be run with all potential combinations of all input values.

Compilers can exploit knowledge about the code generation process in order to provide information about stack usage. However, they cannot take into account the effects of inline assembly code or link-time optimizations. Moreover, automotive software is often composed of libraries and object code integrated from different suppliers. Stack effects of such software parts cannot be safely estimated by the compiler. Measuring the maximum stack usage with a debugger is not a solution since we only obtains the result for a single-program run with a fixed input. Even repeated measurements with various inputs cannot guarantee that the maximum stack usage is observed.

Stack overflows typically occur in corner cases, e.g. related to error handling, which are very difficult to stimulate and often impossible to cover exhaustively by testing.

Measuring the worst-case execution time of software is an ever-growing challenge. End-to-end measurements aim at directly measuring the worst-case execution time of a given task. Since the worst-case path is unknown and hence cannot be explicitly stimulated, again exhaustive testing is required. However, with regard to timing, exhaustive testing not only means stimulating all potential execution paths. Additionally, for each scenario, all possible hardware states have to be considered, since the same code snippet can have very different execution times depending on the initial hardware state of the processor at the beginning of the measurement, as detailed above. The worst-case hardware state for executing a code sequence usually is not known. The resulting search space is gigantic and cannot be exhaustively covered with acceptable effort.

Structural test coverage criteria like the modified condition/decision coverage (MC/DC) [RAD 92] are not applicable as they do not capture the execution paths traversed and there is no indication whether the worst-case path has been observed. It is also not possible to define a reliability metrics for timing measurements based on the time spent for measurements. There is no indication how often a specific execution path has been exercised during the observation period. As a result for software-based systems, no statistical failure rates, which are comparable to those used for hardware components with typical requirements between 10^{-5} and 10^{-9} failures per hour of operation, are available.

In hybrid approaches, the execution times of smaller code sequences are measured and composed to determine critical paths. With timing measurements at the basic block level, there is only one path to measure, but it is often not possible to stimulate it for all potential initial hardware states with acceptable effort. The necessary tracing effort is high. Measuring larger subpaths reduces the tracing effort but incurs the danger of missing valid execution paths. Due to timing anomalies and domino effects, combining measured times for different code blocks is not safe [KAS 13], and it is hard to determine a valid safety margin. On the other hand, combining measurements from different contexts also might lead to significant overestimations of the execution time.

Another problem dimension is how to obtain the measurement data. The simplest approach is *invasive* by adding an instrumentation code to collect a time stamp or read the CPU cycle counter. The instrumentation code interferes with the timing behavior of the software being test and in general, it is not possible to separate the effect of the instrumentation code from the effect of the original code. Assessing the effect of instrumentation is a prerequisite for using invasive test methods in a safety case. As this is not possible in general, one solution is to consider the instrumentation code to be part of the production software. However, this induces further problems, e.g. creating the instrumentation is subject to the same criticality level as developing the application software, and the available processor time is reduced. Mixed hardware/software instrumentation techniques enable a more lightweight instrumentation. Non-intrusive measurements are supported by logic analyzers or hardware tracing mechanisms, e.g. the IEEE-ISTO 5001-2003 (NEXUS) standard and the ETM tracing mechanism.

As a result, with measurement-based testing, in general, it is not possible to derive *safe* bounds on the worst-case execution time. Still, they provide valuable feedback for assessing the timing behavior in soft real-time systems; and play an important role for debugging, and for determining and optimizing the average-case execution time. Testing techniques are required to address transient hardware faults, or incorrect interrupt handling. Measurement-based testing also is instrumental in validating the correctness of hardware models used for static WCET analysis (see section 8.7).

8.5. Verifying non-functional program properties by abstract interpretation

To summarize, investigating non-functional software properties by testing requires high testing effort, the tests require access to the physical hardware and the results are incomplete. An alternative is to use abstract interpretation. Abstract interpretation is a formal verification method that can be applied at the implementation level – a prerequisite for investigating non-functional program properties – and scales up to industry-size software projects (see section 8.9). It enables the soundness of an analysis to be proven: the results are valid for all program runs with all inputs and, hence, provide full data and control coverage. As a static technique, abstract interpretation can be easily automatized and can reduce the verification and validation effort.

Semantics-based static analysis uses an explicit (or implicit) program semantics that is a formal (or informal) model of the program executions in all possible, or a set of possible, execution environments. Often, it is perceived as a technique for source code analysis at the programming language level, but it can also be applied at the binary machine code level. In that case, it does not compute an approximation of a programming language semantics, but an approximation of the semantics of the machine code of the microprocessor.

In the remainder of this section, we will describe how abstract interpretation can be applied to determine worst-case execution times, the worst-case stack usage and to detect all potential run-time errors in C programs. Worst-case execution time analysis and worst-case stack usage analysis are performed at the binary level, because they have to take the instruction set and hardware architecture into account. Run-time error analysis deals with unspecified and undefined behavior according to programming language semantics and therefore works at the source code level. As explained above, a sound analysis computes a safe over-approximation of the concrete semantics and detects all potential errors:

– For worst-case execution time analysis, soundness means that the reported WCET is never below the actual execution time in some execution environment. For instance, if the reported WCET is 1 ms, the actual execution definitely cannot last longer than 1 ms. On the other hand, overestimation may occur: it is possible that actual executions never take longer than 0.9 ms.

– In the same way, the computed stack height must never be below the stack usage in any concrete execution, but overestimations may occur.

– For run-time error analysis, soundness means that the analysis never omits to signal an error that can appear in some execution environment. If no potential error is signaled, definitely no run-time error can occur. When the analyzer reports a potential error, it cannot exclude there being a concrete program execution triggering the error. If there is no such execution, the notification about the potential error is a false alarm.

8.5.1. *WCET and stack usage analysis*

For safe WCET and stack usage analysis, it is important to work on fully linked *binary code*, i.e. here the static analysis is not based on the source code but on the executable code. In general, neither a sound stack usage analysis nor a sound WCET analysis can be based on the source code. The compiler has a significant leeway to generate machine code from the source code given that can result in significant variations of stack usage and execution time. Moreover, for precise results, it is important to perform a whole-program analysis after the linking stage. Finally, for timing analysis, precisely analyzing cache and pipeline behavior is imperative for obtaining precise time bounds. This is only possible when analyzing machine instructions with known addresses of memory accesses.

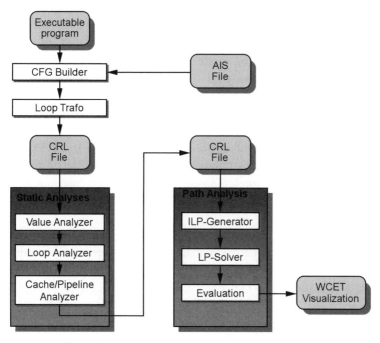

Figure 8.1. *Worst-case execution time analysis phases*

Over the last few years, a more or less standard architecture for timing analysis tools has emerged [ERM 03, FER 01]. It neither requires code instrumentation nor debugs information and is composed of three major building blocks (see Figure 8.1):

– Control-flow reconstruction and static analyses for control and data flow.

– Micro-architectural analysis, computing upper bounds on execution times of basic blocks.

– Path analysis, computing the longest execution paths through the whole program.

The data flow analysis of the first block also detects infeasible paths, i.e. program points that cannot occur in any real execution. This reduces the complexity of the following micro-architectural analysis. There, basic block timings are determined using an abstract processor model (*timing model*) to analyze how instructions pass through the pipeline taking cache-hit or cache-miss information into account. This model defines a cycle-level abstract semantics for each instruction's execution yielding a certain set of final system states. After the analysis of one instruction has been finished, these states are used as start states in the analysis of the successor instruction(s). Here, the timing model introduces non-determinism that leads to multiple possible execution paths in the analyzed program. The pipeline analysis has to examine all of these paths.

This analysis architecture can also be applied to stack usage analysis. While for timing analysis, the entire machine state has to be modeled, for stack usage analysis only stack pointer manipulations have to be covered. The reference architecture is implemented in the abstract interpretation-based static analyzers: StackAnalyzer and aiT WCET Analyzer from AbsInt [FER 06].

StackAnalyzer automatically calculates precise upper bounds on the worst-case stack usage. It shows the critical path, i.e. the path on which the maximum stack usage is reached and that gives important feedback for optimizing the stack usage of the application under analysis. StackAnalyzer depends on the instruction set of the target processor and it is available for a wide range of 16-bit and 32-bit microcontrollers [ABS b].

aiT WCET Analyzer computes safe and precise upper bounds on the worst-case execution time. It is centered around a precise model of the microarchitecture of the target processor and is available for various 16-bit and 32-bit microcontrollers [ABS a]. aiT determines the WCET of a program task in several phases [FER 01] corresponding to the reference architecture described above, which makes it possible to use different methods tailored to each subtasks [THE 98]. In the following, we will give an overview of each analysis stage.

8.5.1.1. *Decoding phase*

The instruction decoder identifies the machine instructions and reconstructs the control-flow graph (CFG) [THE 00]. The reconstructed control flow is annotated with the information needed by subsequent analyses and then translated into control-flow representation language (CRL) [LAN 99] – a human-readable intermediate format designed to simplify analysis and optimization at the executable/assembly level. This annotated CFG serves as the input for micro-architecture analysis. To ensure safety of later analysis results, the reconstructed CFG must be safe, i.e. all possible paths that can occur during execution of the program must be represented. From a static analysis point of view, this can become difficult, for example, in the presence of dynamically computed successors. Such uncertainties may lead to over-approximations of the actual control flow of the analyzed task. This is difficult for, e.g. indirect calls via function pointers or the implementation of high-level programming language constructs like switch tables. If call targets and loop bounds cannot be computed statically, the analyzer asks the user to provide this information. To this end, a formal specification language, which allows us to precisely specify program points where to insert the desired information in a robust way, called AIS is available.

8.5.1.2. *Micro-architectural analysis phase*

Four different data-flow analyses are employed in this phase of the aiT framework: loop analysis, value analysis, cache analysis and pipeline analysis. Loop and value analysis are implemented within a single analyzer, and so are cache and pipeline analysis. Cache and pipeline analysis have to be combined, because the pipeline analysis models the flow of instructions through the processor pipeline and therefore computes the precise instant of time when the cache is queried and its state is updated.

8.5.1.3. *Combined loop and value analysis*

The combined loop and value analysis determines safe approximations of the values of processor registers and memory cells for every program point and execution context. These approximations are used to determine bounds on the iteration number of loops and information about the addresses of memory accesses. Contents of registers or memory cells, loop bounds, and address ranges for memory accesses may also be provided by annotations if they cannot be determined automatically.

Value analysis information is also used to identify conditions that are always true or always false. Such knowledge is used to infer that certain program parts are never executed and therefore do not contribute to the worst-case execution time or the stack usage.

8.5.1.4. *Cache/pipeline analysis*

The combined cache and pipeline analysis represents an abstract interpretation of the program's execution on the underlying system architecture. The execution of a program is simulated by feeding instruction sequences from a CFG to the timing model, which computes the system state changes at cycle granularity and keeps track of the elapsing clock cycles. The correctness proofs according to the theory of abstract interpretation have been conducted by Thesing [THE 04].

The cache analysis presented by [FER 97, FER 98, FER 99] is incorporated into the pipeline analysis. At each point, where the actual hardware would query and update the contents of the cache(s), the abstract cache analysis is called, simulating a safe approximation of the cache effects. Precise analysis of cache behavior still is an active field of research [GRU 09b, GRU 09a, ALT 10].

The result of the cache/pipeline analysis either is a worst-case execution time for every basic block, or a *prediction graph* that represents the evolution of the abstract system states at processor core clock granularity [CUL 13].

8.5.1.5. *Path analysis phase*

The path analysis phase uses the results of the combined cache/pipeline analysis to compute the worst-case path of the analyzed code with respect to the execution timing. The execution time of the computed worst-case path is the worst-case execution time for the program. Within the aiT framework, different methods for computing this worst-case path are available.

8.5.1.6. *Visualization phase and reporting*

The visualization phase enables users to interactively explore CFGs annotated with the results of the other analysis phases. These are the results of decoding and loop/value analysis, plus the results of cache/pipeline and path analysis in case of aiT, and stack levels and stack usage in case of StackAnalyzer. The graphs are displayed by the aiSee graph viewer [ABS 13d] that has been integrated into the graphical user interface.

Figure 8.2(b), shows the graphical representation of the call graph for some small example. The calls (edges) that contribute to the worst-case run time are shown in light grey. The computed WCET is given in CPU cycles and in microseconds provided that the cycle time of the processor has been specified.

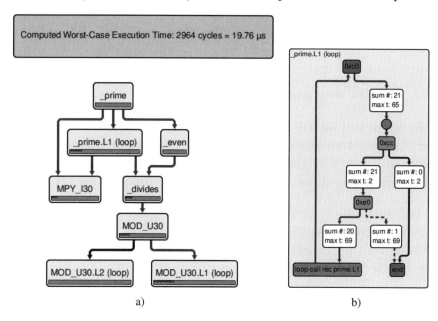

Figure 8.2. *Call graph and basic-block graph with WCET results*

Figure 8.2(a), shows the basic block graph of a loop. The number sum # is the number of traversals of an edge in the worst case, while max t describes the maximal execution time of the basic block from which the edge originates (taking into account that the basic block is left via the edge). The worst-case path, the iteration numbers and timings are determined automatically by aiT. Upon special command, aiT provides information on the origin of these timings by displaying the cache and pipeline states that may occur within a basic block.

The available visualization features are very useful for understanding the analyzed program and the analysis results. With their help, places of high resource usage w.r.t. execution time or stack height can be identified and examined.

Apart from the graphical representation, aiT and StackAnalyzer also support the generation of report files documenting analysis parameters, diagnostic messages, and analysis results. This feature is particularly useful when running analyses in batch mode. There are two kinds of report files: human-readable text-based files without a fully fixed format, and machine-readable XML files conforming to a specific XML Schema Definition.

8.5.2. Run-time error analysis

In this section we will focus on the static analyzer Astrée, which aims to find all potential run-time errors, respectively, proving their absence. Astrée is sound, i.e. it signals all potential run-time errors. If no errors are signaled, this means there are no errors the absence of run-time errors has been proved.

The Astrée analyzer operates on C source code. The run-time errors considered by Astrée include violations of the C standard ISO/IEC 9899:1999 (E), implementation-specific undefined behaviors and violations of user-specified programming guidelines:

– Integer/floating-point division by zero.

– Out-of-bounds array indexing.

– Erroneous pointer manipulation and dereferencing (NULL, uninitialized and dangling pointers).

– Integer and floating-point arithmetic overflow.

– Violation of optional user-defined assertions to prove additional run-time properties (similar to assert diagnostics).

– Code it can prove to be unreachable under any circumstances.

Astrée is sound for floating-point computations and handles them precisely and safely. It takes all possible rounding errors into account.

While the primary goal of Astrée is to prove the absence of run-time errors, the analysis can also be leveraged to compute further program properties relevant for functional safety. Astrée detects read accesses to uninitialized variables, detects shared variables accessed by asynchronous threads and performs a sound value analysis for them, computes detailed control and data flow reports, and enables users to prove user-defined static assertions. The static assertions can be applied to arbitrary C expressions so that functional program properties can be addressed. When Astrée does not report an assertion failure alarm, the correctness of the asserted expression has been formally proven.

The data and control flow reports comprise a detailed listing of accesses to global and static variables sorted by functions or variables, and caller/callee relationships between functions. The reports also cover each potentially shared variable, the list of asynchronous tasks accessing it, and the types of the accesses (read, write, read/write).

The C99 standard does not fully specify data type sizes, endianness nor alignment, which can vary with different targets or compilers. Additionally, there are operating system dependencies, e.g. whether or not global or static variables are automatically initialized to zero. Astrée is informed about these target settings by a dedicated configuration file and takes the specified properties into account.

In the following, we will use the term *alarm* to denote a notification about a potential run-time error. Astrée distinguishes between two different types of alarms:

– Alarms for run-time errors that can cause *unpredictable* results. Examples are write operations via dangling pointers, or dereferences of a misaligned pointer. Since it is not possible to predict what happens after such an error, Astrée only continues the analysis for scenarios where the error did not occur. If there is a context where the error definitely occurs, the analyzer stops for this context since there is no feasible continuation.

– Alarms for run-time errors, which have a *predictable* outcome. The effect of the error can be fully taken into account by the analyzer, which will proceed with an over-approximation of all possible results. Examples are integer overflows, or invalid shift or cast operations.

While Astrée finds all potential run-time errors, it may err on the other side and produce false alarms. The design of the analyzer aims at reaching the zero false alarm objective [BLA 02, BLA 03, COU 05], which was accomplished for the first time on large industrial applications at the end of November 2003.

For industrial use, producing the fewest possible number of false alarms is an important goal. Only with zero alarms is the absence of run-time errors automatically proven. For keeping the initial number of false alarms low, a high analysis precision is mandatory. There is a variety of predefined abstract domains, including the following ones: the interval domain approximates variable values by intervals; the octagon domain [MIN 06] covers relations of the form $x \pm y \leq c$ for variables x and y and constants c. Floating-point computations are precisely modeled while keeping track of possible rounding errors [BLA 03]; the memory domain empowers Astrée to exactly analyze pointer arithmetics and union manipulations. It also supports a type-safe analysis of absolute memory addresses; and the clock domain has been specifically developed for synchronous control programs and supports relating variable values to the system clock [COU 07]. With the filter domain [FER 04b] digital filters can be precisely approximated. It is also possible to incorporate additional abstract domains into Astrée [BER 10].

Any remaining alarm has to be manually checked by the developers and this manual effort should be as low as possible. Astrée explicitly supports investigating alarms in order to understand the reasons for them to occur. When clicking at an alarm message, the corresponding code location is highlighted in the original and preprocessed source code. Alarms can be grouped by source code locations, and all contexts in which an alarm occurs are listed. Alarm contexts can be interactively explored: all parents in the call stack, relevant loop iterations or conditional statements can be visited per mouse click, and the computed value ranges of variables can be displayed for all abstract domains (see Figure 8.3).

Inversely, clicking on the source code location for which an alarm has been produced repositions the focus of the output window to show the corresponding alarm message. In the output window, alarm locations are collected in the order in which they are reached by the analyzer. This is very helpful for alarm investigation since fixing one alarm usually causes several subsequent alarms to disappear so, earlier (root) alarms should be investigated first. The call graph of the software under analysis is visualized taking function pointer calls into account; an example call graph is shown in Figure 8.4.

If there is a true error it has to be fixed. A false alarm can possibly be eliminated by a suitable parameterization of Astrée. If the error cannot occur due to certain preconditions which are not known to Astrée, they can be made available to Astrée via dedicated directives. These annotations make the side conditions explicit that have to be satisfied for a correct program execution. If the false alarm is caused by insufficient analysis precision, steering directives are available that allow to locally tune the analysis precision to eliminate the false alarm. The key feature is that Astrée is fully parametric with respect to the abstract domains. Abstract domains can be parameterized to tune the precision of the analysis for individual program constructs or program points [MAU 05]. This means that in one analysis run, important program parts can be analyzed very precisely while less relevant parts can be analyzed very quickly without compromising system safety.

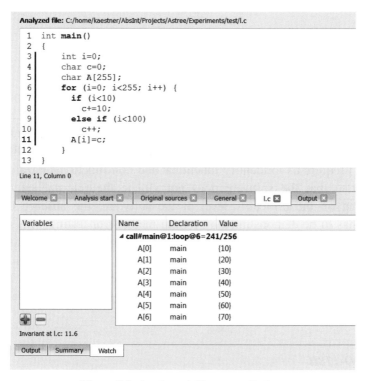

Figure 8.3. *Astrée variable ranges display*

All directives can be specified in a formal language AAL [ABS 13c] and stored in a dedicated file. An AAL annotation consists of an Astrée directive and a path specifying the program point at which to insert the directive. The path is specified in a robust way by exploiting the program's syntactical structure without relying on line number information. The AAL language is a prerequisite for supporting model-based code generators. It makes it possible to separate the annotations from the source code, so that when the code is regenerated, all previously generated annotations from structurally unchanged code parts are still valid, even if the line numbers change.

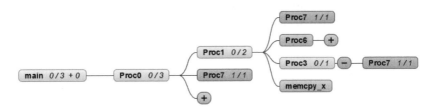

Figure 8.4. *Astrée call graph visualization*

8.6. The safety standards' perspective

Safety standards like DO-178B [RAD 92], DO-178C [RAD 11b], IEC-61508 [IEC 10], ISO-26262 [ISO 11a] and CENELEC EN-50128 [CEN 11] require us to identify functional and non-functional hazards and to demonstrate that the software does not violate the relevant safety goals. Depending on the criticality level of the software, the absence of safety hazards has to be demonstrated by formal methods or testing with sufficient coverage. In the following, we give a short overview on the assessment of non-functional program properties (run-time errors, execution time constraints and memory consumption) by the safety standards for avionics, space, automotive and railway systems, for general electric/electronic systems, and for medical software products.

8.6.1. *DO-178B*

Published in 1992, the DO-178B [RAD 92] was the primary document by which the certification authorities such as FAA, EASA and Transport Canada approved all commercial software-based aerospace systems until the publication of DO-178C (see section 8.6.2).

The DO-178B emphasizes the importance of software verification. Verification is defined as a technical assessment of the results of both the software development processes and the software verification process. Section 6.0 of the DO-178B states that "verification is not simply testing. Testing, in general, cannot show the absence of errors." The standard consequently uses the term "verify" instead of "test" when the software verification process objectives being discussed are typically a combination of reviews, analyses and test. The purpose of the software verification process is to detect and report errors that may have been introduced during the software development processes. Removal of the errors is an activity of the software development processes. The general objectives of the software verification process are to verify that the requirements of the system level, the architecture level, the source code level and the executable object code level are satisfied, and that the means used to satisfy these objectives are technically correct and complete. At the code level, the objective is to detect and report errors that may have been introduced during the software coding process. The non-functional safety properties are explicitly listed as a part of the *accuracy and consistency* verification objective at the code level, including stack usage, worst-case execution timing and absence of run-time errors.

8.6.2. *DO-178C / DO-333*

The DO-178C [RAD 11b], published in December 2011, is a revision of DO-178B to take progress in software development and verification technologies into account. It specifically focuses on model-based software development, object-oriented software, the use and qualification of software tools and the use of formal methods to complement or replace dynamic testing (theorem proving, model checking and abstract interpretation). Each of these key aspects is addressed by a dedicated *supplement* which modifies, complements, and completes the DO-178C core document [RAD 11b]. In this overview, we will specifically focus on the DO-178C core document, the DO-330 (software tool qualification considerations) [RAD 11c] and DO-333 (formal methods supplement to DO-178C and DO-278A) [RAD 11a].

Like the DO-178B, the DO-178C emphasizes the incompleteness of testing techniques. According to the DO-178C, since formal methods are sound, they can completely satisfy some verification objectives while for others, additional verification such as complimentary testing may be necessary. The purpose and objective of the software verification process are defined in the same way as in the DO-178B.

The DO-178C requires software development to be aware of general system aspects including functional and operational requirements, performance requirements and safety-related requirements (see section 2.1 of [RAD 11b]). In particular, timing and performance characteristics require special attention since they affect the system–software and the software–hardware boundaries and have to be included in the respective information flows. As a result, non-functional software properties in general are addressed at all levels of the software verification process. The DO-178C distinguishes between high-level requirements and low-level requirements. High-level requirements are produced directly through analysis of system requirements and system architecture. Low-level requirements are software requirements from which source code can be directly implemented without further information. High-level and low-level requirements blend together when source code is generated directly from high-level requirements.

The software verification process comprises reviews and analyses of high-level requirements, low-level requirements, the software architecture, the source code and requires testing or formal analysis of the executable object code. One common verification objective at all levels is to demonstrate the compliance with the requirements of the parent level. As the system requirements include performance and safety-related requirements, non-functional aspects like timing or storage usage can impact all stages. Consequently, the "compatibility with the target computer" is a verification objective among the high-level requirements, the low-level requirements, and at the software architecture level. In section 6.3. of [RAD 11b] the system response time is given as an example of target computer properties relevant for high-level requirements and low-level requirements. Computing the response time requires the worst-case execution time to be known.

8.6.2.1. *Source-code level*

At the source-code level, the objective *accuracy and consistency* explicitly includes determining the worst-case execution time, the stack usage and run-time errors (memory usage, fixed-point arithmetic overflow and resolution, floating-point arithmetic and use of uninitialized variables). Formal analysis can be used to demonstrate these verification objectives (see section FM.6.3.4 of [RAD 11a]).

8.6.2.2. *Executable object level*

Worst-case execution time and worst-case stack usage have to be considered at the executable object code level. The reason is that the impact of the compiler, linker and of hardware features on the worst-case execution time and stack usage has to be assessed. Both can be checked by formal analyses at the executable object code level (see section FM.6.7 of [RAD 11a]). Run-time errors also have to be addressed at the executable object level, e.g. to deal with robustness issues like out-of-range loop values and arithmetic overflows (see section FM.6.7.b of [RAD 11a]), or to verify the software component integration. The latter implies, for example detecting incorrect initialization of variables, parameter passing errors and data corruption.

At the executable object level, complimentary testing is still required, for example to address transient hardware faults, or incorrect interrupt handling (see section 6.4.3. of [RAD 11b]). Formal analysis performed at the source code level can be used for verification objectives at the executable object code if property preservation between source code and executable code can be demonstrated (see section FM.6.7.f of [RAD 11a]).

8.6.2.3. *Verification objectives*

In general, non-functional aspects contribute to all verification objectives related to the target environment. Stack usage, response times and execution times are determined by the target computer. They can cause violations of high-level requirements, violations of low-level requirements, incompatibility of the software architecture with the target computer, and they can affect the accuracy and consistency of the source code. A formal data and control flow analysis is required to demonstrate consistency between software architecture level and the source code level. Run-time error analysis is required to deal with robustness issues like out-of-range loop values and arithmetic overflows, or to verify the software integration. The latter implies, for example, detecting incorrect initialization of variables, parameter passing errors and data corruption. The verification objectives are summarized in Appedix A of [RAD 11a]. An overview of the non-functional requirements regarding resource usage and run-time errors is given in section 8.11.

While the tables in Appendix A of [RAD 11a] regard the DO-178C, Appendix C of [RAD 11a] contains the equivalent tables regarding DO-278A. They are relevant when using formal methods in the production of software for communication, navigation, surveillance and air traffic management (CNS/ATM) systems. The applicability of aiT, StackAnalyzer and Astrée w.r.t. the tables in Appendix C is identical to the corresponding tables in Appendix A.

8.6.3. *ISO-26262*

In this section we focus on Part 6 of the ISO-26262 standard [ISO 11b], which specifies the requirements for product development at the software level for automotive applications. The safety integrity levels are called ASIL-A (least critical) to ASIL-D (most critical). The ISO-26262 covers the typical software development phases of the V model [VM 06]. In the following, we briefly give an overview of the non-functional requirements regarding resource usage and run-time errors in each of these phases. Section 8.12 contains a summary in tabular form.

8.6.3.1. *Basic requirements*

The ability to handle non-functional program properties is one determining factor for selecting a suitable modeling or programming language (see [ISO 11b], section 5.4.6). The standard requires that real-time software and run-time error handling must be supported. It also states that "criteria that are not sufficiently addressed by the language itself shall be covered by the corresponding guidelines or by the development environment". When run-time errors are not prevented by the language semantics and cannot be excluded by enforcing a language subset, the absence of run-time errors has to be ensured by dedicated tools. Also timing and stack behavior is not captured in contemporary programming language semantics and hence has to be addressed by specific tools.

8.6.3.2. *Safety requirements*

In general, the specification of the software safety requirements considers constraints of the hardware and the impact of these constraints on the software. Among others, safety requirements apply to functions that enable the system to achieve or maintain a safe state, and to functions related to performance or time-critical operations. The standard explicitly lists some requirements, which are part of the software safety, including the hardware-software interface specification, the relevant requirements of the hardware design specification and the timing constraints. Hardware- or configuration-related errors (e.g. stack overflows and run-time errors like erroneous pointer manipulations) can cause globally unpredictable behavior affecting all safety functions and thus have to be taken into account. Timing constraints include the response time at the system level with derived timing properties like the worst-case execution time.

8.6.3.3. *Software architectural design*

The architectural design has to be able to realize the software safety requirements. Section 7.4.17 of [ISO 11b] explicitly demands that "an upper estimation of required resources for the embedded software shall be made, including the execution time, and the storage space". Thus, upper bounds of the worst-case execution time and upper bounds of the stack usage are a fixed part of the architectural safety requirements. The importance of timing is also reflected by the fact that "appropriate scheduling properties" are highly recommended for all automotive safety integrity levels (ASIL) as a principle for software architecture design. All existing schedulability algorithms assume upper bounds on the worst-case execution time to be known, as well as interferences on task switches either to be precluded or predictable. Thus, the availability of safe worst-case execution and response times belongs to the most basic scheduling properties.

Software architectural design requirements also explicitly address the interaction of software components. "Each software component shall be developed in compliance with the highest ASIL of any requirements allocated to it." Furthermore, "all of the embedded software shall be treated in accordance with the highest ASIL, unless the software components meet the criteria for coexistence [...]" (see [ISO 11b], section 7.4.9–7.4.10). Freedom of interference is an essential criterion for coexistence, both in the spatial and the temporal domain. Appendix D of [ISO 11b] focuses on freedom of interference and discusses timing properties like worst-case execution time or scheduling characteristics as well as memory constraints. For memory safety, corruption of content, as well as read or write accesses to memory allocated to other software elements have to be excluded. Such accesses can be caused by stack overflows or run-time errors like erroneous pointer manipulations and dereferences.

8.6.3.4. *Software unit design and implementation*

Chapter 8 of [ISO 11b] defines the three goals of software unit design and implementation as: specification of the software units in accordance with design and safety requirements, implementation of the software units, and static verification of design and implementation of the software units. Thus, static verification plays a very prominent role in the design and implementation stage; it should always precede dynamic testing, which should focus on properties not statically verified.

Table 9 of [ISO 11b] lists the methods for verification of software unit design and implementation, including formal verification, control flow analysis, data flow analysis, static code analysis and semantic code analysis. All these techniques can be considered as aspects of general static analysis. The mentioned static analysis techniques are (highly) recommended for all ASIL levels.

8.6.3.5. *Unit and integration testing*

The absence of run-time errors (division by zero, control and data flow errors, etc.) is considered as a robustness property (section 8.4.4), which has to be ensured during implementation. Resource usage constraints like timing or stack consumption have to be addressed in the software unit testing stage (see Chapter 9 of [ISO 11b]). The software integration phase has to consider functional dependences and the dependences between software integration and hardware-software integration. Again the non-functional software properties have to be addressed; robustness has to be demonstrated, which includes the absence of run-time errors, and it has to be demonstrated that there are sufficient resources to support the functionality that includes timing and stack usage (section 10.4.3).

8.6.4. *IEC-61508*

In 2010, a new revision of the functional safety standard IEC-61508, called Edition 2.0, was published [IEC 10]. It sets out a generic approach for all safety lifecycle activities for systems comprised of electrical and/or electronic and/or programmable electronic (E/E/PE) elements that are used to perform safety functions. The safety integrity levels are called SIL1 (least critical) to SIL4 (most critical). The non-functional program properties are part of the software safety requirements specification, including invalid, out of range or untimely values, response time, best case and worst-case execution time, and overflow and underflow of data storage capacity.

The IEC-61508 states that verification includes testing and analysis. In the software verification stage, static analysis techniques are recommended for SIL1 and highly recommended for SIL2-SIL4. Among these techniques, data flow analysis is highly recommended in SIL2-SIL4, static analysis of run-time error behavior recommended in SIL1-SIL3 and highly recommended in SIL4, and static worst-case execution time analysis is recommended in SIL1-4. Among the criteria to be considered for selecting specific techniques is the completeness and repeatability of testing, so where testing is used, completeness has to be demonstrated. The results of abstract interpretation based static analyses are considered a mathematical proof; their reliability is rated maximal (R3).

The IEC-61508 also provides requirements for mixed-criticality systems: unless freedom of interference can be demonstrated both in the spatial and the temporal domain, or it can be shown that any violation of independence is controlled, all of the software is subject to the highest safety integrity level. For achieving temporal independence the standard suggests deterministic scheduling methods. One suggestion is using a cyclic scheduling algorithm, which gives each element a defined time slice supported by worst-case execution time analysis of each element to demonstrate statically that the timing requirements for each element are met. Other suggestions are using time-triggered architectures, or strict priority based scheduling implemented by a real-time executive [IEC 10].

8.6.5. CENELEC EN-50128

The CENELEC EN-50128 was revised in 2011 [CEN 11]. It provides a set of requirements the development, deployment and maintenance of any safety-related software intended for railway control and protection applications shall comply with. It addresses five software safety integrity levels from SIL0 (lowest) to SIL4 (highest) and identifies and lists appropriate techniques and measures for each level of software safety integrity.

Static analysis is highly recommended for SIL 1 – SIL 4, where the focus of static analysis is mainly on control and data flow analysis.

Throughout all development stages, from requirements specification, software architecture, design and implementation, to the verification and test stage, formal methods are recommended for SIL 1-2 and even strongly recommended for SIL 3-4.

In the verification and test stage and the integration stage performance tests are recommended for SIL 1-2 and strongly recommended for SIL 3-4. As a part of the performance tests it is highly recommended for SIL 1-4 to consider the worst-case response time and storage space limitations. The test coverage criterion strongly recommended for SIL 3-4 is path coverage. Run-time errors are counted to the programming errors subject to boundary value analysis (division by zero, array bound violations, etc.) which is recommended for SIL1–2 and strongly recommended for SIL 3–4.

Abstract interpretation is not included in the list of formal methods in Appendix D.28/D.29. However, this list is not meant to be comprehensive, and it is clear that abstract interpretation belongs to the formal methods. Moreover, as detailed in section 8.2 abstract interpretation is the most efficient way for achieving path coverage for worst-case timing and worst-case stack usage. Establishing path coverage with testing methods requires exponential effort.

To summarize, although abstract interpretation is not explicitly mentioned, there are strong requirements in the EN-50128 to use abstract interpretation to perform run-time error analysis, worst-case execution time analysis and worst-case stack usage analysis.

8.6.6. *Regulations for medical software*

In the medical domain, the most prominent norms are the EN-60601 and IEC-62304. The EN-60601 formulates requirements for the software lifecycle and risk management [INT 96]. The standard IEC-62304 describes a lifecycle for software development with a focus on maintenance and on component-oriented software architectures [DIN 06].

There is no dedicated norm for software-based functional safety as in the domains described above. However, beyond these standards, country-specific requirements have to be respected. Those requirements clearly formulate that for verification, testing is not enough and that the state of the art in verification technology has to be applied. Since there is no dedicated norm defining minimal requirements to the state of the art for medical software, the regulations of related safety norms have to be considered, which includes the norms presented in sections 8.6.1–8.6.5.

In the following, we will briefly discuss the American and German legal regulations. The presentation of the US regulations follows reference 31. Software validation is a requirement of the quality system regulation (see Title 21 Code of Federal Regulations (CFR) Part 820, and 61 Federal Register (FR) 52602, respectively). Validation requirements apply to software used as components in medical devices, to software that is itself a medical device, and to production software. Verification means confirmation by examination and provision of objective evidence that specified requirements have been fulfilled [US 13]. In a software development environment, software verification is confirmation that the output of a particular phase of development meets all of the input requirements for that phase. While software testing is a necessary activity, in most cases software testing by itself is not considered sufficient to establish confidence that the software is fit for its intended use. Additional verification activities are required, including static analysis. In Europe, the validation of medical software has to follow the EU-directive 2007/47/EC [EUR 07], which, in Germany was incorporated into national law in 2010. It states that software in its own right, when specifically intended to be used for medical purpose, has to be considered a medical device. For devices that incorporate software or which are medical software in themselves, the software must be validated according to the state of the art.

8.7. Providing confidence – tool qualification and more

Safety standards like DO-178B/DO-178C, ISO-26262, IEC-61508, or CENELEC EN-50128 require to demonstrate the functional safety of the software. Functional correctness has to be demonstrated with respect to the specified requirements and the absence of critical non-functional hazards – including timing hazards in real-time systems – has to be shown. This substantiation has to be done with adequate confidence. Adequate confidence means that the evidence provided can be trusted beyond reasonable doubt. There are two main sources of doubt: the logic doubt associated with the validity of the reasoning and the epistemic doubt associated with uncertainty about the underlying assumptions [RUS 13].

The logic doubt can be eliminated by using formal methods. The theory of abstract interpretation provides a formal methodology for semantics-based static analysis of dynamic program properties. There is a variety of scientific publications about the theory of abstract interpretation [COU 77, COU 79, COU 81, COU 92, COU 00a, COU 00c, COU 00b], and about Astrée, which give detailed information about the design of Astrée and contain the necessary correctness proofs [BLA 02, BLA 03, MIN 04a, FER 04b, MIN 04b, FER 04a, COU 05, MAU 05, MIN 06, COU 07, KAS 10]. WCET analyzers in general are discussed in [WIL 08], and aiT and StackAnalyzer in [FER 08a, FER 07, KAS 11, KAS 08, SOU 05c, THE 03].

With the soundness of the analysis methodology established, it remains to show the correctness of the underlying hardware model used for WCET analysis, the correctness of the analyzer implementation, and to investigate the underlying assumptions about the physical world. Confidence in the microprocessor model has to be built on empirical evidence. We propose the following strategy: The analytically determined WCET bounds for representative programs or code snippets are compared with measurement data: measured times must always be below the analytically computed WCET bound. Furthermore, automatic trace validation allows a cycle-accurate validation of the model down to the level of individual pipeline events and bus signals, based on the automatic processing of trace files created on the real hardware. For more details about the model validation see [GEB 13, KAS 13]. Implementations of abstract interpretation based program analyzers can be automatically generated from the mathematical analysis specification, hence enabling high implementation quality [MAR 98, KAS 13]. Qualification Support Kits enable tool users to demonstrate the correct functioning of the tool in their operational environment in an automatic way. Part of the tool qualification also is a detailed summary of all underlying assumptions of model, implementation, interfaces and operational conditions. Qualification Software Life Cycle reports document the soundness of the tool development and validation processes. All these measures together enable the epistemic doubt to be eliminated.

8.7.1. *Tool qualification*

To provide high confidence in the correct functioning of a tool it is necessary to demonstrate that the tool works correctly in the operational context of its users. This is a common requirement for most of the current safety standards. The correct functioning of a tool might be affected by the OS version, system libraries installed and software patch levels, etc. Moreover, depending on the user's development process structure and tool landscape the probability for detecting tool errors may vary. Therefore, taking into account the operational context of tool usage is essential for tool qualification.

From the perspective of a tool user, qualifying a software tool causes considerable effort. The functional requirements of the tool have to be specified, a test plan has to be developed, tests have to be executed and documented. Moreover the qualification effort has to be repeated for each development project to be certified. This makes it very desirable to do automatize the tool qualification process. Such an automatic tool qualification can be done by dedicated *Qualification Support Kits (QSKs)* as shipped as a part of a software tool.

In the following, we give an overview of the AbsInt QSKs for aiT, StackAnalyzer and Astrée whose structure is representative for general qualification support kits. They is centered around an automatic validation suite and essentially consists of two parts: a report package and a test package.

The *report part* consists of two different documents: the *tool operational requirements* (TOR) and the *verification test plan* (VTP). The TOR lists the tool functions and technical features which are stated as low-level requirements to the tool behavior under normal operating conditions. Additionally, the TOR describes the tool operational context and conditions in which the tool computes valid results. It summarizes all basic assumptions about the physical world that have to be satisfied for correct tool operation. This includes: unsupported microprocessor options or configurations, system parameters (e.g. scheduling strategy, occurrence of DMA, dynamic RAM refreshes, or exceptions), etc. The VTP defines the test cases demonstrating the correct functioning of all specified requirements from the TOR. Test case definitions include the overall test setup as well as a detailed structural and functional description of each test case. The *test part* contains an extensible set of test cases with a scripting system to automatically execute them and generate reports about the results.

Depending on the safety standard and the criticality level of the application, providing additional confidence about the tool software development processes may be required. The AbsInt *qualification support life cycle data* (QSLCD) reports contain documents which detail the tool development processes, e.g. the software development plan, the quality plan, quality assurance records, the software verification plan and software verification results. The details of QSK and QSLCD and the precise link to the requirements of DO-178B, DO-178C, and ISO-26262 are presented in [ABS 13b].

8.8. Integration in the development process

Static analysis tools are not only applicable at the validation and verification stage, but also during the development stage. One advantage of static analysis methods is that no testing on physical hardware is required. Thus, the analyses can be called just like a compiler from a workstation computer after the compilation or linking stage of the project. For all tools mentioned in section 8.5, aiT, StackAnalyzer and Astrée, there are batch versions facilitating the integration in a general automated build process, or in continuous verification frameworks. This enables developers to instantly assess the effects of program changes on WCET and stack usage and run-time errors. Defects are detected early, so that late-stage integration problems can be avoided.

Model-based development becomes more and more widely used for developing embedded control algorithms, especially for safety-critical applications. The aim is to improve development efficiency and safety by developing the software at a high abstraction level (the model) and by generating the implementation (the C code) automatically from the model. Although model-based development focuses on the models themselves, downstream artifacts such as source code or executable object code have to be considered in the verification stage. As described in section 8.5 abstract interpretation-based static analysis tools, which work at the code level and can prove the absence of such errors, are available. However, the connection to the model level has to be explicitly established. Therefore, it is desirable to integrate static code analyzers with model-based development tools. With such an integration, the static analysis can be invoked automatically from the modeling tool with relevant model-level information automatically being propagated to the analyzer to optimize analysis precision. The results are mapped back to the modeling level. This way, timing bugs, stack overflows, and run-time errors can be detected early in the development process. Implementation-level errors can be traced back to the modeling level, and can be investigated at both the model and the implementation level. This significantly reduces the development effort and allows bugs to be detected early in the development process. To this end, aiT and StackAnalyzer have been integrated in Esterel's SCADE Suite [FER 08b]; also a tool coupling between aiT, StackAnalyzer, and Astrée with dSPACE TargetLink is available [KAS 14]. These couplings enable a seamless integration of static analysis tools in the development process.

8.9. Practical experience

In recent years, tools based on static analysis have proved their usability in industrial practice and, as a result, have increasingly been used by avionics, automotive and healthcare industries. In the following, we report some experiences gained with aiT WCET Analyzer, StackAnalyzer and Astrée.

StackAnalyzer results are usually byte-precise for any given program path. Statements about the precision of aiT are hard to obtain since the real WCET is usually unknown for typical real-life applications. For an avionics application running on MPC 755, Airbus has noted that aiT's WCET for a task typically is about 25% higher than some measured execution times for the same task, the real but non-calculable WCET being in between [SOU 05a]. Trace-based measurements at AbsInt have indicated overestimations ranging from 0% (cycle-exact prediction) till 15% on LEON2, MPC565, MPC5566, Intel 386, AMD 486, M32C, TMS320C33, TriCore TC1197/TC1797/1796, MPC MPC6474F and C166/ST10 [KAS 13, GEB 13].

Astrée has been used in several industrial avionics and space projects. One of the examined software projects from the avionics industry comprises 132,000 lines of C code including macros and contains approximately 10,000 global and static variables [BLA 03]. The first run of Astrée reported 1,200 false alarms; after adapting Astrée the number of false alarms could be reduced to 11. The analysis duration was 1h 50 min on a PC with 2.4 GHz and 1GB RAM.

[DEL 07] gives a detailed overview of the analysis process for an Airbus avionics project. The software project consists of 200,000 lines of preprocessed C code, performs many floating-point computations and contains digital filters. The analysis duration for the entire program is approximately 6 hours on a 2.6 GHz PC with 16 GB RAM. At the beginning, the number of false alarms was 467 and could be reduced to zero in the end.

8.10. Summary

The quality assurance process for safety-critical embedded software is of crucial importance. The cost for system validation grows with an increasing criticality level to constitute a large fraction of the overall development cost. The problem is twofold: system safety must be ensured, yet this must be accomplishable with reasonable effort.

Contemporary safety standards require us to identify potential functional and non-functional hazards and to demonstrate that the software does not violate the relevant safety goals. Tools based on abstract interpretation can perform static program analysis of embedded applications. Their results are determined without the need to change the code and hold for all program runs with arbitrary inputs. Especially for non-functional program properties they are highly attractive, since they provide full data and control coverage and can be seamlessly integrated in the development process. The theory of abstract interpretation provides a formal methodology for semantics-based static analysis of dynamic program properties. It allows provably sound over-approximations of the worst-case execution time and stack usage to be determined and the absence of run-time errors to be proven.

In this chapter, we have presented three exemplary tools: aiT allows us to inspect the timing behavior of real-time tasks. It takes into account the combination of all the different hardware characteristics while still obtaining tight upper bounds for the WCET of a given program in reasonable time. StackAnalyzer calculates safe upper bounds on the maximum stack usage of tasks and can prove the absence of stack overflows. Astrée can be used to prove the absence of run-time errors in C programs. It can be specialized to the software under analysis and achieves very high precision. Industrial synchronous real-time software from the avionics industry could be successfully analyzed by Astrée with zero false alarms. aiT, StackAnalyzer and Astrée have been successfully used as verification tools for the certification according to safety standards like DO-178B or ISO 26262. They are used by many industry customers from avionics and automotive industries and have been proven in industrial practice. The tool qualification process can be automatized to a large extend by dedicated Qualification Support Kits and Qualification Software Life Cycle Data reports.

8.11. Appendix A: Non-functional verification objectives of DO-178C

The table below gives an explicit overview of verification objectives related to WCET, stack usage and run-time errors. The relevant tables in [RAD 11a] are:

– Table FM.A-3 (*verification of outputs of software requirements process*).

– Table FM.A-4 (*verification of outputs of software design process*).

– Table FM.A-5 (*verification of outputs of software coding & integration processes*).

– Table FM.A-6 (*testing of outputs of integration process*).

8.12. Appendix B: Non-functional requirements of ISO-26262

The following table lists the sections of Part 6 of ISO-26262 referring to non-functional program properties and static verification techniques.

Section No.	Section Title	WCET	Stack	Run-Time Errors
FM.A-6 Objective 5	Executable code is compatible with target computer	✓	✓	
6.5.4.6	Criteria for selecting a suitable modeling or programming language	✓	✓	✓
6.5.4.7	Topics to be covered by modeling and coding guidelines			✓
	continued on the following page...			

Section No.	Section Title	WCET	Stack	Run-Time Errors
6.6.2. – General	Specification of Software safety requirements ✓	✓	✓	
6.6.4.1. – Requirements and recommendations	Specification of SW Safety Requirements ✓	✓	✓	
6.6.4.2. – Requirements and recommendations	Specification of SW Safety Requirements ✓	✓	✓	
6.6.4.4. – Requirements and recommendations	Specification of SW Safety Requirements ✓	✓	✓	
6.6.4.8. – Requirements and recommendations	Specification of SW Safety Requirements ✓	✓	✓	
6.7.4.2. – Requirements and recommendations	Software architectural design ✓	✓		
6.7.4.3. – Requirements and recommendations	Software architectural design ✓			
6.7.4.5.	Software architectural design			

continued on the following page. . .

Section No.	Section Title	WCET	Stack	Run-Time Errors
– Requirements and recommendations	✓	✓	✓	
6.7.4.10. – Requirements and recommendations	Software architectural design ✓	✓	✓	
6.7.4.11. – Requirements and recommendations	Software architectural design ✓			
6.7.4.14. – Requirements and recommendations	Software architectural design		✓	
6.7.4.17. – Requirements and recommendations	Software architectural design ✓	✓		
6.7.4.18. – Requirements and recommendations	Software architectural design ✓	✓	✓	
6.8.1. – Objectives	Software unit design and implementation ✓	✓	✓	
6.8.2. – General	Software unit design and implementation ✓	✓	✓	
6.8.4.4.	Software unit design and implementation			

continued on the following page...

Section No.	Section Title	WCET	Stack	Run-Time Errors
– Requirements and recommendations		✓	✓	
6.8.4.5.	Software unit design and implementation			
– Requirements and recommendations	✓	✓	✓	
6.9.4.3.	Software unit testing			
– Requirements and recommendations	✓	✓	✓	
6.9.4.4.	Software unit testing			
– Requirements and recommendations			✓	
6.9.4.6.	Software unit testing			
– Requirements and recommendations	✓	✓		
6.10.4.1.	Software integration and testing			
– Requirements and recommendations	✓	✓	✓	
6.10.4.3.	Software integration and testing			
– Requirements and recommendations	✓	✓	✓	
6.10.4.8.	Software integration and testing			
– Requirements and recommendations	✓	✓		

8.13. Bibliography

[ABS a] ABSINT GMBH, aiT worst-case execution time analyzer website. Available at http://www.AbsInt.com/ait.

[ABS b] ABSINT GMBH, StackAnalyzer website, available at http://www.AbsInt.com/sa.

[ABS 13a] ABSINT, *AIS Quick Reference Guide*, 2013.

[ABS 13b] ABSINT, *Safety Manual for aiT, Astrée, StackAnalyzer*, 2013.

[ABS 13c] ABSINT, *The Static Analyzer Astrée – User Documentation for AAL Annotations*, 2013.

[ABS 13d] ABSINT ANGEWANDTE INFORMATIK GMBH, aiSee, Website, January 2013.

[ALT 10] ALTMEYER S., MAIZA C., REINEKE J., "Resilience analysis: tightening the CRPD bound for set-associative caches", LEE J., CHILDERS B.R., (eds.), *Proceedings of the Conference on Languages, Compilers, and Tools for Embedded Systems (LCTES)*, Association for Computing Machinery (ACM), Stockholm, Sweden, pp. 153–162, April 2010.

[BER 10] BERTRANE J., COUSOT P., COUSOT R., *et al.,* "Static analysis and verification of aerospace software by abstract interpretation", *AIAA InfotechAerospace*, no. AIAA-2010-3385, American Institue of Aeronautics and Astronautics, pp. 1–38, April 2010.

[BLA 02] BLANCHET B., COUSOT P., COUSOT R., *et al.,* "Design and implementation of a special-purpose static program analyzer for safety-critical real-time embedded software", MOGENSEN T., SCHMIDT D., SUDBOROUGH I., (eds.), *The Essence of Computation: Complexity, Analysis, Transformation, Essays Dedicated to Neil D. Jones*, LNCS 2566, Springer, pp. 85–108, October 2002.

[BLA 03] BLANCHET B., COUSOT P., COUSOT R., *et al.,* "A static analyzer for large safety-critical software", *Proceedings of the ACM SIGPLAN Conference on Programming Language Design and Implementation (PLDI'03)*, San Diego, California, CA, pp. 196–207, June 7–14 2003.

[CEN 11] CENELEC EN 50128, Railway applications – Communication, signalling and processing systems – Software for railway control and protection systems, 2011.

[COU 77] COUSOT P., COUSOT R., "Abstract interpretation: a unified lattice model for static analysis of programs by construction or approximation of fixpoints", 4th *POPL*, Los Angeles, CA, pp. 238–252, 1977.

[COU 79] COUSOT P., COUSOT R., "Systematic design of program analysis frameworks", 6th *POPL*, San Antonio, TX, pp. 269–282, 1979.

[COU 81] COUSOT P., "Semantic foundations of program analysis", MUCHNICK S., JONES N., (eds.), *Program Flow Analysis: Theory and Applications*, Prentice-Hall, pp. 303–342, 1981.

[COU 92] COUSOT P., COUSOT R., "Comparing the Galois connection and widening/narrowing approaches to abstract interpretation", BRUYNOOGHE M., WIRSING M., (eds.), *Proceeding of 4th Intternational Symposium on PLILP '92*, Leuven, Belgium, LNCS 631, Springer, pp. 269–295, 26–28 August 1992.

[COU 00a] COUSOT P., "Abstract interpretation based formal methods and future challenges", WILHELM R., (ed.), *Informatics – 10 Years Back, 10 Years Ahead*, vol. 2000 of *LNCS*, Springer, pp. 138–156, 2000.

[COU 00b] COUSOT P., "Interprétation abstraite", *TSI*, vol. 19, nos. 1–3, pp. 155–164, January 2000.

[COU 00c] COUSOT P., COUSOT R., "Temporal abstract interpretation", 27th *POPL*, Boston, MA, pp. 12–25, January 2000.

[COU 05] COUSOT P., COUSOT R., FERET J., *et al.*, "The ASTRÉE analyzer", SAGIV M., (ed.), *Proceeding of the European Symposium on Programming (ESOP'05)*, vol. 3444, *Lecture Notes in Computer Science*, Springer, pp. 21–30, 2005.

[COU 07] COUSOT P., COUSOT R., FERET J., *et al.*, "Varieties of static analyzers: a comparison with ASTRÉE", *First Joint IEEE/IFIP Symposium on Theoretical Aspects of Software Engineering*, pp. 3–20, 2007.

[CUL 13] CULLMANN C., Cache persistence analysis for embedded real-time systems, PhD thesis, Saarland University, 2013.

[DEL 07] DELMAS D., SOUYRIS J., "ASTRÉE: from research to industry", *Proceeding of 14th International Static Analysis Symposium (SAS2007)*, no. 4634LNCS, pp. 437–451, 2007.

[DIJ 72] DIJKSTRA E.W., "The humble programmer", *Commun. ACM*, vol. 15, no. 10, pp. 859–866, October 1972.

[DIN 06] DIN EN-62304, "International electrotechnical commission," *Medical Device Software – Software Life Cycle Processes*, International IEC Standard 62304, First edition 2006-05, 2006.

[DUN 13] DUNN M., "Toyota's killer firmware: bad design and its consequences", *EDN Network*, October 2013. Available at http://www.edn.com/design/automotive/4423428/Toyota-s-killer-firmware–Bad-design-and-its-consequences.

[ERM 03] ERMEDAHL A., A modular tool architecture for worst-case execution time analysis, PhD Thesis, Uppsala University, 2003.

[EUR 07] EUROPEAN PARLIAMENT, Directive 2007/47/EC of the European Parliament and of the Council amending Council Directive 90/385/EEC on the approximation of the laws of the Member States relating to active implantable medical devices, Council Directive 93/42/EEC concerning medical devices and Directive 98/8/EC concerning the placing of biocidal products on the market, 2007.

[FER 97] FERDINAND C., Cache behavior prediction for real-time systems, PhD Thesis, Saarland University, 1997.

[FER 98] FERDINAND C., WILHELM R., "On predicting data cache behavior for real-time systems", MUELLER F., BESTAVROS A., (eds.), *Proceedings of the Workshop on Languages, Compilers, and Tools for Embedded Systems (LCTES)*, of *Lecture Notes In Computer Science: Languages, Compilers, And Tools For Embedded Systems*, Montreal, Canada, Springer, vol. 1474, pp. 16–30, June 1998.

[FER 99] FERDINAND C., MARTIN F., WILHELM R., *et al.*, "Cache behavior prediction by abstract interpretation", *Science of Computer Programming*, vol. 35, no. 2, pp. 163–189, 1999.

[FER 01] FERDINAND C., HECKMANN R., LANGENBACH M., *et al.*, "Reliable and precise WCET determination for a real-life processor", *Proceedings of EMSOFT 2001, First Workshop on Embedded Software*, of *LNCS*, Springer, vol. 2211, pp. 469–485, 2001.

[FER 04a] FERET J., "The arithmetic-geometric progression abstract domain", COUSOT R., (ed.), *Proceeding of 6th VMCAI '2005, Paris, FR*, Springer, vol. 3385 of *LNCS*, pp. 42–58, 17–19 January 2004.

[FER 04b] FERET J., "Static analysis of digital filters", *European Symposium on Programming (ESOP'04)*, no. 2986LNCS, Springer-Verlag, pp. 33–48, 2004.

[FER 06] FERDINAND C., HECKMANN R., KÄSTNER D., "Static memory and timing analysis of embedded systems code", *Proceedings of the IET Conference on Embedded Systems at Embedded Systems Show (ESS) 2006, Birmingham*, 2006.

[FER 07] FERDINAND C., MARTIN F., CULLMANN C., *et al.*, "New developments in WCET analysis", REPS T., SAGIV M., BAUER J., (eds.), *Essays Dedicated to Reinhard Wilhelm on the Occasion of His 60th Birthday*, of *Lecture Notes in Computer Science: Program Analysis and Compilation, Theory and Practice*, Springer, Berlin, vol. 4444, pp. 12–52, February 2007.

[FER 08a] FERDINAND C., HECKMANN R., "Worst-case execution time – a tool provider's perspective", *Proceedings of the International Symposium on Object-Oriented Real-Time Distributed Computing (ISORC)*, Orlando, FL, pp. 340–345, May 2008.

[FER 08b] FERDINAND C., HECKMANN R., LE SERGENT T., *et al.*, "Combining a high-level design tool for safety-critical systems with a tool for WCET analysis on executables", *4th European Congress ERTS Embedded Real Time Software*, Toulouse, France, January 2008.

[GEB 13] GEBHARD G., Static timing analysis tool validation in the presence of timing anomalies, PhD Thesis, Saarland University, 2013.

[GRU 09a] GRUND D., REINEKE J., "Abstract interpretation of FIFO replacement", PALSBERG J., SU Z., (eds.), *Proceedings of the International Static Analysis Symposium (SAS)*, of *Lecture Notes In Computer Science: Static Analysis*, Berlin, Germany, Springer, vol. 5673, pp. 120–136, August 2009.

[GRU 09b] GRUND D., REINEKE J., GEBHARD G., "Branch target buffers: WCET analysis framework and timing predictability", KELLENBERGER P. (ed.), *Proceedings of the International Conference on Embedded and Real-Time Computing Systems and Applications (RTCSA)*, Beijing, China, pp. 3–12, August 2009.

[IEC 10] IEC 61508, Functional safety of electrical/electronic/programmable electronic safety-related systems, 2010.

[INT 96] INTERNATIONAL ELECTROTECHNICAL COMMISSION, IEC 60601-1-4:1996. Medical electrical equipment, Part 1: General requirements for safety, 4 Collateral Standard: Programmable electrical medical systems, 1996.

[ISO 99] ISO/IEC INTERNATIONAL STANDARD, *ISO/IEC 9899:1999 (E) Programming Languages – C.* 2nd ed., 1999-12-01, 1999.

[ISO 11a] ISO/FDIS 26262, *Road vehicles – Functional safety*, 2011.

[ISO 11b] ISO/FDIS 26262, *Road vehicles – Functional safety – Part 6: Product development at the software level*, 2011.

[KAS 08] KÄSTNER D., WILHELM R., HECKMANN R., *et al.*, "Timing validation of automotive software", MARGARIA T., STEFFEN B., (eds.), *Proceedings of the International Symposium on Leveraging Applications of Formal Methods, Verification and Validation (ISOLA), Communications In Computer and Information Science: Leveraging Applications Of Formal Methods, Verification And Validation*, Berlin, Germany, Springer, vol. 17, pp. 93–107, November 2008.

[KAS 10] KÄSTNER D., WILHELM S., NENOVA S., *et al.*, "Astrée: proving the absence of runtime errors", *Embedded Real Time Software and Systems Congress ERTS* [2], 2010.

[KAS 11] KÄSTNER D., FERDINAND C., "Efficient verification of non-functional safety properties by abstract interpretation: timing, stack consumption, and absence of runtime errors", *Proceedings of the 29th International System Safety Conference ISSC2011*, Las Vegas, NV, 2011.

[KAS 13] KÄSTNER D., PISTER M., GEBHARD G., *et al.*, "Confidence in timing", *Safecomp 2013 Workshop: Next Generation of System Assurance Approaches for Safety-Critical Systems (SASSUR)*, September 2013.

[KAS 14] KÄSTNER D., NENOVA S., FLEISCHER D., *et al.*, "Model-driven code generation and analysis", *Submitted to SAE World Congress 2014*, SAE International, 2014.

[LAN 99] LANGENBACH M., *CRL* – A Uniform Representation for Control Flow, Report, Saarland University, 1999.

[MAR 98] MARTIN F., "PAG – an efficient program analyzer generator", *International Journal on Software Tools for Technology Transfer*, vol. 2, no. 1, pp. 46–47, 1998.

[MAU 05] MAUBORGNE L., RIVAL X., "Trace partitioning in abstract interpretation based static analyzers", *14th European Symposium on Programming ESOP'05*, no. 3444LNCS, pp. 5–20, 2005.

[MIN 04a] MINÉ A., "Relational abstract domains for the detection of floating-point run-time errors", *Proceeding of the European Symposium on Programming (ESOP'04)*, vol. 2986 of *LNCS*, Springer, pp. 3–17, Barcelona, Spain 2004.

[MIN 04b] MINÉ A., Weakly relational numerical abstract domains, PhD Thesis, École Polytechnique, Palaiseau, France, December 2004.

[MIN 06] MINÉ A., "The octagon abstract domain", *Higher-Order and Symbolic Computation*, vol. 19, no. 1, pp. 31–100, 2006.

[MOT 14] MOTOR INDUSTRY SOFTWARE RELIABILITY ASSOCIATION (MISRA), MISRA-C:2004 – guidelines for the use of the C language in critical systems, 2014.

[RAD 92] RADIO TECHNICAL COMMISSION FOR AERONAUTICS, RTCA DO-178B. Software Considerations in Airborne Systems and Equipment Certification, 1992.

[RAD 11a] RADIO TECHNICAL COMMISSION FOR AERONAUTICS, Formal Methods Supplement to DO-178C and DO-278A, 2011.

[RAD 11b] RADIO TECHNICAL COMMISSION FOR AERONAUTICS, Formal methods supplement to DO-178C and DO-278A, 2011, RADIO TECHNICAL COMMISSION FOR AERONAUTICS, RTCA DO-178C. Software Considerations in Airborne Systems and Equipment Certification, 2011.

[RAD 11c] RADIO TECHNICAL COMMISSION FOR AERONAUTICS, Software Tool Qualification Considerations, 2011.

[RUS 13] RUSHBY J., "Logic and epistemology in assurance Cases", COFER D., HATCLIFF J., HUHN M., *et al.*, (eds.), *Software Certification: Methods and Tools (Dagstuhl Seminar 13051)*, Dagstuhl, Germany, Schloss Dagstuhl–Leibniz-Zentrum fuer Informatik, vol. 3, pp. 111–148, 2013.

[SOU 05a] SOUYRIS J., LE PAVEC E., HIMBERT G., *et al.*, "Computing the worst case execution time of an avionics program by abstract interpretation", *Proceedings of the 5th Intl Workshop on Worst-Case Execution Time (WCET) Analysis*, pp. 21–24, 2005.

[SOU 05b] SOUYRIS J., PAVEC E.L., HIMBERT G., *et al.*, "Computing the worst case execution time of an avionics program by Abstract Interpretation", *Proceedings of the 5th International Workshop on Worst-case Execution Time (WCET '05), Mallorca, Spain*, pp. 21–24, 2005.

[SOU 05c] SOUYRIS J., PAVEC E.L., HIMBERT G., *et al.*, "Computing the worst case execution time of an avionics program by Xbstract interpretation", WILHELM R., (ed.), *Proceedings of the International Workshop on Worst-case Execution Time (WCET)*, Mallorca, Spain, pp. 21–24, July 2005.

[THE 98] THEILING H., FERDINAND C., "Combining abstract interpretation and ILP for microarchitecture modelling and program path analysis", *Proceedings of the 19th IEEE Real-Time Systems Symposium*, Madrid, Spain, pp. 144–153, December 1998.

[THE 00] THEILING H., "Extracting safe and precise control flow from binaries", *Proceedings of the 7th Conference on Real-Time Computing Systems and Applications*, Cheju Island, South Korea, 2000.

[THE 03] THESING S., SOUYRIS J., HECKMANN R., *et al.*, "An abstract interpretation-based timing validation of hard real-time avionics software", *Proceedings of the International Conference on Dependable Systems and Networks (DSN)*, San Francisco, CA, pp. 625–632, June 2003.

[THE 04] THESING S., Safe and precise WCET determination by abstract interpretation of pipeline models, PhD Thesis, University of Saarland, 2004.

[US 13] U.S. FOOD AND DRUG ADMINISTRATION, Title 21 Code of Federal Regulations (21 CFR) Subpart C – Design Controls of the Quality System Regulation, 2013.

[VM 06] V-MODEL XT, *Part 1: Fundamentals of the V-Modell*, 2006.

[WIL 08] WILHELM R., ENGBLOM J., ERMEDAHL A., *et al.*, "The worst-case execution-time problem—overview of methods and survey of tools", *ACM Transactions on Embedded Computing Systems*, vol. 7, no. 3, pp. 1–53, ACM, 2008.

9

BCARe: Automatic Rule Checking for Use with Siemens

9.1. Overview

Siemens security applications are developed using the B formal methods. These methods are used to demonstrate the conformity of programs to their specifications. Atelier B contributes to this mathematical proof, but certain properties, known as rules, must be proved without tools, i.e. using manual methods.

The BCARe environment has been designed to provide valid, tool-based solutions to replace existing manual activities.

9.2. Introduction

The B method is used for the development of safety applications at Siemens [ABR 96]. To ensure that developed software conforms to the abstract specification of a problem, specifications go through several stages of refinement to produce a program suitable for automatic translation into a compilable language (such as *Ada*). The coherency of each stage is demonstrated formally using B set theory.

The current reference tool for this method is Atelier B [CLE 09]. Supplied with specifications (properties and refinements), the tool allows us to generate

---

Chapter written by Karim BERKANI, Melanie JACQUEL and Eric LE LAY.

proof obligations which must be demonstrated to validate the correctness of a development. The proof assistant supplied with Atelier B facilitates a demonstration but is not able to provide a complete demonstration in its own right. This approach requires the use of intermediate lemmas, demonstrated manually or using an external tool.

The complexity of industrial projects means that proof is an important activity. The quality and cost of proof activities need to be controlled, as the formal correctness of models needs to be validated within fixed time limits. The first successful use of the B method was in the development of the safety aspect of the control-command unit of METEOR (line 14 of the Paris metro). Other successes followed, as this formal approach was applied in the development of other projects, such as the Carnesie line of the New York subway. Projects of this type require the demonstration of a significant number of proof obligations.

Twenty seven thousand eight hundred proof obligations need to be demonstrated in the case of the METEOR project. To do this, proof rules were introduced into Atelier B: 1,400 rules in the METEOR case. These rules extend the capacity of the proof system, and can introduce incoherency if they are not valid; therefore, they must be demonstrated. A proof assistant, technologically linked to Atelier B and independent of the defined rules, was used for validation in the context of the METEOR project. Unfortunately, this tool did not have the necessary capabilities to demonstrate all of the rules, and up until now, it has been necessary to prove these rules manually.

Siemens is currently in the process of capitalizing a database of validated added rules, with approximately 5,300 entries, 2,900 of which have been demonstrated automatically. The other rules in the database have been validated without the use of a proof assistant. This shows the need to develop additional proof tools in order to ensure the consolidation of development demonstration at Siemens, notably to compensate for the weaknesses of existing tools and avoid human error. Our approach centers on proving basic rules (produced by Atelier B) and additional rules added by users.

Siemens has developed a proof environment known as BCARe [LEL 08, JAC 09], which offers services designed to respond to the limits of existing tools in validating basic or added rules. Notably, this environment allows us to ensure that rules are fully protected against variable capture problems, to verify the correctness of typing and prove that a rule clearly denotes a B theorem. The aim of BCARe is to support experts in the use of proof for rule validation.

Other proof-centered approaches have been developed in parallel with the B method. One general aim of BCARe is to provide an environment for the integration of certain theorem demonstrators, such as Coq [COQ 10], with powers of expression that allow simple descriptions of certain B proof problems.

This approach allows us to export the benefits of Coq while providing adequate responses to problems encountered in B. The first experiment was carried out a few years ago, using Coq to validate the basic rules of Atelier B (see [BER 04]). The proof activity was essentially interactive, with no automation; automation would have been of considerable assistance for the execution of repetitive tasks, which made the demonstration process rather burdensome. This first experiment involved the verification of 274 rule proofs, which had been produced by experts using manual approaches. The results showed that 7 of the proofs were incorrect, and 13 of the rules were invalid as the variables were not subject to non-freeness hypotheses. These problems were detected through the use of the Coq language. This experience provided strong motivation for the development of the BCARe approach.

However, the rule validation approach used in BCARe must itself also be valid; notably, we need to ensure that the rules defined in Atelier B are correctly demonstrated in Coq. A rule is translated into a B logic specification using Coq; various tactics can then be used for demonstration. One of these tactics, developed in $\mathcal{L}_{\text{tac}}$, allows us to demonstrate set formulas. In this chapter, we will show justifications for the validity of each step produced in BCARe.

The development of B set theory using Coq in BCARe was based on an extension involving the specification of formula syntax and inference rules in the calculation of inductive constructions using Coq. Other extensions have been produced [BOD 99, CHA 98, CIR 98, JAE 07, COL 09] using different objectives. Note, for example, that BiCoq closely follows the B-Book, but the variable and substitution management systems were constructed using De Bruijn indices. As we are particularly interested in rule validation, we will not consider the demonstration of proof obligations generated by models for the moment.

We will begin this chapter by presenting the rule validation process, with a detailed description of certain aspects of theoretical validation and our proposed improvements using the BCARe environment. We will then consider the tools and their foundations. The final section will be devoted to our current efforts to extend our work.

9.3. Description of the validation process for added rules

In this section, we will present the rule validation process and the improvements offered by the development of BCARe. We will begin by discussing the proof activities associated with a B model, before giving a detailed description of the definition of rules in Atelier B. The use of an incorrect rule can lead to the production of proof for a model that does not respect its invariants. In a context where these invariants act as guarantees for operational safety, this situation cannot be accepted.

9.3.1. *The proof activity*

Atelier B [CLE 09] is a tool developed by Clearsy which uses the B method.

The correctness of models developed using this tool is demonstrated in several stages:

– automatic verification that the model is correctly typed;

– generation of proof obligations;

– demonstration of proof obligations: these properties may be proved automatically by the proof assistant in Atelier B. If this fails, interactive proof is required. Using this approach, the user may apply proof commands to the current goal or to the collection of hypotheses to guide proof. *Theories* may notably be applied to the current goal. A theory is a list of rules, each denoting a B theorem in the Atelier B syntax.

9.3.2. *Rules*

9.3.2.1. *Rules and formulas*

A rule takes the following form:

$$antecedent_1 \wedge \cdots \wedge antecedent_n \Rightarrow consequent$$

An antecedent may be a command (guard or operation, see below) or a *formula*.

A formula is either a *predicate* or an *expression*. Unlike the B-Book, the prover in Atelier B does not distinguish between predicates and expressions: $a + 1$ (expression) is a formula, in the same way that $a + 1 = 0$ is a predicate.

A rule is said to be a *deduction rule* when the consequent is a predicate. It may be applied:

– to the goal (backward mode) when the consequent coincides with the goal. This leads to substitution. Subgoals are then generated by applying the substitution to each antecedent;

– to the hypotheses (forward mode), if an instance of the antecedents of the rule exists to verify them. A new hypothesis, i.e. the application of the substitution to the consequent, is then generated.

A rule is said to be a *rewriting rule* when the consequent takes the form $f_{left} == f_{right}$, where f_{left} and f_{right} are any two given formulas. These rules are only applied in backward mode. If a subformula of the goal coincides with the left-hand side of a rewriting rule, it is replaced by the right-hand side, with application of the substitution produced by the coincidence. The proof then continues using the transformed goals and any subgoals generated by the antecedent;

EXAMPLE 9.1.– $a + b == b + a$ is a rewriting rule without antecedents. Take the goal $\forall value.(value \in \mathbb{N} \Rightarrow value + 1 > value)$, the application of the rule gives us

$$\forall value.(value \in \mathbb{N} \Rightarrow 1 + value > value).$$

EXAMPLE 9.2.– $b > 0 \Rightarrow a + b > a$ is a deduction rule. Taking the goal $value + 1 > value$, the application of the rule gives us $1 > 0$.

9.3.2.2. *Guards and operations*

Guards are special antecedents, interpreted directly by the proof assistant in Atelier B when selecting a rule to apply. They allow us to manipulate the collection of hypotheses (example 9.3) or treat additional conditions (non-freeness).

EXAMPLE 9.3.– $binhyp(P) \Rightarrow P$ is the expression of a basic rule in the B-Book using the proof assistant from Atelier B: if trace P appears as a hypothesis, then P is proved.

In addition to proof activities, operations and guards are used for plot generation during proof, and for all other operations carried out by standard interpreters (file management, processes, etc.).

9.3.2.3. *Rewriting rules*

Rewriting rules allow more powerful term replacements than those defined in the B-Book, as they can be applied to both predicates and expressions; in the B-Book, the replacement rule is only defined for expressions.

If a subformula of the goal corresponds with the left-hand side of a rewriting rule, it is replaced by an instance of the right-hand side. The proof then proceeds using the transformed goal and any subgoals generated using the antecedents. When a subformula coincides with the left-hand side, the rewriting point is the closest node to the root continuing this subformula (example 9.4).

EXAMPLE 9.4.–

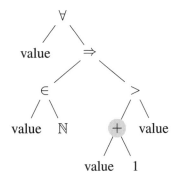

With the rule $a + b == b + a$ and the goal $\forall value.(value \in \mathbb{N} \Rightarrow value + 1 > value)$, the left section coincides with $value + 1$. The rewriting point is therefore at level $+$.

The drawback of the proof assistant in Atelier B is that it does not verify the application context. The rewriting tools are, therefore, not protected against variable capture. This is highlighted in example 9.5.

EXAMPLE 9.5.– Let us take the rule $binhyp(x = a) \Rightarrow x == a$. This rule allows us to replace a value with its value, noted a, as a hypothesis. Let our goal be $xx = 0 \vdash \forall xx.(xx \in \mathbb{N} \Rightarrow xx = 0)$. This goal is false, as, for $xx = 1$, $1 \neq 0$. However, the rule is applied, replacing xx with 0, giving us the goal: $xx = 0 \vdash \forall xx.(xx \in \mathbb{N} \Rightarrow 0 = 0)$. It also produces a second subgoal (the antecedent): $xx = 0 \vdash xx = 0$. These two subgoals are easily provable. The rule therefore allows us to prove a goal which is false.

The error is due to the fact that xx was connected to the rewriting point. This problem is generally solved by protecting the rule using the `blvar` guard and a non-freeness antecedent: `blvar(Q)` instantiates `Q` with variables connected to the rewriting point. Example 9.6 shows how the rule in Example 9.5 may be protected.

EXAMPLE 9.6.– The rule in Example 9.5 becomes $binhyp(x = a) \wedge blvar(Q) \wedge Q \setminus (x, a) \Rightarrow x == a$ where $Q \setminus (x, a)$ means that Q is not free in formula (x, a). $blvar(Q)$ instantiates Q at the only variable linked to the rewriting point: xx. The instantiated rule is thus: $binhyp(xx = 0) \wedge blvar(xx) \wedge xx \setminus (xx, 0) \Rightarrow xx == 0$. The non-freedom antecedent $xx \setminus (xx, 0)$ is not verified as xx is free in xx. Therefore, the rule is no longer applicable.

9.3.3. *Rule validation*

Using the existing process, rule validation involves the three following steps:

Variable capture: The first stage of validation only concerns rewriting rules. It aims to check that a rule is correctly protected against variable capture, as it replaces the subformulas of the goal.

Typing verifications and generation of proof obligations: We begin by ensuring that the rule is syntactically correct and correctly typed. We must then generate proof obligations for the typing, the correct definition of the implemented rules following the definitions set out in article [ABR 02], and ensure that the definition clearly denotes a B logic theorem.

Proof: During this stage, we must demonstrate the proof obligations identified in the previous stage. Demonstration of the typing lemma allows us to validate the inferred type.

In the rest of this chapter, we will highlight the improvements offered by BCARe, with a focus on the aspects not covered by tools in the existing approach. We will also provide elements of justification for our environment.

9.3.3.1. *Variable capture*

Using previously-available methods, variable capture verification was carried out manually, before being automated at Siemens via the definition and implementation of an acceptability criterion. In this section, we will present the definition of two criteria, their theoretical validation and their implementation by a tool, Check_blvar.

The proof assistant in Atelier B is not typed, and so the predicate rewriting approach is implemented in the same way as for expression rewriting. However, this rewriting procedure is not defined in B-Book theory. The lack of a formal definition is problematic when attempting to validate a predicate rewriting rule. We currently translate predicate rewriting rules using a proof of equivalence between the left-hand term and its replacement. In the same way, it is difficult to establish validity criteria in relation to variable capture. Our tool applies the same criteria as those used in rewriting expressions.

9.3.3.2. *Verification of typing and generation of proof obligations*

In addition to ensuring the correct formation of expressions and formulas, typing verification was defined in B to avoid the introduction of incoherences through certain formulas (such as the Russell paradox in naive set theory). However, the rules used in Atelier B are incomplete in relation to the definitions in the B-Book. Certain variables of the rules have an implicit type, due to the hypothesis that the B model and the proof obligations are correctly typed. Thus, this type needs to be reconstructed (inference of supporting sets) before being formally verified using the typing rules defined in the B-Book.

Assistance in this process is currently offered by the *Chaine Validation* tool, presented in the reference document *Validation des rules de l'Atelier B* [STÉ 96] (Rules Validation in Atelier B). This tool allows us to verify typing and automatically demonstrate that the rule clearly denotes a lemma in B logic. However, it is somewhat limited: it does not generate the proof obligation for correct definition and, consequently, does not produce proof. Therefore, we need to use manual methods to ensure that the function is well defined in order for the expression to be considered meaningful (see division by 0). Furthermore, when a rule is not demonstrated automatically, it must be demonstrated manually, i.e. without assistance from tools.

As we will see, the BCARe Chaine_verif tool responds to this shortcoming. It generates lemmas for typing, correct definition and for rule demonstration using B logic. These lemmas must then be demonstrated using the proof tools offered by our environment or by another proof assistant. Finally, the generated results may be analyzed independently in the context of external verification of Chaine_verif.

9.3.3.3. *Proof*

Using the existing validation process, the correct definition of a rule must be demonstrated manually. Furthermore, when proof using *Chaine Validation* fails, the proof that the rule denotes a B lemma is also obtained by manual means.

In the BCARe environment, proof obligations may be demonstrated using the BCoq tool, an implementation of B logic in Coq. This approach presents certain advantages:

– BCoq allows us to produce demonstrations which are correct according to the definitions contained in the B-Book;

– proofs obtained in BCoq are traceable in relation to the B-Book.

The validation activity may require us to present proofs in a format which will be readable during the verification process. We know that proofs carried out in BCoq can be translated into natural language, as they follow the descriptions set out in the B-Book precisely. Moreover, it is also possible to verify these proofs using another proof assistant suitable for use with B.

9.4. The BCARe validation tool

9.4.1. *BCARe: an environment for rule validation*

Siemens currently uses an automatic validation chain based on Atelier B. The main shortcoming of this chain is that it offers no alternatives in cases where automatic validation fails. Therefore, in such cases, rules must be validated manually. The first aim of the BCARe environment, as developed by Siemens, is to provide a modular tool-based approach to validation.

BCARe is currently able to process a subset of the B language (propositional and first-order logic, set operators, functions, unions and generalized and quantified intersections). Integration of the rest of the theory (induction and arithmetic) is currently underway.

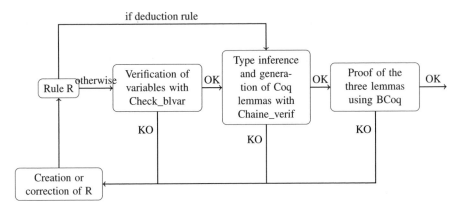

Figure 9.1. *Rule validation process in BCARe*

The validation of a rule R, as shown in Figure 9.1 , is carried out using the following process:

1) For rewriting tools, the Check_blvar tool verifies that the rule is correctly protected against variable capture.

2) Chaine_verif then infers the types of the variables present in the rule and generates three lemmas. The typing lemma validates the type inferred by Chaine_verif. The correct definition lemma needs to be verified in cases where the rule contains function applications. The third and final lemma requests proof of the B theorem represented by the rule.

3) Finally, the three lemmas must be proved using the Coq proof assistant [COQ 10]. These proofs are carried out by an extension of B in Coq, known as BCoq.

9.4.2. *Check_blvar*

Check_blvar is a tool developed to ensure that rewriting rules are correctly protected against variable capture. In Atelier B, a variable of a rule (which may take any value: literal, expression, etc.) is known as a *joker*. Two criteria have been defined for the choice of jokers to protect in a rewriting rule:

– The first criterion is constructed using the jokers of the consequent.

– The second criterion is constructed using the jokers of the antecedents.

Our aim is to express a condition which is sufficient to offer good protection for rewriting rules. For rules to be usable in as many situations as possible, we must identify a reasonably limiting, if not minimal, condition.

The use of multiple approaches allows developers to be more flexible in describing rules: in certain cases, it may be easier to express different criteria. As heuristics have been established, we are unable to state that no less limiting criteria exist. This means that even in cases where none of the criteria are respected, we cannot state that a rule is false.

9.4.2.1. *Criterion for goal E=F*

Let us take a rewriting rule $G \wedge A \Rightarrow E == F$, where G is the conjunction of the guards and A is the conjunction of the antecedents. $P[E]$ is the predicate P containing the formula E. Let $H \vdash Goal[E]$ be the goal in which E is instantiated. The operation carried out by the Atelier B proof assistant (which we wish to verify) replaces $H \vdash Goal[E]$ by $H \vdash Goal[F]$.

1) The goal must firstly be abstracted to include a substitution: $H \vdash [x := E]Goal_x$.

i) This substitution must be clearly defined (calculable using the rules in the B-Book).

ii) x is a fresh variable (and will not create non-freeness issues).

2) The substitution rule from the B-Book is applied:

$$\text{RULE 9} \quad \frac{H \vdash E = F \qquad H \vdash [x := F]P}{H \vdash [x := E]P}$$

This produces the equality condition $E = F$, along with goal $H \vdash [x := F]Goal_x$.

3) The substitution $[x := F]Goal_x$ must also be clearly defined.

Example 9.7 shows the application of this algorithm.

EXAMPLE 9.7.– Take the rewriting rule $binhyp(a = b) => a == b$, and the goal $aa + 1 = 0 \vdash aa + 1 > aa$,

1) Let us include a substitution: $aa + 1 = 0 \vdash [x := aa + 1](x > aa)$. This is applicable.

2) Let us then apply RULE 9. The equality condition $aa + 1 = 0 \vdash aa + 1 = 0$ is an axiom in B. The goal is transformable into $aa + 1 = 0 \vdash [x := 0](x > aa)$.

3) This new substitution is applicable and, therefore, the new goal is: $aa + 1 = 0 \vdash 0 > aa$.

This completes the rewriting process.

The conditions for correct definition of a substitution are the non-freeness conditions. In example 9.8, these conditions are not respected. The problems of application of the substitution are associated with variables which are quantified between the root of the goal and the point of rewriting.

9.4.2.1.1. Protection criterion

We have chosen to stipulate that all rewriting rules must be protected by $blvar(Q) \wedge Q \setminus E = F$.

EXAMPLE 9.8.– Rewriting rule.– $binhyp(a = b) => a == b$ Goal: $aa + 1 = 0 \vdash \forall aa.(aa \in \mathbb{N} \Rightarrow aa + 1 > aa)$ Transformed goal: $aa + 1 = 0 \vdash [x := aa + 1]\forall aa.(aa \in \mathbb{N} \Rightarrow x > aa)$ The substitution is not applicable (see B rules in example 9.14) as $aa \setminus (aa + 1)$ is not verified.

9.4.2.1.2. Proof of the rule

During the verification process, we must also prove that $G \wedge A \Rightarrow E = F$.

9.4.2.2. *Antecedent criterion $G \wedge A$*

The previous criterion is not satisfactory, as it appears to be too strict. Commutativity rules, as shown in example 9.9, have been rejected. From a logical perspective, the criterion does not mention antecedents; however, it is the antecedents that create problems in our example 9.5, page 241.

EXAMPLE 9.9.– Rewriting rule: $s \cap t == t \cap s$

Free variables of $E = F$: s, t These variables are not protected, so the rule is rejected.

A new approach begins by modifying the goal to give us the means of applying a substitution. This removes the conditions on E and F (the left and right sections of the rewriting) and gives us the condition $blvar(Q) \land Q \backslash G \land A$.

9.4.2.2.1. Conversion to prenex form

Before presenting the criterion, we need to introduce the notion of conversion to prenex form.

DEFINITION (Prenex formula).– *A formula of the form $Q_1 x_1 \ldots Q_n x_n \varphi$, with $n \geq 0$, $Q_i \in \{\forall, \exists\}$ and φ (without quantifiers), is said to be prenex.*

EXAMPLE 9.10.– Formula $\exists n.(n \in \mathbb{N} \land \forall m.(m \in \mathbb{N} \Rightarrow m \geq n))$ is not in prenex form. It may be rewritten in prenex form as: $\exists n.(\forall m.(n \in \mathbb{N} \land (m \in \mathbb{N} \Rightarrow m \geq n)))$ (we trace back the quantifier).

9.4.2.2.2. Elimination of variable-binding expressions

Lambda-expressions or sets in comprehension introduce a new context. As expressions, they are not affected by conversions to prenex form; however, they can cause problems when applying substitutions (example 9.11). These expressions need to be eliminated using their definitions and set axioms, as in example 9.12. This transformation is mentioned in the proof diagram presented in article [ABR 02], page 23.

EXAMPLE 9.11.– Let us take the rule $a + b == b + a$ and the goal $a \in \{x | x \in \mathbb{N} \land x + 1 = 1 + x\}$. The goal is in prenex form. The abstraction of the goal gives (where z is a fresh variable) $[z := x + 1](a \in \{x | x \in \mathbb{N} \land z = 1 + x\})$ Substitution $[z := x + 1]\{x | x \in \mathbb{N} \land z = 1 + x\}$ is not applicable, as the bound variable x appears in the substitution.

EXAMPLE 9.12.– Take the rule $a + b == b + a$ and the goal $a \in \{x | x \in \mathbb{N} \land x + 1 = 1 + x\}$. The goal may be transformed using the set axiom SET 3 and becomes: $a \in \mathbb{N} \land a + 1 = 1 + a$. The abstraction of the goal gives (where z is a fresh variable) $[z := a + 1](a \in \mathbb{N} \land z = 1 + a\})$. The substitution is applicable.

9.4.2.2.3. Presentation of the proof process

Let us take a rewriting rule $G \land A \Rightarrow E == F$. G is the conjunction of the guards and A the conjunction of the antecedents. $H \vdash Goal[E]$ is the goal in which E is instantiated.

1) The rewritten goal $(Goal[F])$ is introduced as-is, thanks to the Modus–Ponens rule:

$$\text{MP} \ \frac{H \vdash Goal[F] \qquad H \vdash Goal[F] \Rightarrow Goal[E]}{H \vdash Goal[E]}$$

i) This application is always authorized.

ii) We wish to use the left-hand side of the tree, which allows the user to continue the proof activity.

iii) We wish to show that the right-hand side of the tree is always proved.

2) The rewriting rule is analyzed by following the different cases using an example:

i) If $E = F$ can be proved without the use of a hypothesis (see commutativity, as shown in example 9.9), then H is unnecessary. The collection of hypotheses is therefore removed.

ii) If $G \wedge A$ is necessary to prove $E = F$ (for example, if it contains a $binhyp(..)$), $G \wedge A$ is introduced by application of Modus–Ponens:

$$\text{MP} \ \frac{H \vdash G \wedge A \qquad H \vdash G \wedge A \Rightarrow Goal[F] \Rightarrow Goal[E]}{H \vdash Goal[F] \Rightarrow Goal[E]}$$

iii) The left-hand section $(H \vdash G \wedge A)$ still needs to be proved by the user in the context of application of the rewriting rule using the proof assistant in Atelier B.

iv) In the right-hand section, H is removed and $G \wedge A$ becomes a hypothesis:

$$G \wedge A \vdash Goal[F] \Rightarrow Goal[E]$$

3) Sets in comprehension or derived forms (lambda-expressions) may also need to be eliminated. The variables in question are always quantified in the goal or are fresh variables, so the protection criterion always applies.

4) Finally, we obtain $G \wedge A \vdash Goal'[F'] \Rightarrow Goal'[E']$, such that neither $Goal'[F']$ nor $Goal'[E']$ contains sets in comprehension.

5) $Goal'[F']$ and $Goal'[E']$ have now been transformed in a way that traces the quantifiers back to the root. This conversion to prenex form uses known

logic rules. The transformation is only carried out to the level of the expression to replace. The goal becomes:

$$G \wedge A \vdash \forall(x_0..x_n).(Goal''[F''] \Rightarrow Goal''[E''])$$

E' and F' will have been modified if they included bound variables at the point of rewriting, notably if renaming was required for the conversion to prenex form.

6) The quantifiers have now been eliminated. Two types of eliminations are possible, according to the B-Book:

i) The instantiation of variables using rule DR13, which does not impose limits, for existential quantifiers. A formula $\exists x.P$ thus becomes $[x := Exp]P$, where Exp is an expression.

ii) Quantification removal using RULE 7 for universal quantifiers. The application of this rule transforms goal $H \vdash \forall x.P$ into $H \vdash P$, if $x \setminus H$. This means that the quantified variables must be unfree in the collection of hypotheses. This is the reason why this was reduced as far as possible in step 2.

iii) If we have retained $G \wedge A$, we need a non-freeness condition: $x_i \setminus G \wedge A$. x_i are bound variables at the point of rewriting. Therefore, the condition for the rule to be valid is that all free variables of G and A must be free at the point of rewriting: $blvar(Q) \wedge Q \setminus (G \wedge A)$.

iv) If there are no antecedents, then no validity condition is required for the rule.

v) The goal can then be abstracted to $G \wedge A \vdash ([x := F'']Goal''[x]) \Rightarrow ([x := E'']Goal''[x])$ and the substitutions are clearly defined.

vi) $[x := F'']Goal''[x]$ becomes a hypothesis, and we apply RULE 9 for the substitution.

$$\frac{G \wedge A \vdash E'' = F''}{G \wedge A \wedge ([x := F'']Goal''[x]) \vdash ([x := E'']Goal''[x])}$$

vii) We need to prove $G \wedge A \Rightarrow E = F$ (down to the renamings).

viii) The other section is an axiom.

9.4.2.2.4. Protection criterion

The second validity criterion for a rewriting rule is: $blvar(Q) \wedge Q \setminus G \wedge A$, with no limitations in the absence of antecedents.

9.4.2.2.5. Proof of the rule

We still need to prove the equality of E and F.

9.4.2.2.6. Typing hypotheses

We have yet to address the question of typing hypotheses, which must be retained for certain operations. For example, the intersection between sets presumes the existence of a superset containing these sets. We presume that these hypotheses are present during the proof process.

9.4.2.2.7. Detailed example

We will now give a full example of an application of the algorithm (example 9.13). The chosen rule does not include antecedents, so there is no $blvar$ condition. The goal only contains a single universal quantifier which can be directly eliminated (so there is no need for prenex form conversion), but it contains a comprehension set around the expression requiring substitution.

EXAMPLE 9.13.– Rule.– $s \cap t == t \cap s$

Goal:

$$H \vdash \{x, y | (x_0, y_0) \in \mathbb{P}(S \times S) \wedge x \cap y = x\}$$
$$= \{x, y | (x_0, y_0) \in \mathbb{P}(S \times S) \wedge y \cap x = x\}$$

Instantiation by the Atelier B proof assistant: The left part of the rewriting is instantiated with $s := x$ and $t := y$. It is unified at $x \cap y$ in the left set of the goal, and is replaced by $y \cap x$, giving us the same sets on the left and right, completing the proof with $E = E$.

Proof of the goal: To simplify the written expression, the two comprehension sets are noted $E_{x \cap y}$ and $E_{y \cap x}$

The set equality axiom SET 4 allows us to rewrite the goal (x_0 and y_0 are fresh variables):

$$H \vdash \forall(x_0, y_0).((x_0, y_0) \in E_{x \cap y} \Leftrightarrow (x_0, y_0) \in E_{y \cap x})$$

By definition of the membership (SET 3), we rewrite:

$$H \vdash \forall(x_0, y_0).((x_0, y_0) \in \mathbb{P}(S \times S) \wedge ([x, y := x_0, y_0]x \cap y = x)$$
$$\Leftrightarrow (x_0, y_0) \in E_{y \cap x})$$

The substitution is applied, and the same procedure is repeated on the right of the equivalence:

$$H \vdash \forall(x_0, y_0).((x_0, y_0) \in \mathbb{P}(S \times S) \wedge (x_0 \cap y_0 = x_0)$$
$$\Leftrightarrow (x_0, y_0) \in \mathbb{P}(S \times S) \wedge (y_0 \cap x_0 = x_0))$$

The hypotheses are eliminated, and the universal quantifier (RULE 7 is no longer subject to conditions as there are no more hypotheses):

$$\vdash (x_0, y_0) \in \mathbb{P}(S \times S) \wedge (x_0 \cap y_0 = x_0)$$
$$\Leftrightarrow (x_0, y_0) \in \mathbb{P}(S \times S) \wedge (y_0 \cap x_0 = x_0)$$

This becomes:

$$\vdash (x_0, y_0) \in \mathbb{P}(S \times S) \wedge ((x_0 \cap y_0 = x_0) \Leftrightarrow (y_0 \cap x_0 = x_0))$$

DED allows us to transform the typing terms into hypotheses:

$$(x_0, y_0) \in \mathbb{P}(S \times S) \vdash (x_0 \cap y_0 = x_0) \Leftrightarrow (y_0 \cap x_0 = x_0)$$

A substitution is introduced (z is a fresh variable):

$$(x_0, y_0) \in \mathbb{P}(S \times S) \vdash [z := x_0 \cap y_0](z = x_0) \Leftrightarrow (y_0 \cap x_0 = x_0)$$

The application of RULE 9 produces two goals:

$$(x_0, y_0) \in \mathbb{P}(S \times S) \vdash x_0 \cap y_0 = y_0 \cap x_0$$

and

$$(x_0, y_0) \in \mathbb{P}(S \times S) \vdash [z := y_0 \cap x_0](z = x_0) \Leftrightarrow (y_0 \cap x_0 = x_0)$$

The equality goal is proved by the commutativity property of the intersection: we have retained the typing hypotheses to enable its application.

The second goal is proved by applying the substitution:

$$(x_0, y_0) \in \mathbb{P}(S \times S) \vdash y_0 \cap x_0 = x_0 \Leftrightarrow y_0 \cap x_0 = x_0$$

It is then proved by $P \Rightarrow P$ (DED and BR3).

9.4.2.2.8. Definition of predicate rewriting

We may create rewriting rules to replace predicates in the same way as for expressions. No theoretical justification of this point is given in the B-Book. We have defined a predicate substitution process based on the substitution of expressions. Our approach includes non-freeness conditions similar to those used in the B-Book.

Example 9.14 shows a substitution in the case of universal quantification. The B-Book distinguishes between two cases, as in situations where the variable for substitution is quantified, the substitution disappears. This is not required for predicate substitution, as a predicate is never subject to quantification in B (no higher order).

Let $Pre \rightarrow Post$ be the substitution of predicate Pre by $Post$, $P[Pre]$ the predicate P containing Pre and $E[Pre]$ the expression E containing Pre. In the same way, $P[E]$ is the predicate P containing the expression E.

EXAMPLE 9.14.– Substitution of expressions in the B-Book:

Substitution	Definition	Condition
$[x := E]\forall y.P$	$\forall y.[x := E]P$	$y \setminus x \wedge y \setminus E$
$[x := E]\forall x.P$	$\forall x.P$	

Predicate substitution:

Let $[Pre \rightarrow Post]P$ be the predicate substitution where Pre is to be replaced by $Post$ in P.

Substitution	Definition	Condition
$[Pre \to Post]\forall y.P$	$\forall y.[Pre \to Post]P$	$y \setminus Pre \wedge y \setminus Post$

This definition has the following consequences:

– $(Pre \Leftrightarrow Post) \Rightarrow ([Pre \to Post]P \Leftrightarrow P)$: if the two predicates Pre and $Post$ are equivalent, then the replacement of Pre by $Post$ in P is *equivalent* to P.

– $(Pre \Leftrightarrow Post) \Rightarrow ([Pre \to Post]E = E)$: if the two predicates Pre and $Post$ are equivalent, then the replacement of Pre by $Post$ in E is *equal* to E.

These properties are useful because if we are able to demonstrate $Pre \Leftrightarrow Post$, then the instantiated goal $P[Pre]$ can be replaced by $P[Post]$. The Atelier B proof assistant does this. Therefore, the proof of $Pre \Leftrightarrow Post$ validates a predicate rewriting rule.

9.4.2.2.9. Differences from the Atelier B proof assistant

The replacement approach defined above is different to the predicate rewriting process in the Atelier B proof assistant in two respects:

In our approach, all occurrences of Pre are replaced, whereas Atelier B only applies the replacement process once. However, the user of a rewriting rule may apply the rule as often as required, so the practical difference between the two approaches is minimal.

The replacement defined in this way presents non-freeness hypotheses, unlike the Atelier B prover. In Coq, the system requires the user to prove that these conditions are respected for each use. In the Atelier B proof assistant, the user needs to protect rules using a `blvar` guard.

9.4.2.2.10. Protection criteria

The two protection criteria described above are used for want of a better solution. Their validity for predicate rewriting has not been formally demonstrated.

9.4.3. *Chaine_verif*

Based on an added rule, supplied in text form, the Chaine_verif tool:

– infers a type for each element in the rule;

– interprets the rule to transform it into a BCoq mathematical lemma;

– produces a correct definition lemma for verification in BCoq.

The validity of the inferred type is guaranteed by the generation of a typing lemma, which should be verified in BCoq using the type system taken from the B-Book.

The lemmas are also generated using B syntax to enable them to be proved using another technology, where necessary.

9.4.3.1. *Type inference*

B is a typed language, but type information is often missing for added rules. For example, the rule $s \cap t == t \cap s$ does not specify that s and t share a support type. Similarly, with $i + 0 == i$, the type of i is not stipulated, but deduced from the fact that it is used in an addition operation.

We need to reconstruct this type information in order to prove the rule.

9.4.3.1.1. Type system

The type system defined in the B-Book is intended for type verification rather than for inference.

A natural type system was therefore defined specifically for inference purposes. It operates by declaring a rule for each syntactic construction, defining a rule including type membership as a result and one or more type memberships as antecedents (see example 9.15).

The typing ends with the atoms of the language. Literals (integer, true and false) are always typed. Variables are typed if their type appears in the environment. This is different to the system used in the B-Book, which ends with the equality of support sets.

9.4.3.1.2. Overloaded operators

Multiplication (the Cartesian product) and sustraction are *overloaded operators*, defined by sets and integers. This leads us to duplicate the rules for the two operations. The duplication of rules applicable to the same expression introduces alternatives into the type system (example 9.15).

EXAMPLE 9.15.– Two type rules for a product:

$$\text{TIMES\_SET} \; \frac{TS \vdash S : \mathbb{P}(s) \qquad TS \vdash T : \mathbb{P}(t)}{TS \vdash S \times T : \mathbb{P}(s \times t)}$$

$$\text{TIMES\_INT} \; \frac{TS \vdash S : Integer \qquad TS \vdash T : Integer}{TS \vdash S \times T : Integer}$$

9.4.3.1.3. Correctness property

The equivalence of the two type systems has not been demonstrated, and so the correctness of the proposed system has not been proved. This is taken into account by the methodology: the inferred type is verified in Coq using the type rules from the B-Book.

9.4.3.1.4. Implementation

Type inference applies to the whole rule and follows a three-step process:

– Collection of type constraints and annotation of each node or leaf of the AST with a type variable: the constraints are derived from the type system described above.

– Constraint ordering: the Abstract Syntax Tree (AST) path in the prenex order places constraints resulting from the declaration of a variable above those resulting from its use. This highlights errors linked to incorrect use of a variable.

– Resolution: the Hindley–Milner algorithm is used, with the addition of backtracking for *ad hoc* management of operator overloading.

9.4.3.2. *The BCoq extension*

Our extension of B set theory using Coq is a deep embedding, in which operators and formal systems for typing and proof are defined by induction (see [BER 04]).

Compared to a shallow embedding, in which B theory would be interpreted using Coq logic, this method presents the advantage of being in accordance with the B-Book, as only constructions and rules from the B-Book are used (never those of Coq).

BCoq syntax is defined in Coq in the following manner (we will not give the actual syntax of the inductive types, which will be represented using the reification operator "$\cdot$"):

$$V := I \mid V \mapsto V$$
$$E := V \mid [V := E]E \mid E \mapsto E \mid choice\ (S) \mid S$$
$$S := S \times S \mid \mathbb{P}\ (S) \mid \{V \mid V \in S \wedge P\} \mid BIG$$
$$P := P \wedge P \mid P \Rightarrow P \mid \neg P \mid \forall V.P \mid [V := E]P \mid E \doteq E \mid E \in S$$

where V represents the variables, I represents the identifiers, E represents the expressions, S represents the sets and P represents the predicates. Note that sets defined in comprehension are always typed.

The other logical connectors (such as $\Leftrightarrow$, $\vee$ and $\exists$) and the set operators (e.g. $\cup$, $\cap$) are defined based on the connectors presented here.

9.4.3.3. *Translation into BCoq*

The inferred type is used to add hypotheses to the rule to enable proof in BCoq. The syntax tree, with the addition of the type of each node and the symbol tables, is converted using a data model extracted from BCoq. This transformation is not always transparent, and it is not always possible.

The transformation process involves two main aspects:

– translation of a rewriting rule to give an equivalence or equality lemma;

– interpretation of Atelier B proof assistant specific aspects.

9.4.3.3.1. Translation of guards

Guards may be eliminated, translated systematically, or only translated in certain cases. The presence of non-translatable guards in a rule means that the rule in question cannot be translated.

Guards with no influence on proof (trace collections) are simply eliminated. Other guards are translated systematically (the $binhyp(P)$ guard is translated by P).

The mathematical interpretation of other guards is problematic. For example, $bpattern$, when used as $bpattern(E, (F, G))$, is translated as

$E = (F, G)$; when used as in $bpattern(P, Q \wedge R)$, it is translated as $P \Leftrightarrow (Q \wedge R)$. In all other cases, the translation fails.

Certain guards allowing the use of proof tactics cannot be translated into BCoq, thus forcing us to abandon the translation.

9.4.3.4. *Correct definition*

In formal terms, an ill-defined expression corresponds to a partial function call outside of its domain of definition.

However, assessment of the correctness of a definition cannot be limited to the typing checks described above. The problem must be treated using typing proofs: *context* $\Rightarrow$ *conditions for correct definition.*

Before writing $f(x)$, for example, we need to verify that, in the current context, x belongs to the domain of definition of f.

9.4.3.4.1. Syntactic approach

J.R. Abrial and R. Mussat presented a syntactic approach in [ABR 02]. The aim of this approach is to retain a simple type system and to justify the omission of correct definition conditions during the proof process.

A syntactic filter $\mathcal{L}$ is introduced for use with all predicates. The results of $\mathcal{L}(P)$ contain proof obligations linked to correct definition. The filter is applied before proving the predicate (example 9.16).

EXAMPLE 9.16.– for $1/0 = 1/0$ (which is proved immediately in B by the rule $\overline{E = E}$), filter $\mathcal{L}$ generates the condition $0 \neq 0$, which is false. The predicate will therefore be eliminated before proof.

This filter is defined recursively.

It includes two types of cases: decompositions (e.g. $\mathcal{L}(P \wedge Q) := \mathcal{L}(P) \wedge (P \Rightarrow \mathcal{L}(Q)))$) and atomic cases (e.g. $\mathcal{L}(A) := True$, when predicate A does not contain function applications or sets in comprehension).

The most interesting atomic case is the function application:

$$\mathcal{L}(A_{f(E)}) := \mathbf{fnc}(\mathbf{f}) \wedge \mathbf{E} \in \mathbf{dom}(\mathbf{f}) \wedge \forall y.(y = f(E) \Rightarrow \mathcal{L}(A_y))$$

This has two parts:

– the expression of correct definition obligations for $f(E)$ (where f is a function and E must belong to the domain of the function);

– $\mathcal{L}$ is reapplied to the predicate in which the function application has been replaced by a variable, to treat "nesting" occurrences.

A second filter ϵ is defined. This filter simplifies the goal through unconditional elimination of function applications. The equivalence of $\epsilon(P)$ and P is demonstrated by proof of $\mathcal{L}(P)$.

9.4.3.4.2. Use of $\mathcal{L}$

The proof methodology is, thus:

1) verification of the type of P;

2) calculation of $\mathcal{L}(P)$;

3) proof of $\mathcal{L}(P)$;

4) proof of P (or $\epsilon(P)$, which is simpler, as the equivalence is proved).

9.4.3.4.3. Ill-defined expressions in sets

The filter for sets in comprehension, as presented in [ABR 02], is:

$$\mathcal{L}(A_{\{x|x \in S \land P_x\}}) := \forall x.(x \in S \Rightarrow \mathcal{L}(P_x)) \land \forall y.(y = \{x|x \in S \land P_x\}$$
$$\Rightarrow \mathcal{L}(A_y))$$

In this case, y is a fresh variable and $A_{\{x|x \in S \land P_x\}}$ is a predicate containing an occurrence of the set in comprehension.

Note that $\mathcal{L}(x \in S)$ was not calculated. This means that ill-defined expressions in the supersets of sets comprehension will not have been detected. The authors of the article are likely to have implicitly considered that S is always a support set (INTEGER, BIG, etc.), rendering this verification unnecessary.

We decided to carry out the additional checks, which produced the following case:

$$\mathcal{L}(A_{\{x|x \in S \land P_x\}}) := \forall x.(\mathcal{L}(\mathbf{x} \in \mathbf{S}) \land (x \in S \Rightarrow \mathcal{L}(P_x))) \land$$
$$\forall y.(y = \{x|x \in S \land P_x\} \Rightarrow \mathcal{L}(A_y))$$

9.4.3.4.4. Extension of supported constructions

Article [ABR 02] did not define $\mathcal{L}$ for lambda-expressions (the article only considered function applications and sets in comprehension). We have extended the filter to these constructions, using the following definition of the lambda:

$$\mathcal{L}(A_{\lambda x.(x \in S \wedge P|E)}) := \forall(x, y).(\mathcal{L}(x \in S \wedge P)(y = E)))$$
$$\wedge((x \in S \wedge P) \Rightarrow \mathcal{L} \wedge \forall y.(y = \lambda x.(x \in S \wedge P|E) \Rightarrow \mathcal{L}(A_y))$$

This constitutes a verification of correct definition in S and P, prior to verifying correct definition in E.

9.4.3.4.5. Ill definition and added rules

Added rules include jokers (or metavariables) which are unified to produce complete terms during use of the rule. These terms are not available during rule validation; therefore, we must make the hypothesis so that the introduced terms will be correctly defined.

9.4.3.5. *Examples*

We will now consider two examples of rule validation using BCARe (proofs are discussed in detail in section 9.5).

EXAMPLE 9.17 (Validation of Set 1).– Let us examine the following property (the first property shown in the table on p. 75 of the B-Book):

Set 1: $a \subseteq s, b \subseteq s \vdash a \cup b = b \cup a$

This property is a deduction rule. Therefore, we do not need to check for variable capture using Check_blvar. It does not include function applications, so we have no correct definition lemmas to prove. Chaine_verif produces the following two lemmas:

Lemma type_set1 : **forall** a b s : S,
$\quad a \setminus (b, s) \rightarrow b \setminus s \rightarrow a \subseteq s, b \subseteq s, given(s) \vdash_{\text{type}} check(a \cup b \doteq b \cup a)$.

Lemma r_set1 : **forall** a b s : S,
$\quad a \setminus (b, s) \rightarrow b \setminus s \rightarrow a \subseteq s, b \subseteq s \vdash a \cup b \doteq b \cup a$.

in which *given* introduces the support types, *check* and "$\vdash_{type}$" encode the B type system, and "$\vdash$" is the proof in B.

EXAMPLE 9.18 (Validation of SimplifyRelDorXY.2).– Let us now consider the validation of the rule SimplifyRelDorXY.2:

SimplifyRelDorXY.2: $\text{binhyp}(f \in u \leftrightarrow v) \land \text{binhyp}(a \in \text{dom}(f)) \land$
$\text{blvar}(Q) \land (Q \backslash (f \in u \leftrightarrow v)) \land (Q \backslash (a \in \text{dom}(f))) \Rightarrow a \lhd f == \{(a, f(a))\}$

1) This is a rewriting rule, so we apply the Check_blvar tool. It confirms that the context of application of the rule is correctly protected, as it requires the instantiations of $\{f,u,v,a\}$ to be free at the point of rewriting.

2) Chaine_verif generates the following three lemmas:

Lemma $\text{type\_SimplifyRelDorXY\_2}$:
    forall $t_1 \; t_2 \;:\; S$, **forall** $a \; f \; u \; v \colon \; V$,
$a \backslash (f, u, v, t_1, t_2) \to f \backslash (u, v, t_1, t_2) \to u \backslash (v, t_1, t_2) \to$
$u \in \mathbb{P}(t_2), v \in \mathbb{P}(t_1), f \in \mathbb{P}(t_2 \times t_1), a \in t_2, given(t_1), given(t_2) \vdash_{type}$
$check(f \in u \leftrightarrow v \land a \in \text{dom}(f) \Rightarrow \{a\} \lhd f \doteq \{a \mapsto f(a)\})$

Lemma $\text{rl\_SimplifyRelDorXY\_2}$:
    forall $f \; t_1 \; t_2 \; u \; v \;:\; S$, **forall** $a \colon \; E$, **forall** $s \; t \;:\; V$,
$s \backslash (f, u, v, a, t_1, t_2, t) \to t \backslash (f, u, v, a, t_1, t_2) \to$
$u \in \mathbb{P}(t_2), v \in \mathbb{P}(t_1), f \in \mathbb{P}(t_2 \times t_1), a \in t_2 \vdash$
$f \in u \leftrightarrow v \land a \in \text{dom}(f) \Rightarrow \exists (s \mapsto t).(f \in s \leftrightarrow t \land a \in \text{dom}(f))$

Lemma $\text{r\_SimplifyRelDorXY\_2}$:
    forall $f \; t_1 \; t_2 \; u \; v \;:\; S$, **forall** $a \colon \; E$,
$u \in \mathbb{P}(t_2), v \in \mathbb{P}(t_1), f \in \mathbb{P}(t_2 \times t_1), a \in t_2 \vdash$
$f \in u \leftrightarrow v \land a \in \text{dom}(f) \Rightarrow \{a\} \lhd f \doteq \{a \mapsto f(a)\}$

9.5. Proof of the BCARe validation lemmas

In this section, we will describe the different proof processes used in the BCARe tool to prove the three lemmas generated by Chaine_verif.

A tactic has been developed using the Coq tactical language, known as $\mathcal{L}_{tac}$ [DEL 00], to prove type lemmas. This tactic is based on the type verification decision procedure proposed in the B-Book.

A tactic is also available to automatically demonstrate certain generated lemmas relating to the proof of well-definedness. When this automatic process fails, the process must be carried out interactively. The third lemma is generally demonstrated in an interactive manner.

An automatic proof algorithm has been implemented using $\mathcal{L}_{\text{tac}}$, the Coq tactical language, to reduce the proof workload for users. This tactic can be used to assist in demonstrating correct definition lemmas, or to prove that the lemma denoting a rule is a theorem in B logic. A detailed presentation of this tactic is given below. It only treats operators preceding the introduction of functional abstraction (anonymous functions) in the B-Book. Currently, rules containing other operators must be proved interactively in BCoq, or semi-automatically using certain subtactics.

9.5.1. *Automatic proof using* $\mathcal{L}_{\text{tac}}$

In [ABR 03], J.R. Abrial and D. Cansell provide an explanation of the automatic proof command pp in Atelier B. This includes a solution strategy and a translator from set theory to predicate calculus. For propositional calculus, the command pp implements an algorithm involving the application of rules to transform a sequent without hypotheses into one or more sequents with atomic hypotheses. The sequents are discharged if a contradiction is found in the hypotheses. For predicate calculus, the following two transformations are applied alternately to produce a demonstration:

– The first transformation applies a number of rules, as in the case of propositional calculus; universally quantified subformulas are added as hypotheses. The starting sequent is transformed until it is reduced to FALSE. The appearance of a contradiction in the hypotheses discharges the goal.

– The second transformation instantiates the universally quantified hypotheses.

An expression translator included in pp allows us to transform formulas containing set operators into first-order formulas without set operators. This is attained by applying different axioms or definitions given in the B-Book. This stage is known as normalization. The strategy described above is then applied to demonstrate the first-order formula.

Our set operators removal algorithm has certain points in common with the pp translator. However, our development was carried out in Coq using a deep embedding of B logic, which guarantees correctness in relation to the B-Book. Use of the $\mathcal{L}_{\text{tac}}$ language ensures the conservation of this property of our system. Furthermore, our automatic demonstration method is different; properties are converted to prenex form to allow treatment of quantifiers. The variables are then instantiated as a function of the nature of the quantifier with which they are associated. Our algorithm may be broken down into two consecutive steps:

– normalization;

– treatment of quantifiers.

9.5.1.1. *Normalization*

The first stage in the algorithm consists of converting the input formula into a pure first-order formula, i.e. a formula containing only "$\dot{\in}$" as a set operator. A normalization mechanism is used to obtain these formulas, based on the first four axioms of B set theory, defining the Cartesian product, the power set, the set comprehension and the set equality. These axioms take the following forms:

Take two sets s and t, two expressions E and F, a predicate P and a variable x:

SET 1: $(E \mapsto F) \dot{\in} (s \times t) \Leftrightarrow (E \dot{\in} s \wedge F \dot{\in} t)$

SET 2: $s \dot{\in} \dot{\mathbb{P}}(t) \Leftrightarrow \dot{\forall} x.(x \dot{\in} s \Rightarrow x \dot{\in} t)$, if $x \setminus (s,t)$

SET 3: $E \dot{\in} \{x \mid x \dot{\in} s \wedge P\} \Leftrightarrow (E \dot{\in} s \wedge [x := E]P)$, if $x \setminus s$

SET 4: $\dot{\forall} x(x \dot{\in} s \Leftrightarrow x \dot{\in} t) \Leftrightarrow s \doteq t$, if $x \setminus (s,t)$

The normalization process uses these axioms with the predicate replacement property. The first three axioms are applied from left to right, while the fourth is applied from right to left.

The set operators are deployed according to their definition. For example, the union and inclusion operators are defined as follows:

Inclusion: s and t are two sets. $s \mathrel{\dot\subseteq} t \mathrel{\dot=} s \mathrel{\dot\in} \dot{\mathbb{P}}\,(t)$

Union: Let a be a variable and u, s, t sets with $s \mathrel{\dot\subseteq} u$ and $t \mathrel{\dot\subseteq} u$. $s \mathrel{\dot\cup} t \mathrel{\dot=} \{a \mid a \mathrel{\dot\in} u \mathrel{\dot\wedge} (a \mathrel{\dot\in} s \mathrel{\dot\vee} a \mathrel{\dot\in} t)\}$

This normalization process is illustrated by the following example.

EXAMPLE 9.19 (Normalization of Set 1).– Let us consider example Set 1, introduced in section 9.4.1 above. With three sets a, b, s, the normalization process includes the following steps:

1) $a \mathrel{\dot\subseteq} s, b \mathrel{\dot\subseteq} s \vdash \dot\forall x. x \mathrel{\dot\in} a \mathrel{\dot\cup} b \mathrel{\dot\Leftrightarrow} x \mathrel{\dot\in} b \mathrel{\dot\cup} a$ (SET 4, with $x \setminus (a, b)$)

2) $a \mathrel{\dot\subseteq} s, b \mathrel{\dot\subseteq} s \vdash x \mathrel{\dot\in} a \mathrel{\dot\cup} b \mathrel{\dot\Leftrightarrow} x \mathrel{\dot\in} b \mathrel{\dot\cup} a$ (RULE 7, with $x \setminus a \mathrel{\dot\subseteq} s$ and $x \setminus b \mathrel{\dot\subseteq} s$)

3) $a \mathrel{\dot\subseteq} s, b \mathrel{\dot\subseteq} s \vdash x \mathrel{\dot\in} a \mathrel{\dot\cup} b \mathrel{\dot\Leftrightarrow} x \mathrel{\dot\in} b \mathrel{\dot\cup} a$ (def. inclusion)

4) $a \mathrel{\dot\subseteq} s, b \mathrel{\dot\subseteq} s \vdash x \mathrel{\dot\in} \{x \mid x \mathrel{\dot\in} s \mathrel{\dot\wedge} (x \mathrel{\dot\in} a \mathrel{\dot\vee} x \mathrel{\dot\in} b)\} \mathrel{\dot\Leftrightarrow} x \mathrel{\dot\in} \{x \mid x \mathrel{\dot\in} s \mathrel{\dot\wedge} (x \mathrel{\dot\in} b \mathrel{\dot\vee} x \mathrel{\dot\in} a)\}$
(def. union)

5) $a \mathrel{\dot\subseteq} s, b \mathrel{\dot\subseteq} s \vdash x \mathrel{\dot\in} s \mathrel{\dot\wedge} (x \mathrel{\dot\in} a \mathrel{\dot\vee} x \mathrel{\dot\in} b) \mathrel{\dot\Leftrightarrow} x \mathrel{\dot\in} s \mathrel{\dot\wedge} (x \mathrel{\dot\in} b \mathrel{\dot\vee} x \mathrel{\dot\in} a)$
(SET 3, with $x \setminus s$)

Note that certain steps of the normalization process generate hypotheses with non-free variables. For the sake of simplicity, when we introduce a new variable, we presume that it is a fresh variable in relation to the hypotheses and the goal. For this example, we obtain the hypothesis $x \setminus (a, b, s)$.

After normalization, if no quantifiers appear in the formula, it is considered to be a propositional formula. We may then apply a specific tactic for this type of proof, based on the proof strategy given in the B-Book.

EXAMPLE 9.20 (Continuing with the Set 1 example).– $a \mathrel{\dot\subseteq} s, b \mathrel{\dot\subseteq} s \vdash x \mathrel{\dot\in} s \mathrel{\dot\wedge} (x \mathrel{\dot\in} a \mathrel{\dot\vee} x \mathrel{\dot\in} b) \mathrel{\dot\Leftrightarrow} x \mathrel{\dot\in} s \mathrel{\dot\wedge} (x \mathrel{\dot\in} b \mathrel{\dot\vee} x \mathrel{\dot\in} a)$ may be rewritten as follows: $H1, H2 \vdash P_s \mathrel{\dot\wedge} (P_a \mathrel{\dot\vee} P_b) \mathrel{\dot\Leftrightarrow} P_s \mathrel{\dot\wedge} (P_b \mathrel{\dot\vee} P_a)$ This may be demonstrated rapidly using the appropriate tactic.

9.5.1.2. *Treatment of quantifiers*

Using our algorithm, the formula must undergo an initial conversion to prenex form in order to remove quantifiers.

9.5.1.2.1. Conversion to prenex form

If the formula still contains quantifiers after the normalization stage, we need to convert the formula to prenex form (see definition, page 247).

The following properties are used to convert a formula to prenex form.

PROPERTIES 9.1.– Renaming of quantified variables
$\exists x.P \Leftrightarrow \exists y.[x := y]P \ \forall x.P \Leftrightarrow \forall y.[x := y]P$

PROPERTIES 9.2.– Definition of $\Rightarrow$ and $\Leftrightarrow$ $(P \Rightarrow Q) \Leftrightarrow (\neg P \vee Q)$ $(P \Leftrightarrow Q) \Leftrightarrow (P \Rightarrow Q \wedge Q \Rightarrow P)$

PROPERTIES 9.3.– Morgan's laws
$\neg \forall x.P \Leftrightarrow \exists x.\neg P \ \neg \exists x.P \Leftrightarrow \forall x.\neg P$

PROPERTIES 9.4.– Distributivity
$\forall x.P \wedge Q \Leftrightarrow \forall x.(P \wedge Q)$ si $x\backslash Q$
$\forall x.P \vee Q \Leftrightarrow \forall x.(P \vee Q)$ si $x\backslash Q$
$\exists x.P \wedge Q \Leftrightarrow \exists x.(P \wedge Q)$ si $x\backslash Q$
$\exists x.P \vee Q \Leftrightarrow \exists x.(P \vee Q)$ si $x\backslash Q$

PROPERTIES 9.5.– Monotony
$\forall x.(P \Rightarrow Q) \Rightarrow (\forall x.P \Rightarrow \forall x.Q)$
$\forall x.(P \Leftrightarrow Q) \Rightarrow (\forall x.P \Leftrightarrow \forall x.Q)$

PROPERTIES 9.6.– $\exists (x, y).P \Leftrightarrow \exists x.\exists y.P$

The method used to convert a formula to prenex form is as follows:

– introduce fresh variables if a variable is quantified twice;

– eliminate all $\Rightarrow$ and $\Leftrightarrow$;

– propagate $\neg$ below the quantifiers; ;

– pull up the quantifiers.

9.5.1.2.2. Introduction of fresh variables

As the properties in group 9.4 can only be applied if the quantified variable in question is not free in the other part of the formula, a variable may only be quantified once. To do this, we replace the first occurrence of variables, which have been quantified twice by applying the properties in group 9.1.

EXAMPLE 9.21.– Let $(\dot{\exists}\, x.P \;\dot{\wedge}\; \dot{\exists}\, y.Q) \;\dot{\vee}\; \dot{\exists}\, y.Q$ be the formula for conversion to prenex form. Taking $x \setminus Q$ and $y \setminus P$, without introducing fresh variables, the conversion to prenex form involves the following steps:

$$
\begin{aligned}
(\dot{\exists}\, x.P \;\dot{\wedge}\; \dot{\exists}\, y.Q) \;\dot{\vee}\; \dot{\exists}\, y.Q &\equiv (\dot{\exists}\, x.(P \;\dot{\wedge}\; \dot{\exists}\, y.Q)) \;\dot{\vee}\; \dot{\exists}\, y.Q \\
&\equiv \dot{\exists}\, x.((P \;\dot{\wedge}\; \dot{\exists}\, y.Q) \;\dot{\vee}\; \dot{\exists}\, y.Q) \\
&\equiv \dot{\exists}\, x.(\dot{\exists}\, y.(P \;\dot{\wedge}\; Q) \;\dot{\vee}\; \dot{\exists}\, y.Q) \\
&\equiv \dot{\exists}\, x.\, \dot{\exists}\, y.((P \;\dot{\wedge}\; Q) \;\dot{\vee}\; \dot{\exists}\, y.Q) \text{ (as } y \setminus \dot{\exists}\, y.Q)
\end{aligned}
$$

The second $\dot{\exists}\, y$ cannot be removed as y is free in Q. Therefore, we need to add a step to rename variables that have been quantified twice.

Let $R' \equiv Q[y := z]$. By applying the first of the properties in group 9.1, the formula becomes:

$$
\begin{aligned}
(\dot{\exists}\, x.P \;\dot{\wedge}\; \dot{\exists}\, y.Q) \;\dot{\vee}\; \dot{\exists}\, z.R &\equiv (\dot{\exists}\, x.(P \;\dot{\wedge}\; \dot{\exists}\, y.Q)) \;\dot{\vee}\; \dot{\exists}\, z.R \\
&\equiv \dot{\exists}\, x.((P \;\dot{\wedge}\; \dot{\exists}\, y.Q) \;\dot{\vee}\; \dot{\exists}\, z.R) \\
&\equiv \dot{\exists}\, x.(\dot{\exists}\, y.(P \;\dot{\wedge}\; Q) \;\dot{\vee}\; \dot{\exists}\, z.R) \\
&\equiv \dot{\exists}\, x.\, \dot{\exists}\, y.((P \;\dot{\wedge}\; Q) \;\dot{\vee}\; \dot{\exists}\, z.R) \\
&\equiv \dot{\exists}\, x.\, \dot{\exists}\, y.\, \dot{\exists}\, z.((P \;\dot{\wedge}\; Q) \;\dot{\vee}\; R) \text{ (as } z \setminus (P, Q))
\end{aligned}
$$

Thus, the conversion to prenex form has been accomplished without difficulty.

9.5.1.2.3. Removal of $\dot{\Rightarrow}$ and $\dot{\Leftrightarrow}$

To do this, we simply apply properties of group 9.2.

9.5.1.2.4. Propagation of $\dot{\neg}$

This step is only applied in cases including quantifiers located after the $\dot{\neg}$. In this case, it is useful to propagate the $\dot{\neg}$ beyond the quantifiers to trace back the $\dot{\forall}$ before $\dot{\exists}$, using properties of group 9.3.

EXAMPLE 9.22.– Let us take the property $\dot{\neg}\, (P \;\dot{\wedge}\; (\dot{\forall}\, x.Q \;\dot{\vee}\; \dot{\exists}\, y.R))$ with $x \setminus (P, R)$ and $y \setminus (P, Q)$.

– If we convert this formula to prenex form directly using properties of group 9.4 we obtain:

$$\dot{\neg}\,(P \wedge \dot{\forall}\,x.(Q \vee \dot{\exists}\,y.R)) \equiv \dot{\neg}\,\dot{\forall}\,x.(P \wedge (Q \vee \dot{\exists}\,y.R))$$
$$\equiv \dot{\exists}\,x.\,\dot{\neg}\,(P \wedge (Q \vee \dot{\exists}\,y.R))$$
$$\equiv \dot{\exists}\,x.\,\dot{\neg}\,(P \wedge \dot{\exists}\,y.(Q \vee R))$$
$$\equiv \dot{\exists}\,x.\,\dot{\neg}\,\dot{\exists}\,y.(P \wedge (Q \vee R))$$
$$\equiv \dot{\exists}\,x.\,\dot{\forall}\,y.\,\dot{\neg}\,(P \wedge (Q \vee R))$$

The quantifier $\dot{\exists}$ is situated before $\dot{\forall}$.

– If the $\dot{\neg}$ is propagated before conversion to prenex form, then:

$$\dot{\neg}\,P \vee \dot{\neg}\,(\dot{\forall}\,x.Q \vee \dot{\exists}\,y.R) \equiv \dot{\neg}\,P \vee (\dot{\exists}\,x.\,\dot{\neg}\,Q \wedge \dot{\forall}\,y.\,\dot{\neg}\,R)$$
$$\equiv \dot{\neg}\,P \vee \dot{\forall}\,y.(\dot{\exists}\,x.\,\dot{\neg}\,Q \wedge \dot{\neg}\,R)$$
$$\equiv \dot{\forall}\,y.(\dot{\neg}\,P \vee (\dot{\exists}\,x.\,\dot{\neg}\,Q \wedge \dot{\neg}\,R))$$
$$\equiv \dot{\forall}\,y.(\dot{\neg}\,P \vee \dot{\exists}\,x.(\dot{\neg}\,Q \wedge \dot{\neg}\,R))$$
$$\equiv \dot{\forall}\,y.\,\dot{\exists}\,x.(\dot{\neg}\,P \vee (\dot{\neg}\,Q \wedge \dot{\neg}\,R))$$

The quantifier $\dot{\forall}$ is correctly placed before $\dot{\exists}$.

9.5.1.2.5. Removal of $\dot{\forall}$ and $\dot{\exists}$

This step is carried out using properties of group 9.4. Quantifier propagation is no longer possible after conversion to prenex form, as the formula $\dot{\forall}\,y.\,\dot{\exists}\,x.P(x,y) \Rightarrow \dot{\exists}\,x.\,\dot{\forall}\,y.P(x,y)$ is not valid. Therefore, the order in which the quantifiers are pulled up determines the resulting prenex form. We have chosen to begin by pulling up the $\dot{\forall}$ quantifiers in order to facilitate quantifier elimination, which is the next stage in the resolution process. In the same way, when choosing which of the two $\dot{\exists}$ to pull up, we need to check for $\dot{\forall}$ after these $\dot{\exists}$. If this is the case, we begin by pulling up the branch where the $\dot{\forall}$ is nearest to the root of the subformula tree. Note that these branches must already be in prenex form.

EXAMPLE 9.23.– Take $P \equiv \dot{\exists}\,x.\,\dot{\forall}\,y.Q \wedge \dot{\exists}\,z.\,\dot{\exists}\,t.\,\dot{\forall}\,u.R.\,\dot{\forall}\,y$ is at depth 1 and $\dot{\forall}\,u$ is at depth level 2. The first part of the conjunction therefore has priority. The result of the conversion to prenex form is then $P \equiv \dot{\exists}\,x.\,\dot{\forall}\,y.\,\dot{\exists}\,z.\,\dot{\exists}\,t.\,\dot{\forall}\,u.(Q \wedge R)$ instead of $P \equiv \dot{\exists}\,z.\,\dot{\exists}\,t.\,\dot{\forall}\,u.\,\dot{\exists}\,x.\,\dot{\forall}\,y.(Q \wedge R)$.

9.5.1.2.6. Quantifier elimination

Once the formula has been converted to prenex form, we need to eliminate the quantifiers. Quantifier $\dot{\forall}$ is eliminated by applying RULE 7. This rule allows us to eliminate the $\dot{\forall}$, if the quantified variable is not free in the hypotheses.

To remove the quantifier $\dot{\exists}$ in $\dot{\exists}\ x.P$, our heuristic involves searching for a reference variable y such that $P[x := y]$ is true. The substitution is carried out using rule DR 13. To facilitate removal of the $\dot{\exists}$, all existential variable couples are removed using property 9.6.

Our algorithm is therefore as follows:

– For each existential variable, establish the list of variables which may be used as substitutes for the quantified variable. The selected substitutions are those which are universally quantified in the goal.

– Test all of the replacement possibilities using rule DR 13 until the proof succeeds using the designated tactic for propositional calculus, as described earlier in this chapter.

If none of the combinations leads to the finalization of proof, the algorithm stops and the tactic has failed.

This heuristic is illustrated in the two following examples.

EXAMPLE 9.24.– Let us retain one of the examples used to illustrate conversion to prenex form. Let $\dot{\forall}\ x.\ \dot{\forall}\ y.\ \dot{\exists}\ z.\ \dot{\neg}\ P\ \dot{\lor}\ \dot{\neg}\ Q\ \dot{\lor}\ Q'$ be the formula to prove. After two applications of RULE 7, if the non-freeness conditions for the variable have been verified, we obtain $\dot{\exists}z.\ \dot{\neg}\ P\ \dot{\lor}\ \dot{\neg}\ Q\ \dot{\lor}\ Q'$. Therefore, the variables which may potentially be used as replacements for z are x and y. The two test cases are: $[z := x]\ \dot{\neg}\ P\ \dot{\lor}\ \dot{\neg}\ Q\ \dot{\lor}\ Q'$ and $[z := y]\ \dot{\neg}\ P\ \dot{\lor}\ \dot{\neg}\ Q\ \dot{\lor}\ Q'$. In our example, the second combination is correct because, by definition, Q' is $Q[y := z]$. The algorithm has been completed successfully.

EXAMPLE 9.25.– Let $\dot{\exists}\ x_1 P_1\ \dot{\Leftrightarrow}\ \dot{\exists}\ y_1 Q_1$ be the formula to prove. The conversion to prenex form involves the following steps:
Take $P_2 \equiv [x_1 := x_2]P_1$ and $Q_2 \equiv [y_1 := y_2]Q_1$

$$
\begin{aligned}
\dot{\exists}\ x_1 P_1 \dot{\Leftrightarrow} \dot{\exists}\ y_1 Q_1 &\dot{\Leftrightarrow} \dot{\exists} x_1 P_1 \dot{\Rightarrow} \dot{\exists} y_1 Q_1 \dot{\land} \dot{\exists} y_1 Q_1 \dot{\Rightarrow} \dot{\exists} x_1 P_1 && \text{(Def. of } \dot{\Leftrightarrow}) \\
&\dot{\Leftrightarrow} \dot{\exists} x_1 P_1 \dot{\Rightarrow} \dot{\exists} y_1 Q_1 \dot{\land} \dot{\exists} y_2 Q_2 \dot{\Rightarrow} \dot{\exists} x_2 P_2 && \text{(Property 9.1)} \\
&\dot{\Leftrightarrow} (\dot{\neg} (\dot{\exists} x_1 P_1) \dot{\lor} \dot{\exists} y_1 Q_1) \dot{\land} (\dot{\neg} (\dot{\exists} y_2 Q_2) \dot{\lor} \dot{\exists} x_2 P_2) && \text{(Def. of } \dot{\Rightarrow}) \\
&\dot{\Leftrightarrow} (\dot{\forall} x_1 \dot{\neg} P_1 \dot{\lor} \dot{\exists} y_1 Q_1) \dot{\land} (\dot{\forall} y_2 \dot{\neg} Q_2 \dot{\lor} \dot{\exists} x_2 P_2) && \text{(Property 9.3)} \\
&\dot{\Leftrightarrow} \dot{\forall} x_1((\dot{\neg} P_1 \dot{\lor} \dot{\exists} y_1 Q_1) \dot{\land} (\dot{\forall} y_2(\dot{\neg} Q_2 \dot{\lor} \dot{\exists} x_2 P_2))) && \text{(Property 9.4)} \\
&\dot{\Leftrightarrow} \dot{\forall} x_1 \dot{\forall} y_2((\dot{\neg} P_1 \dot{\lor} \dot{\exists} y_1 Q_1) \dot{\land} (\dot{\neg} Q_2 \dot{\lor} \dot{\exists} x_2 P_2)) && \text{(Property 9.4)} \\
&\dot{\Leftrightarrow} \dot{\forall} x_1 \dot{\forall} y_2 \dot{\exists} y_1 \dot{\exists} x_2((\dot{\neg} P_1 \dot{\lor} Q_1) \dot{\land} (\dot{\neg} Q_2 \dot{\lor} P_2)) && \text{(Property 9.4)}
\end{aligned}
$$

Thus, we are able to eliminate the quantifiers. After two applications of RULE 7, the goal becomes $\exists\ y_1\ \exists\ x_2((\dot\neg\ P_1\ \dot\vee\ Q_1)\ \dot\wedge\ (\dot\neg\ Q_2\ \dot\vee\ P_2))$. Let x_1, y_2 be the non-quantified variables of the goal. The possible replacement variables with the corresponding properties are:

	Variable for y_1	Variable for x_2	Property to demonstrate
Test 1	x_1	x_1	$[(y_1, x_2) \doteq (x_1, x_1)](\dot\neg\, P_1\ \dot\vee\ Q_1)\ \dot\wedge\ (\dot\neg\, Q_2\ \dot\vee\ P_2)$
Test 2	x_1	y_2	$[(y_1, x_2) \doteq (x_1, y_2)](\dot\neg\, P_1\ \dot\vee\ Q_1)\ \dot\wedge\ (\dot\neg\, Q_2\ \dot\vee\ P_2)$
Test 3	y_2	y_2	$[(y_1, x_2) \doteq (y_2, y_2)](\dot\neg\, P_1\ \dot\vee\ Q_1)\ \dot\wedge\ (\dot\neg\, Q_2\ \dot\vee\ P_2)$
Test 4	y_2	x_1	$[(y_1, x_2) \doteq (y_2, x_1)](\dot\neg\, P_1\ \dot\vee\ Q_1)\ \dot\wedge\ (\dot\neg\, Q_2\ \dot\vee\ P_2)$

If one of the tests is successful, then the correct combination has been found; otherwise, the algorithm will fail.

9.5.1.2.7. Limitations

Note that the contraction rule ($P \Leftrightarrow P \dot\vee P$) is never used in the algorithm, which only considers the intuitionist semantics of the existential quantifier. Consequently, it can only prove formulas with the property of the witness, i.e. formula such as $\exists\ xF$, which is true if a witness term t exists such that $F[x := t]$ is true. However, as the B method uses classical logic, the algorithm cannot be complete.

EXAMPLE 9.26.– Peirce's law $((A \Rightarrow B) \Rightarrow A) \Rightarrow A$ cannot be demonstrated without the contraction rule. Our algorithm is, therefore, unable to demonstrate this law.

Similarly, the B-Book property $dom(p \mathbin{\lhd\mkern-9mu-} q) = dom(p) \cup dom(q)$, where p and q are the relationships between two sets s and t, cannot be demonstrated without the contraction rule.

Moreover, the instantiation is too specific; it does not involve unification, and terms other than the variables are not taken into account.

EXAMPLE 9.27.– Property $P(1) \Rightarrow \exists\ x.P(x)$ cannot be demonstrated by this algorithm as x must be replaced by the term 1.

While this heuristic is somewhat naive, it allows us to prove around 200 of the properties from the B-Book. In certain cases, it raises performance issues, as we will see in section 9.5.2.

9.5.2. *Evaluation and tests*

In this section, we will present the results of implementation using a number of examples. These tests are based on several properties contained in the B-Book, on added rules from Atelier B and on added rules from the Siemens rule database. Our results are summarized in Table 9.1. For the B-Book properties, the "Set" formulas were extracted from the set properties in the "Derived Constructions" section of B-Book (p. 75), the "Domain" formulas from the "Domain Property" table (p. 100) and the "Overriding" formulas from the "Overriding Property" table (p. 114). The number associated with each formula is the line number in the corresponding tables.

Type	Formula	FOL	Total
B-Book properties	Set 1	0.28	0.80
	Set 2	0.28	0.66
	Set 3	0.56	2.10
	Set 4	0.56	1.92
	Domain 2	0.80	3.38
	Domain 3	14.96	61.37
	Domain 4	26.58	536.43
	Domain 5	0.46	0.77
	Overriding 1	5.01	–
	Overriding 3	1.44	6.71
	Overriding 4	4.36	11.06
	Overriding 5	5.31	45.26
Added rules	SimplifyRelDoaXY.20	1.30	2.90
	SimplifyX.79	6.98	77.65
	SimplifyRelFonXY.7	3.82	41.63
	SimplifyRelComXY.20	25.89	51.80
	Rule no928	3.39	–
	Rule no2466	0.65	28.97
	Rule no2470	3.10	9.61
	Rule no2496	19.98	–

Table 9.1. *Test results for the $\mathcal{L}_{\text{tac}}$ tactic*

We considered the following added rules from Atelier B:

SimplifyRelDoaXY.20: $\mathrm{dom}(r) \lhd r == \emptyset$

SimplifyX.79: $a \lhd b = \emptyset == (\mathrm{dom}(b) \in \mathbb{P}(a))$

SimplifyRelDoaLongXY.7: $u \lhd (r \lhd\!\!- s) == u \lhd r \lhd\!\!- (u \lhd s)$

SimplifyRelComXY.20: $(r; \{a \mapsto b\}) == r^{-1}[a] \times \{b\}$

and the following added rules from the Siemens database:

Rule no928: $(a \cup b)[A] == a[A] \cup b[A]$

Rule no2466: $\mathsf{binhyp}(a \cup b = c) \wedge \mathsf{binhyp}(a = \emptyset) \Rightarrow b = c$

Rule no2470: $a \in \mathbb{P}(b) \wedge c \in d \wedge \mathsf{blvar}(e) \wedge e \backslash (a, b, d, c) \Rightarrow a \triangleleft b \times c \triangleright d ==$
$a \times c$

Rule no2496: $\mathsf{binhyp}(a \cup b = c[d]) \wedge a = \emptyset \wedge c = e^{-1} => b = e^{-1}[d]$

These tests were carried out using an Intel 3.40GHz/4Gb processor. The two columns in Table 9.1 show the time taken to execute the $\mathcal{L}_{\text{tac}}$ approach. All execution times are given in seconds. "FOL" shows the normalization time. The symbol "−" means that the tactic took longer than 4 hours to obtain proof, or was unable to do this without manual application of the contraction rule.

The problem with this approach is that the more complex the formulas, the more variables are introduced, thus increasing the demonstration time. The time taken to choose the correct instantiation of the existential quantifiers depends on the path times of the variable lists, given that the algorithm needs to demonstrate or invalidate an instance each time. The worst cases occur when the correct variables are situated at the end of the list. This complexity problem was apparent in our tests, particularly for property "Overriding 1". However, this tactic appears to be appropriate (as the time involved is reasonable) for rules containing few quantifiers, such as "SimplifyRelDoaXY.20".

The general tactic has allowed automatic proof of a significant number of properties. However, it only addresses a subset of the logic contained in the B-Book. When a property from outside of this set needs to be proved, subtactics may offer some assistance, for example, by removing sets in comprehension or Cartesian products. Similarly, the prenex conversion subtactic can be useful for complex proof cases, allowing us to test a strategy which is difficult to implement manually.

9.6. Conclusion

In this chapter, we have presented the BCARe environment, used to assist experts in verifying rules, whether those contained in the Atelier B base or those added later. This environment includes a variety of different tools, used to verify that the variable capture problem is correctly treated in the case of rewriting rules, to verify correct typing, to demonstrate well definedness and to show that definitions clearly denote theorems in the B-Book. A deep embedding of the B set theory using Coq allows us to solve B proof problems (such as non-freedom), which previously required manual treatment. In addition, we have implemented automatic demonstration tactics with the aim of reducing validation costs, using the Coq $\mathcal{L}_{tac}$ language. First-order logic formulas are derived from set formulas, then converted to prenex form. Finally, quantifiers are eliminated in order to obtain a formula suitable for evaluation using a valid propositional logic algorithm. This approach has been used to automatically validate around 200 lemmas from the B-Book, alongside rules from the Atelier B rule base and from the internal database used at Siemens.

This work offers a number of perspectives for future extensions. The first possibility concerns the generation of the three proof obligations by the Chaine_verif tool; we wish to develop this aspect in order to obtain formally-certified proof obligations. One possible approach would involve extracting a typing inference algorithm using an adaptation of the type inference specification defined for Chaine_verif in Coq. We also need to establish a formal demonstration of coherence properties relating to the B-Book type system. This improvement would remove the need to demonstrate the typing lemma, and, consequently, the need to generate this lemma. Another possible improvement concerns changes to the user interface to allow easier access to errors highlighted by our tools.

Another possibility concerns full validation of the B-Book lemmas: BCARe currently allows us to validate all of these lemmas, but not all automatically. Moreover, the proof tactic developed in $\mathcal{L}_{tac}$ is subject to significant increases in complexity when the number of variables involved in the formula increases. Therefore, we need to consider other automatic proof strategies offering better performance. Work is currently underway on another approach involving the use of an external theorem demonstrator, Zenon [BON 07]. This allows us to benefit from the algorithmic developments of the tool. More generally, we wish to integrate other proof demonstrators into BCARe in order to produce adequate responses to our problems.

Therefore, the BCARe environment needs to adapt to the introduction of new proof assistants. In addition to our work on demonstrating the lemmas contained in the B-Book, efforts are currently being made to validate the rules used in Atelier B (with a special focus on the 600 rules which cannot be demonstrated automatically with the elementary prover used in Atelier B) and in the Siemens rule base, which includes around 1,800 rules which have not been validated using automatic methods.

9.7. Acknowledgments

The authors thank all of those involved in rereading this chapter, particularly Catherine Dubois and David Delahaye, whose remarks have been invaluable in improving our work.

9.8. Bibliography

[ABR 96] ABRIAL J.-R., *The B-Book, Assigning Programs to Meanings*, Cambridge University Press, Cambridge, UK, 1996.

[ABR 02] ABRIAL J.-R., MUSSAT L., "On using conditional definitions in formal theories", BERT D., BOWEN J.P., HENSON M.C., *et al.*, (eds.), *ZB 2002: Formal Specification and Development in Z and B, Proceedings of the 2nd International Conference of B and Z Users,* Lecture Notes in Computer Science, Springer, Grenoble, France, vol. 2272, pp. 317–322, 23–25 January 2002.

[ABR 03] ABRIAL J.-R., CANSELL D., "Click'n'prove: interactive proofs within set theory", BASIN D., WOLFF B., (eds.), *16th International Conference on Theorem Proving in Higher Order Logics - TPHOLs 2003,* Lecture notes in Computer Science, Springer, Rome, Italy, vol. 2758, pp. 1–24, 2003.

[BER 04] BERKANI K., DUBOIS C., FAIVRE A., *et al.*, "Validation des règles de base de l'Atelier B", *Technique et Science Informatiques (TSI)*, vol. 23, no. 7, pp. 855–878, 2004.

[BOD 99] BODEVEIX J.-P., FILALI M., MUÑOZ C., "A formalization of the B-method in Coq and PVS", *B Users Group Meeting, Toulouse, France*, FM'99 – B Users Group Meeting – Applying B in an industrial context: Tools, Lessons and Techniques, Springer-Verlag, September 1999.

[BON 07] BONICHON R., DELAHAYE D., DOLIGEZ D., "Zenon: An extensible automated theorem prover producing checkable proofs", *Logic for Programming Artificial Intelligence and Reasoning (LPAR)*, LNCS/LNAI, Springer, Yerevan, Armenia, vol. 4790, pp. 151–165, October 2007.

[CHA 98] CHARTIER P., "Formalisation of B in Isabelle/HOL", *B Conference*, Montpellier, France, LNCS, Springer, vol. 1393, pp. 66–82, April 1998.

[CIR 98] CIRSTEA H., KIRCHNER C., "Using rewriting and strategies for describing the B predicate prover", *Strategies in Automated Deduction*, Lindau, Germany, pp. 25–36, July 1998.

[CLE 09] CLEARSY, *Atelier B 4.0*, February 2009, available at http://www.atelierb.eu/.

[COL 09] COLIN S., MARIANO G., "BiCoax, a proof tool traceable to the BBook", *TFM B'2009: From Research to Teaching Formal Methods – The B Method*, June 2009, http://www.lina.sciences.univ-nantes.fr/apcb/BDayNantes2009/.

[COQ 10] THE COQ DEVELOPMENT TEAM, Coq, version 8.3, INRIA, October 2010, available at http://coq.inria.fr/.

[DEL 00] DELAHAYE D., "A tactic language for the system Coq", *Logic for Programming and Automated Reasoning (LPAR)*, LNCS/LNAI, Springer, Reunion Island, France, vol. 1955, pp. 85–95, November 2000.

[JAC 09] JACQUEL M., Automatisation de la preuve B, Master's Thesis, Pierre and Marie Curie University, Siemens, September 2009.

[JAE 07] JAEGER E., DUBOIS C., "Why would you trust B?", *Logic for Programming Artificial Intelligence and Reasoning (LPAR)*, LNCS/LNAI, Springer, Yerevan, Armenia, vol. 4790, pp. 288–302, October 2007.

[LEL 08] LE LAY E., Automatiser la validation des règles, Master's Tthesis, INSA, Rennes, Siemens, 2008.

[STÉ 96] STÉRIA., Validation de la base de règles - guide méthodologique, RATP, 1996.

10

Validation of Railway Security Automatisms Based on Petri Networks

10.1. Introduction

10.1.1. *Note to the reader*

This chapter does not aim to teach readers everything about the method of proof by assertion applied to concurrent constraint automata. This has already been the subject of several academic articles.

Instead, we will confine ourselves to giving a few pointers that will help the reader to understand the domain of application and the points in favor of using a method based on Petri networks, while also setting forth the main concepts of this method.

We will not go into the details of the mathematics of the method. Our emphasis will be on the conceptual aspects linked to the practical and industrial application of this proof method, particularly within the railway sector.

10.1.2. *Summary*

The development of information technology (IT) and automation has led us to new, increasingly effective solutions. However, they have also led us to a new level of complexity, which makes it even more difficult to design

---

Chapter written by Marc ANTONI.

sustainably and economically, and to evaluate the operating safety of the equipment and transport systems. Real-time computing is widespread in systems that manage human lives. It now seems that the current methods and standards are not always sufficient to address what is expected in terms of availability and security.

The risk of software system errors cannot be ignored. Our work consisted of defining and instrumenting a method of design and validation. We showed that it is indeed possible to apply a formal validation method to industrial automatisms.

We focus, in particular, on the case of railway automatisms. Our method is based on several design actions:

– taking the specific railway context to be highly important, identifying security properties and operating postulates;

– making a distinction between the functional software and the basic software (equipment management and interpretation of business functions);

– specifying the functions in the form of automata written in AEFD language (*Automate à Etats Finis Déterministe* – Deterministic Finite Automaton). This language makes it possible to write Petri networks (concurrent constraint automata) and interpret in a deterministic way which is accessible to those involved in signaling.

Under these conditions, it is possible to carry out formal validation of a railway automatism, such as a signal box.

The central idea is to develop an industrial security automaton which behaves like an abstract machine (a concurrent constraint automaton with zero transition time), which could, once it has been developed, eventually be used for formal validation. The writing of the functional graphs is designed for those with a working knowledge of the railway sector, but who may not have in-depth IT knowledge.

Petri networks are a language for conceptualization. We used these networks, written in AEFD language, as a language for interpretable specifications. The safety properties and the operating postulates were written in the same way.

Under these conditions, our method makes it possible to carry out a formal proof of the system functions in an industrial process for the commissioning of safety installations.

10.2. Issues involved

10.2.1. *Introduction*

For over 20 years, computerized systems have been involved in the management of train traffic on railways, all around the world. Where once they were applied only to peripheral operations, now they are involved in the central commands at all critical points. They are now at the heart of the systems. Yet we all know that our mobile phones and other home automation equipment based on processors and market software contain many faults that are impossible to identify, even after thousands of hours of factory testing.

When we communicate on the telephone, or browse the Internet, these faults do not pose any risk to our life. However, this is not the case when these same types of information technologies, which are becoming ubiquitous, are applied to the command of railways around the world. The risk of faults becomes a danger to the life of the user when the software interferes with the safety and security of vital functions.

In these cases, there is the risk of death, explosion, fire, or possibly even aggression, which may originate from a virus or another disruptive factor. Mechanics, electrotechniques, electronics, automation and computerization all play a role in the railway system. As a result, any failure in the computerized component leads to dangerous risks, even certain death in some situations, which, however, are not clearly defined. This is why there are many commissions that are not successful, through lack of conclusiveness.

It should be noted that carrying out functions in software which relate to physical equipment has made some of these functions more complex. This is because the quantity of design functions necessary to fulfill the main functions has become very large in relation to the quantity of main functions properly speaking, and this has substantially increased complexity. Designing a critical or complex software system involves a certain number of theoretical problems and practical "on-the-job" applications, which we will address in the sections that follow.

10.2.2. *An industry context: railways*

The railway system is based on many technical components that ensure safety and quality for the transport of passengers and goods. The functions carried out by these components are varied, whether they are infrastructure (track, signaling, overhead lines, etc.) or part of the rolling stock (locomotives, cars, metro trains, etc.).

Computerized or IT systems play a role, which will soon be one of the leading ones, in systems based on automatisms. The safe operation of these automatisms is an essential prerequisite for delivering a quality service and reducing costs caused by malfunction and incidents.

These costs include:

– direct costs resulting from losses caused by the failure (loss of life, loss of revenue, repair costs, replacement costs, costs for return to operation, etc.);

– indirect costs caused by preventative design and maintenance measures aimed at reducing occurrences and consequences of failures (interruption of traffic due to maintenance or modification operations, application of regulation procedures, etc.).

To arm themselves against the risk of unsafe failure[1] of the automatisms of safety installations, those managing infrastructures that govern these systems have adopted and implemented various policies for preventative maintenance and the (re)commissioning of equipment. These aim to ensure, as efficiently as possible, the maximum possible availability for the use of these automatisms so as to limit the number of safe failures and to avoid any unsafe failures for safety installations[2].

The arrival of computerized systems means that earlier validation procedures and practices need to be reassessed. The application of standards does not provide answers regarding the required safety level. Safety installations are constantly in use (24 hours a day and 365 days a year) and the only acceptable level for unsafe operational error is: none at all.

---

1 Safe failure: a safe failure does not have any influence on the safety of people or traffic.

2 Security measures: these cover signaling installations and oversee the automatisms.

Otherwise, because these are computerized installations, we would accept one or more unsafe failures.

The quest for zero faults in the development and modification of IT automatisms for safety installations requires, with current methods, a high level of manual or automatic validation of operation, without any guarantee of success. The level of effort required is judged to be economically unviable, and naturally leads constructors of railway equipment and the authorities guaranteeing safety to accept the change to computerization and to opt for a probabilistic safety approach for critical IT systems, both at the level of the implementation of the functionalities and at the definition of these functionalities.

This comes down to reducing the safety level in Europe for new computerized safety installations, through a lack of means for efficient and economically acceptable validation. And therein lies the field of formal methods.

Thus, in order to address the issues cited above, it would seem useful to raise some initial questions about determinism and probabilism.

10.2.3. *Determinism versus probabilism for the safe management of critical computerized systems*

Aiming to identify a general principle for solving the problem in the railway sector due to the introduction of computerized systems, we will address the following topics: the constitution of the real system, determinism, probabilism, interrelation, system layers, the three levels of a critical system, the basic system, the deterministic system and effectively handling the long life of the system.

10.2.3.1. *The constitution of the real system*

In everyday reality, whatever our situation, we cannot ever (and we will never be able to) exhaustively describe the entire constitution of the system. The same applies for every system. As a result, all railway systems are also impossible to describe completely. Whatever organization is deployed, it always comprises some gray areas. The railway system is made up of multiple parts – mechanical, electrical, automatic, computer – all interdependent. This leads to so many possibilities that it is totally impossible to envisage a complete, exhaustive description of them.

The same applies for each of the parts of the system, however, as far as our gaze stretches. In other words, the elementary functions over which the activities of the computer programs are today spread are extremely wide. At present, no program has yet claimed to be able to characterize to a level of 100% all the possibilities, functioning and non-functioning.

To understand this, we can take the following as a hypothesis: two elements in a series make 4 combinations, 4 possible functions, 3 give 8, 4 give 16, n elements give 2^n. Our second hypothesis is the following: a system (computerized) is made up of n elements in a series. The result is that it can yield 2^n possible functions. As a conservative estimate, it is made up of several tens of millions of basic components (let us presume that there are 50,000,000 logic gates). The result is that it can yield $2^{50,000,000}$ possible functions, with or without fault. Testing times quickly become immeasurable, and when we add in the possible redundancies and loops, the situation worsens considerably.

This explains why no computerized system, no computer, in the world can be completely tested. Thus we restrict ourselves to testing only the parts that are considered essential for a level of safety that is deemed to be sufficient. The same applies for computer systems that command trains on railways, if we do not take action. Our aim here is to show that there is a solution that can considerably reduce the number of possible functions to only several functions, and these several functions can be sufficient to manage an entire system, whatever the complexity. This small number means that we can be sure of the result that we should expect.

That it is impossible to describe with 100% certainty the required functions, and yet we must[3] guarantee 100% safety for passengers, is the paradox with which all managers of railway networks around the world are confronted.

However, from the viewpoint of empirical work, the "commitment to the experience of the senses, distrust of speculation and claimed knowledge born of intuition, preference for logical rigor in deductions, striving towards

---

3 Or "should", because in this competitive world, nothing is perfect.

plainness and clarity in presenting findings"[4], paths of research which follow an approach that is deterministic as much as probabilistic start to appear.

10.2.3.2. Determinism

Determinism, or a "set of causes or conditions necessary to determine a phenomenon"[5], is a notion that basic rationalism seems to accept as an immediate practice. For a precise, focused question, it consists of making the hypothesis that everything can be determined *a priori*. The work is then to define the following: the objective sought, its domain, its field of operation, each of the functions that will be activated in it, precisely when and how, and their cause/effect.

We take as a strong hypothesis that under these conditions, nothing will change for the entire lifetime of the system under study.

These conditions can be possible following a systematic approach in the context of the management of rail infrastructures, all around the world. We will, therefore, only work on that which is necessary for the proper functioning of these infrastructures, and that alone. We will proceed by level of abstraction directly linked to a relevant operational context.

In the past, determinism in rail signaling has been interpreted as the notion of intrinsic safety, which is based on hypotheses of failure of the components used. It follows, then, that we can only use simple components, or a combination of simple components with this concept. As a result, the treatment capacity of the equipment is limited. This is compared to probabilistic safety, which allows an unsafe residual risk.[6] This risk is taken as the objective and divided into allocations for each subsystem, with the formidable problem of interdependencies and latency times. From this point of view, the deterministic approach makes it possible to use computerized systems.

---

4 http://www.cnrtl.fr/definition/empirisme (definition translated).

5 http://www.cnrtl.fr/definition/déterminisme (definition translated).

6 The risk allowed for the occurrence of an unsafe situation is not merely random and dependent on the hardware. It also covers deterministic faults in the definition and creation of software. This risk is therefore unsuited to being quantified using a level of failure.

Figure 10.1. *Illustration of deterministic versus probabilistic safety: the locking bed of a 1945 mechanical interlocking (Stevens tappets)[7]. Determinism: definition of the conditional incompatibility between the lever of a warning signal and the two levers controlling a square signal. Probabilism: occurrence of the risk of poor physical achievement of the interlockings, which turns this physical incompatibility into an event. The physical principle applied: incompressibility of a piece of steel*

Determinism and safety: the strong hypothesis with the deterministic approach is that only the control-command of rail infrastructures is achieved safely (to be understood here: control-command then action in the automatic sense). The approach does not introduce any (*a priori*) safety risk (because all the states of control-command are determined). From this point of view, the term "intrinsic deterministic safety" may be defined.

For this, we can cite two definitions:

– The definition provided by the standard NF 001-101 [NF 93] relative to railway equipment:

- "Method using known physical properties of components regarding their behavior in case of break-down or disruption, so that a safe configuration is obtained as a result".

---

7 Photo: Marc Antoni.

– The definition from [DAV 88]:

- "A system is said to be intrinsically secure if it is certain that any failure of one or several components cannot bring it to a situation less permissive that the situation in which it is found at the moment of the failure, the least permissive situation being a total standstill".

In rail transport, taking into account the physical situation and the current rules regarding signaling, we can, in fact, stop a train or halt traffic on a portion of the track in the case of a subsystem fault[8].

Two basic notions should be highlighted here:

– Intrinsic safety "uses the physical properties of the components", which means that only those components for which we have a perfect knowledge of their "behavior in case of failure" may be used.

– "The failure of one or several components" must maintain the system in a safe state in the presence of simple breakdowns, but also of combinations of breakdowns. The occurrence of this last assertion, maintaining the system in a safe state, is greatly increased by a construction which deliberately puts the system in a safe state as soon as the first failure of a first component appears.

These first remarks suggest the design and development of a deterministic approach in the railway sector.

Consideration of the deterministic approach in railways meant that engineers were faced with the lack of reliability of the components (paradox of the deterministic and the random).

Their answers to this situation may be summarized as follows:

– In 1949, Murphy's law was first stated: "anything that can go wrong, will go wrong" [PON 08].

– This law changes a probability into a certainty. It creates the equation: the probability of an unfavorable event is equal to 1.

---

8 In fact, a train must be able to come to a stop at any place and be able to start again by itself, a train is only permitted to drive at a given speed if the portion for free track ahead of it is sufficient for it to come to a stop by itself at the end of this portion.

– The time delay before an unfavorable event occurs is of no significance: the number of events is sufficiently large for the probability of an unfavorable event occurring within a limited time to be actually quite high.

So what can we do to ensure the safety of an entire (rail) system when the components are unreliable [PON 08]? The tactic used has been to call upon solidly established principles (logic, etc.), physical laws (gravity, Lenz, etc.) which may be considered to be very reliable, and upon which it is tempting to rely on to assume certain, local, reliability of the components.

For example, the principle following which a body that is subject to no mechanical action other than its weight falls. It should be noted that in this case safety is not based on the reliability of the apparatus, but on the reliability of several physical laws and an "oriented design" of the components. It is said oriented in the sense that all possible changes of the component are not equivalent. They are hierarchical, and used following these principles: some states (i.e. physical states) are more stable than others, "spontaneous" alteration in the subsystem always progresses toward the most stable state, and it is possible to make the most stable state correspond to the most secure situation.

By this (physical) principle, any "system" which combines technical components is designed in such a way that none of the results of the proof of the testing of their operation (whatever the probability of occurrence of corresponding stresses) leads to the occurrence of an event which "compromises safety".

Note that this understanding of safety, which is separate from reliability, nonetheless has a significant other side: rigorous preventative maintenance. It is not enough for an installation to place itself in a "secure" state when it breaks down for safety to be ensured. In addition, the operators, under production constraint, must not be pushed to accept an installation which displays faults too frequently. Therefore, despite appearances, this safety model is not based on technique alone[9]. So human

---

9 Operational experience with the electromechanical relays confirms this reasoning: a relay is, on average, several billion times more likely to remain raised despite a break in supply than it is likely to fall. And it is people, in this case maintenance agents, who constrict, in a preventative or corrective sense, the automaton that makes up a signalling installation, so that it remains within its realm of operation.

resourcefulness, in the context of procedures, plays a leading role in the railway system [REA 93, REA 95].

Determinism and the closed railway world: deterministic reasoning is only possible in a "closed world"[10]. This principle of closure is involved in all thought in industrial safety because "the safety of an automated system may only be envisaged in the case of a closed system; as soon as there is interaction, there is a risk of the unforeseeable" [PON 08].

Thus, the principle of an organization isolated from its environment was one of the foundations of the conception of safety. Indeed, in 1846, the law imposed the principle of the railway as a closed system, including at level crossings. Thus, for the development of a railway system, the boundaries must be clearly defined, in an operational sense, through regulation, and physically.

Three types of properties must absolutely and categorically be defined:

– those that directly guarantee the "safety" of the system in itself and in its interactions;

– those that guarantee the "operational availability" of the system in itself and in its interactions;

– those that describe the interaction with its "environment" (postulate).

Moreover, such a system must, in the context of railways, have at least one safe state. This is a state in which the risk from the system is qualified as safe: safe fallback system[11]. It is agreed that the system is in a safe state when it is operated within the rules of operation. The safe state is usually a lower energy state which is in agreement with operational rules. The fail-safe position should be accessible within a short time and by deactivating the system functions.

---

10 The supersystem and its interfaces with the system must be defined. These interfaces must be defined physically, temporally and functionally so as to delimit the domain of accessible system states authorized by the system. If the modes of solicitation of the system are exhaustively known, along with the accessible system states, it is then possible to arrive at a logical demonstration of the impossibility to access a non-safe system state.

11 This fallback system which is labeled safe is not so indefinitely. The management of the degraded mode created in this way requires the application of procedures which are themselves subject to the risk of error in interpretation or application.

Figure 10.2. *Illustration of deterministic versus probabilistic safety: an S3 Aster relay box from the former Poste 1, Strasbourg[12]. Determinism: definition of the conditional incompatibilities between relay positions. Risk of poor definition and implementation of electric diagrams leading to these conditional incompatibilities. Probabilism: occurrence of maintenance risks in the upper position of the relay when it is not receiving supply, commutation outside the time and energy forks fixed by the CT (conditions techniques – technical conditions). The physical principle applied: gravity*

Due to the long life of signaling installations, their design and maintenance in working order[13] must be such that no gap in the

12 Photo: Marc Antoni.

13 There are over 2,000 signal boxes in operation on the French national railway system. Some of them have been in operation for more than 100 years, most of them for more than 50. This creates a probability of a waiting period for an unsafe situation.

interlocking[14] or uncertainty regarding safety is possible, whether software is involved or not. For computerized systems, it is thus essential to find a way to provide an absolute guarantee that the implementation is correct.

10.2.3.3. *Probabilism*

Probabilism, a "doctrine according to which the human mind cannot arrive at absolute certainty but only at probable propositions"[15], refers to any probabilistic system, and thus to that "which is relative to probability: which is founded in theory, on the calculation of probabilities". It requires a system of functions based on hypotheses of probabilities, which are the result of past experience (on the basis of statistical evidence and hypotheses of likelihood models).

Although it is possible to deduce the probabilities for a large production number, as is the case in factories, with a sure degree of likelihood, it is, however, completely impossible to do this for functions that are only rarely or partially used, even if these functions are vital. Probability becomes inoperative in this case. It can also lead to catastrophes, conclusions that are dangerous because it is impossible to foresee them.

For a question, the probabilistic hypothesis consists of defining the objective sought, as well as its domain, its field, each of the functions that will be activated in it, and how, precisely, it is associated each time with the levels of probabilities. We take as a hypothesis that under these conditions, everything will change during the entire life of the system under study. This is reassuring because it resembles reality. Since we have no idea of the development of the levels of probability of each of the elements of the system considered, management of the rail infrastructure becomes increasingly risky, perhaps even dangerous over long periods (e.g. decades).

This raises the need to discuss the notion of probabilism and safety in railways.

---

14 The interlockings are the way to physically realize the incompatibilities in position of different controlling bodies or operational states. Therefore, two interlockings are necessary to achieve a binary incompatibility: (A- B-) ⇔ (A active engages B rest) and (B active engages A rest). An "interlocking hole" is a result of the absence or incomplete accomplishment of an interlocking, which leads to non-coverage for a dangerous situation, covered *a priori* by an incompatibility [DES 98].

15 http://www.cnrtl.fr/definition/probabilisme (definition translated).

Probabilism and safety: probabilistic safety arrived late on the scene, nearly 150 years after the railway began, during the 1980s. It involves attributing safety objectives to the system, which are expressed in the number of victims or accidents per year. Probability calculations, which may be of varying rigors in practice, are then used to show that the system design makes it possible to achieve these objectives (which, in fact, lack rigor as far as those from the sector are concerned. Those from within the railways sector will notice that for many elements it is impossible to know the probability for the fault. Therefore, approximations are used as long as practice does not disprove them, and safety is not proved).

The standard NF F 00-101 [NF 93] provides the following definition of probabilistic safety: "A method which consists of showing *a priori* that the probability of appearance of scenarios of a feared event is less than a threshold previously defined".

Besides the fact that one of the basic principles of probabilistic safety means allowing that zero risk does not exist[16], what we then need to do is reduce the probability of occurrence of a risk as a function of its gravity. Thus, we encounter diagrams of this style in publications concerning the safety of systems [LIE 76].

Probabilism and computerized systems: it is commonly held to be true in certain circles that a software package cannot be exhaustively validated and that the application of standards leads to the acceptance of an uncertain residual probability[17] of an unsafe fault. This probability is judged to be easier to achieve than a logical demonstration of the safety would be. Reducing the endemic safety weakness in computerized systems has a basis in the assurance of quality of the design and development methodology (therefore, implementation) for the integration of computerized control-command systems for railway infrastructure as it is being rolled out (with the following software safety paradox: obligation of means for the software, but no obligation regarding result).

---

16 This is true, including for a closed world, with reference to the section above.

17 "It should be recognized that, for software, the delivery of absolute numerical safety targets is generally considered to be impossible, and the methods contained in EN 50128 [CEN 01] produce a probability that certain failure will be archived rather than an absolute safety". Guidance on the application of safety assurance processes in signalling industry – May 2010 – IRSE.

With the integration of these computerized systems by the new standards, the constraints imposed are essentially based only on the hardware architecture (probabilistic approach) and on the quality assurance approach of the software package. It then becomes quite sensitive to quantify (in the form of probabilities) the level of safety of functions carried by an entire software package (a whole part of which, as we have seen, we cannot approach using probabilistic methods, because it is impossible to do so).

We then reach a point where we cannot go further; the occurrence of rail accidents becomes increasingly expensive, for companies and for society, due to the way these accidents are presented on the Internet, and the relationship between this presentation and the constantly high level of demand for safety in Western societies.

Although it may be relatively easy to identify the probability levels for hardware faults, it is impossible to do this for software systems. Many researchers have concluded that dealing with IT safety as soon as design has begun might be more economical in the long term, when compared with money-saving in development, which leads to systems that are less safe and less profitable.

The application of these principles, adapted for use in IT, to the issues surrounding safety of operation, economic and regulatory constraints and the history and experience of each realm of activity forms a "state of the art" which makes it possible to design, manufacture and operate safe systems, i.e. systems that have a risk level which is tolerated by society [BAR 09].

Due to this "state of the art", most of the safe system risks no longer come from random faults, but from "systematic faults" [LEV 00, LEV 01, BIE 03, STA 08]. These affect the entire system. For example, faults from a common cause have an impact simultaneously on all the equipment of a redundant system. Systematic faults in software due to design errors, faults linked by domino effects, faults due to malicious action or natural catastrophes all simultaneously affect initiatory events and gates.

Systemic risk can thus be defined as the potential for systematic faults. Systemic approaches have been and still are put in place to control the complexity, in particular through the creation of global installation models which make it possible to study the significant properties, such as safety or availability.

The representation of purely hardware elements (random faults) is quite well accepted for these FMDS models[18] [VIL 88], which are based on probabilistic approaches. However, their representation of the deterministic aspects of computerized systems (systemic or systematic faults) is less well accepted [LEV 00, LEV 01, BIE 03, GAR 09, BOM 05, LOT 07, LOT 08].

In fact, in programmed equipment, it is impossible in practice to guarantee the absence of specification and design faults, particularly in the software. In very high quality, highly reliable programmed equipment, these residual errors are usually linked to the things we have not thought of yet. Therefore, it is extremely difficult, if not impossible, to determine the nature, the impact and the number of residual errors.

Because numerical techniques have a strongly deterministic and repeatable character (the same behavior will occur each time the equipment is exposed to the same conditions), these residual design errors can leave the equipment vulnerable to a risk of fault through common cause, or in several pieces of equipment sharing the same error and subject to identical conditions, a fault may occur concomitantly [BIE 03, NGU 08].

In contrast to failures due to hardware faults, which appear randomly (outside common mode), we cannot always foresee the damaging effects of residual design errors using redundancy. An "unsafe" error in specification can be "awoken" by a particular combination of inputs, and then irreparably affect outputs, whatever the number of redundant units[19].

10.2.3.4. *Interrelation*

As previously mentioned, all management systems for railway infrastructures are made up of many different elements (which are systems in themselves): mechanical, electrical, electronic, automatic and computerized. From this point of view, we can understand that these systems are a set of elements (of systems) made up of multiple relationships between each other, sometimes in a loop, which form multiple interrelationships to address

---

18 Fiabilité, Disponibilité, Sécurité, Maintenabilité – reliability, availability, security, maintainability.

19 All these chains of events, which are true for both the software and the equipment, were established around 18 years ago by Mr Gérard Collas (ex Bull and ex ImdR – for more information on ImdR, visit http://www.imdr.fr/). Unfortunately, we have been unable to locate the exact reference for this discovery.

multiple management requirements for multiple railway infrastructures, which themselves address multiple passenger requirements, all around the world.

In fact, we can instantly understand that a system may here also be described as "a group of elements that inter-relate to perform a given task"[20]. The path that we must always follow is that of understanding its situation(s), its inclination(s) and its construction principles for safety and its safety. Remember that there is no system for which all elements, interrelations, causes and consequences have been identified. We therefore need to arbitrarily define safe local user conditions for a length of time which is (as) determined (as possible), and as long as possible.

Signaling principles and procedures that were defined over a century ago may still, fortunately, be applied today with new technologies. However, a systemic approach is necessary in order to gain a better understanding. In other words, if we were to take a small area of focus, we could, usefully and pragmatically, put a deterministic approach in place, by zone and level to be treated. This involves defining the objective, the field, the area, the functions that should be filled and the (total) ban on going outside of the area under consideration. This is what makes our general (total) safety hypothesis for the management of railway infrastructures around the world. To get to this point, we need to determine the layers of operation, which cannot be crossed.

10.2.3.5. *System layers*

All systems may be viewed and characterized through an approach in multiple layers, one on another. While some of them intrinsically function in a probabilistic mode (the lower layers), others function according to a purely deterministic model. Those of the second type will be obliged to remain in their area of operation, which will have been predefined. This system, because it is totally identified in its operation, will control and command any electromechanical (electrotechnical) system.

This system will command and manage the entire electrotechnical system which makes up the railway network under consideration. The management of the railway infrastructure is once more under control, and more rapidly so,

---

20 Gestion de risque – concepts – Denis Lebey – QSE CNAM 2008, 10 October 2008, LAAS Toulouse; http://mindmedia.fr/prod_MM/~pagesCNAM/lebey.html.

following the criteria of use developed since the origin of the train, since the end of the 19th Century at the latest.

Mechanical signal boxes already make the distinction between formally provable notions of interlocking program [DES 98] (as a result of incompatibilities) and the means of achieving these interlockings (a tappet carries out the two interlockings which make up the incompatibility). However, a non-indicated use of the transition to computerization leads us to purely functional aspects (during programming of the interlockings in mechanics, cabling and relay box) and technical IT aspects of equipment use (during the tappets in mechanics and the relays in electrical installations) being combined in the same software package. There is then a risk that it might be believed that software safety rules may replace the rules for safety of rail traffic (uniquely through a probabilistic approach, when a great part of this IT system cannot follow the safety rules).

10.2.3.6. *Three levels of critical system*

In order to avoid this confusion, which implicitly leads to a "probabilistic" vision (which is totally impossible, and thus risky) concerning the evaluation of the safety of these railway systems, it would appear to be necessary to make a clear distinction (in a manner which is non-negotiable in terms of duration) between three levels of critical system. This means imagining a safety automaton which can easily dissociate the following three levels:

– at a functional applicative software level defined by the symbolism it uses, its interpretation rules and its writing rules. This level may be understood by experts at the on-the-job level of the field[21], and does not include any modalities which they cannot understand, and does not require any specific IT knowledge. For example, we might be concerned with concurrent constraint automata (an interesting case of interpretable event Petri nets) with rules for creating and interpreting graphs (deterministic operation which fixes in particular the management of events propagated on a group of graphs);

---

21 When it comes to this, France has two points in its favor. First, the training that the technicians receive allows them to easily understand and master certain abstract, quasi-formal languages such as Grafcet. Second, the delegated infrastructure manager controls all of the principles of signaling of the mechanical, electrical or computerized signal boxes. This control allows them to graph all these principles. The same is not the case in Germany, for example.

– a basic software level, the role of which is to manage the equipment level, to interpret the functional software, while respecting interpretation rules, keeping the rules for graph formation in mind. This level is defined without the need to take the functional job-level aspects into account, but by creating a predetermined list of basic functions or of interpretation (or emulation) rules;

– an equipment level which includes input, output and communication aspects. The calculation units may be redundant and linked by an AND voter so that their rate of acceptable unsafe random failure is controlled, in a way that corresponds to the safety objectives.

Together, the equipment and the basic software make up a coherent whole which may be reproduced many times for potentially different applications. Because this list of functions necessary for the emulation of interpretation rules further defined is limited, the volumetry of the basic software is very limited, which makes a very efficient development and test possible. Originating from possible hardware faults, rates of safe and unsafe faults can then be provisionally and experimentally estimated for a significant population (λ_{PD}, λ_{PNS} for the hardware managed by it basic software).

The functional applicative software level translates, in a deterministic and interpretable formal language, the expectations of those within the industry, in a way that can be understood and mastered by them, regarding the system functions.

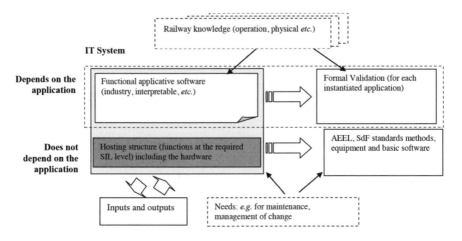

Figure 10.3. *Hardware and software architecture in three levels*

At this level, no probabilistic failure can be envisaged. The translation is either entirely correct with regard to the operation postulates (of the definition of the supersystem in which the system is operating), or it is not correct, and no confidence can be attributed to the system as a whole. The hardware and software architecture is illustrated in Figure 10.3.

In general, this approach makes it possible to return to a "fail-safe" approach[22], which has existed in France since the time of mechanical and electromechanical signal boxes [DES 98, PIC 86]. This approach makes it possible to significantly reduce the complexity of the system and to attribute a share corresponding to abilities to each of the parties involved in the development as follows:

– to the infrastructure management or the railway company, the definition of the system functionalities and interfaces with regard to the pre-existing supersystem in which it has to operate;

– to the manufacturer, the definition of the hosting structure, which includes hardware aspects (e.g. communication, interfaces, ensuring safety) and the basic software necessary for its activity and concerned with the surrounding conditions.

It is then possible to reuse functionalities that have been proved through use alongside the associated regulations, to obtain systems that are easy to adapt and to maintain, and are safe and thus economical. In fact, besides what it can contribute in terms of safety, the use of a formal method in an industrial process for the validation of a critical computerized system also results in a significant reduction in the costs of development, initial validation of software and management of change, and also in a reduction in the time and resources necessary for the implementation of any functional change to the software.

10.2.3.7. *The basic system*

The hosting structure or basic system is an inseparable group of equipment and software which makes it possible to ensure, with the required level of safety, the management of the peripherals (inputs, outputs, communication, ensuring safety, etc.) and also to ensure a deterministic and real-time interpretation of the job functionalities of the system.

---

22 Security logic, or any fault, exterior disruption or incorrect request, leads to placing in safe position (degraded safe mode).

This involves designing a basic system with constant characteristics for all possible application cases (for all stations, etc.) Considering the weak relative complexity of operation around a reduced group of interpretation rules, we may consider that the command automaton (basic software) does not need to be complex, and may be identical whatever the functional software of the system. The basic system determines the type of software interpreter for the functional software (Petri networks, for example), and this should not change during the lifetime of the system[23]. These rules must be recognized by all, and must be binding to all.

SNCF[24] Infra has written all the functional applicative rules with Petri nets (in AEFD language defined by a French/German academic research project [ANT 09]). So it is possible to hypothesize that this group of basic equipment and software behaves according to a reliability law similar to that of electronic equipment.

10.2.3.8. *The deterministic system*

What hypothesis must be related to the design for it to be possible to say that a three-level system functions in deterministic mode, while it is based on a basic system which functions in probabilistic mode?

The hypothesis is that it is possible to build a deterministic system that is operated by a system in probabilistic mode (safe and unsafe failures), but which interacts with the functional level in a field of constraints fixed to the design in such a way that the constraint field limits the functioning domain to a deterministic space (strong rules defining *a priori* the finite verification space).

10.2.3.8.1. Complementarity of the probabilistic and deterministic approaches

Systemic approaches attempt to represent the different mechanisms that might lead to faults or serious accidents in an installation with a global probabilistic model. For this reason, they decide to opt for a macroscopic vision rather than a detailed study of the mechanisms. Traditionally, they only represent the random breakdowns of the equipment. It has, however, proved necessary to take two other types of phenomena into account:

---

23 Less than 30 RdP emulation rules for French signalling boxes.
24 For more information, visit http://www.sncf.com/.

– errors in the human–machine interactions, particularly in the application of regulatory measures ⇨ stochastic faults;

– systematic failures caused by specification, design or other similar faults ⇨ deterministic faults.

Normally, the probabilistic and deterministic approaches are in opposition regarding the evaluation of the level of safety and availability of a computerized system. This is true for all organizations (operators, safety authorities, suppliers, etc.) and in all countries involved with railways and all industries involved with safety.

Complex industrial systems involve both physical functions and computerized functions. It is useful to define a general method, based on our three-level architecture, to evaluate the impact of programmed equipment in the probabilistic safety studies which combine the two approaches.

To answer this question, further barriers must be eliminated. In particular:

– The formal verification of the programmed equipment, in particular the software: "classic" verification methods are generally based on the examination of the development processes, tests, and reviews of design and coding. Formal verification techniques, which are now accessible, make it possible to detect faults in programming or specification. Some methods enable the identification of all the sequences of inputs which lead to a given feared state, which makes it possible to encode the occurrence.

– Improvement of the quality of functional specifications: experts in operational safety of programmed equipment recognize that the weakest point in the development process for programmed equipment at the level of the highest demand is the functional specification. It is thus important to significantly improve this key development phase.

– The quantification of probabilities[25] for "systematic" failure of the redundant programmed architectures: the problem is even more difficult for failure probabilities which are correlated for several pieces of equipment.

– Accounting for the aging of circuits and electronic cards in the models, in particular, due to technological developments in electronics (increasingly developed integration with more detailed geometries).

---

25 Probabilistic aspect defined based on occurrence probabilities for all or a part of external inputs leading to dangerous situations.

– The representation of the impact of the command control and the programmed equipment on the availability, and not just the reliability, of an installation.

These two approaches, probabilistic and deterministic, are complementary. They can feed into each other in the context of a process as follows:

– General system safety study, as well as its usual results, which should:

- identify the critical functions performed by the computerized systems,

- define the operating postulates which relate to these functions,

- define the safety properties that these functions must fulfill (predicates, proof obligations, etc.).

– Study of the safety of the computerized system, which should:

- encode, according to the generally used methods, the level of safe and unsafe failures attributable to equipment that supports the function (as a function of the architecture in particular);

- identify the complete list of ordered sequences of inputs that lead to states considered "unsafe". If there are none, the level of unsafe failure from the software may be considered to be zero;

- ensure that the greatest possible use is made of the conditional occurrence probabilities of the various sequences in order to estimate the level of safe and unsafe breakdowns linked to possible demands on the critical functions.

– Completion of the general study of system safety by integrating the levels of occurrence of safe and unsafe behaviors estimated in this way.

This process may only be considered with a "formal validation of the functional software". Some methods, including the one that we will describe in this Chapter, are able to completely describe all the sequences that lead to feared situations.

In this case also, we should note how important it is to exhaustively define the following notions, on the basis of either expressions of needs at the highest level (functions of interlocking and signaling), or the written specification, believed to be correct, which has been handed over by the project management:

– operating postulates: physical, technical and regulatory;

– expected safety properties for the installation in its context;

– independence conditions between the architecture (hardware and basic software) and the application software (as independent as possible from the architecture).

Figure 10.4 illustrates this issue.

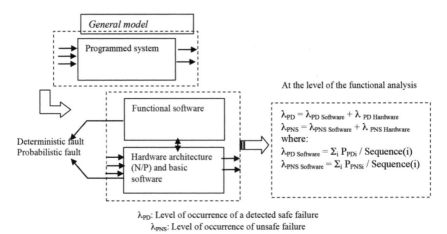

λ_{PD}: Level of occurrence of a detected safe failure
λ_{PNS}: Level of occurrence of unsafe failure

Figure 10.4. *Suggestion of a quantification model for a programmed system*

10.2.3.9. *Continuing control throughout the lifetime of a system*

The distinction between the functional software and the basic structure makes it possible to flexibly manage the difficult questions of equipment obsolescence, functional changes in the system, and questions regarding the verification and validation of the system.

This approach enables us to prove that the functional software for the system cannot lead to a dangerous situation in the application of such a method as it should be applied [ANT 09].

The specification process for a new system or for any desired functional changes may require, over and above the functional written specifications alone, the principle of architecture on three levels so as to ease the subsequent management of the system for its complete lifecycle.

This approach may then be advantageously used by any infrastructure manager. First, it can aid them to specify the "railway-specific" functionalities of the system in development and, second, to have at their disposal the elements necessary to ensure the progressive integration of the global system. The responsibilities and industrial risks for the infrastructure managers and the supplier in charge of development can then be clearly identified.

The applicative functionalities, formally described by the infrastructure manager, are interpreted by the target machine. The manufacturer in charge of the development in this way creates a hosting structure (equipment and basic software) which can interpret, with the required safety level, the functional specifications provided by the infrastructure manager (functional software). The target machine may also be reused in this way, without additional development, for other applications.

The infrastructure manager thus obtains the possibility to ensure that the systems will last for a long time (modifying the functions of the product without requiring the support of the product provider, and ensuring a system integration of the developed product) (see Figure 10.5).

This approach is very useful in the long term for both parties. The product can be redesigned in this way, without the need to re-work its functionalities. The functionalities can be modified, without requiring the redesign and redevelopment of the product/hosting structure.

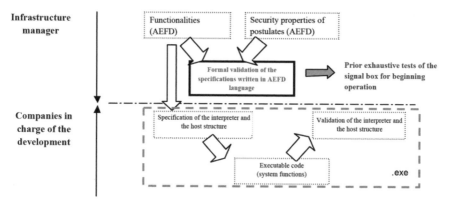

Figure 10.5. *Suggestion of process for programmed development of a long-lasting system*

The unambiguous and comprehensive formalization of the functionalities, possibly formally proved, makes it possible to create the conditions for placing equipment providers in competition with each other in the best possible conditions. This is both in terms of sharing responsibilities and of controlling the economic and safety implications (see Figure 10.6), and is the only way to ensure long life for these systems, which incur significant development costs.

The range of unfortunate experiences since 2000 in the context of the development and the rolling out of the European Rail Traffic Management System, ERTMS[26] (see [ERA 08]), demonstrate that the absence of unambiguous and comprehensive high-level specifications inevitably leads to unsafe situations, and potentially even accidents [LOT 08, OFT 08].

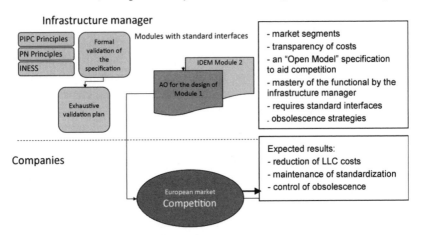

Figure 10.6. *Suggestion of process for programmed development of a long-lasting system.*

10.2.4. *A key element: formal validation*

Our hypothesis is that there is a path which allows us to ensure that the railway system around the world works well, and the proof exists that this is in fact the case (more than 350 installations in operation around the world). To achieve this, we should constrict the description of the functional software to the format of interpretable deterministic graphs. If necessary, we should use simple functions included in the basic software, which may be

---

26 To find out more information on this, visit http://www.ertms.com.

summoned by the actions of a Concurrent Constraint Automaton, and its result, which is translated by the generation of an *ad hoc* event. This approach has been tested by more than 15 years of use, both on the French national network and on railways around the world.

Therefore, a key element in the establishment of new, more efficient strategies is to create the application and industrial implementation conditions for formal validation methods of the functionalities of computerized safety installations. The process required is to define the design and formal validation conditions for the automatisms of the computerized safety installations, in their *ad hoc* railway supersystem, so as to maintain the notion of "fail-safe" installations and the previous levels of safety, and to objectively evaluate the level of safety of a system that combines equipment and a software component. As the problem in question is an industrial problem with safety and economic issues at stake, it is addressed with an attitude that is both pragmatic and theoretical.

The need for pragmatism arises from several issues:

– we need to start out from the context of industrial railways and from real practical problems;

– the suggestions that we make must absolutely reduce the costs of creation and maintenance in operational condition. If not, they will never be applied, whatever the safety benefits they may offer;

– the human factor must be included in our calculations, notably in the definition of safety properties.

10.3. Railway safety: basic concepts

The application of formal methods to signal boxes requires that we render the safety properties and the operation postulates totally explicit. Therefore, it is necessary to take the railway context on board, to observe and formalize the safety and the logical and physical properties of its critical computerized systems.

The demonstration of the safety of such a technical system cannot be undertaken without taking its integration into its environment into account, within the system in which it participates.

10.3.1. *Control of safety properties and postulates*

10.3.1.1. *Signaling*

The notion of safety may have different implications depending on the nature of the activity under consideration. The safety of rail traffic is founded in particular – and principally – on the possibility of bringing it to a halt. When no train is circulating, any danger linked to the traffic in itself is removed. This is where the system of basic equations comes from: stopped train = safety (unavailability) at least initially, and moving train = danger (availability).

The "system" combines technical systems designed in such a way that none of the results of the testing of their operation leads to the occurrence of an event which runs "counter to safety". It is not enough for an installation to place itself in a "secure" state when it breaks down for safety to be ensured. In addition, the operators, under production constraint, must not be pushed to accept an installation which displays faults (frequently). Therefore, this safety model is not based on technique alone. People, in the context of procedures, play a leading role in the railway system [REA 93, REA 95].

Taking into account their technical characteristics and the tools they have at their disposal, we traditionally make a distinction between:

– the safety of the traffic, which concerns interaction of traffic with other traffic or the treatment of unexpected changes in the environment which interfere with traffic. This is based on operators who use their tools and apply procedures;

– technical safety, which aims to allow a train to circulate on an infrastructure, through the conservation of dimensional and functional characteristics. This comes under the responsibility of the maintenance operators for fixed installations and the maintenance operators for the rolling stock. Their interventions with respect to the traffic agents and the drivers take place within the context of procedures.

Any modification of a system component may possibly have a knock-on effect on another component, and thus endanger the balance of the safety of the system itself. Therefore, it is necessary to watch out for this at all phases of the lifecycle of the system. This is illustrated in Figure 10.7. The crosses represent the transitions, the existence of which should be proved. In this case, the computer system functions in the same way as a "fail-safe" system.

It should be noted that the driving agent for a rail journey (or mechanic) should take into account the braking distances which are greater than those allowed by directly looking at the infrastructure[27] and that it is impossible to change route to avoid a collision. The driver thus cannot, under normal operation, drive the train "by view" and does not have control over the direction of the train. As a result, a sedentary operator needs to be put in place, which is in charge of commanding the fixed installations and organizing traffic.

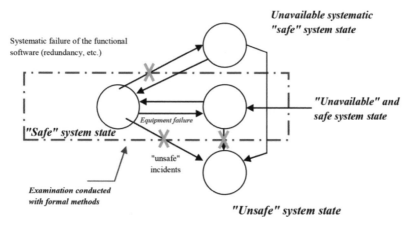

Systematic failure of the functional software (redundancy, etc.)

Unavailable systematic "safe" system state

"Unavailable" and safe system state

Equipment failure

"Safe" system state

"unsafe" incidents

Examination conducted with formal methods

"Unsafe" system state

Figure 10.7. *System states which translate functional and dysfunctional states*

The agent operating the signal boxes needs to respond to the necessity of scheduling traffic. This is because trains can only follow each other between two successive installations, where it would be possible to modify their succession. It is also because it is necessary, usually using technical installations, to warn the driver of an order to stop or slow sufficiently in advance, and also to maintain a clear space ahead of the train of sufficient length so that the transmitted order may be carried out.

The operation of railways on an infrastructure involves, among other things, ensuring the operational management of traffic. The principal components of the railway system which are involved in operation are the

27 Compared to road vehicles, the possible stopping distances are (they are not used in the normal course of events in order to limit effort for the breaking system), respectively, in the order of 1,000 m for freight trains travelling at 100 km/h and 3,500 m for passenger trains travelling at 300 km/h.

infrastructure, the rolling stock and the signaling. The signaling is the set of means and installation which make it possible to plot "safe" itineraries for trains and to send orders to drivers. It allows the train to avoid the set of risks that result from the circulation of trains and crossing routes. It is considered to include the installations which are concerned with the technical safety of traffic, and does not include those that supervise the track, the platform and the building hardware.

The design and maintenance in operational condition of signaling installations do not permit any interlocking hole or uncertainty regarding safety. For these installations, it is thus essential to find a way to provide an absolute guarantee that the implementation is correct.

10.3.1.2. The railway system

There are three components of the railway system: people, procedures and installations. It is not possible to define the safety function without defining the usage and environmental context. The railway system involves ground and onboard operators who work on an infrastructure and on rolling stock, applying a procedure of which the common parts define the interactions between them.

Figure 10.8 shows the secure operation of an installation (its ability to fulfill the various expected functions with the correct level of safety). For each main point, there are degraded modes and it is possible to manually override. The railway system is thus made up of four subsystems which involve four types of actors.

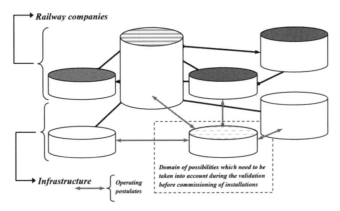

Figure 10.8. *Current global view of the railway system*

Coherent procedures guarantee perfect understanding of the dialogues and coherence of action. They are thus the nexus of the system's safety. They are the product accumulated experience obtained over 150 years of railway operation.

10.3.1.2.1. People

People are a central feature of the safety system and the reliability of the system rests as much on human reliability as on technical reliability. Only people, operating within the regulatory procedures suited to the tools, are able to cope with all the situations for their use, and this is particularly the case if there is some disruption.

The conditions for the application of procedures by operators [BEL 08] are thus an integral part of the operating postulates that should be taken into account in any validation of a safety system such as a signal box.

If blocking or safe breakdown of the installations occurs, this leads to a reduction in the global level of safety. It is essential to detect any possible excesses that might paradoxically reduce the global safety level of an "Operator–Procedures–Installation" group [HOL 07].

10.3.1.2.2. Procedures

The procedures are designed to ensure coherence of the actions of the different actors involved, among themselves and with the operation of the installations and the equipment. Railway procedures are implemented by operators who are generally on their own.

They thus attempt to codify the required behavior in all situations, with all types of rolling stocks and on all infrastructures. On computerized systems, which are highly automated, the procedure is reduced to cases where the installations are disturbed, and its application is rare and must be approached sensitively. It should be noted that it is essential to allow at least a minimum amount of traffic to circulate with degraded performances, and, at the very least, to evacuate trapped trains. The application of procedures by operators, particularly based on safety checks provided by tools, is one of the postulates that needs to be taken into account for the validation of a safety system.

10.3.1.2.3. Installations

The installations comprise onboard safety equipment and track-side safety installations. They make it possible for operators to ensure that the actions they perform are safe, and to improve their performance. They use very reliable, very safe components. The current trend is to transform the installations into automatisms, which progressively replace people and human error in performing safety tasks.

The risks covered by signaling fall under three fundamental rules:

– a one-dimensional system ⇨ two trains cannot be at the same place at the same time;

– limited adherence and friction ⇨ a train must have an available free distance that is at least equal to its braking distance;

– geometry in one dimension only ⇨ a train cannot proceed unless it is assured of the non-deformability of the route and the non-presence of another train.

Seven types of dangerous events result from the application of these rules. A set of safety properties corresponds to each risk. These should always be respected by one or the other of the railway system components, in particular the track-side safety installations (signaling and signal box) and the rolling stock.

A signal box is an infrastructure element which commands the various types of track equipment and the protection signals. Its role is to manage rail traffic inside a geographically demarcated track space. Management of traffic involves, among other tasks, shaping the itineraries that the trains must take and giving movement instructions to each train in the station, which take the itineraries shaped for other trains and their current positions into account. Operation always takes place in successive phases which take the successive positions of the track equipment into account, as well as the zones which correspond to the regulation areas. Table 10.1 formalizes the functional states linked to the implementation of an itinerary.

The creation of an itinerary is the necessary conclusion of the creation and the completion of successive phases: the command giving the itinerary, its recording, its preparation through commanding the required resources, its shaping through immobilizing the resources positioned using the transit interlocking, the controlling of track-side resources for the itinerary and the command at the opening of the protection signal. Signaling functions are activated in successive layers. These take the successive positions of command instances of the considered resources, the positioning and the occupation of these resources by a train.

The correct application of these different operational phases, in line with the regulation in vigor for the management of potential degraded modes by operators, is one of the safety properties that should be verified when a safety system is being validated.

For more detailed information on the internal functioning of signal boxes, articles on the subject of railways may be consulted [RET 87, ANT 09].

Phase	Action	PRS Translation	Result
Command	Pushing the command button	Lifts the route command relay (CIt), makes the command button flash	Closes the relay circuits commanding the switches (CAg)
Preparation	Puts the route switches into position, along with the protecting switches, if they are not controlled by another route (untaken transit) or occupied by traffic	Switch command relays (CAg) move if the transit relays involved in the route are high and the track circuit relays are free	The placing into position of all the switch command relays (CAg) involved in the route makes it possible for the interlocking relay for the route to move into open position for the relevant entry signal (EIt)
Shaping and interlocking	Ensures the immobilization of the route – prevents the formation of incompatible itineraries	Cuts power to the transit relays that ensure interlocking for the transit, makes the route repeater relay (RIt) rise, which ensures constant monitoring of the position of the CAg and EIt	Makes the command button light constantly, shuts the control circuits for the itineraries
Monitoring (establishment)	Ensures that the route has been effectively created and opens the entry signal	Imperative control of the switches is ensured after they have been effectively placed in position by the KAg relays – this makes it possible to raise the route control relay of the Kit C1 entry signal	Opening of the entry signal Extinction of the control light for the closing of the entry signal

Table 10.1. *Functional states for the setting of a route*

10.3.2. *Aspects that should be considered for carrying out a formal validation*

10.3.2.1. *Independences and weak independences*

The operation of a route signal box in France, whatever technology it uses, is based on the same operation phases, which are:

– command: memorization of the operator request to plot a route;

– preparation: requisitioning the positioning resources to ensure the task can be carried out and the memorized route is protected;

– shaping: immobilization (interlocking) of the resources that need to be reserved to ensure that the memorized route can be created and protected;

– checking: constant verification of the establishment conditions (control of the switches, control of the protections, control of individual properties such as level crossings, etc.).

We can use these independences or quasi-independences to carry out several independent proofs (for example, by route) and to reduce their combinatory burden. It should be noted that these properties are currently in use for carrying out tests on electromechanical and electric signal boxes.

This possibility for "segmenting" the functional application software is based on an *a priori* knowledge of the job-level functional software and makes it possible to carry out several complementary proofs. This knowledge is only accessible in manual design which respects the establishment principles for signaling functions. This excludes languages written automatically in code.

10.3.2.2. *Operation postulates*

Before proceeding to a formal validation, it is essential to formalize all the conditions that define the domain of safe operation, and the interfaces of the system with the supersystem in which it operates.

Among other things, these conditions allow us to limit the domain of possibilities for system inputs: the regulation limits the possibilities at the disposal of operators and those who maintain the system [RET 87]. Exterior installations themselves limit the development possibilities for inputs, the modes of safe failures for exterior equipment, etc.

Whatever mode of validation an installation uses, the domain of possibilities for system inputs must be defined. We will see that this is also necessary in order to fix the limits for automatic exploration of attainable system states.

The operation postulates are of various types. We should mention, in particular:

– the respect of procedures by the various operators involved in or using the system that needs to be validated;

– that due consideration has been given to the limitations of inputs resulting from the existence of cabled interlocking functions exterior to the system that needs to be validated.

These postulates convey:

– the organizational, procedural and regulatory conditions for the operation of a signal box;

– the conditions for interactions of rail traffic with signal boxes (particularly at the level of the captors and the resources occupied);

– the interaction conditions for exterior installations, resources occupied and/or surrounding signal boxes, with the signal box.

These postulates may vary from one supersystem to another, from one country to another, from one type of traffic to another and from one setting to another. These operation postulates must be generically defined for a given route. These rules will then be used to delimit the space of possibilities for inputs, which will limit that of the attainable system states in the functional software of the signal box. The operation postulates are based on the formal and on-the-job training of agents.

These postulates formalize workplace know-how, which is, to a very large extent, distinct from the computerized nature of the installations. These postulates are largely unknown to the manufacturers creating modern signal boxes.

10.3.2.3. *Safety properties and incompatibilities*

As we have seen in the preceding sections, incompatibilities for ensuring safety of operation are created using two corresponding "interlockings":

– the incompatibilities are the expression of the exclusions of states of resources, physical or otherwise, which are managed by the safety installations;

– binary incompatibilities are created by means of two interlockings. Ternary conditional interlockings are carried out by means of nine interlockings.

In general, whatever the technology in use, an incompatibility is created by carrying out the set of corresponding interlockings. By reference to the signaling principles presented in the preceding sections, the safety properties may be directly deduced from the incompatibility or interlocking functions required by the track plan.

In particular, the functions identified above are relevant: interlocking for route shaping, interlocking for the control of the correct positioning of the resources necessary for a route, approach interlocking, transit interlocking, interlocking for the immobilization of the switches or other resources, direction interlocking, or for a single track or a clash, etc.

It is much easier to translate these than it is the operation postulates, particularly because of the rigorous formalization (and conservation), in spite of the changes that have been made to signaling principles at SNCF Infra over a number of years. It should be noted that the increase in the share of system development which is entrusted to manufacturers and the high level of renewal of study agents leads to the rethinking of the principles behind certain technology.

So, while in the past there was a principle which involved defining the "interlocking principles" independently of the technology selected to carry it out, we are obliged to notice that this principle is gradually disappearing in practice. Eventually, abandoning this situation leads to potentially dangerous situations.

10.3.2.4. *Non-overload properties*

The incompatibilities which ensure safety should not get in the way of the required functionalities. The existence of parasite or superfluous interlockings may be a source of lapses in safety. This is through the potentially risky application of the regulatory manual procedures by the operators, and also because the non-conformity of the installation may disguise unsafe faults which have not yet appeared (access to unforeseen system states).

Reduction in the operational availability of a signal box has a certain impact on its overall safety level. Therefore, any unjustified reduction of the possibilities of the box in terms of safety must be detected and remedied. What is required is that operators should be given an installation which is as available and as flexible as possible, so as to reduce the occurrence of situations that require the application of regulatory procedures.

It is necessary to find those abnormally restrictive situations which could indirectly lead to a lack of safety, whether through an application of the regulations or through potentially disguising other faults. We should note that a signal which always remains in the closed position will always respect the properties of simultaneous non-opening with another signal. However, this does not guarantee safe and operational functioning of the signal box.

10.3.2.5. *Summary*

In order to carry out an operational proof of a railway functional software package, it is necessary to consider the total supersystem that surrounds it, and all the interfaces between it and the supersystem. In fact, we should bear in mind that we may gain a false impression if we apply a formal method without formalizing:

– the rules for physical considerations, both explicit and implicit, and for the technical, functional, human and regulatory considerations. The agents involved in manufacturing are largely unaware of these rules;

– the functional software of an existing system without knowing its existing independences and dependences;

– the rules, dependences, physical considerations, system considerations, human considerations, etc., may be interpreted using postulates, functional properties and safety properties.

A given system, whether computerized or not, may only be considered "safe" or "unsafe" as a function of the supersystem within which it operates. This includes the context, the modes of operation, the possible faults, etc. Safety is not within the system alone but also in its compatibility with the supersystem in which it is placed, or, in other words, in the working context. Therefore, before validating any computer system for railway, the job-level functionality must be taken into account, with all its general features and complexity.

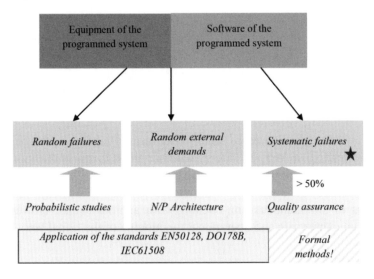

Figure 10.9. *Common points with standards*

The application of formal methods leads to a prior reflection which is significantly different from that mentioned by the standards which are concerned with the operating safety of the software package. Therefore, in the first case, particular attention should be given to the writing of safety properties and the postulates that define the domain within which they are valid. In the second case, identification of the dangerous situations which should be treated is required [MON 96].

In any case, the standards still only touch upon the aspects of development of the basic software and the software that handles the non-correction and the completeness of the application functionality. To this end, only organization recommendations and quality assurance procedures for the software are mandatory for covering any possible gaps in specifications, formalization of functional applicative software.

A distinction should be made between two major groups of formal methods: those known as formal design and those known as formal validation. In the industrial context, the formal validation is more in demand and more effective, particularly when an interpretation of the formal language itself is possible. Whatever formal methods used, the main issue remains the clear description by workplace experts of the proof obligations (safety properties and postulates).

10.4. Formal validation method for critical computerized systems

10.4.1. *The interlocking module for modern signal boxes*

10.4.1.1. *Design principles for the interlocking module*[28]

The interlocking modules (MEI)[29] of the modern computerized signal boxes (PAI) designed by SNCF Infra follow the principles of separation given in section 10.2. The exhaustive description of the critical functionalities of the installation is created using Concurrent Constraint Automata (ACC). The mathematical properties of these no longer need to be shown.

The computerized interlocking module (MEI) physically carries out the treatments so as to interpret the functional software in real time, while guaranteeing at all times that the operation postulates of the ACC are fulfilled, and thus that all the properties which characterize it are also fulfilled. To that end, it is necessary to define:

– a description language for the functional software which is accessible to operators and agents studying signaling (the language AEFD for "Automaton with Deterministic Fixed States" which is described above);

– a rule for the interpretation of graphs by the host structure (equipment architecture and basic software);

– a rule for the writing and composition of signaling graphs.

All of the signaling principles, all of the functions that address an operational need and make it possible to operate while ensuring the safety of the traffic, have been written in the form of ACC written in AEFD language.

---

28 By "interlockings", we understand the physical means necessary to carry out one or several incompatibilities between resources positions managed by a signal box, for example. These means guarantee that the resources can never take on combinations for functional states which are forbidden by incompatibilies imposed by the railroad operators and the track plan.

29 To find out more about the architecture of computerized signal boxes, we recommend Chapters 4 and 5 of [BOU 09].

Readers who would like to have more detailed information on how installations of the PIPC type work may consult [BOU 09, Chapter 4].

The computerized interlocking module ensures that these functions can be carried out. It employs the signaling principles necessary to carry out the commands of the control command level and sends the information necessary for the coordination of the human–machine interface intended for the operator.

The architecture of the PIPC signal box has thus been intentionally designed in three layers:

– equipment which is not specific to the railway milieu: these are PC to industrial standards which conform to the standards CEI 1004.4 (2oo2 architecture for safety, doubled for availability);

– a basic software package, independent of the equipment and the functional software. This manages the computerized resources (inputs, outputs, messages, memories, communication, temporizations, archiving, etc.) and interprets the application functional software using the imposed rules. This basic software is a hosting structure (software common to all the possible functional software applications). In particular, it includes the execution engine for running functional specifications modeled in graphs written in AEFD language;

– application software for the definition of the interlockings (graphs) and the interfaces with the control-command post. This functional software is based on generic asynchronous state graphs, which are configured for each site.

In the following, the term "interpreter" will be used to designate the second-level software package that interprets the functional graphs. The interlocking module is a deterministic machine which makes it possible to:

– carry out signaling functions with a very high safety level (SIL4)[30];

– make a clear distinction between probabilistic and deterministic risks. This makes it possible to find simple and suitable solutions for our

---

30 The reference body CENELEC [CEN 01, CEN 00, CEN 03] introduces the notion of SIL for Safety Integrity Level, which can have four possible values, from 1 to 4. To find out more about the management of the SIL, we recommend Chapter 7 of [BOU 11].

requirements regarding maintaining the system in operational condition over long time frames.

A workshop for making functional graphs makes it possible to generate all of the graphs useful for the signal boxes, rapidly, and with a high level of confidence.

Beyond these general aspects, it is useful to note that the distinction between the functional applicative software and the basic software makes it possible to prove the functional software (the functionalities to be carried out by the module), independently of the basic software. The basic software can be developed with or without the use of formal methods. It can be re-used for a target machine with different applicative software.

The complexity of the proof which must be provided is then largely reduced, and can be applied industrially.

10.4.1.2. *Consequences for the proof*

The interlocking module (MEI) is strictly deterministic and includes properties for applying the suggested method. In this way, it:

– maintains the chronology of all external events, whatever the gap between these events. All these events will then be taken into account in the order in which they appear;

– handles a single external event at a time. When an external event is taken into account, this event is "propagated" for all of the graphs which make up the application functional software. Once the internal propagation is finished, the next external event is then taken into account;

– interprets the graphs as they are, without any rewriting or algorithmic programming;

– involves fixed interpretation rules. Transition equations, with their grammar and vocabulary, are read in a defined order;

– behaves like an abstract machine with zero commutation time (instantaneous transitions).

Figure 10.10 clarifies what is specific to the interpretation of graphs which create the functional software of the module.

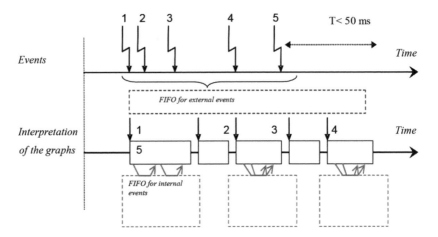

Figure 10.10. *Managing the inputs – operation of an automaton with zero transition time*

The use of interpreted graphs makes it possible to avoid resorting to algorithmic writing. This option allows us to obtain an easily accessible way of writing and reading workplace functionalities, and to combine formal descriptive language and the language that is interpreted by the target machine. The functional specifications of signal boxes are solely based on graphs that interpret ACC describing the necessary sequential processes and combinations.

10.4.2. *AEFD specification language*

10.4.2.1. *An interpretable specification language*

The functional application software of the signal box is described in the form of a network of concurrent constraint automata. These graphs describe the operation of signal interlocking. Each graph can only be found in a finite number of states, and can only be in a single state at a given time. Each state of a graph is shown by *one single* space.

The states within a graph are linked by transitions. A transition is made up of an event field, a condition field and an action field. The elements defined in the transitions are known as functional entities and they serve to identify physical elements outside the system and variables inside the system.

Each functional entity is a *Boolean* variable, and its type is determined by an identifying prefix, as shown in Table 10.2.

Prefix	Type of functional entity
CTL	On-the-ground entry check (reading the state of a relay or switch)
CMD	On-the-ground exit command (relay command)
ACT	Automaton activator (used to synchronize automata)
IND	Indicators (internal variable)
MSG	Message (command sent by an operator)
FCI	Computerized command function (call for this function)
DTP/ATP	Beginning of temporization / halting of temporization
FTP	End of temporization

Table 10.2. *Type of logical variable that can be managed by the graph interpreter*

At a given space, an indicator always takes the same value. An indicator of the functional software may be changed by a single automaton, but all the automata may access its value or take it into account in a transition (i.e. as an event or condition). Table 10.3 recapitulates the usage possibilities.

Prefix	Event	Condition	Action
CTL	X (if change of state)	X	
CMD			X
ACT	X		X
IND	X (if change of state)	X	X
MSG	X		
FCI			X
DTP			X
ATP			X
FTP	X		

Table 10.3. *The use of logical variables managed by the graph interpreter*

The functionalities (signaling principles) of a signal box are a set of graphs which communicate with each other. They interact with their environment. The change in state of a graph is always linked to a single external change.

The description language for the functional software is a language specific to concurrent constraint automata, which is compatible with the creation of a deterministic industrial automaton with FIFO stacks. It is also compatible with carrying out mathematical proofs on the definite automata for the description of the functional software in the form of multiple communicating graphs.

Concretely, it contributes the following properties to systems composed in this way:

– The interpretation of events by the network is deterministic, whatever the order of interpretation of the graphs. The constraints of this are that only one event may be handled at a time, external events occurring simultaneously are treated in a decidable way and the graphs are not temporized.

– The automaton thus defined must behave like an automaton with a finite number of states.

– It must be possible to interpret the automaton thus defined in real time using the hosting software of a target machine.

We have called our language of description AEFD. With this language, it is thus never necessary to use "priorities" or "temporizations" between transitions. It is different from the more traditional ways of writing in that:

– it includes the writing of the graphs in the form of a text file known as "6 lines";

– it includes the notion of Indicator which refreshes after the changes in highlighting have run out;

– time does not feature as such in the graphs, only an event called "end of temporization" is used;

– it introduces the notions of external and internal events to ensure an interpretation "with zero commutation time".

It should be noted that certain design rules should be followed during the writing of the application functionality (application software). These guarantee a correct interpretation of the graphs, which enables the removal of any possibility for indecision in the interpretation of the graphs and the management of communication.

10.4.2.2. *Graph and transitions*

Generally, a graph comprises:

– spaces;

– transitions which link spaces;

– conditions for crossing the transitions;

– actions associated with these transitions;

– a marking. A "token" occupies the state in which the graph is found. We will turn our attention solely to graphs with unique marking in what follows.

These graphs formalize signaling functions in a text file format. The description of the functioning of the application software may always be expressed in the form of graphs, independently of the technical solution used to arrive at it.

The graphs work in the following way:

– a graph may be in a certain number of states, which are represented by spaces;

– when a graph is in a particular state, the space that represents the state is marked. At each moment, only one space in a graph can be marked;

– the transitions link the spaces on the graph. They make it possible to move the token from one location to another and thus for the marking to develop. The crossing of a transition is associated with the appearance of an event and with the respect of conditions. For it to be possible for a transition to be crossed, the space preceding the transitions needs to be marked and the conditions associated with crossing must be verified. When the marking crosses a transition, the actions associated with the transition are accomplished.

In order for it to be possible to interpret them in real time with a target machine, the graphs are grouped together in a single text file. This file thus describes the entire application automaton. The graphs are described in it in an order, which does not have an effect on the determinism of their interpretation.

Each graph is made up of a finite number of transitions between its spaces. Each transition is described by six lines, which have the following meanings:

– name of the graph;

– starting space for the transition;

– ending space for the transition;

– text line translating a Boolean expression, which concludes with "Event";

– text line translating a Boolean expression, which concludes with "Condition";

– text line representing an order list of actions to perform, separated by semicolons and which concludes with "Action".

Let us consider the theoretical example of Figure 10.11.

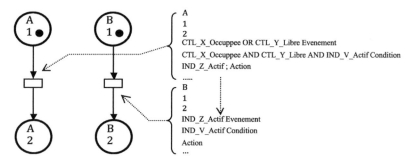

Figure 10.11. *Transitions and writing in six lines – the case of an event which activates two graphs*

Therefore, knowing that the initial state vector of the global automaton at the i-1st injection of an exterior event:

VE[(*i*-1)th injection] = [*A*=1 ;*B*=1 ;*IND_Z_Actif*=0 ;*IND_V_Actif*=1 ;...]

If the occurrence of an external event in a context satisfies the conditions of the receiving transition:

T⟨*CTL_X_Occupé*   OU   *CTL_Y_Libre*=1| *CTL*   *X_Occupee*   ET *CTL_Y_Libre* ET *IND_V_Actif*⟩

will lead the global automaton in the state which corresponds to the following state vector:

$$VE[(i)\text{th injection}] = [A=2 ; B=2 ; IND\_Z\_Actif=1 ; IND\_V\_Actif=0 ;...]$$

So, if the treatment is external (CTL_X_Occupee corresponding to the ith injection, for example) *in interruptible* until the final state is reached, we obtain the operation of a concurrent automaton. Constraint automata describe "automata with a finite number of states".

Constraint automata (ACC) [NAR 01] are automata where we can associate for each transition a generic expression of the type:

$$VE[(i)\text{th injection}] \leftarrow VE[(i\text{-}1)\text{th injection}] \neg T\langle\text{event}\,|\,\text{condition}\rangle$$

The expression can be read and understood in three ways:

– knowing the state of the automaton after the ith external event treated and the nature of the valid transition to be treated $\Rightarrow$ the state of the automaton at the $(i\text{-}1)$th treated external event is defined logically;

– knowing the state of the automaton after the $(i\text{-}1)$th external event treated and the valid transition to be treated $\Rightarrow$ the state of the automaton at the ith treated external event is defined logically;

– knowing the state of the automaton after the ith treated external event and that of the preceding event (at the $(i\text{-}1)$th treated external event) $\Rightarrow$ the transition conditions are defined logically.

We obtain equivalent interpretation on the mathematical, immediate internal transition, and physical planes, bearing in mind that the external events are treated interruptibly.

10.4.2.2.1. Indicators

Particular attention should be given to the notion of indicators (IND). These allow us to make a distinction between the development of markings during the treatment of an event and the state which the automaton was in at the moment when the event being treated occurred. They are fundamentally different compared with classical Petri networks and the interpreters available on the market. In particular, the indicators make it possible to do without any definition of the evaluation priorities of the transitions, and not to be sensitive to the order of development of the automaton graphs. These points are necessary in order to make the running of the automaton deterministic.

Their use must follow certain writing rules for functional graphs:

– an indicator is only updated by a single graph;

– an indicator state is fixed for a group of graph spaces, the complementary state is imposed for the other graph spaces;

– an indicator may be operated as an event as well as a condition in all the transitions of other graphs of the automaton.

10.4.2.2.2. Temporization

In order to conserve the ACC properties, which are required to run a proof, we need to externalize the function of measuring time outside of the graphs. To do this, the DTP, ATP and FTP prefixes are used. From a functional point of view, four cases should be considered for each temporization. They each correspond to a stable state:

– the temporization is not armed. No event occurs;

– the temporization is armed by a functional graph automaton. A "DTP"-type action is performed. Temporization is in progress. Whatever the current value of the temporization, what is involved is a state in which the temporization has been armed but has not yet arrived at term. For example, for a 3 min temporization, whether 1 or 2 min have passed, only the current state of the temporization (temporization in progress) is of significance. The precise value of the temporization does not have functional significance;

– the temporization in progress has failed. The "FTP"-type event is generated by the basic software and is injected into the functional graphs;

– the temporization in progress is stopped by a functional graph automaton (whatever the value of the temporization). The "ATP"-type action has been carried out. The basic software deletes the associated temporization.

Let us consider the theoretical example of Figure 10.12.

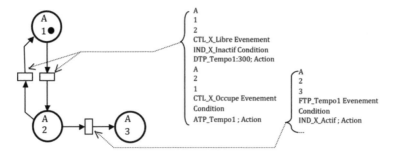

Figure 10.12. *Transitions and writing in six lines – the case of an event which activates two graphs*

In this way, for the generation of accessible states, no particular treatment is necessary for the management of temporizations:

– actions of the "ATP" and "DTP" type should be treated like command-type "CMD" actions. It all happens as if we were concerned here with the command of a timer, except it is the basic software that takes on the action, rather than external equipment;

– management of time (physical clock) is external to the graphs;

– "FTP"-type events should be treated like external "CTL"-type events;

– the graphs which we have retained for consideration are not temporized state graphs. This way of managing time makes it possible to conserve a finite state automaton.

10.4.2.3. *Rules of writing*

In order to simplify the writing of marking graphs, the practical interpretation of the graphs has only one token available to it:

– the marking of the graph is thus the number of the space occupied. The marking of the spaces is never used as an event or a transition condition;

– the transitions starting from the same space must always be exclusive, either by means of the events or by means of the execution conditions for the transition;

– to each ground-level input at a given moment there corresponds one single eligible transition.

These rules result in a deterministic interpretation of the graphs.

10.4.2.4. *Accessible states and combinatorics*

Writing the functional software of an application using this language makes it possible to exhaustively explore all the accessible states of the automaton starting from its initial state. To this end, we define the following state vector for the automaton:

VS [marking of the graphs; States of the Indicators; States of the inputs]

Thus, starting from the state vector VS_0, it is possible to generate all the system states that can follow it according to the pivot method. It should be noted that if the crossing of a transition has an internal action (i.e. a communication between two automata situated in the same machine) as its associated action, the transition is immediately treated.

The system is thus immediately in the state which results from this activation. Thus, we do not take the intermediary state into account, where this activation is to be treated: if a message is treated from the state vector VS_α and the system moves into the state vector VS_β, with an internal activation, to be sent, then the activation is treated instantly, and the system is then in a state vector VS_γ. The system passes directly from the state vector VS_α to the state vector VS_γ.

The number of accessible states of the system is directly associated with the number of events still occurring and the receptivity of the transitions. The problem of combinatory explosion is due to external events, and their combinations which do not have functional meaning. It is interesting to note the power of this method in terms of reduction of the combinatory effect during the generation of the list of states accessible to the system. The theoretical number of accessible states is far greater than the number of accessible states reached by this method and the hypotheses retained.

The proof applies to a group of automata describing a functional process. This is the notion that defines the segmentation of automata from the application on which the formal proof will be run. If it is possible to identify several independent functional processes (even if they both contribute to a product or sum function), then it is also possible to run as many formal proofs of independent specifications (reduction of the combinatory effect).

10.4.3. *Method for proof by assertions*

10.4.3.1. *Principle*

The application of a proof method by assertions is based on the following principles:

– The functional software of the automaton to be validated needs to be a finite state automaton, which can be described in the form of concurrent constraint automata. The current state vector is written as VS_F. The initial state vector $VS_F[0]$ is known and unique.

– The safety properties and the operation postulates, which may exist there, must be written in the same form: i.e. finite state automata. Non-respect of a property leads to reaching a particular well state. The current state vector is written as VS_P. The initial state vector $VS_P[0]$ is known and unique.

– The state vector of the automaton to be considered is the concatenation of the two preceding state vectors. The current state vector of the automaton is then written as $VS = [VS_F; VS_P]$.

– The exploration of accessible states of the automaton is carried out on the complete state vector VS.

– During this exploration, none of the well states should ever be reached.

Thus, using the fact that with concurrent constraint automata we can associate a generic expression with each exterior event which leads to a transition of at least one graph and through this an automaton transition, the generic expression is of the following type:

$$VS[(i)^{th} \text{ injection}] \leftarrow VS[(i\text{-}1)^{th} \text{ injection}] \neg T\langle event \,|\, condition\rangle$$

This produces:

– the initial state of the automaton: $VS[0] = [\, VS_F[0] \,;\, VS_P[0]\,]$

– the accessible states from the first rank obtained by considering all the injectable events starting from the state vector $VS[0]$:

$$VS[1] \leftarrow VS[0] \neg T\langle event \,|\, condition\rangle$$

– and then the accessible states from the second rank obtained by considering all the injectable events starting from the state vector $VS[1]$:

$$VS[2] \leftarrow VS[1] \neg T\langle event \,|\, condition\rangle$$

And so on by recurrence until the state vector previously reached is found again.

Using the fact that knowing the state of the automaton after the (i-1)th external event and the valid transition to be handled implies knowledge of the unique state of the automaton at the ith external event handled, it is thus possible to logically identify all the accessible states and to write:

$\text{Post}^*(\mathbf{VS}[0])$

Conducting a formal proof of this type of automata means verifying a list of logical properties for each state attained, and thus answering the question: Is the design in line with the specifications? The proof is based on the detection of the well state, the use of mutual exclusions and of invariance properties.

It is based on an analysis of the accessible system states and can be summarized by the expression:

$\text{Post}^*(\text{VS}[0]) \cap \{\mathbf{VS}[i]\ \text{unsafe}\} = \varnothing$

where $\{\text{VS}[i]\ \text{unsafe}\}$ is the set of state vectors where at least one of the state vectors VS_P from the graphs representing the safety properties has reached a well state.

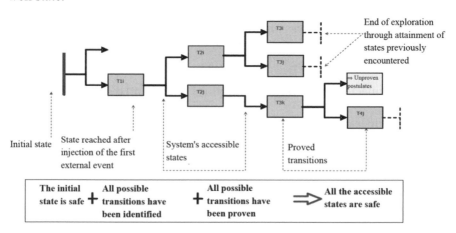

Figure 10.13. *Exploration and formal proof of the safety properties formalized in the form of an AP (automate de preuve – proof automaton) as the accessible states of the functional automaton are being explored*

This expression represents the fact that the intersection between the set of the accessible state of the system and the set of feared events (unsafe) is an empty set. Thus, the proof that the system cannot attain one of the non-safe states is assured. The proof is rejected if this is not the case.

The principle of the method is thus simple. The basic idea is: "if a property is true in an occupied (marked) state and if keeping this property during the transition following this state is guaranteed, the property will be true in the new state occupied. The demonstration may be continued for as long as the property is maintained" (see Figure 10.13).

This principle is used for safety and functional properties. Much work has been carried out on automata with a finite number of states. Our method, which we consider particularly suitable because it is simple and possible to automatize, has been inspired by the one suggested by Bielinski [BIE 93] in the context of work on the validation of integrated encoding and decoding circuits for cyclic redundancy check (CRC) code.

The functional application software of the signal box to be proved (or if not, the automatism) is specified and created in the form of a finite state automaton, where:

– E1 an input vector;

– S1 a vector of outputs without error;

– S2 a vector of outputs with error;

– P3 a state vector of the prover (with existence of a well state, for example).

Proving an automaton means showing that if there is a treatment error, then the expression [E.6.1] is true.

(E.6.1)

The method used is based on that of invariants, transposing it to the case of automata:

– an invariant is attached to each state of the automaton (or at least to each state of a functionality to be proved);

– the invariants are directly inspired by the writing of the incompatibilities between graph positions of the signal box, or more exactly, the corresponding interlockings. The system's (functional automaton) accessible states are identified by a well-known state exploration method.

Demonstration is based on an analysis of accessibility of the system states (global automaton). If the proof method is particularly simple, this is because the difficulties have been transferred to other aspects that are easier to manage, which are:

– the creation of a target machine which has the properties that are required in order to make it possible to refer to it as a constraint automaton;

– the writing of the safety properties and the operation postulates, taking into account the supersystem in which the final automaton will be operating;

– the automation of the process using tools that can be handled by operators or study agents of the job of signaling.

10.4.3.2. *Automation of the proof*

10.4.3.2.1. Principle for the automation of the proof

The method can thus be applied to railway interlocking functions specified in the form of interpretable graphs by modern signal boxes. However, its application may not be automatized: the writing of safety properties and postulates necessary to the proof is manual.

Therefore, we need to innovate in order to automatize the properties and the postulates, on the one hand, and the application of the method, on the other hand. What is of concern here is verifying that an automaton (set of graphs) constantly verifies one or several properties: these properties are described by specific graphs known as "proof automata".

In order to prove an automaton, we need to be able to:

– emulate its operation: functional automaton and proof automaton;

– describe the operation of its environment (postulate automaton);

– explore all its accessible states;

– verify that all the properties are respected in each of the explored states.

We end up with the diagram of Figure 10.14.

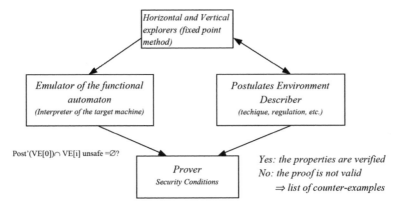

Figure 10.14. *Principle of automation and the proof method*

10.4.3.2.2. Method stages

What is required here is the establishment of a proof that feared events (associated with risks) have not occurred, starting from the specification of an automaton, which is at once the representation (modeling) of the installation and the executed application on the target machine. The demonstration is based on the study of automata transitions, and can be divided into several phases:

– Listing all of the possible states and transitions starting from the initial state: it should be noted that the enumeration of the possible system states is not a simulation of the overall system. In fact, we are here operating from the point of view of the automatism, and not of an observer. This listing is constructed starting from the initial state (state of the signal box at commissioning), making a ramification on the accessible states. This method of fixed point also yields all the possible transitions from each state (arborescence);

– Putting in place safety properties and postulates that show that if in a state a property is verified, then, after the possible transition is crossed, this property remains verified. For each transition, a postulate established using hypotheses on the operation of the ground level is required;

– A recurrence in time: the demonstration uses a recurrence in time – in the initial state S0, the properties are verified: the safety properties and postulates have demonstrated that if the properties are verified before a possible transition, the properties remain verified after it. Therefore, whatever the sequence of transitions (thus, the time), it does not lead to a forbidden state, and the safety properties are verified;

– We have sought a solution which would make it possible to demonstrate the lemmas automatically, easily and rapidly.

10.4.3.2.3. Proof automata

The safety properties to be proved need to be defined by the operators Never or Always applied to the components of the current state vector of the automaton. When a property is valid, whatever the current state of the automaton (system state of the installation), it can be the subject of a proof automaton (AP) with two spaces. When a feared (forbidden) situation occurs, the automaton must take a particular space and the indicator P_5 (Contrary to Safety, wrong side failure) is positioned at True.

When a property only needs to be valid when the current state of the automaton belongs to a subgroup of accessible states for the automaton (system states of the signal box), it can be the subject of a proof automaton (AP) with more than two spaces. When the current state of the system belongs to a target subgroup, the AP takes a particular space, activating the transition which represents the property that needs to be verified. At this moment, when the feared (forbidden) situation has occurred, the proof automaton must take a specific space (AP[9] and the indicator P_5 (contrary to safety, wrong side failure) is positioned at True.

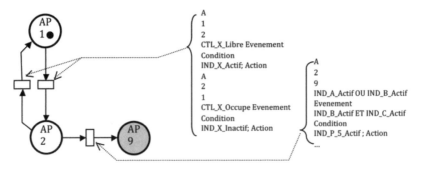

Figure 10.15. *Proof automata for the verification of a safety property*

The safety property which needs to be verified can be expressed by the conditional incompatibility between the internal indicators *IND_A_Actif* = True and *IND_B_Actif* = True, knowing that to the extent that a postulate positions another indicator, *IND_X_Actif* =True. Thus, the indicators should never be simultaneously at the active state when the postulate is verified.

Si ∃VS[i] / [(*IND_A_Actif* ET *IND_B_Actif*) / *IND_X_Actif*] ⇒ *IND_P_5_Actif*

where:

IND_A is an indicator of the functional software;

IND_B and *IND_P_5* are indicators of the proof graphs;

IND_X may be an indicator of the functional software or of a proof graph which relates that a postulate has been verified.

Similarly, we can say that:

VS[(*i*)th injection with *IND_P_5_Actif*] ← **VS**[(*i*-1)th injection with *IND_X_Actif*] ¬ **T**⟨*IND_A_Actif* OR *IND_B_Actif* | *IND_A_Actif* AND *IND_B_Actif*⟩

The postulates generally translate sequences with memorization (sequential aspect of a property that needs to be proved, for example) and position an indicator at True in case of success. This can then be used in a safety property that needs to be proved. This is why the postulates are generally the subject of specific proof graphs.

It should be noted that this method thus makes it possible to simultaneously prove all the properties as exploration of the accessible states of the automaton produced by the signal box progresses.

10.4.3.2.4. Postulates and redundancies

In addition to the information obtained from the signaling program, from the technical plan and from the analysis of the topology of the track plan, proof graphs make it possible to verify, upon the same principle as the safety properties, additional properties:

– The properties of redundancy. For example:

- the conditions necessary for the checking of a route are satisfied and the opening command of the signal is not effective;

- the conditions necessary for the shaping of a route are satisfied and the command for the shaping of the route is not effective;

- the sequence required for automatic destruction is satisfied and destruction does not occur, etc.

The non-respect properties of the operating postulates. For example:

- the control circuits of the switches do not allow (SIL4) the two controls left and right to be established at the same time;

- the action on the passage detector is used so as to only generate one impulse (assembly SIL4 through discharging of capacity), etc.

10.4.3.2.5. Practical achievement of the proof

The proof is achieved by carrying out AP, taking as inputs the functional inputs that are accompanied by outputs produced by the functional software following the application of these inputs. In this way, the proof graphs make it possible to verify that the functional software responds correctly to variation in the exterior environment.

The proof motor is made up of the resolution power motor for the graphs of the functional software. The external events to which the proof graphs are sensitive are ground-level inputs (CTL), messages (MSG) and the indicators of the functional software (IND) of which the value change has made "True" at least a transition of the functional software and the temporization ends (FTP).

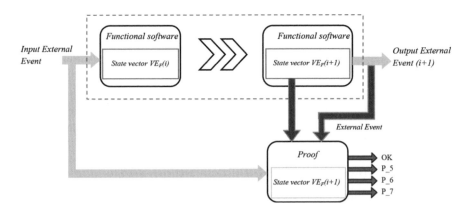

Figure 10.16. *Principle of application of the proof method*

The prover will then run through all of the accessible states to verify that none of them corresponds to a situation which is counter to safety. All possible sequences of external events will be tested. Unfortunately, it is possible that this method might suffer from a combinatory explosion. It happens that an appropriate writing of the proof graphs is able to make this inconvenience less severe and to obtain acceptable calculation times in relation to the temporal constraints imposed during the trial process.

10.4.3.2.6. Proof graphs

The proof graphs are the most sensitive part of the method because the following items depend on them:

– the validity of the proof: is that which is proved necessary and sufficient for safety to be guaranteed?

– the calculation time necessary to carry out the proof;

– the adoption of the method: the genericness of the AP must be ensured for it to be possible for signaling experts to use the method.

Crossing a transition of proof graph positions specific indicators:

– *IND_P_5*: translates to True the fact that at least one safety property has not been fulfilled;

– *IND_P_6*: translates to True the fact that one of the postulates has not been respected;

– *IND_P_7*: translates to True the fact that there is a redundant interlocking condition.

These indicators are thus used to check whether an expected sequence has correctly taken place or not. This nicely reflects the fact that the proof graphs are passive observers, and do not interact with or act on functional graphs. This constraint also has the effect of avoiding the possibility of proof automata becoming the mirror of functional automata. Here, we focalize only on what the functionality needs to achieve, and not the way in which it does this.

Events counter to safety (*IND_P_5*): the detection of situations counter to safety is the reason why this method has been designed. When such a situation occurs, the proof graph under consideration positions the indicator *IND_P_5* at True as soon as an incompatibility is noticed.

Redundant conditions (*IND_P_7*): what is of concern here is verifying that there is not a superfluous constraint in the functional software which could lead to a dangerous situation in the context of the management procedure for the degraded mode created in this way. For example, a route where the protection signal always remains closed while the route is shaped and checked is not counter to safety in itself. In fact, no train can follow the route. It is important, however, to mention that functional graphs do not answer the rules of signaling which require that the signal should open in this case.

The postulates (*IND_P_6*): the exploration of all the accessible states could lead to a combinatory explosion on industrial systems. However, signal boxes are governed by precise rules and ground-level safety equipment, which we can use to overcome this problem.

Figure 10.17 summarizes the positioning of the preceding indicators in all the accessible states and in relation to the proof process. The writing of proof graphs requires job-level knowledge of signaling and railway safety principles.

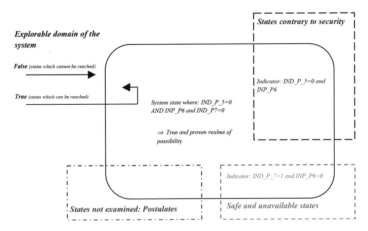

Figure 10.17. *Positioning of the indicators in all system states*

What is involved is the description of the following in the form of automata:

– the railway system's feared configurations, risks and events: indicators *IND_P_5*;

– the conditions of the railway system's operation, in nominal and in degraded mode: indicators *IND_P_6*;

– the functionalities of the signal boxes which are necessary for the operation of the railway system: indicators *IND_P_7*.

The writing of new proof automata usually follows this general approach:

– Step 1: describe, in the form of automata, the sequences of external events that lead to the appearance of a feared situation, a wrong side failure (indicator *IND_P_5*).

– Step 2: complete the preceding automata by writing sequences which highlight the absence of the expected functionalities of the system (indicator *IND_P_7*).

– Step 3: write, in the form of new automata, the sequences of external events that are not authorized by the regulations or that are not possible as a result of the technical environment of the computerized system (indicators *IND_P_6*).

In order to generate proof graphs as rapidly as possible by operators responsible for trials, a tool chain has been developed. This makes it possible to generate the instantiation of the generically useful proof graphs, using the installation's track plan and data from the signaling program.

10.4.3.3. *Tools for carrying out the proof*

The industrial application of our method has required the development of instruments suitable for defining the safety properties, evaluating the conservation of safety properties for each transition between the system states, defining an initial state before the proof is launched (the initial state where all the safety properties are true) and, finally, evaluating the safety properties at each transition between the system states. The safety properties are evaluated until all the safety properties are no longer true; otherwise, the proof is stopped.

SNCF Infra has developed a suite of tools which make it possible to carry out the treatments necessary for executing the process previously described industrially, and to conduct useful trials before the system will be put into service.

This chain of treatment of data (see Figure 10.18) was developed internally in SNCF Infra in order to provide various engineering centers with the most efficient means to conduct formal validation of the functionalities of signal boxes before they begin operation.

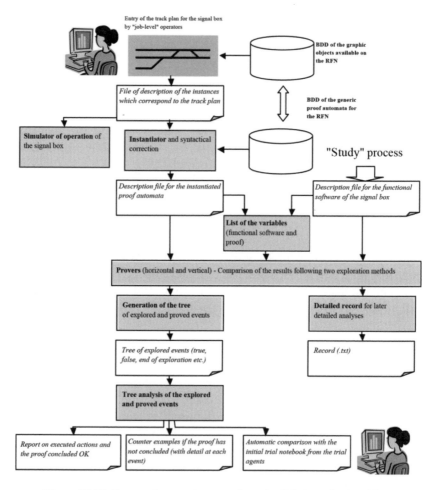

Figure 10.18. *Process for carrying out a formal validation of a signal box*

So, for the case of a real signal box, it is possible to illustrate the various stages described by the previous figure. This makes it possible to arrive, route by route, at the creation of a formal proof of the implanted functionalities.

10.5. Application to a real signal box

10.5.1. *Introduction*

The method has been applied to the functional of several real signal boxes of PIPC-type (which are currently in operation or about to enter operation shortly) using tools that automate its execution. The subject of the work was functional graphs (which will actually be interpreted by the target machines).

We present the results obtained without entering into great detail. In order to verify how effective the process is, we voluntarily introduced design errors of different types into the graphs, at different levels of operation. This is an action which always leads to a justified detection by the tools, and which thus validates the tools and also the method in its concrete application to industrial cases.

10.5.2. *Presentation of the track plan and the signal box program*

The Nurieux signal box is a signal box for a single track line with automatic block. Nonetheless, it reuses around 60% of the generic principles of the signal boxes currently in use in France. Figure 10.19 shows one of the zones of action of the box, as captured by the agents responsible for the validation of the box before it begins operation. A double click on each object makes a window appear, which is not shown here, a dialog box, for configuration, and visualization of parameters which have been topologically and automatically identified.

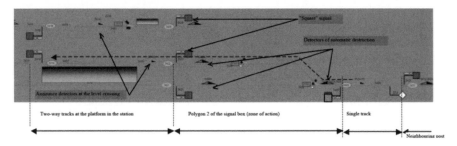

Figure 10.19. *Track plan from the Nurieux signal box (extract)*

In the following, we will present the validation of route 3422 toward 3414 (dotted arrow).

10.5.3. *Safety properties and postulates*

The following safety demands relative to this route are identified by the agents responsible for the validation of the signal box before it finally begins operation:

– the existence or non-existence of interlocking functions attached to the route as a function of the functional program expected of the box;

– the configuration of these functions as a function of the layout and the real distances of implantation of the resources (signal, switch, insulating joints, detectors, etc.).

This work is carried out independently of the study process (which generally takes place externally) and in particular without the influence of the choices made during the study process.

The elements are brought together, examined and validated by the agents on the basis of the information returned by the tools (in particular, the track plan from Figure 10.19). This information makes it possible to automatically instantiate the generic proof graphs required by this route (postulates, safety properties): the postulates that are useful for the explorer and the prover.

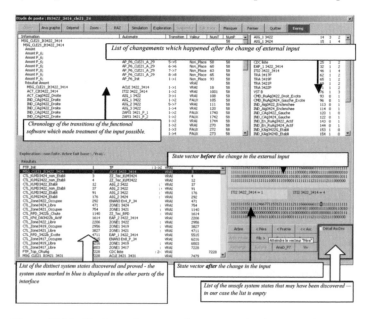

Figure 10.20. *Checking of automated treatments for the route 3222-3114*

10.5.4. *Exploration and formal validation of the application functional software of the signal box*

The treatment of a route will serve as a concrete example to illustrate the procedure, the treatments and the interfaces available to the users. Route 3322-3114 has been investigated and it leads to the following results. The number of state changes of explored internal inputs is approximately 250,000, of which:

– 25,079 were followed by valid transitions (condition: true & properties: true);

– 117,114 were rejected by the functional software of the signal box (false condition);

– the other transitions were explored but, as they did not respect the operation postulates, they were not reinjected;

– 7,000 distinct functional transitions were discovered by the fixed point method;

– 920 system state vectors were temporarily memorized before reinjections.

The checking table allows a signaling operator to follow, if necessary (abnormal operation or non-respect of a safety property) step by step: the chronology of the system's internal events, the state changes of the graphs and the indicators, etc.

The analysis of these makes it possible to find the origin of any possible gap between the observed operation and the expected operation from the viewpoint of safety requirements.

The above process for exploration and proof can then be applied simultaneously or consecutively (or simultaneously using as many calculation units) to all the signal box's itineraries. In this way, a certain number of combinations will be treated several times, ensuring coverage of proofs and, through this, the coverage of all of the possibilities of the signal box.

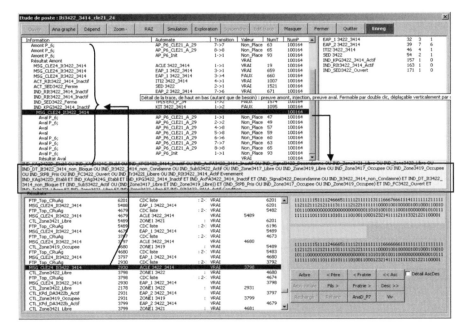

Figure 10.21. *Checking of automated treatments for the route 3222-3114*

10.6. Conclusion

10.6.1. *From a general point of view*

The main difficulties for the development of a computerized signaling system with a high safety level revolve around taking its future integration in the railway system into account during design. This stage is an absolute necessity for the contributions of the computerized systems and the related digital communication to be used well and for their weaknesses to be reduced as far as possible. Thus, during the definition of any new computerized signaling system, the system manager and the agent responsible for maintenance must be involved starting from the project launch. What is at stake here is the definition of the level of technical knowledge desired for their strategic objectives and the mode of functional specification which will guarantee the level of knowledge desired regarding the technical options required for integration in the railway supersystem.

Purely functional specifications have been proved to be insufficient for obtaining a system that can be formally validated and maintained for the entire lifetime of the system. Our development has shown that it is possible to create safety automatisms at reasonable cost, which are long-lasting and which can be validated. In particular, it has been possible to show that the use of a formal method in place of traditional trials makes it possible to significantly reduce costs, while at the same time avoiding taking a safety risk that could not reasonably be taken.

Our original method can be applied industrially for the validation of the functional specifications of signal boxes, in this way making it possible to prove that the specifications carry out all the expected requirements and that the product is correctly designed from a functional point of view. This method could be used to formalize, in a common way, the new specifications for new signal boxes, new Communication-Based Train Control (CBTC) systems (see [IEE 04]) or vital elements of ERTMS (see, e.g., [ERA 08]).

It has the following advantages:

– the creation of safety properties will be conducted by railway experts who have knowledge of the regulations context for the use and maintenance of the railway system, and not by mathematicians who do not have an in-depth knowledge of signaling systems;

– the possibility of applying the proof to existing functional software applications or functional software applications that have been independently modified;

– for manufacturers, the possibility, if they wish to directly interpret the functional specifications which can be given to them, of reducing their level of design and validation effort;

– the automatic and systematic exploration of the accessible states makes it possible to verify all the event chronologies which are not included in the trials (the economic constraint limits the trial time allocated, etc.) or in all the scenarios which can possibly occur (the occurrence of several events within a short time frame, etc.). This goes beyond the limits inherent to more traditional test methods;

– the use of Petri networks means that the results are easy to read, are easy to use and understand, and provide a link to the rich resource of past experience;

– the method is applied industrially for those involved in the railroad, removing the drawbacks cited above: the users need not have any knowledge of mathematical techniques, the formalism makes it possible to reduce production and maintenance costs for the functional software created by a critical information system. Industrial tools exist; the proof of a box may be split into several partial proofs, making the treatment of a complete signal box possible to conduct within a reasonable time frame.

This method has taken a position in the process of carrying out trials before a signal box is put in service at SNCF Infra, without any change in the level of safety required for the tests.

10.6.2. *The use of the method*

At present, formal methods based on modeling are generally, wrongly, considered to be costly in terms of resources (human and hardware) and are often reserved for the most critical software. They are also considered to require both job-level and mathematical knowledge. Their improvement and the broadening of their fields of practical application have inspired much scientific and IT research. Above all, the knowledge of how to use modeling processes, and make them profitable, needs to be based on organizational and cultural changes within companies, which will make the use of models and the formal treatments, of which they may be a subject, widespread. We must, however, never forget that a model is a partial description of a system according to a particular point of view, which limits itself to represent only certain relevant aspects of the system being modeled. It is thus essential to bear in mind that a model will always highlight one or several partial point(s) of view on a software application. Even if all the intrinsic behavioral aspects of a software application can be covered by a modeling language, it is highly unlikely that all of the combinations of the interactions of this application with the different components of its environment can be covered by one single model.

It is thus important to learn to precisely qualify the perimeter of coverage and interpretation of a model and the associated results, through precise knowledge and formalization of the initial postulates that it supposes (behavior hypotheses, interaction with the environment, etc.). Added to this should be the domains of definition, of variation and of validation of all of the desired or non-desired inclusions.

From our point of view, the ideal would be to directly run the formal model which produced the proofs, and to show the properties in an absolute manner in a given context (supersystem), without going through a process of generating an algorithmic code.

As soon as these precautions and reservations have been correctly handled, it is clear that the use of formal methods is the method of choice for the establishment of a guarantee on the behavior of a software application: it is then truly possible to show that a feared situation will never occur, or that a property will always be verified[31]. This is the case whatever random cases occur within the interaction of the application with its environment. In other words, it becomes possible to show the "never" or the "always", and not only the "maybe" modulated by a figure of probability or gravity, etc.

In fact, the methodological and technical reference method of model engineering makes it possible to modulate and control the area for application and the interpretation of results from formal methods even more precisely, as a function of the physical and software layers that make up the environment of the application.

Model engineering allows us to handle other issues linked to the long life of applications and the safety statutes established on the application at a given moment in its lifecycle:

– proof, demonstration of safety properties at a given time;

– independence from these proof statutes regarding the software and physical levels of implementation of the application;

– long life of these safety properties in time, as a function of change or obsolescence phenomena which may characterize the immediate and less immediate environment of the application;

– minimizing the costs of the maintenance of these safety statutes in time.

Research has led to a unique method which can be applied industrially to carry out the validation of executable functional specifications of signal boxes. In this context, there is the possibility to automatically prove that the specifications really do embody all of the expected requirements and that the product is correctly designed. The defined AEFD language is used by SNCF

---

31 Descubes already began discussing "absolute security" in 1898 [DES 98].

Infra to formalize, in a common way, the specifications of new signal boxes or associated products.

The method may be applied industrially, and it avoids all the usual setbacks: the users do not need to have any knowledge of mathematical techniques, the formalism makes it possible to reduce production and maintenance costs for the critical software, industrial tools are available, the proof of a signal box may be split into several partial proofs, which makes the treatment of a complete box possible to perform within a reasonable time frame, etc.

10.6.3. *From a research point of view*

This approach may build bridges between the academic and industrial worlds, in the interests of both as individual parties and as a group working together. Researches have a wealth of theory at their disposal, methods and approaches relative to Petri networks and particularly to "finite state automata" in their various formulations. Presently, manufacturers need to design, maintain and allow the systems to evolve (live): many critical safety systems and computerized systems where all the functionalities can be specified by finite state automata.

The approach demonstrates that it is possible to physically create, within the inherent development constraints of the SIL4 system, a target machine which behaves exactly like a finite state automaton. The "model" which specified the functional application software changes from the status of "abstraction of reality" and "specification to be carried out" to that of "real description" or "specification which has been carried out".

It may be hoped that this method will make it possible to transfer the results of researchers from all countries on Petri networks, in general, and on finite state automata, in particular, to the industrial world. To a certain extent, this gives new life to the initiative which began in the 1970s for GRAFCET, but with a different outcome.

10.6.4. *From the railway industry perspective*

There are code generation tools available on the market. Some of these are associated with a risk analysis, which aims to obtain a better-quality code using a formal or semi-formal process. However, this is then only effective to the extent that the model (abstraction of reality) already contains all the functional information necessary for creating software which is run without algorithmic transformation.

In a simplified way, the model becomes "the specification which can be obtained" (or which should be obtained) so as to carry out the test scenarios of the analyses of structures at the level of the model as soon as possible. This comes down to recognizing that the current models of development of software generate specification errors, design faults or (high level) implementation faults which should be identified as soon as possible so that their treatment does not require too much cost and effort.

Considering models prior to this is incontestably an advance, but only if the designers take all of the elements of the railway context and the environment of the future system into account. Nevertheless, there still remains the considerable (risky) step of the practical (physical) implementation on the target calculators. We have shown that our combined "equipment and software" approach makes it possible to handle these risks efficiently, from a practical and economic point of view. In a simplified manner, the model becomes "the specification which can be carried out" so as to run, as soon as possible, the formal proof of the functional application software defined in this way, and that will be run in a deterministic manner.

Due to the fact that the safety functions are executed to a large extent within the software, both national and European legislative bodies naturally require the guarantee of a high level of safety (the quality and the reliability of the software) through standards. The European standard CENELEC EN 50128 [CEN 01][32], which currently is in application in the domain of railways, presents a process, procedures and principles. If these are followed, the software should logically be acceptable with regard to safety requirements. The standard CENELEC EN 50128 [CEN 01] is a process standard, and it defines a development process for software (essentially the basic software). The standard requires a top-down process in the management of projects, modular design, verification after each step in development, traceable and verifiable documentation, and test procedures. This is a standard process for ensuring the quality of the design and generation process of software.

---

32 For more information, visit http://www.cenelec.eu/Cenelec/Homepage.htm.

Due to the long-term use of systems involved in train circulation (30 years minimum), many applications are still programmed in assembly language, Pascal, or C. As a result, many requirements for change appear, for example changes in specification or hardware obsolescence, that need to be tested manually beyond the modifications are carried out. This represents a considerable cost factor, without providing any total guarantee in return.

The suggested architecture, with a basic software package which can be reused as it is, has as its only configuration the functional software linked to the site's needs, and it is not very dependent on the hardware platform. For this reason, it quickly becomes potentially very useful.

Since the model represents the complete description of the application, all the tests, except the integration test and the tests on the target machine, may be conducted. Conducting a validation/formal proof makes it possible to check the model's properties using mathematical methods. In contrast to tests with a limited number of test cases, a mathematical proof that the specifications are correct may be carried out on the entire domain of possibilities of the inputs.

10.6.5. *The model and its implementation*

The final source code is produced on the basis of models for the target machine (options for compilations to be integrated onto the target machine). In order to reduce the risk of error, some workshops use a compiler, which checks the correct translation of the linguistic constructions and the physical configurations.

This translator is "certified" for the identified target machines so that it can cover, without additional tests, the end of the design procedure of the specification into executable compiled code.

What level of confidence may we give to these "certified" tools, target by target in practice? What level of confidence is attributed to these code checks? It has been proved, to the extent which the application allows, that it is always preferable to reckon on the absence of any transformation between the proven model and that which has been run on the target machine. The added value of formal methods, including the application and its environment, covers the entire development cycle.

This is the main advantage of "the executable specification". It is thus no longer necessary to carry out coverage level analyses of tests carried out, required by the standard CENELEC EN 50128 [CEN 01], because validation is total and valid on the target machine.

The *ex nihilo* design of a critical software is relatively rare. Generally, what is of concern are modifications, extensions or adaptations to existing software. In order to face the future, it is thus necessary to take this need into account, and leave those involved in the trade with the power to adapt the functionalities of the system without totally reworking the functions previously developed.

The approach we have presented is based on a changing library of generic instantiable graphs. If we respect the design rules pronounced, these do not bring the deterministic and provable character of new functional software into doubt. The application of a "formal validation" method thus makes it possible to prove the entirety, preceding code and new code, without distinction and in hidden time.

What we suggest here is a formal method which makes it possible, besides the expected advances in terms of cost and safety, to ensure:

– success conditions for the application of formal methods in the specific field of the railway industry;

– the maintenance of functional and technical control of safety installations by those involved in the railway industry.

We hope that we have shown that these goals may be achieved as soon as we stop conducting our procedures in "IT", "mathematics" and "safety of operation" as we so often do today, without taking the particular attributes of the job and the railway system into account.

10.7. Glossary

ACC: concurrent constraint automata

AEFD: deterministic finite automaton

AP: proof automaton

CBTC: communication-based train control

CENELEC: *Comité Européen de Normalisation Electrotechnique* (European Committee for Electrotechnical Standardization)

CRC: cyclical redundancy code

CT: technical condition

ERTMS European Rail Traffic Management System

FIFO: first in first out

IMdR: Institut de Maitrise des Risques (Risk Control Institute)

MEI: computerized interlocking module

PAI: computerized signal boxes

PIPC: computer-based station with PC technology

RAMS: reliability, availability, maintainability and safety-harmlessness

RdP: Petri network

SIL: safety integrity level

SNCF: *Société Nationale des Chemins de fer Français* (French National Railway Company)

SSIL: SIL Software

VE: state vector

10.8. Bibliography

[ANT 09]   ANTONI M., Petrinetzbasierte Validation von Eisenbahnsicherungssystemen – Validation d'automatismes ferroviaires de sécurité à base de réseaux de Petri, PhD Thesis, TUBS, 2009.

[BAR 09] BARBIER C., *Le frisson d'Icare*, L'Express, June 2009.

[BEL 08] BELMONTE F., Impact des postes centraux de supervision de trafic ferroviaire sur la sécurité, PhD Thesis, University of Technology of Compiègne, 2008.

[BIE 93] BIELINSKI P., Méthode de validation formelle – Thèse soutenue en 1993 à l'Université Paris 6 – P. Bielinski, Implantation VLSI d'un algorithme de code correcteur d'erreur et validation formelle de la réalisation, 1993.

[BIE 98] BIED-CHARRETON D., *Sécurité intrinsèque et sécurité probabiliste dans les transports terrestres* – Synthèse n 31 de l'INRETS, 1998.

[BIE 03] BIED-CHARRETON D., "Informatique et sécurité ferroviaire (Informatik und Sicherheit bei der Eisenbahn)", *Revue RGCF*, December 2003.

[BOM 05] BOMBARDIER TRANSPORT, "Analyse technique – Rame 105 – La Tour de Carol – Septembre 2005", Rapport d'expertise Bombardier Transportation/ Document interne SNCF – 10/2005.

[BOU 09] BOULANGER J.-L., *Sécurisation des architectures informatiques – exemples concrets*, Hermes-Lavoisier, 2009.

[BOU 11] BOULANGER J.-L., *Sécurisation des architectures informatiques industrielles*, Hermes-Lavoisier 2011.

[CEN 00] CENELEC, NF EN 50126, "Applications Ferroviaires. Spécification et démonstration de la fiabilité, de la disponibilité, de la maintenabilité et de la sécurité (FMDS)", January 2000.

[CEN 01] CENELEC, NF EN 50128, "Applications Ferroviaires. Système de signalisation, de télécommunication et de traitement – Logiciel pour système de commande et de protection ferroviaire", July 2001.

[CEN 03] CENELEC, NF EN 50129, "Norme européenne, Applications ferroviaires: systèmes de signalisation, de télécommunications et de traitement systèmes électroniques de sécurité pour la signalisation", 2003.

[DAV 88] DAVID Y., "L'évolution des méthodes de certification de la sécurité face au développement des applications de la microinformatique dans les transports terrestres", *Annales des Ponts et Chaussées*, 1er trimestre, 1988

[DES 98] DESCUBES M., "Etude sur les enclenchements – Introduction des enclenchements conditionnels dans les tableaux et détermination de tous les enclenchements secondaires qui en sont la consequence", (Ingénieur en chef adjoint de la voie à la compagnie de l'est) – *Revue RGCF* (revue générale des chemins de fer et des tramways), 11/1898.

[ERA 08] ERA, "ERTMS/ETCS – system requirement specification – Chapter 2 – basic system description", ref Subset-026-2, issue 3.0.0, 2008.

[GAR 08] GARTNER RESEARCH, *Datarequest Insight: Unplanned Downtime Rising for Mission-Critical Application*, Gartner Research, 10/2008.

[GAR 09] GARTNER CONSULTING, "Worldwide trends of formal methods application and the issues in information systems to secure software dependability", Gartner Consulting Japan, March 2009.

[HOL 07] HOLLNAGEL E., Functional Resonance Accident Model (FRAM), Pôle Cindynique, Sophia Antipolis, France, 2007.

[IEE 04] IEEE, 1474.1, "IEEE standard for communications-based train control (CBTC) performance and functional requirements", 2004.

[LIE 76] LIEVENS C., *Sécurité des Systèmes*, CEPADUES, 1976.

[LEV 00] LEVESON Pr N.G., "The role of software in spacecraft accidents", Aeronautics and Astronautics Department, Massachusetts Institute of Technology, AIAA, 2000.

[LEV 01] LEVESON Pr N.G., "Systemic factors in software-related spacecraft accidents", Aeronautics and Astronautics Department, Massachusetts Institute of Technology, AIAA 2001-4763, 2001.

[LOT 08] ETCS Software Error led to Derailment", *Railway Gazette International*, January 2008.

[MON 96] MONIN J.-F., *Comprendre les méthodes formelles, Panorama et outils logiques*, Masson et CNET-ENST, 1996.

[NF 93] NF F 00 101, Fonctions de sécurité - Méthode de détermination et règles de traitement, Norme Française homologuée NF F 00-101 Paris, 1993.

[NGU 08] NGUYEN T., GILLES D., Performance et sûreté des installations – impact des équipements programmés, EDF R&D – 3SGS08, 03/2008.

[OFT 08] Schlussbericht der Unfalluntersuchungsstelle Bahnen und Schiffe über die Entgleisung von Güterzug 43647 der BLS AG auf der Weiche 34 (Einfahrt Lötschberg-Basisstrecke) vom Dienstag, 16. Oktober 2007 in Frutigen – Reg. Nr. 07101601 – Unfalluntersuchungsstelle Bahnen und Schiffe UUS Service d'enquête sur les accidents des transports publics SEA Servizio d'inchiesta sugli infortuni dei trasporti pubblici SII – 06/2008.

[PIC 86] PICHON L., "Note sur une solution générale des enclenchements ternaires – (ingénieur principal de l'exploitation à la compagnie des chemins de fer du nord)", *Revue RGCF* (revue générale des chemins de fer), June 1886.

[PON 08] PONCET F., L'accident serait dû à une erreur humaine – Université de Paris X -Nanterre – mémoire de sociologie des organisations, September 2008.

[REA 93] REASON J., *L'erreur humaine* – Paris, Editions PUF, Collection "le travail humain", 1993.

[REA 95] REASON J., "A system approach to organizational error", *Ergonomics*, vol. 38, no. 8, 1995.

[RET 87] RÉTIVEAU R., *La signalisation ferroviaire*, Presses de l'école nationale des Ponts et Chaussées, pp. 1708–1721, 1987.

[LOT 07] "Umfall im Lötschberg-Basislinie Tunnel mit ERTMS", *Eisenbahn is a revue*, April 2008.

[STA 08] STAFFELBACH T., "Each time you change a bit or byte in your system, you have to run through the whole process again – Dr T. Staffelbach – head of Train Protection, SBB Infrastructure, Terrapinn's EuroRail 2008, Milano, February 2008.

[VIL 88] VILLEMEUR A., *Sûreté de Fonctionnement des systèmes industriels*, Eyrolles, 1988.

11

Combination of Formal Methods for Creating a Critical Application

11.1. Introduction

This chapter, written by Philippe Coupox of AREVA TA, aims to formalize the experiences of AREVA TA in the use of formal methods in the project of developing the software for its security platform DRACK, and for the development of the wayside CBTC software applications named Zone Controller (ZC) and Input Output Controller (IOC), which had DRACK as their execution support. These software developments are relevant to the highest level of software development, following the standard EN50128:2001, see [NF 01], i.e. level SSIL4. These two developments have been evaluated by the independent organization CERTIFER.

The two developments are linked in terms of software architecture because the DRACK platform makes it possible to offer run-time support for application software, which can make it independent of the equipment. The acquisitions and outputs are carried out by the platform functions. The application software is made up of two main components: a hosting structure, which interfaces with the platform, and an application. Through this design feature, the development of a level SSIL4 application does not need to involve handling the problems linked to the treatments of random faults of the run-time support or the management of aspects related to the interface with the equipment. The use of a formal method for the development of applications thus makes it possible to focus uniquely on

---

Chapter written by Philippe COUPOUX.

converting the functional requirements into security "software". Appendix 1, section 11.5.1 presents, in a simplified form, the architectural aspects in terms of software.

11.1.1. *A history of the use of formal method in AREVA TA*

Given its principal activity, which is linked to the design and creation of nuclear reactors for French nuclear-powered vessels (submarines and aircraft carriers), and also, in particular, to the control-command systems for these reactors, AREVA TA has great experience in the development of security software (Level A, according to standard CEI 60880, see [CEI 06]). However, it also has a great depth of experience in the field of control-command security systems for rail transport. In fact, since 1992, the domain of rail transportation has been gaining ground as the alternative domain for activities linked to nuclear propulsion. The cycles of development for nuclear propulsion are very long, nearly 10 years, and the number of objects produced per project is quite small: four new generation ballistic missile submarines and six attack submarines have been planned.

For the development of the security applications for these reactors, AREVA TA does not currently apply formal methods. The use of these methods has been studied several times since 1990, and it has not become widespread, following the analysis of various criteria that concern the context of these developments, and in particular on account of the characteristics of these applications (the applications principally treat the thresholds on the thermodynamic pressure and temperature values), and because the method currently in use is accepted by the sector assessor (IRSN). The perspective of this chapter introduces a part of the lifecycle where these methods are being considered for use.

In the context of the transport sector, the use of formal methods was introduced during the development of the ATP software for the project OCTYS for RATP through the use of SCADE 5 for development, in particular the odometer applications. This project served as a test project for the use of this method to complement the method traditionally in use (formalized SA/RT and SD method).

In the context of the development of its security platform DRACK and wayside CBTC application software, AREVA TA proceeded with the use of formal methods for the SSIL4 software developments. It was decided to use the SCADE 6 suite from Esterel Technologies (now Ansys), alongside the B method for the ZC security application. The development of the SSIL4 software of the platform should be harder to place within an approach for software developed by the formal method, through the very nature of the instructions that need to be conducted. However, it was decided to create this software also using the SCADE 6 formal method, and the functionalities of the tool that make it possible to insert objects developed through more traditional methods (C language) into the model. These objects then become parts of the model as a whole. A low-level interface layer with the equipment was created entirely with imported operators developed in C language.

11.2. Use of SCADE 6

11.2.1. *Reasons for the choice of SCADE 6*

In order to improve its development process for security software, AREVA TA decided to use the tool SCADE V6 to obtain the following:

– A formalized modeling environment, with a power of expression available to engineers of the process. This is in order to avoid, or at least to limit, interpretation errors or bias introduced during semantic change.

– An environment that has the capacity to simulate and check the test coverage from the generated code, and check the formalism of the model, so as to detect specification errors as soon as possible.

– A certified code generation for the highest levels of security, which is really recognized, so as to avoid unnecessary rewriting in programming language. This will render unecessary unitary tests of the code and integration tests of code for the functions covered by the code generator. This removal of the need for a unitary test of the generated code does not, however, remove the need for tests on the model itself.

– An environment which can adapt to general development principles for security software at AREVA TA, and in particular the principle of cyclicity:

- The semantics of the SCADE language are based on the synchronous language Lustre, and as a result, the principles of modeling and code generation are founded on a pattern of cyclical execution:

– waiting for the start of the cycle;

– cyclical initialization of non-memorized information;

– acquisition of inputs;

– evaluation of the cycle instructions;

– production of outputs;

– within this cycle, the instructions are not sensitive to the environment. These semantics are thus completely compatible with the generic architecture of AREVA TA security software.

- to obtain a "language" which has a power of expression including the notions of state machines or iterative patterns (The SCADE 5 suite does not have iterative operators and the state machines are generated in another product component).

11.2.2. *SCADE 6 in the context of the lifecycle of a software package*

The implementation of a methodology-oriented model, backed by a formal language and a tool for automatic code generation, which is qualified for the required level of security, as is possible with the SCADE 6 suite, has a significant impact on the software lifecycle. This methodology has not yet been strictly regulated within the rail transportation reference system (CENELEC EN 50128, level 4 of July 2001 or 2011). The standard CEI60880 of 2006 introduces this notion, particularly in its informative Appendix C, where it is recommended. Extract from standard CEI 60880, Appendix C.3: "When it conforms to this standard, the methodology for automatic code generation ensures the production of high-quality software and significantly reduces the probability of the introduction of human error".

The challenge posed by a formal method is that this model is a conceptual response to the requirements allocated to the software or to another part of these requirements. For this reason, it formally describes not only what the software should do but also, in a certain manner, how it should do it (the requirements expressed formally could be expressed in another way while using the same formalism).

A tool like SCADE 6 could be considered to be a software specification tool, a design tool or a language for the creation of a software package.

11.2.2.1. *Initial analysis*

At the outset, in order to combine the advantages of using a highly recommended method with financial efficiency, it was decided to use the SCADE 6 suite as the specification method for the software requirements. Following this procedure, the model is the specification of the software, which formalizes the requirements allocated to the software in earlier documents. Once it is finalized, this model becomes the specification for the generator of the source code. Software "development" activities concentrate on the upper part of the traditional lifecycle, therefore, at the level of the specification.

The traditional phases at the lower end of the cycle of software development – detailed design of the modules, coding of the modules, testing of the modules and integration of the modules – are integrated within the automated process conducted in SCADE 6 by the certified tool KCG. Since there is no manual coding of the modules, there are no unitary tests of the module, that is, there are no unitary tests of the source code generated by the tool KCG. Similarly, the integration task for the modules is no longer present because the code generator ensures that the generated code is complete and coherent.

This automated production chain for the program ensures that it conforms to the specifications (the model). The tests at code level are replaced by verification tests and the level of the model of a high-level semantic impact, in order to verify that the model closely corresponds to the requirement expressed for the software.

This verification, which can be conducted even before the target system equipment has been made, contributes to the improvement of the quality of the software, because it provides early detection of the possible faults which could mar the software.

The end of the cycle for this type of "software" is composed of carrying out the software/equipment integration on the target machine. This has, as its main aim, the verification of the performance and endurance requirements. Function oriented tests are conducted to complete the achievement of these first two objects, during the validation tests for the software on the target machine.

To summarize, in the initial diagram, the SCADE 6 suite is implemented in the following way:

– Identification and traceability of the requirements allocated to the software, using the notion of commentary associated with diagram-type SCADE objects. These commentaries are structured so that they regulate functionalities of the software in the form of requirements. During this phase, it is also possible to create a preliminary architecture of the model. Using this model as a starting point, the documentation associated with the traceability of the requirement is produced using the SCADE suite's REPORTER tool.

– The model is then refined until a model which can be executed is obtained, and which conforms to the expected requirements. If imported operators are identified, the design of these is defined within the model in the commentary field of a diagram associated with the operator.

– This model is then verified by an independent team, using simulation possibilities available with an AREVA TA tool that encapsulates the SCADE 6 simulator and the MTC model coverage tool.

– The coding of the software is carried out by the certified automatic generation tool KCG (SSIL3/4), which produces a code which can be simulated on the host machine or exported to the run-time support. In the case where the model uses imported operators, the coding of the operators is carried out manually.

– SCADE 6's Compiler Verification Kit suite (CVK) is used to qualify the target compilers.

The following diagram provides a synthesis of the imagined initial lifecycle.

On paper, this model seems have many points in its favor, particularly the elimination of interpretation and specification errors, and the reduction in development costs, especially by eliminating the need for unitary tests at the C-code level. However, as soon as we first began to discuss this with the assessor it became clear that these points in its favor could not help it to obtain an evaluation which conformed to the standard EN 50128, see [NF 01]. The approach from the standard requires the application of several successive phases in the descending part of the lifecycle: specification, architecture, design and coding. Therefore, it is not possible for the creation of a model, even of a formal model, to completely replace these phases. In addition, the verification and test activities encounter a significant issue. If the model is the "specification", then what can we use to formally verify or test it? A model cannot be both the expression of the software need and the response to this need.

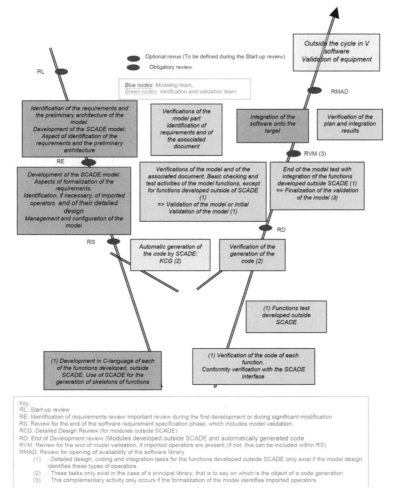

Figure 11.1. *Initial pattern of application for SCADE 6. For a color version of this figure, see www.iste.co.uk/boulanger/industrialsystems.zip*

However good the idea of an approach oriented toward a formal model might seem, it should be used as a means to verify a specification written in natural language, in design phase which complies with the requirements of the standards.

11.2.2.2. *Final analysis*

Following the remarks from the assessor, the use of SCADE 6 was repositioned to become a design method in a more global lifecycle.

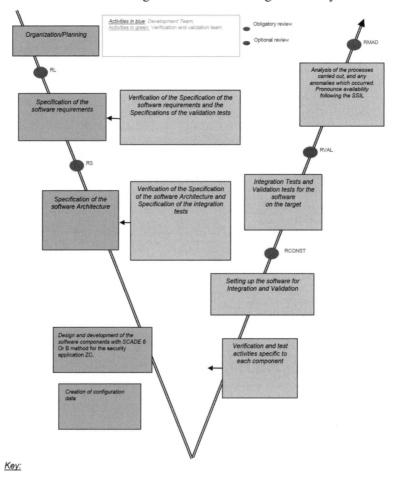

Key:

RL: *Start-up review/Planning*
RS: *Review of end of Specification*
RCONST: *Review of the (end of) creation of the standard application software (and starting up the integration/validation tests)*
RVAL: *Review of end of validation (may be grouped together with RMAD)*
RMAD: *Availability review of the application software by the validation team*

Figure 11.2. *Global lifecycle for application software. For a color version of this figure, see www.iste.co.uk/boulanger/industrialsystems.zip*

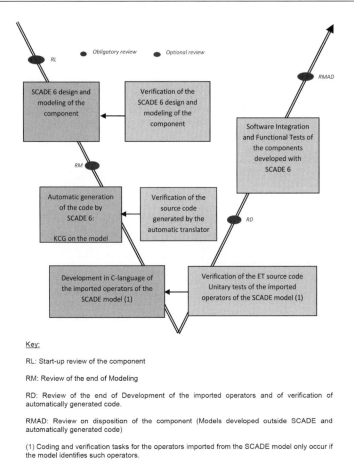

Figure 11.3. *Final SSIL4 with SCADE 6 design lifecycle. For a color version of this figure, see www.iste.co.uk/boulanger/industrialsystems.zip*

11.2.3. *Organization and development rules of a SCADE 6 model*

Through analogy with the organization required by the standard EN 50128, an agent responsible for independent design and an agent responsible for independent verification are named. In addition, a document which regulates the implementation of the tool and the modeling rules (composition of the nodes, naming of the nodes and data fluxes, typing data flows and use of the SCADE operators) and which formalizes the consideration of the constraints exported from the certificate associated with the use of the KCG code generator.

The main stages of a development that uses a SCADE model are identified in the following way:

Activities of the agent responsible for model design	Activities of the agent responsible for verification
Identification of the requirements: development of the model: inventory of requirements	
	Verification of requirements.
Formalization in SCADE language of the software requirements. Identification, if necessary, of imported operators and of their detailed design. A "bench" of the model may be created to verify execution performances. Generation of a design document for the component using the REPORTER tool.	
	Verification of the model: – verification of respect for rules; – verification of the functionality; Verification of the document.
Generation of the code certified by KCG.	Verification of the generation.
Development, if necessary, of imported operators.	Verification and test of the operators imported by unit.
Integration of imported operators into the model, if necessary.	Integration test for operators imported into the model.

11.2.3.1. *Identification of the requirements and documentary production associated with the model*

The management of the requirements allocated to the software component is an important activity within the SSIL4 development procedure of the standard EN 50128. It must be possible to show that no prior requirement has been neglected, and that the all design requirements originate from at least one prior requirement. If not, a justification needs to be produced. During the initial evaluation of the SCADE 6 suite, it was decided not to use the RM_Gateway available within the SCADE 6 to manage the requirements within the SCADE 6 model. The ergonomics of the tested version was not deemed to meet our requirements. A traceability mechanism was put in place at the level of the model, in a commentary field of the diagram associated with a root node. These requirements are then exported into a document with the utilitarian use of access to the models (particularization of the REPORTER tool).

In the context of a project, the model on its own is not enough. It is necessary to produce a document which includes all the elements of the model. The document associated with the model is obtained using the "Reporter" model of SCADE. This module generates, for example, files in RTF format, which will be included in a design document. The objective of producing a document is, in particular, to be able to get past any possible disappearance of the tool, and in any case, forms a part of the "deliverables" of a project specified by the standard.

11.2.3.2. *Training*

In order to be able to use the suite, the team will need to attend training sessions. Some initial support from the company which produces the suite makes it possible to roll out use of the suite more effectively. For software engineers who know how to use other modeling tools, learning how to model with SCADE 6 does not require any additional, high-level skills.

11.2.3.3. *Use of the property proof, techniques for static analysis on the model*

In addition to the syntactic and semantic verifications of the language and the test techniques, the complementary modules allow the operator to carry out property proofs and static analyses (worst-case execution time and stack size).

The tests carried out at earlier phases of the project have not made it possible to show a convenient and useful placement within the project. Therefore, we decided not to use these modules.

11.2.4. *Usage summary SCADE 6*

Except for the change in the positioning for the use of the SCADE 6 suite within the lifecycle, as explained above, the strengths/weaknesses we encountered are the following:

11.2.4.1. *Weaknesses*

11.2.4.1.1. Product maturity

We started to use this suite from the very first versions (6.0). Evidently, the project was not mature at this stage, particularly at the level of the stability of the editing functions. Given the initial investment cost and the reputation for stability that SCADE 5 had, these problems led to an initial negative reaction toward the product. Fortunately, the current version 6.3 is stable. One recommendation might be not to use the initial beta version of the product within an operational project. A maturity of two years would seem to be necessary. The qualification of tools has become an important component of the standard, and it would seem difficult to deliver a qualification for a non-mature version.

11.2.4.1.2. Performance of the generated code in relation to iterative patterns

One of the reasons for changing to SCADE 6 (from SCADE 5), was the availability of the iterative pattern. Among wayside CBTC applications, this was an important argument for the functional part of these applications, where a type of instruction needs to applied to several "objects" of the same type. Examples include management of all trains, management of all switches and of all the signals of a railway plan.

We quickly realized that the performance of the generated code was not present during use of these operators on a large number of objects. Solutions to bypass this were implemented, which notably reduced, at least for the time being, the usefulness of these operators. This is one of the reasons that led us to develop the core of the ZC application in B method.

11.2.4.1.3. Performance of the test tools and the test coverage tools

The availability of an editing suite and a certified code generator is not enough. As outlined in the previous sections, it is necessary to be able to conduct tests on the model and to show its coverage.

In the initial versions used, the suite did not offer a tool that allowed the creation of test scenarios with the positioning of input data and checks on the results obtained in relation to the expected results. Thus, it was necessary to develop a tool of this kind on the basis of the existing SCADE simulator. Since then, the suite has begun to offer a similar test tool.

The test coverage is dedicated to the Model Test Coverage tool. Despite the extensive effort on the implementation of this suite, we notice that currently the instrumentation choices that have been made do not make it possible to use this tool productively. As soon as a model reaches a certain size and in particular if it contains iterative patterns with several levels of depth, the tool requires, at the same time, high-powered machines and a very long instrumentation and execution time. This means that the test phases are critical in terms of planning and cost.

11.2.4.1.4. Cost of the product and of maintenance

The KCG code generator may be certified, but the costs of the SCADE 6 suite are quite high. Each component has an individual license, editor, KCG, MTC and in some cases it is not possible, for example to run an MTC coverage test without having a KCG license.

Depending on the function and the makeup of the team, the cost of beginning use and maintenance may thus be very high, which makes access difficult for small organizations.

11.2.4.2. *Drawbacks*

11.2.4.2.1. Unavailability of SCADE 6 for Linux users

The suite is only available with Windows. A Linux version would be very advantageous, and would allow us to get past certain limitations of Windows.

11.2.4.2.2. Limitations of KCG

Some KCG choices are currently factors in reducing productivity. For example, if the definition of a type of structured data is not modified, KCG redefines internal types upon detection of the modification of certain aspects of a graphic board. As a result, the generated code is functionally identical, but not identical, which leads to exhaustive recompilations. In the same manner, KCG does not detect the non-modification of a part of the model, and systematically regenerates all of the code of a model.

11.2.4.3. *Strengths*

11.2.4.3.1. Method strongly recommended by the standard reference system

The use of a formal method such as SCADE 6 is one of the methods deemed highly recommended in the standard 50128 for the design phase. Its implementation makes it possible to demand strict conformity.

11.2.4.3.2. Elimination of coding-type faults

Due to the formal nature of the SCADE 6 language and the native checks associated with it (syntactical and semantic), the traditional faults of a non-formal language are eliminated by the developers themselves. However, the fact remains that a SCADE design may very well be syntactically and semantically correct, but still not fit for requirements. Therefore, tests are still necessary.

11.2.4.3.3. Accessibility of the language

The SCADE 6 language is formal and in addition the SCADE 6 suite offers a graphic interface that makes it possible to implement operators native to the language or to create new ones without it being necessary to know the textual syntax of the language. As for the training necessary, even though it is essential to know the meaning of the blocks, getting to the level of being able to program with SCADE is quite quick and it is quite intuitive to use.

11.2.4.3.4. State machine

The SCADE language makes it possible to use state machines alongside data batch-type operators or iterative patterns. This is really a positive addition for the description of some functional requirements, and it makes it much more readable than a program which processes this type of algorithm with conditional instructions.

11.2.4.3.5. Certified code generator KCG

In spite of the limits identified on the generated code associated with the use of the iterative pattern, the use of KCG is a very positive attribute. In this version of SCADE 6, among the models that we created, we did not encounter any code generation bugs. This allowed us to concentrate all our attention on the conformity of the model to the requirement. The generated code may be implemented on any type of final processor, because it is by portable code by specification. The CVK makes it possible to show how suited a compiler is to the forms for the C ANSI language which is used by KCG.

11.2.4.3.6. Ease of modification, reuse

The notions of nodes, library and package make it easier to reuse and modify than with a more traditional programming language.

11.3. Implementation of the B method

11.3.1. *The reasons for choosing the B method for the ZC application*

The wayside CBTC application software called ZC is responsible for preparing what is known as the limit of movement authorization for mobiles under CBTC controls, that is, the position up to which the mobile can develop, and which is guaranteed secure. The mobile is responsible for respecting this limit. This position is developed cyclically, taking the information issued by traditional signaling into account, along with the occupation of the track circuit, the position of the switch, the position of the signals, and based on the positioning information provided by the mobiles under CBTC control. The ZC can manage a railway line on which mobiles that are not under CBTC control circulate, such as work trains.

The development of a ZC application is particularly well suited to a modeling in B method based on first-order logic, and of which the basic notion is the set. Thus, the designer will be able to intuitively represent the various objects, such as trains, track circuits, signals and switches, and associate properties with them that need to be "proven". For more a more detailed description on the modeling approach in B, see [ABR 96].

The performance limitations identified on the KCG SCADE 6 generator associated with iterative patterns led us not to use SCADE 6 for the ZC security application part. SCADE 6 was maintained for the other parts of the software components. The implemented software architecture made it possible to use two different methods.

The implementation of this method during this project was the first time it had been used by AREVA TA. Therefore, a project organization was put in place with French workers from the domain: the company SYSTEREL, which also works in partnership with AREVA TA in the context of its software development. Even after training, it is necessary to regularly use the B method in order to completely master it. The underlying concept, the first-order logic, which is often presented as being easy for an engineer to master, requires a new way of thinking in order to produce efficient and relevant models. In addition, in the context of an industrial project, the model must meet criteria linked to the proof. Designed without taking the constraints of the proof tools into account, many hours of "manual" proof of the model are required. Three levels of knowledge are identifiable, reader of B Model, designer of B Model and proof operator of B Model.

In this organization, after training, we carried out verification activities, as understood in the standard EN 50128, see [NF 01], for the specification and design phases of the ZC security application component. Although this takes place during the design phase of the ZC software, we, in fact, carried out a specification phase for the ZC security application (level 2 component in the architecture indicated in the appendix) and applied the SA/RT method widely used by AREVA TA in its security software developments. We decided that, for reasons of maintenance and readability, the transition from expression in natural language into expression in B was an excessively large semantic jump. The following section details the implementation of the method in the context of this project.

11.3.2. Positioning the B method in the V cycle of the ZC software

Thus, the B method is employed for the development of the security application of the ZC, following the architecture defined in Appendix 1.

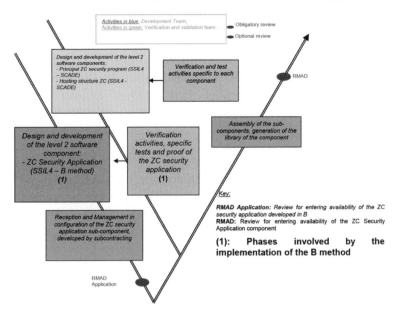

Figure 11.4. *Global lifecycle for ZC application software component. For a color version of this figure, see www.iste.co.uk/boulanger/industrialsystems.zip*

The approach presented here becomes involved during the descending phase of the V cycle, beginning at the design phase of the highest level software. The aim of this approach is to support the classical development process with the use of a formal method. This leads to:

– specifying the ZC security application using a formalized method;

– applying an incremental procedure for the design of the ZC security application, which results in a deterministic model (CGF);

– tooling the verification of the coherence of the model by formal proof;

– tooling the traceability between the general formal design (CGF) and the detailed formal design (CDF) by formal proof;

– automating certain steps of the detailed design and the coding by automatic translation using a code generator.

The approach makes it possible to model the ZC security application by successive refinements until a compilable code is obtained. The development cycle is described in Figure 11.5. The use of the formal B approach has an impact on the boxes with double borders.

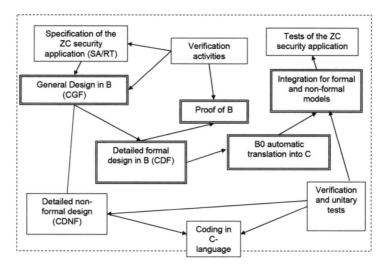

Figure 11.5. *Detailed lifecycle of the ZC security application in B*

The specification phase for the ZC security application is carried out in the form of a word document and an SA/RT model (DSL). This document is the entry point for the general design. The aim of this is to federate the allocated requirements to the ZC security application and present an intermediary stage before modeling in B.

The general formal design is composed of:

– a document (DCG) which presents the architecture of the ZC security application, and in particular the modular segmentation of the B model, and identifies the non-formal SSIL4 modules coded in C;

– a first part of the B model (CGF) which completely specifies, in a way that is as deterministic as the DSL with regard to the inputs and outputs from the software, the functional requirements and the sequencing of the functions that carry out these requirements.

The verification of the conformity of the general design with respect to the software specification is performed by verification activities (verification of the traceability table, proofreading of the design folder, etc.).

Starting from the detailed design, the cycle continues in two branches for the SSIL4 development:

– The first branch is concerned with the security development in C (detailed design then coding), following a conventional approach. Detailed design and coding rules documents regulate these activities.

– The second branch corresponds to the development in B (CDF), up to the coding of the implantations known as B0, which can be automatically translated into C.

For both the branches, phases, designs and coding rules documents regulate the activities.

The re-ascending phase of the cycle begins with:

– a proof phase for formal modules in B which makes it possible to:

- verify the conformity of the CDF with respect to the CGF (replacing the traceability matrix and manual verifications of the detailed design). These verification activities are covered by the proof if the CGF is as deterministic as the DSL and completely specifies the expected behavior of the software with respect to the inputs and outputs. Therefore, the CGF does not allow the CDF to add or suppress behavior,

- verify the coherence of the CGF and the CDF (by swapping the unitary test and integration phases between formal models),

– a verification phase of the source code and unitary tests for non-formal modules.

The two branches of the cycle then rejoin during an integration phase for the formal models developed in B and automatically translated into C with non-formal modules coded in C. Tests make it possible to verify this integration phase.

The functional configuration data are identified in specification phase on the basis of the system data identified in the technical equipment specification. The actual configuration data of the software are then identified in the design phase.

11.3.2.1. *Method B tools aspects*

The use of the B method is currently closely linked with the use of Atelier B (see http://www.atelierb.eu/), which is distributed by the company Clearsy. It provides support for the method, and in particular the whole environment linked to the notion of property proof (generator of proof obligation and proof tools).

Although this component is indispensable, Atelier B does not offer a native translation tool for the final form of B, i.e. B0, into a traditional language such as C, or an ADA certified language, as is the case with the KCG translator of the SCADE 6 suite. Within an industrial project which it is planned to evaluate with SSIL4, this is an important part of the development, which should not be underestimated. Even if the final B0 form of B is not syntactically complex, the development of a B to C or ADA qualified language translator is a task which requires a team dedicated to the development. In this context, a B to C translator made up of two diversified chains was developed by AREVA TA and its partner SYSTEREL. The specifications of this translation chain were established in line with the detailed modeling and design rules of the B model, which limit the forms of B0 used.

In keeping with the standard objectives, the development of such a tool requires a quality development process, and the involvement of operation security teams in the analysis of the process.

Atelier B does not offer a test or simulation environment either. Therefore, a simulation environment was created which would make it possible to test the ZC security software on a host machine. This is something to bear in mind when deciding to use the B method.

The notion of management by requirement is not specifically addressed by Atelier B. Therefore, specific rules must be obtained in order to ensure the traceability which is required by the reference standard.

Although the B method contributes rigor in its design phases, its use via Atelier B does not answer all the questions raised by an SSIL4 development in line with the standard EN 50128.

11.3.3. *B Method Usage Summary*

The implementation of this method during this project was the first time it had been used by AREVA TA, although this was not the case with SCADE. We encountered the following strengths/weaknesses:

11.3.3.1. *Weaknesses*

11.3.3.1.1. Accessibility of the method

Although it is presented as being easy for software engineers to use, due to its syntax and semantics, use of the B method requires regular practice. Although the method is formal, and thus unambiguous, the process of designing with notions of sets and the associated properties may be more difficult for engineers with experience primarily in programming traditionally or by object. Also, the proof techniques require specific skills and an in-depth knowledge of the proof verification tools in order for these phases to be effective in terms of time frame, and thus cost. Therefore, it is essential to establish a partnership with specialists in the domain during the implementation of the method for an industrial project.

11.3.3.1.2. Tooled environment

The use of Atelier B makes it possible to have access to the modeling and tools linked to the proof. However, the environment does not offer a translator or a test environment. These two types of tools are fundamental in software development. It is useful to have a proven B Model, but it cannot be used if we do not have a translator. There is currently no compiler available for the final form of B, i.e. the B0.

11.3.3.1.3. Management of the requirements

The B method is not specifically designed for design based on requirements. Thus, it is necessary to put in place a specific complementary process in order to respond to the requirements of standards.

11.3.3.1.4. Limit of the proof

The "conforms and is correct through proof" characteristic of software in B cannot be applied to all of the developments in B. Some early parts of the model, such as sequencers, need to be created in "code B0", and also all the interfaces require basic machines. The final implementation of these is conducted in the form of a non-formal module. The method thus requires an implementation in the context of a more complete process.

11.3.3.1.5. Spread of the method outside France and outside of the domain of rail transport

The method is used very little or not at all outside of France and the domain of rail transport. Thus, the industrial environments are very limited. For this reason, it is valid to ask questions in terms of maintenance and the long life of the method.

11.3.3.2. *Strengths*

11.3.3.2.1. Method Highly Recommended by the standards reference body

The use of a formal method like the B method is one of the methods named Highly Recommended in the standard 50128 for the design phase SSIL4. Its implementation makes it possible to demand strict conformity. Another advantage of the method is the confidence that the assessors have in it.

11.3.3.2.2. Residual faults

The B process of development associated with functional tests of the application based on the SA/RT model and on detailed verifications resulted within a few iterations in operational software with very few residual errors. The evaluated version only currently contains one error.

Through the nature of the method, the design requires the establishment of the properties that are required. Thus, this involves a process where the ambiguities are handled systematically.

11.3.3.2.3. Product maturity

The B method has been used for several years in France, by other manufacturers in the railway transport industry. Thus, the method and Atelier B benefit from a significant level of prior learned knowledge.

11.3.3.2.4. Performance of the generated code

Although the method is complex, the generated code makes it possible to obtain very good performance in terms of memory occupation and execution time. Our opinion is that the code obtained is equal in value to the code that would have been produced manually by a programming specialist. This criterion was particularly important to us. Even if it is possible today to have execution supports which perform very well, when it comes to SSIL4 execution platforms, there are always problems with the performance.

11.3.3.3. *Size of the created model*

11.3.3.3.1. SA/RT specification

– number of DFD (Data Flow Diagram): 39;

– number of P-spec (Process Specification): 93;

– number of pseudo-code lines: approximately 21,000 (excluding empty lines but including commentaries).

11.3.3.3.2. B Model

– number of B files: 290 (CGF=142/CDF=148);

– number of C-code lines produced by translation: approximately 34,700;

– number of proof obligations: approximately 23,600;

– levels of automatic proof (forces 0 and 1): 78% (approximately 5,000 interactive proofs remain);

– number of SYSTEREL proof rules: approximately 2,000.

11.3.3.4. *Non formal C code modules*

– number of C modules written: 18;

– number of lines of C code written: 6,157.

11.3.3.5. *Integration tests formal modules/non-formal modules*

– number of test scenarios: approximately 30;

– number of test cases: approximately 120.

11.3.3.6. *Tests on the model of the conformity to specification requirements type*

– number of test scenarios: approximately 260;

– number of test cases: approximately 1,200.

11.4. Conclusion

Development with formal methods is the current trend for SSIL4 development. So, it is important to monitor them. Nevertheless, our historical culture for SSIL4 (EN 501298) or level A (CEI 60880) software development is to use functional analysis methods like SA/RT SD.

In the nuclear field, the use of such methods is now recommended (see IEC 60880: 2006). So, we should follow the evolution of the assessor's requirement.

For the nuclear propulsion domain, we have to balance these requirements to confront this position with the type of application that we have to achieve, i.e. application of size controlled with instructions involving implementation concepts of time, representation floating number calculations (derived, exponential, logarithm and power). For these types of application, use of the formal method is less relevant. We consider using formal methods to verify the system specification. If a system model is established, it may be used to produce a sequence of tests for the validation of the final software.

Nevertheless, we learn by the experience of the development of the wayside CBTC software and the development of the software of the platform DRACK, that it is undeniable that these methods contribute much to the process of development and, in particular, by the confidence gained from the assessors, but they do not provide the gains expected on associated development costs (deletion unitary tests on code and validation tests).

They may well say that safety has no price, but it does have a cost and it is clear that this cost will not decrease. To limit its impact, we need to continue to apply a product strategy even if it is difficult and requires R&D projects to manage the obsolescence of products in terms of technology and regulatory application.

11.5. Appendices

11.5.1. *Appendix 1: SOFTWARE architecture on DRACK platform*

The application software for ZC or IOC equipment corresponds to the application layer of wayside CBTC software. The software architecture is broken down into three layers:

– *Level 1* (linked to the material architecture of the platform)

Each ZC and IOC software application may be broken down into:

A software application component for helping with maintenance classed SSIL0 and a security software application component (security functions) classed SSIL4.

NOTE.– We only talk of one software security application (AppQ) although there are two generated and charged instances on two distinct processors on the DRACK target. This is because there is only one version of source code for this component, compiled and generated for each target CPU.

The diagram below shows the main components of the application software, along with the data linked to the platform architecture.

– *Level 2*

Each of the application software components is broken down into subcomponents, following a generic architecture which aims to segregate the application instructions from the instructions linked to the execution constraints linked to the platform.

The following notions are defined for this:

– "application subcomponent" in charge of CBTC functional treatments (also conventionally known as: "application software component" or simply "application");

– "DRACK platform host structure subcomponent" (also conventionally known as: "host structure software component" or simply "host structure"), and which is responsible for:

- presenting the entry and exit points of the DRACK platform to generic software,

- checking the integrity of configuration data and current cycle data transmitted by platform generic software via the VME.

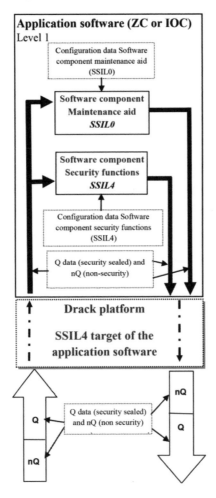

Figure 11.6. *Simplified architecture for a software application on DRACK*

In input, decompressing, if required, the data in 32 bit or Boolean integers to make them available to the application;

In output, compressing the data produced by the application and intended for the platform generic software;

"Principal Program Subcomponent", which is responsible for gathering together and sequencing the instructions of the two sub-components listed above.

This architecture makes it possible to develop the "application subcomponent" with formal methods associated with code generators, without the need to be concerned with access to resources in equipment which cannot be represented formally. The implementation of the formal development method can thus be fully effective while it only "is concerned" with purely application aspects.

AREVA TA implemented, in addition to the formal design methods, a method for verifying the data used by the security application that made it possible to verify formal properties on the binary data. The properties had been expressed during the design cycle of the software.

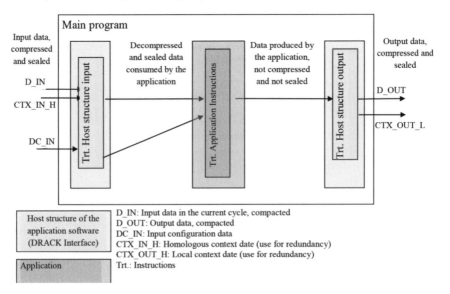

Figure 11.7. *Simplified architecture of an application component on DRACK*

– Level 3

Each subcomponent is finally broken down into "modules", the precise nature of which depends on the design method chosen for the subcomponent, SCADE or B method.

11.5.2. *Appendix 2: detailed description of the approach chosen for the B method*

The approach suggested is based on the B method defined by Jean-Raymond Abrial (see [ABR 96]). It has already been in use for more than 10 years for the development of security software in the railway sector.

The aim of the B method is to formally specify the critical software, and then to formally prove the defined models. The process of modeling is modular and incremental, by stages of refinement:

– First, an abstract formal model of the software is created (which corresponds to a general design), which specifies the software architecture and the distribution of requirements of the software specification in functions.

– Then, following each stage of refinement, each element of the model is specified (data and function) so as to obtain an executable code (which corresponds to a detailed design).

At the final level of refinement, the model is made up of implantation in B0 language (subset implantable in B-language). These implantations are then automatically translated in a classical programming language (e.g. C and ADA), which can run under different platforms. In the context of AREVA TA developments, the execution language used is the C language. The required integrity level of the software security is obtained by using two redundant translators developed to have no common mode except their common specification, which has been submitted for double verification by two people. For a more detailed description on the modeling approach in B, see [ABR 96].

The verification of the formal B model comprises several steps:

– a critical proofreading of the abstract model with the construction of a traceability matrix with regard to the software specification;

– tooled verifications of structures, syntaxes and types of the B models;

– the formal proof of the B model which includes:

- the automatic generation of proof obligations,

- discharge of automatically provable proof obligations,

- the assisted manual proof of the remaining obligations, if necessary, with added proof rules.

The B model is considered verified when the complete traceability matrix has been verified, the syntactic and type checks have been successfully conducted, the model has been proven to 100% and the added proof rules have been verified.

For more information on the mechanisms for proof and the writing of rules, see [ABR 96].

The following sections detail the modalities used for the phases where the B method is implemented in the context of the ZC security application.

11.5.3. *General design of the ZC security application*

Under this approach, the general design of the ZC security application is based on the SA/RT specification model. The description of the ZC security application is formalized in B (see [ABR 96]), except at the level of the external interfaces (entry point, basic modules and management of context), for which only an abstract machine formally models the interface constraints (accessible data, classification of data, etc.)

11.5.3.1. *Architecture of the ZC security application*

The architecture of the ZC security application is described by a B-modular architecture, which includes the B modules (machine, elaboration and implantations) and links between these modules (REFINES to express an elaboration link, IMPORTS to express a composition link and SEES to express a link for the use of data being read).

To make this work of verification and traceability with the software specification of the ZC security application easier, the B architecture is structured to correspond as much as possible with the breakdown of the

SA/RT model of the specification. In particular, the following principles are applied (insofar as they are feasible in relation to the B architectural constraints):

– The segmentation of function into SA/RT sub-functions is modeled in an implantation by sequencers.

– Each sequence of operations defined in an activation table at the SA/RT level is specified by a sequencer operation in a B implantation.

– The data of outputs of a function are modeled by B machine variables that model the function.

– Access to the input data of a function is obtained through an SEES link to a machine which models these input data or by the variables of the B module which consumes them.

Additionally, the configuration data can be defined or refined during general design of the software. These data are plotted in the appendix of the DCG so they can be refined by concrete data during the detailed design.

11.5.3.2. *Modeling the functionalities*

The content of each module is modeled in B-language, which makes it possible to produce a clear and precise modeling of the application.

Verification of the modeling by formal proof ensures that it is coherent and unambiguous.

The use of the B method, supplemented with the stage of formal proof, makes it possible to guard against the introduction of mistakes in the detailed design of the software.

The B-modeling must respect modeling and naming conventions, which are detailed and formalized in a document.

Most of the modules are developed formally in B. Only those which concern the software interfaces cannot be implanted in B. In this case, a B machine known as "basic" contains a modeling of the expected constraints on the interface (accessible data, classification of data, etc.).

The expected behavior of the functions of the basic machines is specified in B. Only the modules which cannot be created in B are developed in C, in a non-formal way. The non-formal modules in C only then form a thin and minimal layer in interface between the formal part and the host structure (see Appendix 1, architecture).

11.5.3.3. *Constraints exported by the equipment*

The constraints imposed by the equipment on the software must be globally described in the DSL of the ZC application software, and detailed in the DCG:

– cycle time;

– size of configuration data;

– size of manipulated data.

11.5.3.4. *Data and interface exchanges*

The exchanges of data between modules are modeled in B:

– The input data of a module are those defined in the machines of the SEES clause or variables. The constant data can be directly accessed; the variable data are accessed by reading operations.

– The output data of a module are modeled by the variables or constants of a B machine. If the variables can be used by other modules, a reading operation must be defined.

The data exchanged with the environment are modeled in B machines called "basic":

– the definition, the typing and the initialization of data, and also the specification of reading operations are specified in an abstract machine;

– the coding and the link with the interfaces are performed directly in C (detailed non-formal design). These modules must use defensive programming to ensure that the predicates of the abstract machine are satisfied by the C implantation.

The model implements a detection of the faults which are relevant to the range of values from the configuration as well as those that originate from values produced in outputs.

11.5.3.5. *Traceability in relation to the DSL*

The general design should respect the requirements defined in the specification of the ZC security application. This is shown using a traceability matrix in the general design folder.

In order to make this traceability easier, the general design reuses the names of data defined in the software specification (dictionary of SA/RT data of the specification model).

In addition, the tags of the requirements of the software specification are reused in the header of the corresponding B modules.

11.5.4. *Detailed design ZC security application*

Under the suggested approach, the detailed design is in direct continuity with the general design. Here the functional modeling of the general design is detailed until an implantable model is obtained.

11.5.4.1. *Formal detailed design*

For the CDF, the modeling principles in B language from the CGD are reused.

The modules must be readable and comprehensible or automatically generated (using the automatic Bart refinement tool integrated into the Atelier B platform).

An implementable code is obtained by successive refinement of the B modules, until a model in B0 is obtained. During these refinements, detailed design submodules are created, in addition to the general design modules. The submodules of a given module correspond to an internal organization within the model, in order to facilitate the refinement and the proof.

The particular technical choices such departures from general principles as well as the remarkable particularities of the formal software are formalized in a document in order to facilitate maintenance.

11.5.4.2. *Detailed design of the non-formal modules*

The external interfaces of the software are not formalized in B. The formalization of inputs and outputs external to the software is thus limited to the specification of the basic machine that models the inputs necessary to the function on which it depends.

The detailed design of the non-formal modules, which models the interfaces (basic machine) and the interactions with the host structure is conducted in accordance with design rules and is given in the document DCD: document of detailed design.

11.5.4.3. *Traceability in relation to general design*

The traceability between the detailed formal design and the general design is carried out by the formal proof. More precisely, the static checks of the model guarantee that the architecture defined by the general design is maintained by the detailed design, and the proof properly speaking guarantees that the detailed design is coherent and complete with respect to the general design.

The traceability between the detailed non-formal design and the general design is carried out by a traceability matrix of the DCD.

11.5.5. *Proof of the formal model*

This phase's aim is the mathematical proof of the B model, and it consists of:

– the generation of the proof obligations;

– the proof of the coherence of the model;

– the proof of the conformity of the CDF to the CGF.

This verification of the B modules by mathematical proof replaces the verification by unitary tests of these models, the integration between formal modules, the stages of verification of the detailed design and the coding of formal modules (if the code generator is qualified to produce the SSIL4 code).

The mathematical formalization of the design makes an automatic reasoning on the design model possible, in order to verify:

– the coherence of the model: no contradiction is detected between the various modules;

– the specified properties (including the correct definition of the data, the respect of the types, the boundaries, etc.);

– the traceability between the CGF and the CDF up to the implantable modules.

The tool "Atelier B" gives a platform to conclude the verification of a model by:

– a syntactic analysis and a static checking of the model;

– verification of the architecture of the B model;

– the exhaustive generation of the model's proof obligations;

– tools for automatic and interactive demonstration of the proof obligations.

As with any tool, a qualification folder of Atelier B is created.

A formal proof folder describes the result of the proof activity.

11.5.5.1. *Verification of the architecture, syntactic analysis and checking of the types*

The first stage of verification concerns the structure of the model (see [BRE 08]), in the order:

– the architecture of the model should be valid (respect of the constraints on the SEES and IMPORTS links for example);

– the syntax of each module is correct;

– all of the data are correctly typed (in the sense of the types of B).

These verifications are automatically carried out by the tool. If the architecture of the project is not respected, the following verifications cannot be carried out. For a given module, the checking of the types can only be carried out once the syntactic analysis has been verified.

11.5.5.2. *Generation of proof obligations*

For each module which is syntactically correct and correctly classified, Atelier B generates an exhaustive set of proof obligations:

– to verify the semantic coherence of the module with the seen and imported modules;

– to verify the specified properties (in the form of invariants or of postcondition of an operation);

– to verify the refinement links (which makes it possible, among other things, to validate the CDF with respect to the CGF).

For each proof obligation, the tool archives a commentary that traces its origin.

11.5.5.3. *Demonstration of the proof obligations*

The demonstration of the proof obligations (which may be performed module by module) can be broken down into two stages:

– The automatic demonstration to discharge a maximum number of obligations: Atelier B automatically applies a set of predefined proof tactics;

– The interactive demonstration to treat the residual proof obligations: the designer directs the proof by choosing the proof tactics and rules to apply, and Atelier B assists the proof by the application of the rules and the tactics.

During this last stage, the designer may need to define new proof rules. These rules are defined in the proof files, one per non-proven module, automatically. These files also contain a recording of the manual proofs which could also be replayed automatically in this way. The aim of this stage is to reach 100% of the generated proof obligations proven.

The status of the proof for all of the modules, listing the number of proof obligations generated and automatically proven, is given in the proof report.

The proof report also contains the list of the added rules and their demonstrations.

11.5.6. *Coding of the ZC security application*

This phase consists of generating an executable code, on the basis of a detailed formal and non-formal design.

11.5.6.1. *Automatic code generation starting from the CDF*

A double chain of translation of B into C makes it possible to automatically obtain a code that can be evaluated at the SSIL4 level starting from the B model.

The specification of the translators is verified by two independent pairs of editor and expert in B modeling to ensure that this specification preserves the semantics of the B model during translation (no bias introduced by translation).

The differentiation of translators is then ensured by an independent development (two independent agents) and the use of distinctive software techniques to avoid any common mode.

The formal proof of the original B model covers the unitary tests and the integration tests between formal modules that might be performed on these modules. The formal proof shows mathematically that, whatever these inputs are, a formal module will run in accordance with its formal specification (providing that all the other activities described in this document are correctly conducted).

11.5.6.2. *Manual coding and verification based on the CDNF*

The modules which come from the detailed non-formal design are coded in C, following coding rules. The C modules are simple and are not broken down.

A verification process and unitary tests are implemented for these modules, following a methodology described in a Software Verification Plan.

11.5.7. *Integration of the ZC security application*

This stage consists of integrating the various software bricks (from the translation chain or manually coded) to obtain a complete application.

The integration, as far as possible, is conducted incrementally.

The formal proof ensures that the B modules fulfill the functional requirements of the CGF and interface correctly amongst themselves. Thus, the integration tests only apply to the points that are not covered by the proof:

– interfaces between the application software and its hosting structure;

– interfaces between non-formal modules;

– interfaces between formal and non-formal modules (manually coded);

– performance of the application software on the target.

An integration test plan is defined to verify these points following the process defined in the software verification plan.

11.5.8. *Tests of the ZC security application*

In this final stage, the aim is to verify through tests that the obtained, proven and integrated object satisfies the objectives of the specification of the ZC security application. This stage, outside the pattern of the B method techniques, is nonetheless essential. Even if the verification activities are carried out between the specification and design phases, these activities are not infallible and may possibly leave a residual group of functionalities that do not conform to requirements. The object obtained is correct, but does not conform to requirements. Thus, the proof of a B model is an activity which is necessary, but is not sufficient.

The test activity takes place on a host machine and is completed by tests on the target machine to verify, in particular, the performance, memory occupation and conformity with the final compiler chosen.

11.6 Glossary

CBTC: Communication Based Train Control

CDF: Detailed formal design

CGF: General formal design

DCD: Detailed design folder

DCG: General design folder

DRACK: D – Dependable, R – Reliable, A – Available, C – Configurable, K – Kit

DSL: Software specification folder

IOC: Input Output Controller KCG: Code generator of the SCADE suite

SA/RT: Structured Analysis/Real Time

SD: Structured Design

SSIL: Software Safety Integrity Level

ZC: Zone Controller

11.7. Bibliography

[ABR 96] ABRIAL J.-R., *The B-Book*, Cambridge University Press, 1996.

[BRE 08] B Reference Manual, Clearsy, 3 November 2008.

[CEN 01] CENELEC 50128, "Railway applications – communication, signalling and processing systems", *Software for Railway Control and Protection Systems*, July 2001.

[CEI 06] CEI 60880, "Nuclear power plants – instrumentation and control systems important to safety", *Software Aspects for Computer-based Systems Performing Category A Functions*, May 2006.

12

Mathematical Proofs for the New York Subway

12.1. The CBTC of the New York subway Line 7 and the system proof

The project for the modernization of Line 7 of the New York subway involves installing a Communication Based Train Control (CBTC) on this line, and updating the signaling in line with this change. THALES Toronto was entrusted with this project. The benefits expected from this modernization are:

– an increased service level as a result of the reduction in the interval between trains;

– a simplification of the track equipment (reduced number of track circuits/signals);

– increased possibilities in terms of special movements of trains, for example in the case of a track obstruction.

This project began in 2010, and the new system is due to begin operation in 2016.

The authority responsible for the New York subway, New York City Transit authority (NYCT), chose to include formal mathematical proofs at the system level as an element of the security demonstration of the system. The French company *ClearSy* was chosen for these proofs, using the formal B method and the Atelier B toolkit, which is already in used for the creation of security software, including many software packages equipped with CBTC.

Chapter written by Denis SABATIER.

Figure 12.1. *Line 7, with its track equipment and its signals*

12.2. Formal proof of the system

12.2.1. *Presentation*

The main aim of this formal proof is to establish the impossibility of collision between trains, and the impossibility of derailment. Here are the demonstrated properties in more detail:

– At each moment, the movement space of each train contains no other train and only contains switches that are locked into the correct position;

– At each moment, no train is overspeeding.

As can be seen, if the above properties are assured, then the security of the system is guaranteed with respect to a very large category of accidents and hazards, except hazards independent of the system, such as fire or people falling onto the track.

The formal demonstration aims to obtain a mathematical proof of these properties, which are based on a set of assumptions, which have been explained and well defined. These "assumptions" (in the mathematical sense of the term) should thus contain everything necessary, from the braking or train tracking algorithms to the definition of the various limit conditions such as, for example, the minimum radius of curvature with which localization precision can be guaranteed. The whole context must be introduced in the form of assumptions in the proof tool, which, of course, has no knowledge of mathematical rules.

The CBTC algorithms, the mechanical behavior of the trains, the behavior of the signaling system, and the characteristics of possible slippages: all these elements are part of the properties known as "assumptions" in the formal demonstration, which is, in fact, the mathematical description of all of these elements. Of course, it must be established that these assumptions match the reality:

– The mathematical description of the design must correspond to the real, final design.

– The mathematical description of the behavior of the elements with which the CBTC interfaces (signaling, train systems, etc.) must match the reality.

– The assumptions on the external conditions (train slippages, mechanical limits, etc.) must be approved by experts.

If the mathematical proof is established and these assumptions are validated, then we have obtained a *logical guarantee in the mathematical sense* that the two target properties explained above are always verified.

12.2.2. *Benefits*

What are the concrete benefits obtained at the end of this work? At what points does this proof activity eliminate potential errors?

The benefits are already apparent during the stages of constitution of the proof:

– During the stage of "demonstration in natural language" (which we will further explain; this is the stage of analysis of the system and of choice of the path of reasoning and the assumptions), the difficulties encountered show a potential problem: the design is based on assumptions which are not explained or are poorly explained, or the reasoning for correct functioning is not explicit on an aspect, or a case has been omitted. At this stage, the proof activity leads to the completion of these gaps, during the exchanges between the proof team and the designers.

– During the finalization of the formal proof, cases which are hard to define and understand, and which require unexpected tests, always appear (for example: a case where residual traction may exert a reverse force at the beginning of the emergency braking of a train). These cases can then be taken into account in an informed manner.

Once the formal proof has been completed, we are sure that *all* the elements necessary to the guarantee of the desired properties have been revealed: if not, the proof would not have been able to conclude. These elements are then consigned to the "set of system verifications", which is a set of documents in natural language which brings together everything upon which the proof is based. These documents are written in order to make the verification or re-verification of these assumptions as accessible as possible, and they contain precise indications on how to verify each assumption (how to find the concrete elements which correspond to them, who should carry out the verification, etc.). The set of verification of assumptions allows us to:

– check that all the points have been correctly validated, when the system begins operation;

– to find out if the validity of the proof is conserved during any change in the system or its environment, and to find out how to restore it, if it is not.

Of course, the proof is hierarchically decomposed: establishment of the two main properties needs to be based on lower level properties, which themselves need to be proven, and so on through the hierarchy. The level of detail at which we stop determines the level of the proof assumptions. For example, as concerns counting the impulsions produced by the wheels equipped with rotation captors, an assumption may be formulated for the relationship between the counting and the real rotation, or we can continue down a level by analyzing the firmware which detects these impulsions.

This choice of level of detail at which we stop conditions the type of errors that the proof is likely to detect. For the software, the *system* proof carried out is based on a documentary description of the algorithms. The computer code itself has not been examined. Low level errors for example, errors in indices in the tables. are not the target of a proof such as this. We can nonetheless bank on the fact that the clear explanation in the written assumptions of the properties that each algorithm should establish, clarifies the objectives for the programmers and in this way contributes to the elimination of these low level errors.

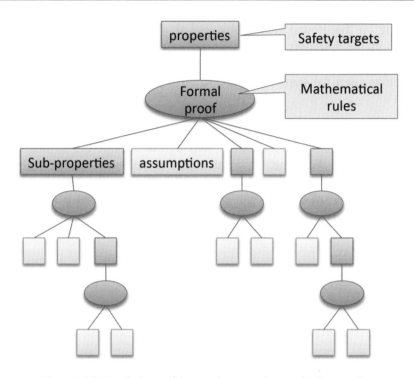

Figure 12.2. *Break-down of the proof: assumptions and subproperties*

12.2.2.1. *Method*

We use two main stages:

– Understanding and explaining in a text in natural language *why* the system guarantees the required properties. We call this the "demonstration in natural language" (in quotation marks because this is not a true formal demonstration).

– Constructing formal B models so that the demonstration obtained with Atelier B is the formal equivalent of the demonstration in natural language.

The first stage is linked to the fact that understanding *why* and *how* a CBTC system guarantees non-collision and non-overspeed is first and foremost an on-the-job issue. The system has been designed to ensure that these properties are fulfilled; it is thus necessary to understand all of the details of its designers' reasoning before trying to formalize it. At this level, the use of very precise formal notation could mar exchanges with those working on the ground. The problem at this stage is that the explanations written by the designers usually describe *how* the system works, and not *why* it is designed in a particular way. This is the difference between knowing an algorithm (step by step) and understanding why it produces the required result.

This first stage of "demonstration in natural language" is a way of stabilizing this understanding before making the transition to writing formal models. Without this stage, the development of the understanding of the *why* could possibly lead to repeated, costly modifications of the formal models, if they are written too early in the process. However, this stage must form a real step towards a rigorous demonstration. In order to guarantee that this is the case, it should be verified that these demonstrations in natural language only contain:

– well-defined assumptions;

– non-subjective stages of logical reasoning;

– the established properties.

At this stage, in natural language, there is no tool for checking these characteristics. The most important characteristic is the first one: all of the assumptions must be unambiguous and well defined. We check this, using the following criterion:

> Well defined assumptions: in any imaginable scenario on the real system, it must be possible to unambiguously determine whether the assumption is satisfied or not.

We will test this criterion on a sentence chosen at random: "The house is red". We can immediately see to what extent the terminology needs to be precise: what is the house? The inside, the outside, the roof? Matte red, glossy red, dark red? The criterion in the box above, although quite informal, is very effective for verifying the precision of definitions. Thus, risks of imprecision relating to notions that at first might seem simple, are avoided. This leads, for example, to the precise definition of the slippage of an axle. At corners, it is always possible that the difference in length between the outside and inside rail is not exactly compensated for by the conicity of the wheels: one of the wheels of the axle then lightly slips outside of any explicit slippage.

The second stage consists of modeling the B language so that the proof carried out by Atelier B corresponds to the demonstration in natural language. This stage brings the complete guarantee of the exactness of the reasoning conducted, because Atelier B reruns this reasoning uniquely through the mathematical rules that it contains. This second stage might seem to hold no surprises, however, experience shows that the demonstrations are still evolving at this time: things which seemed obvious prove to be sometimes difficult, even sometimes false. This leads to the examination of tricky cases with the system's designers.

12.2.3. *Obtaining the first demonstration: organization and communication*

Putting an effective method in place, for conducting this formal proof is not solely a technical problem. Far from it. For the first stage of "demonstration in natural language" there is also the challenge of coordinating organization and communication with the system's designers.

The main stumbling blocks to be avoided are:

– spending too much time on this stage. The system is complex. Therefore, the proof team must focus only on the matters that are necessary for the establishment of the required properties;

– finding a reasoning independent of the system's designers. It is very unlikely that such a reasoning would be relevant.

The first point is an optimization problem: the system is described by a large volume of documents, the complete reading of which would take too much time, and many details in them are unimportant for guaranteeing the required properties. In order to find the most direct way to the desired results – the simplest reasons for which the desired properties must be guaranteed – we use a process which is applied in conjunction with the system's designers:

– We play the scenarios quickly and cleverly, while trying to violate the target property (for example: looking for a scenario which leads to a collision). Proceeding in this way, we can see the reasons why the property cannot be broken.

- We present these scenarios to the designers: because the desired properties (for example, the absence of collision) are their concern, they will easily be able to explain how and why the property is maintained in the case in question, unless there really is a pitfall.

- Once these reasons which guarantee the desired property have been revealed, the reasons are explained, first informally, and then more and more rigorously, until a demonstration based only on well-defined assumptions and steps of purely logical reasoning has been obtained.

- Once again, these *simplest reasons for which the required property is actually guaranteed* are presented to the designers. Their opinion is fundamental and these reasons must exactly match what they know about the system.

As mentioned above, writing well-defined assumptions is crucial. By testing these written assumptions using the informal criterion "*in any imaginable scenario on the real system, it must be possible to unambiguously determine whether the assumption is satisfied or not*", we remove a large number of questions before arriving at a satisfactory formulation. Another very effective criterion for each assumption involves looking for a realistic accident scenario if the condition of the assumption is not true: these scenarios should then be stored with the assumption of which they are a good explanation.

12.2.4. *A method based on exchange*

The two stages of this method – the stage of "demonstration in natural language" and the stage of "formal proof" – are accompanied by multiple exchanges between the proof team and the experts in the field (system designers and those responsible for the infrastructure).

In the first stage, the large number of exchanges makes it possible to understand why it is intended for the system design to ensure the required properties. It might seem surprising that it is necessary to develop a stage like this when the system has been designed to guarantee these properties. However, experience has shown that the existing documents always describe the *how* of the design and not the *why*. Therefore, the *why* needs to be brought together and recreated by a large number of exchanges. These exchanges then form a general "along with the flow" clarification, which raises many points which it is useful to define further, and works alongside the finalization of the design.

There are fewer exchanges in the second phase (formal proof), because they are limited to unexpected cases revealed during the complete formulation in B language and the proof with Atelier B. Experience has shown that such cases always occur. It might even be said that the reasoning which is finalized once the formulation in B language has been completed and the proof has been carried out in Atelier B is generally quite different to its informal version, in particular regarding the paths it takes.

These exchanges are shown in the diagram below:

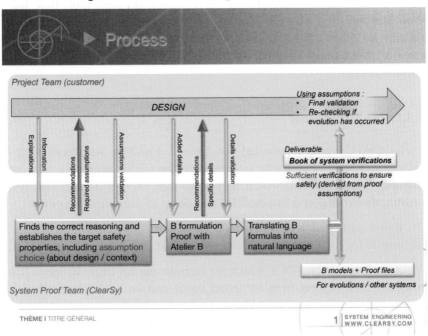

Figure 12.3. *The formal proof process for the system: interface with the design*

At the end of the process, the client receives the B models, the proofs and the set of system verifications. This last element does not require any knowledge of the B language in order to use it in practice. It makes it possible to know all of the conditions which determine whether the assumptions we are handling are those for which the proof is valid. It also lets us know how to verify if these conditions are established, how these conditions have been checked up until the present moment, and how to check them again.

During the Flushing project, in order to help others involved in the process to be able to use these documents efficiently, we conducted an in-depth presentation of them (which took several days) to the NYCT experts and the experts from THALES Toronto.

12.3. An early insight into the obtained proof

As previously mentioned, the first target property for this formal demonstration is: "At each moment, the movement space of each train contains no other train and only contains switches locked into the correct position". Let us now examine how this guarantee may be logically deduced from the design.

12.3.1. *The global proof*

The CBTC system intended for Line 7 Flushing interfaces with the existing signaling. The trains overseen by the CBTC receive a Movement Authority Limit (MAL), which they must not exceed. The global system ensuring that collision is impossible is made up of the following parts:

– trains equipped with OBCU (On Board Computer Units), which are responsible for their localization and ensure that they respect their MAL;

– Zone Controllers (ZC), which are responsible for tracking trains (based on localization reports from equipped trains and on track circuits for other trains), and which transmit MALs to trains. These ZC ensure that the trains remain on the itineraries that have been authorized and are in progress, with a correct amount of space between them and other trains;

– the signaling system, which is responsible for the interlocking and the authorization of the itineraries;

– unequipped trains or trains which are operated line-on-sight, the use of which, following procedures, must be compatible with the new context.

To simplify slightly, we might say that signaling opens the protected spaces within which the trains are circulating in the same direction and following one another in function of their ability to control the space between them. Within one of these spaces, segmented off by the signaling, it is thus possible to have several trains where CBTC guarantees the space between them, or one manual train, the security of which is then certain for all of this space. If maximum reverse distance of a manual train in such a situation is limited, it is also possible to have a manual train followed by trains where CBTC ensures there is enough space between them. Of course, this is on the understanding that within these spaces opened up by the signaling, the switches are locked into the correct position; the signaling has modified and then controlled their state *before* opening or increasing the space which they are authorized to occupy.

When the CBTC trains, within one of these protected spaces with locked switches, guarantee there is enough space between them for them to be secure, it is in fact the ZC which create "bubbles" for each train. These "bubbles" are then used by the ZC to deduce the MALs which should be sent to the trains. We thus have protected subspaces within the spaces created by signaling. As a result of transmission delays and random events, the spaces known to each CBTC train are slightly different to the spaces known to the ZC: these "train" spaces remain included within the ZC spaces. The following image gives an example of how these spaces are distributed.

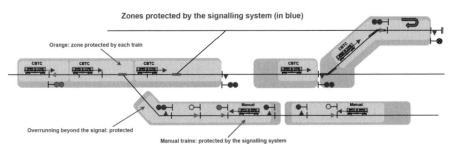

Figure 12.4. *The spaces protected by the signaling and those protected by the trains*

We should note that the signaling in the New York subway obliges us to use systematic stop measures at each signal. These are "trip stops", little yellow levers which are raised when the signal is restrictive and which the trains mechanically detect and then activate their emergency brake. The space beyond a restrictive signal which is accessible to a train is thus limited, even for a manual train.

It is in paying attention to all of these different protected spaces that the anti-collision property is obtained. This is a "proof by induction": by starting from a state where the arrangement of the protections makes it possible to find a space for each train in which the train is alone and only encounters locked switches, we show that for all the possible changes, these properties are maintained.

Figure 12.5. *A "trip stop" just after a signal, in lowered position (open signal)*

On the basis of this principle, real demonstration requires a large number of assumptions which involve various verifications of the CBTC, the signaling, and the operating procedures. For example, a CBTC train which starts operating in manual mode must proceed line-on-sight in order not to exceed and pass the next restrictive signal. This is because the marked limited space past the "trip stop" will not necessarily be engaged in this case. Generally, this global part of the proof in the process of scenario cycles and exchanges with experts in the domains has led to many conditions being formulated and verified, and in particular:

– changes in train type (breakdowns, resumptions, couplings, etc.);

– the turning of trains (and any possible reversing).

We have mentioned above that signaling opens protected spaces within which all the trains circulate *in the same direction*: in fact, this is a simplification. The new CBTC makes it possible to manage two-directional zones when there are only CBTC trains and the signaling is able to use this fact. This new function creates increased possibilities in terms of special movements of trains, for example in the case of a track obstruction. The movements are defined by the *virtual signals* of the CBTC.

12.3.2. Proof that localization has been correctly achieved

The global proof above is based on an important property: when a CBTC train provides its location to the ZC (in the form of a maximum interval), this train must absolutely be within this interval.

In order to enable the CBTC trains to detect their position, the track is equipped with radio localization transponders and the trains are equipped with transponder interrogation units. Between two transponders, the localization is updated by detection of movement. The trains of Line 7 are modified to ensure that movement is detected. This is done by assigning a bogie to measurements. This bogie is not motorized, it therefore has a free axle and an axle which is braked only in order to install two rotation captors, minimizing the impact of potential slippages. The onboard calculator is equipped with more than three pendulous accelerometers installed in redundancy to compare the measured accelerations with those of the equipped axles. This gives a high level of detection of slippages.

Here too, the exercise of deducing the property "localization always correct" of a group of explained assumptions using a completely unsubjective reasoning makes it possible to formulate and reveal all the necessary elements, from the correct placement of the transponders to the principles which govern whether changes in direction are taken into account.

A crucial point in these elements concerns slippages: if one of the equipped axles begins to slip in an undetected manner, this obviously can compromise the measurement. In the installation on the flushing line, the fact that there was one free axle and one only braked axle available made it possible to assume that a simultaneous slippage of an entire bogie is unlikely, all the more so, because prolonged slippage of one of the axles leads to the activation of slowing. In these assumptions, the fact that a correct localization between transponders has been maintained is shown on the basis of the precise nature of the measurements and the frequency of the beginnings of slippage, while taking into account the time delay which is necessary before they are detected.

In this part of the proof, it was necessary to be wary of assumptions which seemed to be self-evident but could prove to be false: a curious example is that of the impossibility of skating (slippage with a rotation greater than the distance traversed) of a free axle. This seems obvious, however, it is theoretically false if the train brakes strongly from all its other axles while the free axle crosses a slippery portion: its rotation momentum can then lead to skating. We take the following to be a rule: assumptions about mechanical behavior must either be well-known physical laws or it must be possible to deduce them from these. Cases such as the one just mentioned can be detected in this way, and decided upon in an informed manner (and not implicitly and through omission).

Along with the position, the measurement of speed is also important. The global demonstration is based, in fact, on a subproperty which needs to be proven: the speed measured by the train needs to be a majoring value of the real speed. The speed measured using the same captors as for the position is corrected using many tuned Kalman filters; representing the action of these filters in the reasoning of the proof is a particular challenge. Here too, the key is to proceed in such a way that the formal proof reproduces the natural reasoning of understanding of the operation. In this natural reasoning, we can understand, for example, that the property which links real speed and measured speed is only established due to the fact that speed does not vary too quickly. This is true because the train undergoes limited accelerations (except in the case of an accident).

12.3.3. *Proof of correct braking*

The respect by CBTC trains of "movement authority limits (MALs) is also a subproperty upon which the global demonstration is based, and which needs to be proven. More exactly, the subproperty is stated as follows: if at t0 a train has accepted a MAL, then it will never exceed this MAL as long as it remains in CBTC mode, unless it receives a new MAL which goes beyond the first MAL.

In order to prove this property, we need to involve the cycles of the onboard OBCU calculator. The real mechanical apparatus which is constituted by the train is controlled discontinuously by the OBCU; the cycle time thus obviously has an influence. After a first phase of reasoning, the following property to be proven is obtained: if the OBCU activates the emergency brake in the current cycle, when, during the preceding cycle its calculation confirmed respect of a MAL, then the emergency braking sequence – which covers all of the time delays necessary, including the time necessary for lifting traction and establishing braking – will lead to stoppage of the train before the MAL.

There are specific challenges related to formalizing the reasoning which establishes this property: it is a reasoning which includes (tiny) physical changes and all of the physical laws involved must be explained and then added to the proof. To make this reasoning easier, we firstly compare the real train to a "worst-case" train: an imaginary train with the same masses that is circulating on the same portion of track but which always presents the worst-case scenario in terms of timing and braking effectiveness. As always, interesting cases appear during the natural reasoning phase, and trickier cases appear during the complete formulation.

An example of a case which appeared in the first phase is that of the energy potentially concealed in the traction axles that skate: if the train is at low speed and accelerates suddenly, some of these axles may skate (modulo the anti-skating devices, which are not safety critical). The energy in these axles is then only visible by the movement captor axle. As a result, the braking calculation could be compromised. The estimation of the possible energy delta shows, however, that it can be compensated for, by the margins taken in the timeframe necessary to establish braking. Another example of a "tricky" case revealed by complete formulation is that of the direction of the residual traction during the release of an emergency braking action. This direction can be reversed (specific failure of the traction). This seems to help the braking, but in certain cases, this can bring a slope behind the train into the action, which has not been taken into account. Here too, estimations including the value of the timeframes for cutting traction and for braking make it possible to avoid the occurrence of these cases.

12.4. Feedback based on experience

This project of formal proof began at the end of 2010 with a completion date at the end of 2012, when the desired demonstrations with B models proved by Atelier B would be obtained, and the collections of system verifications written, itemized and proofread.

In order to obtain this result, the first phase (making the demonstrations available in natural language) represented slightly over 50% of the overall work. During this phase, as we have stated above, communication with the designers and with experts in the field is essential. The challenge is to ensure that the members of the proof team are seen as being helpful rather than critical. More than a simple exercise in logic, this phase requires a strong and renewed desire on the part of the modelers to face the system's real problems, and those of the people who manage them.

In the communication between these parties, the format of the exchanges is of capital importance. It must be possible to rapidly share information which has not yet been finalized. Meetings which allow this exchange to occur orally are thus essential, but not in themselves sufficient. "Light" supports need to be used to fix and clarify the elements, all the while avoiding the pitfall of a complete anticipated documentation before validation by Atelier B. At the end of this demonstration phase in natural language, a detailed account of the reasonings obtained was presented to the experts in the field.

The phase of formal proof properly speaking represents approximately 35% of the overall effort. At this stage, what is at stake is trying to find the simplest and most effective model for reproducing the reasoning in natural language, so that any error necessarily produces a proof error. The models obtained must thus contain the desired properties as properties to be proven, and all the other elements provided to the proof system (properties allowed, assumptions on the changes, etc.) must match a validated assumption from the reasoning, which should be plotted in the final set of the system verifications. At this stage, the level of contact with the designers is less intense, but it remains essential: tricky cases are discovered, which require new precautions.

The final phase consists of running through the obtained models step by step to form the final sets of system verifications, while checking that all the elements found therein have already been seen by the designers and the experts in the field and have been validated by them. In addition, this involves a significant amount of writing work, because it should be possible to re-verify each system verification using the final documents only, independent of the common understanding which may have grown up between those involved in the operation. Proofreading by a second set of eyes is thus absolutely essential. In this way, the meaning of the terms is checked, along with how easy the documents are to use, and whether there is a risk of incorrect interpretation. This work is far from insignificant: in this project it represented 15% of the overall work effort. Finally, it is important to present and explain these documents to their future users: a final presentation was organized over several days.

The final collections of system verifications for the CBTC Flushing Line are divided in line with the hierarchical break-down of the proof, to make it possible, if necessary, to separately verify the conditions necessary to the proof of one subproperty alone. The number of conditions and verifications is around 250; each of these requires several pages of explanation.

A mathematical demonstration of this kind is thus an accessible method for *finding out why* the system's security function is established, and to obtain a *strong assurance* that this understanding is not marred by errors. Obtaining strong assurances is the central and basic issue for security. The operation of the software may be tested, it is possible to check by view if the train is stopping correctly and if the doors action with sufficient speed. Security involves events *which should never happen*: accidents that can be seen are accidents that have already happened. When we see them, it is already too late! This is why the assurance provided by a mathematical demonstration is so completely invaluable.

Conclusion

C.1. Introduction

Formal techniques (simulation, model-checking, abstract interpretation, proof, etc.) have been in use for quite a while. Indeed, the first papers written on the subject date from the 1970s (see for example, [HOA 69, COU 77, DIJ 76]). However, the application of these methods began in the 1980s [SPI 89, JON 90, HAL 91], with industrial use of them beginning in the 1990s [BEH 93, ARA 97].

In [BOW 95] and [ARA 97], we find the first feedback on the industrial use of formal techniques, and particularly on the use of the B method [ABR 96], the LUSTRE language [HAL 91, ARA 97] and SAO+, the precursor of SCADE[1]. Other works, such as [MON 00, HAD 06], provide an overview of formal methods from a more academic point of view.

In the present book, we have shown various different uses of formal methods within the railway sector. Several different environments and formal methods have been presented (ASA+, B method, SCADE, Design Verifier, etc.).

Conclusion written by Jean-Louis BOULANGER.

1 It should be noted that SCADE was initially a development environment based on the LUSTRE language. However, since Version 6, SCADE has become a language in its own right (the code generator for Version 6 takes a SCADE model as the input, and not a LUSTRE code).

This conclusion will aim to bring together everything that has been presented in the book, and to take stock of the changes that are occurring in the domain of railway applications.

The aim of this series of four books (i.e. this one and [BOU 11c, BOU 12a, BOU 12b]) has been to provide an overview of the use of formal techniques (simulation, model-checking [BAI 08], proof, abstract interpretation, etc.) and formal methods (for example, the B method [ABR 96], LUSTRE [HAL 91, BEN 03, HAL 05], SCADE [HAL 05, DOR 08], AltaRica, SPARK Ada [BAR 03], etc.) in industry contexts. Therefore, we will not embark on a discussion of the scientific challenges and possible uses (in 5, 10 or 15 years).

First, we will discuss how formal methods and techniques currently feature in the standards. Then, we will discuss the current uses to which formal methods (and formal techniques) have been put, and the difficulties which have been encountered. Finally, we will examine the future prospects for these methods and techniques.

C.2. Formal methods and the standard CENELEC EN 50128

C.2.1. *E/E/PE System*

The standard CEI/IEC 61508 [IEC 08] is a generic standard which can be applied to all complex systems with an electronic and/or programmable electronic basis, known as E/E/PE (electric/electronic/programmable electronic). This standard has been published by the International Electrotechnical Commission[2] (IEC), the international standardization organization which is responsible for the electrical and electronic sectors and associated techniques.

The standard CEI/IEC 61508 [IEC 08] suggests a globalized approach for safety, in the sense of safety/innocuity[3], which could be compared to the quality system ISO 9001:2008 [ISO 08]. The standard CEI/IEC 61508 is completely coherent with the convergence which can be observed between

2 To find out more about the IEC, see the site www.iec.ch/.

3 The standard CEI/IEC 61508 [IEC 08] does not cover confidentiality and/or data integrity. These are linked to put precautions in place, which aim to prevent unauthorized people from damaging and/or having an impact on the safety functions created by the E/E/PE safety systems. In particular, this involves network management for avoiding intrusions.

the various industrial sectors involved (aeronautical, nuclear, railway, automobile, manufacturing, etc.). However, the content of the standard CEI/IEC 61508 is so complex, and even unusual, that some background reading may be necessary to understand it. The following references may be useful in this case: [ISA 05] or [SMI 07].

The standard CEI/IEC 61508 [IEC 08] defines the notion of the Safety Integrity Level (SIL). The SIL makes it possible to quantify the safety level of a system. Safety Integrity Level 1 (SIL1) is the lowest SIL and Safety Integrity Level 4 (SIL4) is the highest.

The standard lists the requirements necessary to reach each SIL. These requirements are stricter at the higher safety levels, in order to guarantee a lower probability of dangerous failure.

The SIL makes it possible to specify the prescriptions concerning the integrity of safety functions which should be allocated to E/E/PE systems.

For several years the generic standard CEI/IEC 61508 [IEC 08] has been adapted to its purpose through related standards which cover various sectors, as shown in Figure C.1.

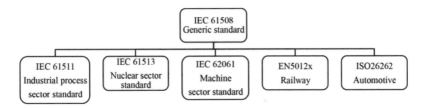

Figure C.1. *The standard CEI/IEC 61508 and its related, adapted versions*[4]

The standard CEI/IEC 61508 [IEC 08] is very widely used for the development of "critical" software in the automation and automobile sectors, and also for control installations in industrial processes. Part 3 of standard CEI/IEC 61508 concerns the software design.

---

4 Figure C.1 shows a link between standard CEI/IEC 61508 and standard CEI/IEC 61513 [IEC 01], but this link is not correct. In fact, the nuclear standards were in existence before standard CEI/IEC 61508 and this link is in name only.

C.2.2. *Railways*

Railway projects are currently governed by texts (e.g. decrees, orders, etc.) and a referential standard (CENELEC[5] EN 50126 [CEN 00], EN 50129 [CEN 03], and EN 50128 [CEN 01a, CEN 11]) which aims to define and reach certain reliability, availability maintainability and safety objectives (RAMS).

The three standards (see Figure C.2) cover the aspects which concern the safety-innocuity (SAFETY) of the system up to the equipment and/or software elements.

For the notion of safety-confidentiality, the reference standard CENELEC is supplemented by the standards EN 50159 [CEN 10], which can be applied if the application uses open or closed networks.

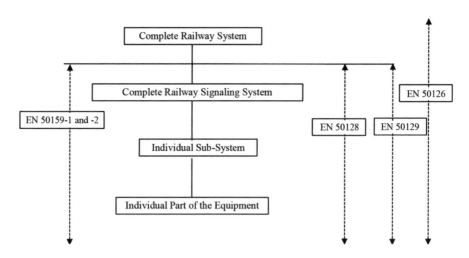

Figure C.2. *CENELEC reference standard*

The standards CENELEC EN 50126 [CEN 00], EN 50129 [CEN 03], and EN 50128 [CEN 01a, CEN 11] describe requirements in terms of construction and of demonstration of the RAMS of programmable

---

5 CENELEC stands for Comité Européen de Normalisation ELECtrotechnique – European Committee for Electrotechnical Standardization, see the website www.cenelec.eu/.

electronic systems for railway applications. These standards now have a Europe-wide status, as they apply to all the Member States of the European Community, and have been taken on by the International Electrotechnical Commission CEI/IEC 61508 [IEC 08], which has given them international status.

Safety, as an element of Operating Safety, is obtained by putting in place certain concepts, methods and tools, throughout the entire lifecycle. The analysis of system failures is necessary for the preparation of a study of safety. When this is conducted, the aim should be to identify and quantify the seriousness of any potential consequences and also to forecast the potential frequency of these failures.

The standard CENELEC EN 50129 [CEN 03] describes several actions to reduce risk, among which is the allocation of safety objectives to system and subsystem functions. The SIL is defined as one of the discrete levels for specifying the safety integrity requirements of the safety functions allocated to the safety systems. The SIL scale is from 1 to 4.

It should be noted that the notion of SIL in the sense of the standard CENELEC EN 50129 [CEN 03] is not the same as the notion of SIL in the sense of the standard CEI/IEC 61508 [IEC 08]. The differences between these concern the method of identification and the impacts. Their use within the standards is identical.

The standard CENELEC EN 50128 [CEN 01a, CEN 11] is more particularly concerned with the development of software for railways. For software, the Software SIL (SSIL) defines several risk levels from 0 (no danger) to 4 (critical).

The standard CENELEC EN 50128 specifies the procedures and the technical prescriptions applicable to the development of programmable electronic systems for use in railway command and protection applications. Therefore, the standard CENELEC EN 50128 cannot normally be applied to all railway software applications. The standard EN 50155 [AFN 01] may normally be applied for all onboard train applications. However, the standard EN 50155 requires reference to the standard CENELEC EN 50128.

C.2.3. *Taking formal techniques and methods into account*

It may be useful to note that the definition in Appendices B and C (Part 7 of the standard CEI/IEC 61508) use articles dating between 1970 and 1998 as references. This might benefit from an update.

C.2.3.1. *Definitions*

C.2.3.1.1. *Semi-formal method*

According to the standard IEC 61508 (B.2.3), a *semi-formal method* provides a way to develop a description of a system at a stage of development (specification, architecture and/or design). The description may be analyzed or animated in order to verify that the modeled system satisfies the requirements (real and/or specified). The standard indicates that state diagrams (finite automata) and temporal Petri nets are two semi-formal methods.

In the new standard CENELEC EN 50128, semi-formal methods no longer feature as techniques. This is due to the ambiguity which existed: where does the limit between formal and semi-formal lie? Some of those involved in industry believed that the existence of a modeling tool was sufficient for them to claim the implementation of a semi-formal method.

C.2.3.1.2. *Formal method*

Section B.30 of EN 50128:2001 indicates that a formal method (HOL, CSP, LOTOS, CCS, Temporal logic, VDM[6] [JON 90] and Z[7] [SPI 89]) makes it possible to create an unambiguous and coherent description of a system at a stage of development (specification, architecture and/or design). The description takes a mathematical form and can be subjected to a mathematical analysis. This mathematical analysis can be tooled.

---

6 In the standard IEC 61508, references to VDM include VDM++ [DUR 92], which is a real-time object-oriented extension of VDM. To find out more, see the website http://www.vdmportal.org/.

7 It should be noted that in the standard CEI/IEC 61508, the B method [ABR 96] is viewed as a method associated with Z.

A formal method generally provides a notation, a technique for creating a description using this notation and a verification process for checking that the requirements are correct.

Standard CEI/IEC 61508 indicates that it is possible to make transformations right down to "a logical design circuit"[8].

Petri nets and state machines (listed among semi-formal methods) may be considered to be formal methods depending on the degree of conformity of their uses to a rigorous mathematical basis.

C.2.3.1.3. *Structured method*

The aim of *structured methods* (EN 50128 – B.60) is to promote the quality of software development by examining the first phases of the lifecycle. These types of methods require precise and intuitive notation (generally computer-assisted) in order to produce and document the requirements and the installation characteristics of the product.

Structured methods are tools for analysis. They are based on a logical order of thought, an analysis of the system which takes its environment into account, the production of the system documentation, the break-down of the data, the break-down of the functions and the elements which require verification. They should be quite easy to understand (they should be simple, intuitive and pragmatic). The following are some examples of structured methods: SADT [LIS 90], JSD, CORE, Real-time Yourdon and MASCOT.

Structured specification is a technique which aims to show the simplest visible relationships between the partial requirements and the functional specification. The analysis is refined by stages until clear small partial requirements are obtained. We then obtain a hierarchical structure of partial requirements which makes it possible to specify the complete requirements. The method emphasizes the interfaces between the requirements and makes it possible to avoid interface failures.

C.2.3.1.4. *Computer-assisted specification tools*

In the standard CEI/IEC 61508 section B.2.4, it is indicated that the use of computer-assisted specification tools allows the agent to obtain a

---

8 These are the terms used in the standard CEI/IEC 61508.

specification in the form of a database which can be automatically inspected to evaluate coherence and comprehensiveness. The tool can make animation possible. It can be applied during the various different phases of specification, architecture and/or design. For the design phase, use is recommended as soon as tools are available. However, it is necessary to show that the tool is correct (through feedback based on experience and/or independent verification of the results).

C.2.3.2. Specification of the software requirements

C.2.3.2.1. Need

The requirements of the software should conform to at least the following three points (EN 50128:2001– 8.4.2):

– They must be clear, precise, unequivocal, verifiable, testable, maintainable and possible to create.

– They must be traceable with the input elements.

– They must be unambiguous and it must be unlikely that they could be incorrectly understood.

	SSIL0	SSIL1	SSIL2	SSIL3	SSIL4
Formal methods, including, for example, CCS, CSP, HOL, LOTOS, OBJ, temporal logic, VDM, Z and B[9]	–	R	R	HR	HR
Semi-formal methods	R	R	R	HR	HR
Structured methodology, including, for example, JSD, MASCOT, SADT, SDL, SSADM and YOURDON	R	HR	HR	HR	HR

Table C.1. *EN 50128 – Table A.2*

Table C.1 shows the complementary requirements that need to be applied in order to guarantee that the requirements are clear and precise. Thus, the standard CENELEC EN 50128:2001 recommends that the specification of a

---

9 It should be noted that in contrast to the standard CEI/IEC 61508 [IEC 08], the standard CENELEC EN 50128:2001 recognizes the B method as a formal method properly speaking.

software application should be made up of a textual description of the problem (the requirements) and all the necessary notations.

C.2.3.2.2. Managing the requirements

The standards which are applicable in the various domains make the identification of the requirements of the software application obligatory. It should be noted that the literature uses several terms which seem to be equivalent to one another: prescriptions, recommendation, requirement, constraint and property. The general standard CEI/IEC 61508 [IEC 08] uses "prescription", but "requirement" remains the more widely used term.

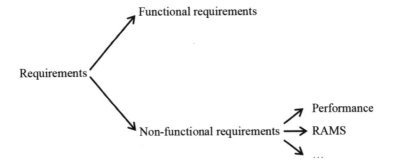

Figure C.3. *Different kinds of requirements*

As can be seen in Figure C.3, there are at least two types of requirements: functional and non-functional (safety, reliability, performance, etc.).

In Chapter 2 of [RAM 09] and Chapter 3 of [RAM 11] we showed some examples of the management of requirements in the automobile and railway sectors.

Table C.2 is taken from [STA 94]. It clearly shows that more than 30% of the causes of failure during the creation stage come from incomplete requirements, from a gap in the description of the needs and from unrealistic needs.

[STA 01] mentions that using a management environment for the requirements is the best way to have a major impact on the success of a project. Defining a minimum set of requirements makes it possible to have a basis which can be managed. In this case, the tool becomes a vector for communication between the teams.

Description	%
Incomplete requirement	13.1%
Lack of user involvement	12.4%
Lack of resources	10.6%
Unrealistic expectations	9.9%
Lack of executive support	9.3%
Changing requirement/specification	8.7%
Lack of planning	8.1%
Did not need it any longer	7.5%

Table C.2. *Distribution of the causes of failure*

Defining what a "requirement" is, in this case, becomes a difficult matter. There are several works which attempt to identify what a requirement is and how a requirement should be handled. [HUL 05] provides one of the clearest outlines. We will use the following definition, which is taken from work carried out by industrialists.

DEFINITION C.1.– (REQUIREMENT[10]).– *A requirement is a statement which illustrates a need and/or constraints (techniques, costs, timeframes, etc.). This statement is written in a language, which may be natural, mathematical or other.*

Figure C.4 shows how the recommendations of the client can be adjusted to the system, and how the process may be continued right up to the software and equipment elements.

In the n_i level verification phase, it should be shown that the requirements of this level relate to the higher level n_{i-1}. This relationship is established through a traceability action.

Traceability is assured by the definition of at least one link between two objects. In the context of requirements, the traceability links must show that a level n_i requirement is linked to a need from the preceding level n_{i-1}. The inverse link shows that no link has been neglected during the creation process.

---

10 AFIS stands for "Association Française d'Ingénierie Système" – French Association for Systems Engineering. One of these working groups is dedicated specifically to the management of requirements. For more information, see: www.afis.fr.

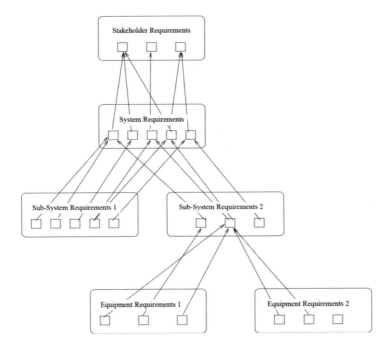

Figure C.4. *Partial traceability between the client requirements and the requirements linked to the equipment*

As shown in Figure C.5, there are several basic transformations of requirements. These include two particularly interesting cases, adding and abandoning a requirement. In each of these cases, a justification must imperatively be attached to the requirement.

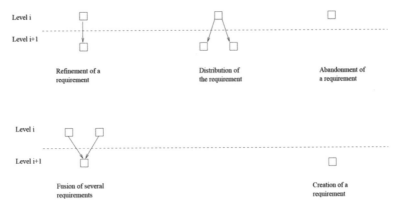

Figure C.5. *Basic transformation of the requirements*

C.2.3.2.3. Specification

The specification of a software application is thus at least one set of requirements. Figure C.6 shows the suggested process. A preliminary analysis of the written specification provided by the client should make it possible to identify the functional requirements.

Alongside this work, it is possible to begin analyses linked to the safe operation, which aim to define the non-functional requirements. These include safety requirements, but also availability, reliability and other requirements.

However, it is necessary to know a bit more about the needs of the software application. Therefore, the following should be included in the specification:

– the interfaces with the environment;

– the notion of state, putting in place a partition between the states of correct operation, the states of shutdown and the dangerous states;

– the notion of correct and of dangerous behavior;

– the notion of requirement linked to safety. This type of requirement must make it possible to characterize dangerous behaviors;

– the integrity level of the software (notated SSIL/DAL).

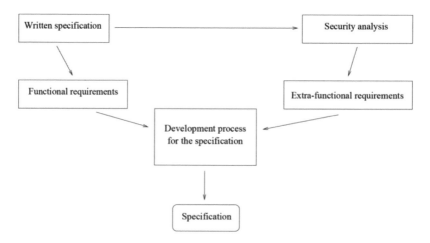

Figure C.6. *Development of the specification*

The environment of the software application is made up of interfaces with the equipment (memory, specific address, inputs/outputs, watchdog, etc.), with other software applications (basic software, linked application, etc.) and/or with the operating system.

Figure C.7 shows an environment of the software application which is made up of three inputs (E_i), two outputs (S_j) and three interfaces (I_k) with equipment (e.g. access to a specific memory address).

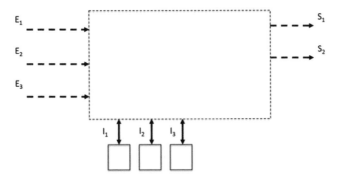

Figure C.7. *Environment of the software application*

C.2.3.2.4. Application

Usually, the designers of a software application go directly to the code from the textual requirements without verifying the coherence of the requirements and without having perfect knowledge of all of the requirements (Figure C.8).

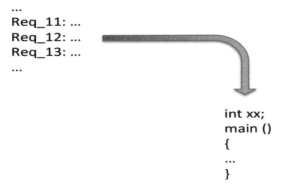

Figure C.8. *From requirements to code*

Successful development of a maintainable software application goes through at least two stages:

– a phase of the formalization of the requirements (see Figure C.10). This formalization phase may be based on structured methods (for example, Figure C.9 in SADT[11] makes it possible to apply a functional analysis etc.), semi-formal methods or formal methods (e.g. automaton, Petri net, Graphcet, B method[12], SCADE[13], etc.).

– an architecture phase (section C.2.2.4).

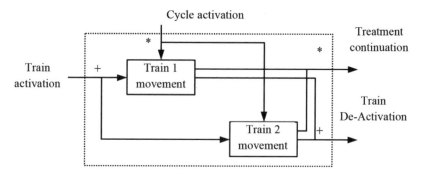

Figure C.9. *Example of a static modeling which introduces different types of communication*

The formalization phase is important because it translates an abstract requirement into elements which can be modeled, such as the following property P1:

P1: "there must be no risk of collision"

In first-order logic, we can express P1 by $\forall \{t_1, t_2\} \in [T]$, *alors* $D_{t_1} \cap D_{t_2} = \phi$, *si* $t_1 \neq t_2$ where D_{ti} is the domain where the train t_i is authorized to move i.

---

11 S.A.D.T. stands for Structured Analysis and Design Technic. This method has been developed by Softech in the USA. The SADT method is an analysis method by successive levels of descriptive approach of any set.

12 In [BOU 12b – Chapter 2], we have provided an example of the use of SADT [LIS 90] and of the B method [ABR 96, BEH 96] during the SAET-METEOR project ([BOU 06].

13 In [BOU 12b – Chapter 6] we have provided some examples of the use of SCADE [DOR 08].

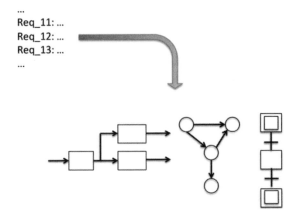

Figure C.10. *Formalizing the requirements*

C.2.3.2.5. Summary

In the railway sector, structured, semi-formal and formal methods are used in specification phase to formalize the need (SADT, B method and SCADE).

Models created in this way allow us to:

– acquire the need;

– formalize the need and verify the coherence and the comprehensiveness of the need;

– have some help in selecting the cases for validation tests; etc.

The new version of the standard CENELEC EN 50128 [CEN 11] replaces the notion of semi-formal method with the notion of modeling (see Table C.3).

	SSIL0	SSIL1	SSIL2	SSIL3	SSIL4
Formal methods (based on a mathematical approach)	–	R	R	HR	HR
Modeling	R	R	R	HR	HR
Structured methodology	R	R	R	HR	HR
Decision table	R	R	R	HR	HR

Table C.3. *EN 50128:2011 – Table A.2*

C.2.3.3. *Model*

The creation of an M model is a way to understand and/or approach a problem/situation. In general, the specification phase, which allows us to make the written specification our own, includes the creation of an M model.

A model may be more or less close to the studied system, in which case we talk of "abstraction". The closer the model, the closer the results obtained will be to those observed on the final system.

Another characteristic of models comes from whether the support language has a semantics available or not.

If it has a semantics, then reasoning techniques can be applied which guarantee that the results obtained will be correct.

A model (Figure C.11) is generally made up of two complementary parts:

– A static modelling (Figures C.9 and C.12), which describes the entities of which the system is composed and the states that can be associated with them;

– A dynamic modeling, which describes the authorized state changes.

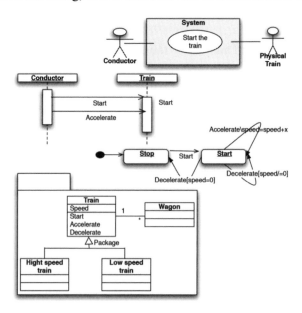

Figure C.11. *Example of a UML model*

Figure C.11 shows an example of an UML model[14] [OMG 06a, OMG 06b, OMG 07, etc.] from a railway system which uses different modelings: usage case, sequence diagram, state/transition diagram and class diagram.

Use of UML raises several issues [BOU 07, OKA 07], among which are the following: how can we use a notation which does not have any semantics? How can we evaluate an application based on UML notation? Several works aim to suggest responses to these questions, for example [OOT, 04] and [MOT, 05].

UML notation [OMG 06a, OMG 06b, and OMG 07] has not yet been recognized as a structured and/or semi-formal method in all of the standards, even if many of them wish to apply it completely or partially.

In [BOU 07, BOU 09a] and [RAM 09], we have shown how UML notation can be used to create models of critical systems.

During the projects RT3-TUCS, ANR-SAFECODE and ANR-RNTL-MEMVATEX we studied different ways of introducing UML as a means for modeling a critical system. See, for example, [RAS 08, BOU 08, IDA 07a, IDA 07b, OKA 07 and BOU 05].

Over the last few years, several works have suggested a formalization of UML notation through a transformation into formal languages. This may be seen, for example, in [IDA 09, IDA 06, MAR 04, MAR 01, MAM 02, LED 02]. We should also mention work such as [MOT 05], which has suggested complementary rules for verifying UML models.

C.2.3.4. *Architecture of the software*

Once the specification of the software application has been created, it is then possible to put an architecture in place. This architecture aims to break the software application down into components (or modules, depending on the vocabulary in use).

Figure C.12 shows an example of the architecture. The software application has been broken down into three components (C_1, C_2, and C3). There are interfaces between the environment (E_1, E_2, S_1, and S2) and the components, and interfaces between the components. For each component, the list of requirements that needs to be taken into account is given.

---

14 To find out more, see OMG's website: http://www.omg.org/.

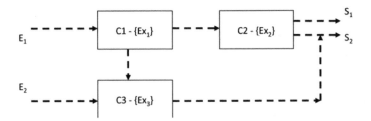

Figure C.12. *Example of the architecture of a software application*

The earlier version of the standard CENELEC EN 50128 [CEN 01a] did not identify any specific requirement for the architecture phase. The new version of the standard CENELEC EN 50128 ([CEN 11] – Table A.3) recommends that the architecture of the software application should be based on a structured method (e.g. SADT). However, it is also possible to create a modeling which is based on the techniques from Table A.17 (see Table C.4).

	SSIL0	SSIL1	SSIL2	SSIL3	SSIL4
Modeling the data	R	R	R	HR	HR
Organizing the data	–	R	R	HR	HR
Diagram of the command flux	R	R	T	HR	HR
Fixed-state automata / transition diagrams	–	HR	HR	HR	HR
Formal methods	R	R	R	HR	HR
Sequence diagrams	R	HR	HR	HR	HR

Table C.4. *New CENELEC EN 50128: 2011 – Table A.17*

A specification and/or the architecture is much more than a simple list of requirements. A model support of the requirements must also be available. This model support (see Table C.4) provides the possibility of verifying the coherence and the comprehensiveness of the requirements.

C.2.3.5. *Software design*

The architecture phase of the software application has provided identification of the main components, the interfaces between these components, and the interfaces with the environment. It is now necessary to define the content of each component. This stage includes the identification of services carried out by the components and the definition of the associated algorithms.

The design phase may be described by two stages, a preliminary design phase which identifies the services and the main algorithms, and a detailed design phase which precisely defines the manipulated data and the algorithms employed.

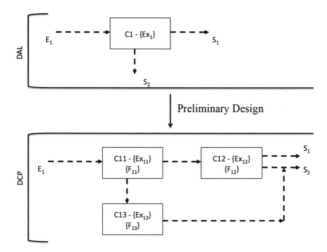

Figure C.13. *Example of preliminary design*

The preliminary design is a stage in the creation of the software which makes it possible to finalize the break-down of the components into basic units. The basic units will depend on the design methodology used. They may be modules (in the sense of independent files), packets (in the sense of ADA, where they are made up of a specification part and a design part), classes, and/or components (in the sense of the literature on components, which describes the component as an independent autonomous entity).

Each base unit (C_{ij}) is associated with a set of requirements, notated $\{Ex_{ij}\}$, and with a set of functions/services/methods, notated $\{F_{ij}\}$. The software preliminary design document (SwPDD) must identify the basic units C_{ij} and describe the services and requirements that need to be carried out for each C_{ij}. The preliminary design folder must show that all the components identified at the level of the architecture of the software application (SwAD – Software Architecture Document) are properly taken into account, and that there is traceability between the requirements of the DAL and the requirements of the SwPDD.

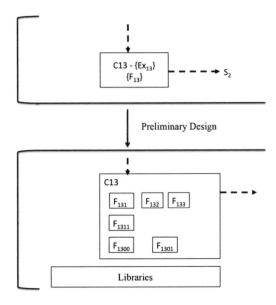

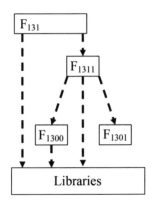

Figure C.14. *Example of detailed design*

Figure C.14 shows how the function F13 of the component C13 has been broken-down into three subfunctions: F131, F132 and F133. The subfunction F131 is based on an internal service F1311, and F131, F132 and F133 are based on two internal functions F1300 and F1301. We have also introduced the fact that all of the services of the component C13 may be based on one or more libraries. Figure C.15 shows the call graph of the function F131.

Figure C.15. *Example of call graph*

As can be seen in Table C.5, the standards advise that at least one SADT-type structured method is used to describe the architecture.

	SSIL0	SSIL1	SSIL2	SSIL3	SSIL4
Formal methods, including, for example, CCS, CSP, HOL, LOTOS, OBJ, temporal logic, VDM, Z and B	–	R	R	HR	HR
Semi-formal methods	R	R	R	HR	HR
Structured methodology, including, for example, JSD, MASCOT, SADT, SDL, SSADM and YOURDON	R	HR	HR	HR	HR

Table C.5. *EN 50128 [CEN 01a] – Table A.4*

The new version of the standard CENELEC EN 50128:2011 reinforces the need to create models for the design phase.

	SSIL0	SSIL1	SSIL2	SSIL3	SSIL4
Formal methods	–	R	R	HR	HR
Modeling	R	HR	HR	HR	HR
Structured methodology	R	HR	HR	HR	HR

Table C.6. *EN 50128:2011– Table A.4*

C.2.3.6. *Coding*

C.2.3.6.1. Presentation

The traditional development process for a software application is based on the use of a programming language such as ADA, C and/or C++. Even if these languages are of a certain level of abstraction in relation to the code executed on the final calculator, the writing of code lines is necessary for them.

It is not possible to analyze all the programming languages in existence for all domains, so in the rest of this section, we will analyze the developments that have occurred in the railway sector.

	SSIL[15]0	SSIL1	SSIL2	SSIL3	SSIL4
ADA	R	HR	HR	R	R
MODULA-2	R	HR	HR	R	R
PASCAL	R	HR	HR	R	R
C or C++ without restriction	R	–	–	NR	NR
Subset of C or C++	R	R	R	R	R

Table C.7. *CENELEC EN 50128:2001 – Table A.15*

C.2.3.6.2. The language Ada

The first railway applications in France were programmed, in the mid-1980s, with the language Modula 2. Since then, the language Ada 83 [ANS 83] has become the reference language for the development of critical applications [RIC 94]. As can be seen in Table C.7, in highly critical applications (SSIL3/SSIL4), the Ada language itself is only R (Recommended), a language subset must be put in place for the use of Ada to be HR.

The Ada language was designed at the instigation of the Department of Defense (USA D.O.D.) to bring together over 400 languages or dialects which were used in that organization in the 1970s.

```
with Ada.Text_IO;
procedure Hello is
begin Ada.Text_IO.Put_Line("Hello, world!");
end Hello;
```

Figure C.16. *Example of ADA code*

The Ada language is very widely used in the context of onboard aircraft software applications (Airbus), in space (the Ariane rocket) and in the railway sector. The main characteristic of these systems is that they require a correct execution.

---

15 The reference standard CENELEC [CEN 01, CEN 00, CEN 03] and the standard CEI/IEC 61508 [IEC 08] both introduce the notion of SIL for SIL, which may take four values, from 1 to 4. To find out more about the management of the SIL, we recommend Chapter 7 of [BOU 11]. The notion of SSIL concerns the allocation of a safety level to the software. The SSIL level concerns systematic failures.

The Ada 83 language has developed into a second major standard, Ada 95 [ISO 95], which is the first standardized object language. It contributes the possibility of constructed object-oriented models. The latest version is called Ada 2005.

As for the certification of Ada compilers, because there is a standard and a sufficiently refined semantics for Ada, it is possible to define a certification process for a compiler. This process has been implemented on various different compilers. It is a process which is based on a suite of tests called Ada Conformity Test Suite (ACATS). For more information on these tests, see the standard [ISO 99a]. To find out more about Ada, see [ADA 01].

At present, these new versions of the Ada language have not yet been adopted for use in onboard systems, due to the object-oriented aspect. However, the Ada 95 compilers, due to their effectiveness, are used for compilation. This is bearing in mind that we remain on a subset of the language that does not use the "object-oriented" traits.

The "object-oriented" aspect is not taken into account by standards which apply to critical applications: CENELEC EN 50128 [CEN 01], DO 178 [ARI 92], CEI/IEC 61508 [IEC 98], and ISO 26262 [ISO 09]).

To avoid this potential pitfall, ISO 15942 [ISO 00] defines a restriction on the constructions of Ada 95 and defines usage rules (programming style) which make it possible to create an application which is said to be certifiable.

The language SPARK Ada [BAR 03] is a programming language which is a subset of Ada. All the complex structures of Ada which are considered to be risky or which do not allow easy demonstration of safety are absent from SPARK Ada. A mechanism which allows the addition of annotations in the code has been included.

The SPARK Ada tools contain a compiler, but also an annotation verifier. It should also be noted that there is a free version of the SPARK Ada tools[16]. Chapter 3 of the third volume in this series presents the tool SPARK Ada and industrial examples of its application.

---

16 To find out more about AdaCore and free versions of tools such as GNAT and SPARK Ada, see the site www.libre.adacore.com.

C.2.3.6.3. The language C

The language C[17] [KER 88] is one of the first languages that was made available to developers in order to create complex applications for them. The main difficulty of the C language is in the partial definition of the language. This means that different compilers generate an executable with different behaviors. It has been subject to a standardization process by ANSI [ISO 99].

For the use of the C language [ISO 99], depending on the required safety level, the standard CENELEC EN 50128 [CEN 01a] recommends defining a subset of the language (see Table C.7), the execution of with can be controlled.

	SSIL0	SSIL1	SSIL2	SSIL3	SSIL4
ADA	R	HR	HR	HR	HR
MODULA-2	R	HR	HR	HR	HR
PASCAL	R	HR	HR	HR	HR
C or C++	R	R	R	R	R
C#	R	R	R	R	R
JAVA	R	R	R	R	R

Table C.8. *New CENELEC EN 50128 [CEN 11] – Table A.15 (partial)*

Table C.8 (taken from the new version of the standard CENELEC EN 50128 [CEN 11] shows that a judgment has been made that enough knowledge based on experience of use is available for the languages Ada, C and C++. This means that we do not need to explicitly mention the notion of subset of the language, because this is taken to have been already established.

Figure C.17 shows a piece of C code which can yield two different codes due to the anomaly (a) or (b) which applies here. This example clearly shows the weakness of C: little errors in programming are not detected at compilation. However, this type of error is detected if Ada is used for programming.

---

17 Even though Kerdigan and Ritchie [KER 88] do not describe the ANSI C language [ISO 99], their book is still one of the most useful on this topic.

The following C-Program
fragment:

```
if (TheSignal == clear)                                      if (TheSignal == clear) ;
{                                (a)                         {
        open_gates();         -------------→                       open_gates();
        Start_train();            fault                           Start_train();
}                                                           }


           (b)   ┆  fault


if (TheSignal = clear)
{
        open_gates();
        Start_train();
}
```

Figure C.17. *Example of a fault in C*

Some of the weaknesses of the C language can be avoided by putting programming rules in place. For example, in order to avoid an anomaly of the type if (a = cond) rather than if (a == cond), we can add a rule in the form "in the context of the comparison with a variable, this variable must be in the left-hand side of the expression".

As early as 1994, feedback based on experience of the use of C (see, for example, [HAT 94]), showed that it is possible to define a subset of C which can be used to create software applications which should be able to offer a high level of safety (SSIL3-SSIL4).

In fact, since the end of the 1990s, the standard MISRA-C [MIS 98, MIS 04] has become the most widely accepted standard for C. It was developed by the Motor Industry Software Reliability Association (MISRA[18]).

MISRA-C [MIS 04] specifies the programming rules (see the examples in Table C.9) which make it possible to avoid execution errors caused by poorly defined constructions, unforeseen behaviors (some structures of the

---

18 To find out more, see www.misra.org.uk/.

C language have not yet been completely defined), and misunderstandings between the people in charge of the software creation (legible code, code with implicit cast, etc.). Several tools allow automatic verification of the MISRA-C rules.

Id	Statutes[19]	Description
Rule 1.1	Required	All of the code must conform to the standard ISO 9899:1990 "Programming languages – C", amended and corrected by ISO/IEC9899/COR1: 1995, ISO/IEC/9899/AMD1: 1995 et ISO/IEC9899/COR2: 1996.
Rule 5.4	Required	Each tag is a unique identifier
Rule 14.1	Required	There must not be any dead code.
Rule 14.4	Required	No unconditional branching (goto) in the programs.
Rule 14.7	Required	A function must have a unique output point at the end of the function.
Rule 17.1	Required	Pointer arithmetic may only be used for pointers that address a table or a tabular element.
Rule 17.5	Advisory	An object declaration must not contain more than two levels of pointer indirection.

Table C.9. *Some rules[20] MISRA-C: 2004 [MIS 04]*

The standard MISRA-C [MIS 04] repeats some rules which are explicit in several standards (see for example, rules 14.4 and 14.7):

– Rule 14.4: In the standard EN 50128 – Table A.12 or the standard IEC 61508 – Table B.1;

– Rule 14.7: In the standard EN 50128 – Table A.20 or the standard IEC 61508 – Table B.9; etc.

MISRA-C [MIS 98] was created in 1998 and updated in 2004 [MIS 04], which shows that some feedback based on experience is available.

The main difficulty with the C language remains the choice of a compiler which has a sufficient amount of feedback based on experience available to it for the chosen target and required safety level. Given that there is no precise and comprehensive standard, there is no certification process

19 An MISRA rule can be "required" or "advisory". A "required" rule has to be applied by the developer, and an "advisory" rule cannot be ignored, even if it is not obligatory to apply it.
20 [MIS 04] introduces 122 "required" rules an 20 "advisory" rules.

currently available for C compilers, even if initiatives such as [LER 09] do exist[21].

C.2.3.6.4. Object-oriented language

As has already been stated above, the "object oriented" aspect is not taken into account by the standards CENELEC EN 50128 [CEN 01a], DO 178 [ARI 92], CEI/IEC 61508 [IEC 98], ISO 26262 [ISO 09], which apply to critical applications.

	SSIL0	SSIL1	SSIL2	SSIL3	SSIL4
No dynamic objects	–	R	R	HR	HR
No dynamic variables	–	R	R	HR	HR
Limited use of pointers	–	R	R	R	R

Table C.10. *CENELEC EN 50128:2011 – Table A.4*

The object oriented aspect is mentioned in standard CENELEC EN 50128 [CEN 01], but the constraints which apply to the languages do not allow us to develop critical applications (with SSIL3 and SSIL4) with this type of language (see Table C.10).

As can be seen in Tables C.7 and C.8, the language C++ [ISO 03] is mentioned as being one that could be used. However, some of the recommendations are not compatible with the use of an object-oriented language. This is shown in Table C.10.

C++ was developed in the 1980s, as an improvement on C. C++ introduces the notions of class, inheritance, virtual functions and overloading. It was standardized by the ISO in 1998 and in 2003 [ISO 03]

From 2000 onwards, much work has been undertaken with the aim of defining a framework within which C++ can be used [ISO 03] for the development of high-safety applications (SSIL3-SSIL4).

---

21 It should be noted that [LER 09] shows the verification work of a limited C compiler. However, even though the term "certification" is used, this does not refer to certification by an external organization. Certification does not only involve the demonstration that the compiler is correct, but should also apply to the process employed, to the elements that are produced (documents, sources, etc.) and to the tools that are used (Ocaml, Coq, and other free tools must be demonstrated to be safe).

Here we should mention the work:

– of the Object Oriented Technology in Aviation[22] (OOTIA), which has published several guides [OOT 04a, OOT 04b, OOT 04c, OOT 04d];

– of the JSF++ (Join Strike Fighter C++), which has published a guide [LM 05] tackling development in C++. This guide makes use of pre-existing studies, and in particular the standard MISRA-C [MIS 98];

– of MISRA, which developed the standard MISRA-C++:2008 [MIS 08].

The language C++ [ISO 03] is thus quite an old language. Approaches which identify the weak points of C++ and suggest rules appeared quite early on [SCO 98, SUT 05]. However, the definition of a framework for the use of C++ for high-safety applications is quite recent [OOT 04, LM 05, MIS 08]. This is why we find applications in C++ up to the safety level SSIL2.

	SSIL0	SSIL1	SSIL2	SSIL3	SSIL4
Classes should only have a single objective.	R	R	R	HR	HR
Inheritance used only if the derived class is a refinement of its base class.	R	HR	HR	HR	HR
Depth of inheritance is limited by coding standards	R	R	R	HR	HR
Neutralization of operations (methods) under close supervision	R	R	R	HR	HR
Multiple inheritance used only for interface classes	R	HR	HR	HR	HR
Inheritance based on unknown classes	–	–	–	NR	NR

Table C.11. *CENELEC EN 50128:2011 – Table A.23*

As a result of various influences (a reduction in the number of Ada and C programmers, for example), when CENELEC EN 50128 or DO 178 were updated, the opportunity was taken to attempt to introduce object-oriented languages.

The new version of the standard CENELEC EN 50128:2011 has increased the list of object-oriented languages which may be used to include JAVA and C#, as shown in Table C.8. However, this new version of the

22 To find out more, see http://www.faa.gov/aircraft/air_cert/design_approvals/air_software/oot/.

standard introduces several restrictions (limitations on inheritance). This can be seen in Table C.11.

The C version of the standard DO 178 should have a specific appendix which will aim to define the constraints relating to applying an object-oriented language for the creation of a critical application.

As is the case with C, the difficulty with C++ remains demonstrating that the compiler for the chosen target and the associated libraries comply with the safety objectives which were defined in the safety studies. There is currently no certification available for C++ compilers, so a justification based on experience and/or qualification needs to be established.

C.2.3.6.5. Advantages/disadvantages

The programming language used must aid the detection of anomalies. In order to achieve this, strong typing must be implemented, alongside modular, structured programming.

As can be seen in Table C.12, one of the main difficulties while using a language such as C or C++ is in demonstrating the "tested" character of the translator.

	SSIL0	SSIL1	SSIL2	SSIL3	SSIL4
Programming language	R	HR	HR	HR	HR
Strongly typed programming language	R	HR	HR	HR	HR
Subset of the language	–	–	–	HR	HR
Validated translator	R	HR	HR	HR	HR
Tried and tested translator	HR	HR	HR	HR	HR
Library of secured/verified modules and components	R	R	R	R	R

Table C.12. *CENELEC EN 50128:2001 – Table A.4*

The new version of the standard CENELEC EN 50128 [CEN 11] introduces the need to create a qualification folder for the tools used (the depth of the folder depends on the impact of a failure of the tool on the executable or on the V&V).

For the creation of a safety software application it is necessary to ensure that it is possible to follow the process through (Figure C.18) from the specification up to the design phase, if not the coding phase.

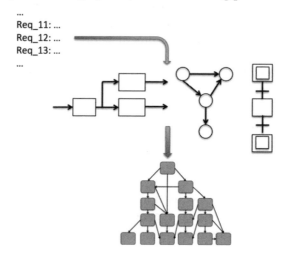

Figure C.18. *From requirements to code generation*

C.2.3.7. *Verification and validation*

The development of a certifiable software application is constrained by the requirements of the standards associated with each domain (Aeronautics [ARI 92], Automobile [ISO 09], Railway [CEN 01, CEN 11], Nuclear [IEC 06], and Generic [IEC 98]). These requirements from the applicable standards recommend implementing a "V cycle" type development process. This is based on the verification and validation techniques, which in turn are based on the creation of a test (TU, TI and TV).

	SSIL0	SSIL1	SSIL2	SSIL3	SSIL4
Formal proof	–	R	R	HR	HR
Static analysis	–	HR	HR	HR	HR
Analysis and dynamic tests	–	HR	HR	HR	HR
Metrics	–	R	R	R	R
Traceability	R	HR	HR	M	M
AEEL	–	R	R	HR	HR
Test coverage by the code	R	HR	HR	HR	HR
.....					

Table C.13. *CENELEC EN 50128:2011 – Table A.5*

The implementation of test activities faces several issues. These are:

– the high cost and highly demanding nature of test activities;

– the late detection of a fault;

– the difficulty of carrying out all the tests, etc.

This is why we need to implement other practices which should provide early and more widespread detection of faults in the software application.

One of the possible orientations consists of using formal methods (for example the B method [ABR 96], SCADE[23] [DOR 08], VDM [JON 90], Z [SPI 89], etc.) based on a model and a set of properties which make it possible to show that the software produced verifies the above-mentioned properties.

However, it can also be useful to explore the behavior of the program on the basis of more classical development languages (such as C) and to show that it verifies a certain number of properties. Demonstration is possible only through the addition of annotation describing the local conditions (pre-condition, post-condition, invariant) and through a propagation and/or proof mechanism. This analysis of the behaviors may be performed through the implementation of static code analysis techniques based on abstract interpretation [COU 00] and the proof of the program [HOA 69]. The first volume of this series [BOU 11a] is concerned with abstract interpretation.

It should be noted that one of the difficulties with implementing these techniques lies in the fact that they are not recognized in the standards currently applicable. Indeed, certain standards (see Tables C.1, C.3, etc. from the standard CENELEC EN 50128) recommend using formal methods but they do not mention the notion of abstract interpretation (or methods derived from it).

C.3. Modeling

This book, in all of its chapters, has shown the experience within the railway sector of the use of formal methods (Z, B method and SCADE) and

---

23 SCADE is distributed by ESTEREL-TECHNOLOGIES. See http://www.esterel-technologies.com.

formal techniques (proof, model-checking and abstract interpretation of programs), through an insight into several concrete and complex projects.

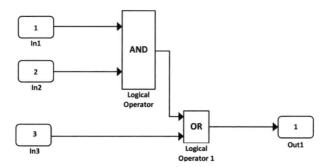

Figure C.19. *Example of model*

From all of these experiences a common thread emerges: modeling is an essential requirement for the different phases of creation of a software application. The main development made in recent years is in the recognition of the necessity to create models (see Table C.6, for example). Figure C.19 shows an example of a SIMULINK model.

C.4. Conclusion

In this book, we have presented various industrial uses of formal techniques and methods. We have seen that the main methods used are either structured methods such as SADT and SART or formal methods such as SCADE and the B method.

The B method [ABR 96] and SCADE 6 [DOR 08] have this in their favor: they offer an approach which goes from the specification of the software through to coding (while also traversing the phases of architecture and design). The Atelier B code generator is considered, for some versions, to be qualified by use, and the SCADE 6 code generator is certified.

We would expect the following two major changes over the next few years:

– The use of models at all levels and of all kinds. The difficulty with this point is that modeling tools have no semantics (UML notation, SIMULINK model and/or MATLAB, etc.).

– The qualification of tools used to create models, for the creation of verifications and for the generation of code.

Once again, I would like to take the opportunity to thank everyone who was involved in writing and publishing this book.

C.5. Glossary

ASA: Automata and Structured Analysis

ASIL: Automotive SIL

BDD: Binary Decision Diagram

CdCF: *Cahier des Charges Fonctionnel* – Functional Written Specification

CENELEC: *Comité Européen de Normalisation Électrotechnique* – European Committee for Electrotechnical Standardization

DAL: Design Assurance level

E/E/EP: *électrique/électronique / électronique programmable* – electric/electronic / programmable electronic

HR: Highly Recommended

IEC[24]: International Electrotechnical Commission

ISO[25]: International Organization for Standardization

METEOR: *METro Est Ouest Rapide* – Rapid East West Metro

MISRA[26]: Motor Industry Software Reliability Association

OMG[27]: Object Management Group

R: Recommended

SACEM: *Système d'Aide à la Conduite, à l'Exploitation et à la Maintenance* – Assisted Driving, Control and Maintenance System

SADT: Structured Analysis and Design Technic

24 See: http://www.iec.ch/.
25 See: http://www.iso.org/iso/home.htm.
26 See: www.misra.org.uk/.
27 See: http://www.omg.org/.

SAET: *Système d'Automatisation de l'Exploitation des Trains* – Train Automation and Operation System

SAO: *Spécification Assistée par Ordinateur* – Computer-Assisted Specification

SCADE: Safety Critical Application Development Environment

SIL: Safety Integrity Level

SSIL: Software SIL

UML: Unified Modeling Language

V&V: Verification and Validation

C.6. Bibliography

[ABR 96] ABRIAL J.R., *The B-Book.*, Cambridge University Press, 1996.

[ARA 97] ARAGO, "Applications des Méthodes Formelles au Logiciel", *Observatoire Français des Techniques Avancées* (OFTA), vol. 20, June 1997.

[ARI 92] ARINC, Software Considerations in Airborne Systems and Equipment Certification, no. ED12, DO 178B and l'EUROCAE, 1992.

[ARI 00] ARINC, Design Assurance Guidance for Airborne Electronic Hardware, no. ED80, ARINC and EUROCAE, 2000.

[AST 10] ASTRUC J.-M., BECKER N., "Toward the application of ISO 26262 for real-life embedded mechatronic systems", *ERTS2, Toulouse, France*, 19–21 May 2010.

[BAI 08] BAIER C., KATOEN J-P., *Principles of Model Checking*, The MIT Press, 2008.

[BAR 03] BARNES J., *High Integrity Software: The SPARK Approach to Safety and Security*, Addison-Wesley, 2003

[BEH 93] BEHM P., "Application d'une méthode formelle aux logiciels sécuritaires ferroviaires", in *Atelier Logiciel Temps Réel, 6ème Journées Internationales du Génie Logiciel*, 1993.

[BEN 03] BENVENISTE A., CASPI P., EDWARDS S.A., *et al.*, "The synchronous languages 12 years later", *Proceedings of the IEEE*, vol. 91, no. 1, January 2003.

[BOU 05] BOULANGER J.-L., BERKANI K., "UML et la certification d'application", *ICSSEA 2005*, Paris CNAM, 1–2 December 2005.

[BOU 06] BOULANGER J.-L., Expression et validation des propriétés de sécurité logique et physique pour les systèmes informatiques critiques, PhD Thesis, University of Technology of Compiègne, 2006.

[BOU 07a] BOULANGER J.-L., BON P., "BRAIL: d'UML à la méthode B pour modéliser un passage à niveau", *Revue RTS No. 95*, pp. 147–172, April–June 2007.

[BOU 07b] BOULANGER J.-L., "UML et les applications critiques", *Proceedings of Qualita'07, Tangier, Morocco*, pp. 739–745, 2007.

[BOU 08] BOULANGER J.-L., "RT3-TUCS : how to build a certifiable and safety critical railway application", *17th International Conference on Software Engineering and Data Engineering, SEDE-2008*, Los Angeles, CA, pp. 182–187, 30 June–2 July 2008.

[BOU 09a] BOULANGER J.-L., IDANI A., PHILIPPE L., "Linking paradigms in safety critical systems", *Revue ICSA*, September 2009.

[BOU 11a] BOULANGER J.-L., *Sécurisation des architectures informatiques industrielles*, Hermes-Lavoisier, 2011.

[BOU 11b] BOULANGER J.-L., *Utilisation industrielles des techniques formelles – interpretation abstraite*, Hermes-Lavoisier 2011.

[BOU 11c] BOULANGER J.-L. (ed.), *Static Analysis of Software*, ISTE, London, & John Wiley & Sons, New York, 2011.

[BOU 99] BOULANGER J.-L., DELEBARRE V., NATKIN S., "METEOR: validation de spécification par modèle formel", *Revue RTS*, vol. 63, pp. 47–62, April–June 1999.

[BOU 12a] BOULANGER J.-L. (ed.), *Industrial Use of the Formal Method*, ISTE, London, & John Wiley & Sons, New York, 2012.

[BOU 12b] BOULANGER J.-L. (ed.), *Formal Methods Industrial Use from Model to the Code*, ISTE, London, & John Wiley & Sons, New York, 2012.

[BOW 95] BOWEN J.P., HINCHEY M.G., *Applications of Formal Methods*, Prentice Hall, 1995.

[CEN 00] CENELEC, EN 50126, Applications Ferroviaires – spécification et démonstration de la fiabilité, de la disponibilité, de la maintenabilité et de la sécurité (FMDS), CENELEC, EN 50126, January 2000.

[CEN 01a] CENELEC, EN 50128, Railway applications – communications, signalling and processing systems – software for railway control and protection systems, CENELEC, EN 50128, May 2001.

[CEN 03] CENELEC, EN 50129, Norme européenne, applications ferroviaires: systèmes de signalisation, de télécommunications et de traitement systèmes électroniques de sécurité pour la signalisation, CENNELEC, EN 50129, 2003.

[CEN 10] CENELEC, EN 50159, Norme européenne, applications aux chemins de fer: systèmes de signalisation, de télécommunication et de traitement, CENELEC, EN 50159, 2010.

[CEN 11] CENELEC, EN 50128, Railway applications – communications, signalling and processing systems – software for railway control and protection systems, CENELEC, EN 50128, January 2011.

[COU 77] COUSOT P., COUSOT R., "Abstract interpretation: a unified lattice model for static analysis of programs by construction or approximation of fixpoints", *Conference Record of the 4th Annual ACM SIGPLAN-SIGACT Symposium on Principles of Programming Languages (POPL'77)*, Los Angeles, CA, pp. 238–252, January 1977.

[COU 00] COUSOT P., "Interprétation abstraite", *TSI*, vol. 19, nos. 1–3, 2000. Available at www.di.ens.fr/~cousot/COUSOTpapers/TSI00.shtml.

[DIJ 76] DIJKSTRA E.W., *A Discipline of Programming*, Prentice Hall, 1976.

[DOR 08] DORMOY F-X., "Scade 6 a model based solution for safety critical software development", in *Embedded Real-Time Systems Conference*, 2008.

[DUR 92] DURR E.; VAN KATWIJK J., "VDM++, a formal specification language for object-oriented designs", *CompEuro'92, Computer Systems and Software Engineering Proceedings*, pp. 214–219, 1992.

[HAD 06] HADDAD S., KORDON F., PETRUCCI L., *Méthodes formelles pour les systemes repartis et coopératifs*, Hermes, Lavoisier, 2006.

[HAL 91] HALBWACHS N., CASPI P., RAYMOND P., *et al.*, "The synchronous dataflow programming language Lustre", *Proceedings of the IEEE*, vol. 79, no. 9, pp. 1305–1320, September 1991.

[HAL 05] HALBWACHS N., "A synchronous language at work: the story of Lustre, *MEMOCODE '05"*, *Proceedings of the 2nd ACM/IEEE International Conference on Formal Methods and Models for Co-Design*, 2005.

[HAT 94] HATTON L., SAFER C., *Developing Software for High-integrity and Safety-critical Systems*, McGraw-Hill, 1994.

[HOA 69] HOARE C.A.R., "An axiomatic basis for computer programming", *Communications of the ACM*, vol. 12, no. 10, pp. 576–580, 583, 1969.

[HUL 05] HULL E., JACKSON K., DICK J., *Requirements Engineering*, Springer, 2005.

[IDA 06] IDANI A., B/UML : mise en relation de spécifications B et de descriptions UML pour l'aide à la validation externe de développements formels en B, PhD thesis, Joseph Fourier University, November 2006.

[IDA 07a] IDANI A., BOULANGER J.-L., PHILIPPE L., "A generic process and its tool support towards combining UML and B for safety critical systems", *CAINE 2007*, San Francisco, November 7–9, 2007.

[IDA 07b] IDANI A., OKASA OSSAMI D-D., BOULANGER J.-L., "Commandments of UML for safety", 2nd *International Conference on Software Engineering Advances IEEE CS*, Press, August 2007.

[IDA 09] IDANI A., BOULANGER J.-L., PHILIPPE L., "Linking paradigms in safety critical systems", *Revue ICSA*, September 2009.

[IEC 08] IEC, IEC 61508: Sécurité fonctionnelle des systèmes électriques électroniques programmables relatifs à la sécurité, International Standard, 2008.

[IEC 06] IEC, IEC 60880: Centrales nucléaires de puissance – instrumentation et contrôles-commande importants pour la sécurité. Aspects logiciels des systèmes programmés réalisant des fonctions de catégories A, International Standard, 2006.

[IEC 01] IEC, IEC 61513: Centrales nucléaires de puissance – instrumentation et contrôles-commande importants pour la sûreté. Prescription Générales pour les systèmes, International Standard, 2001.

[ISO 00] ISO. IEC 15942: Technologies de l'information – Langages de programmation –Guide pour l'emploi du langage de programmation Ada dans les systèmes de haute intégrité, 2000.

[ISA 05] ISA, Guide d'interprétation et d'application de la norme iec 61508 et des normes dérivées iec 61511 (isa s84.01) et iec 62061, April 2005.

[ISO 08] ISO 9001: 2008, Systèmes de management de la qualité – Exigences, 2008.

[ISO 09] ISO, ISO/CD-26262, Road vehicles – Functional safety – in press.

[ISO 95] ISO/IEC Information technology – Programming languages – Ada, ISO/IEC 8652, 1995.

[ISO 99a] ISO, ISO C standard 1999. Technical report, 1999. Available at http://www.open-std.org/jtc1/sc22/wg14/www/docs/n1124.pdf.

[ISO 99b] ISO/IEC 18009:1999, Information Technology – Programming Languages – Ada: Conformity Assessment of a Language Processor, 1999.

[KER 88] KERNIGHAN B.W., RITCHIE D.M., *The C Programming Language*, 2nd edition, Prentice Hall, 1988.

[JON 90] JONES C.B., *Systematic Software Development using VDM*, Prentice Hall International, 1990.

[LED 01] LEDANG, H., Des cas d'utilisation à une spécification B. AFADL'2001 : Approches Formelles dans l'Assistance au Développement de Logiciels, 2001.

[LER 09] LEROY X., "Formal verification of a realistic compiler", *Communication of ACM*, vol. 52, no. 7, pp. 107–115, July 2009.

[LIA 08] LIAIGRE D., "Impact de ISO 26262 sur l'état de l'art des concepts de sécurité automobiles actuels", *LambdaMu'08*, Avignon, France, October 2008.

[LIS 90] LISSANDRE M., *Maîtriser SADT*, Armand Collin, 1990.

[MAM 01] MAMMAR, A., LALEAU, R., An automatic generation of B-specification from well-defined uml notations for database applications, cnam, Paris, 2001.

[MAR 01] MARCANO, R., LÉVY, N., Transformation d'annotations ocl en expressions B. Journées AFADL, Approches formelles dans l'assistance au développement de logiciels 2001.

[MAR 04] MARCANO, R., COLIN, S., MARIANO, G., "A formal framework for uml modeling with timed constraint: Application to railway control system", *SVERTS, Specification, Validation of uml models for Real Time and Embedded Systems*, Lisbon, 2004

[MAT 98] MATRA, RATP, "Naissance d'un Métro. Sur la nouvelle ligne 14, les rames METEOR entrent en scène, PARIS découvre son premier métro automatique", Numéro 1076 -Hors-Série, *La vie du Rail & des transports*, October 1998.

[MON 00] MONIN J-F., *Introduction aux methodes formelles,* Hermès, 2000.

[MOR 90] MORGAN C., *Deriving Programs from Specifications*, Prentice Hall International, 1990.

[MOT 05] MOTET, G., Vérification de cohérence des modèles UML 2.0. Première journée thématique Modélisation de Systèmes avec UML, SysML et B-Système, Association française d'ingénierie système, Toulouse, France, 2005.

[OMG 06a] OMG, Unified modeling language: superstructure, version 2.1, OMG document ptc/06-01-02, January 2006.

[OMG 06b] OMG, Unified modeling language: infrastructure, version 2.0, OMG document formal/05-07-05, March 2006.

[OMG 07] OMG, Unified Modeling Language (UML), version 2.1.1, 2007.

[OKA 07] OKALAS OSSAMI D.D., MOTA J.-M., THIRY L., *et al.*, "A method to model guidelines for developing railway safety-critical systems with UML", *ICSOFT'07 – International Conference on Software and Data Technologies*, Barcelona, Spain, 2007.

[OOT 04a] OOTIA, Handbook for Object-Oriented Technology in Aviation (OOTiA), Handbook Overview, Revision 0, vol. 1, October 26, 2004.

[OOT 04b] OOTIA, Handbook for Object-Oriented Technology in Aviation (OOTiA), Considerations and Issues, Revision 0, vol. 2, October 26, 2004.

[RAS 08] RASSE A., BOULANGER J.-L., MARIANO G., *et al.*, "Approche orientée modèles pour une conception UML certifiée des systèmes logiciels critiques", *CIFA, Conférence Internationale Francophone d'Automatique*, Bucharest, Romania, November 2008.

[SMI 07] SMITH D.J., SIMPSON K.G.L., *Functional Safety, a Straightforward Guide to Applying IEC 61508 and Related Standards*, 2nd ed., Elsevier, 2007.

[SOM 07] SOMMERVILLE I., *Software Engineering*, 2007.

[SPI 89] SPIVEY J.M., *The Z notation- a Reference Manual*, Prentice Hall International, 1989.

[STA 94] The Standish Group, The chaos report, Technical report, 1994.

[STA 01] The Standish Group, Extreme chaos, Technical report, 2001.

Glossary

AADL	Architecture Analysis and Design Language
ACATS	Ada Conformity Assessment Test Suite
ACU	Alarm Control Unit
AFIS	French: Association française d'ingénierie système English: French Association of Systems Engineering
AMN	Abstract Machine Notation
ANSI	American National Standards Institute
APU	Auxiliary Power Unit
ASA	Automata and Structured Analysis
ASIL	Automotive SIL
ATO	Automatic Train Operation
ATP	Automatic Train Protection
ATS	Automatic Train Supervision
BDD	Binary decision diagram
CAN	Controller Area network
CAS	Computer-assisted specification
CBTC	Communication Based Train Control
CbyC	Correct by Construction
CCP	Centralized control point

CdCF	French: Cahier des Charges Fonctionnel
	English: Functional Requirements Specification
CENELEC[1]	European Committee for Electrotechnical Standardization
CMMI	Capability Maturity Model Integration
CPU	Central Processor Unit
DAL	Design Assurance level
DV	Design verifier
DoD	Department of Defense
DV	Design Verifier
E/E/PE	Electric/electronic/programmable electronic
EAL	Evaluation assurance level
ECU	Electronic Control Units
ERTMS	European Rail Traffic Management System
FADEC	Full Authority Digital Engine Control
FBD	Function Block Diagram
FC	Failure Condition
FDA	Food and Drug Administration
FMECA	Failure Mode and Effects Criticality Analysis
FT	Functional Testing
GPS	GNAT Programming Studio
GSL	Generalized Substitution Language
GUI	Graphical User Interface
HIL	Hardware In the Loop
HR	Highly recommended
IDE	Integrated development Environment

---

1 See www.cenelec.eu.

IEC[2]	International Electrotechnical Commission
iFACTS	interim Future Area Controls Tools Support
IL	Instruction List
IMAG	French: Institut de Mathématiques Appliquées de Grenoble English: Institute of Applied Mathematics of Grenoble
IPSN	French: Institut de Protection et de Sûreté Nucléaire English: Institute of Nuclear Protection and Safety
IRSN	French: Institut de Radioprotection et de Sûreté Nucléaire English: Radioprotection and Nuclear Safety Institute
ISO[3]	International Organization for Standardization
ISSE	International Symposium on Software Reliability Engineering
IT	Integration testing
KCG	Qualifiable Code Generator
KLOC	1000 LOC
LaBRI	French: Laboratoire Bordelais de Recherche en Informatique English: Bordeaux Laboratory for Computer Research
LD	Ladder Diagram
LOC	Lines of Code
MaTeLo	Markov Test Logic
MBD	Model-Based Design
MBT	Model-Based Testing
METEOR	METro Est Ouest Rapide, train operation system used by the Paris metro
MISRA[4]	Motor Industry Software Reliability Association
MMI	Man-Machine Interface
MPU	Main Processor Unit

2 See www.iec.ch.
3 See www.iso.org/iso/home.htm.
4 See www.misra.org.uk.

MTC	Model Test Coverage
MTTF	Mean Time To Failure
MU	Multiple Unit
NHMO	NATO HAWK Management Office
NR	Not recommended
NSA	US National Security Agency
NSE	No Safety Effect
OCR	Optical Character Recognition
OFP	Operational flight plan
OMG[5]	Object Management Group
OOTIA[6]	Object Oriented Technology in Aviation
OPRI	French: Office de protection contre les rayonnements ioisants English: Office of Ionising Radiation Protection
OS	Operating System
PADS	French: pilote automatique double sens English: two-way autopilot
PAI-NG	French: poste d'aiguillage informatisé de nouvelle génération English: next generation computerized signaling control
PO	Proof obligation
PTS	Problem of the traveling salesman
PWM	Pulse With Modulation
QTP	Quick Test Professional
R	Recommended
R&D	Research and Development
RAMS	Reliability, availability, mantainability, and safety
RAT	Ram Air Turbine

5 See www.omg.org.
6 See www.faa.gov/aircraft/air_cert/design_approvals/air_software/oot.

RATP[7]	French: Régie autonome des transports parisiens English: Autonomous Operator of Parisian Transports
RER	French: Réseau Express Régional English: Regional Express Train
RFT	Rational Functional Tester
RM	Requirement Management
ROM	Read Only Memory
SACEM	French: Système d'Aide à la Conduite, à l'Exploitation et à la Maintenance English: Assisted Driving, Control, and Maintenance System
SADT	Structured Analysis and Design Technic
SAET	French: Système d'Automatisation de l'Exploitation des Trains English: Automation System of Train Operations
SAO	French: Spécification assistée par ordinateur English: computer-aided design
SAS	Software Architecture & design
SAT	Satisfiability
SCADE	Safety Critical Application Development Environment
SFC	Sequential Function Chart
SHOLIS	Ship/Helicopter Operational Limits Instrumentation System
SIL	Safety Integrity Level
SIS	Safety Instrumented System
SMDS	Software Module Design Specification
SMTP	Software Module Test Plan
SOC	System On a Chip

---

7 See www.ratf.fr.

SPIN	French: Système de Protection Intégré Numérique English: Digital Integrated Protection System
SRS	Software Requirement Specification
SSIL	Software SIL
ST	Structured Text
SU	Single Unit
SUT	Software Unit Test
TCMS	Train Control Management System
TCO	French: Tableau de Contrôle Optique English: Visual Control Panel
TFTA	Terrain Following Terrain
TIS	Tokeneer ID station
TOR	French: Tout ou Rien English: hit-or-miss
UML	Unified Modeling Language
UT	Unit Testing
V&V	Verification and Validation
WCET	Worst Case Execution Time
WP	Weakest Precondition

List of Authors

Marc ANTONI
SNCF
Paris
France

Salimeh BEHNIA
RATP
Fontenay-sous-Bois
France

Karim BERKANI
Siemens SAS I MO
Chatillon
France

Jean-Louis BOULANGER
CERTIFER
Anzin
France

Nicolas BRETON
Prover Technology S.A.S.
Toulouse
France

Stéphane CALLET
SNCF – INFRA IG
La Plaine Saint Denis
France

Paul CASPI
(Formerly) Research Director at
CNRS and Member of Verimag
laboratory
Grenoble
France

Mathieu CLABAUT
Systerel
Aix-en-Provence
France

Philippe COUPOUX
Areva TA
Aix-en-Provence
France

Evguenia DMITRIEVA
RATP
Fontenay-sous-Bois
France

Saïd EL FASSI
SNCF – INFRA IG
La Plaine Saint Denis
France

Hervé FEDELER
SNCF – INFRA IG
La Plaine Saint Denis
France

Laurent FERIER
ERTMS Solutions
Brussels
Belgium

Sylvain FIORONI
RATP
Paris
France

Mélanie JACQUEL
Siemens SAS I MO
Chatillon
France

Daniel KÄSTNER
AbsInt GmbH
Saarbrucken
Germany

Damien LEDOUX
SNCF – INFRA IG
La Plaine Saint Denis
France

Eric LE LAY
Siemens SAS I MO
Chatillon
France

Pierre LESOILLE
Ansaldo STS
Les Ulis
France

Svitlana LUKICHEVA
ERTMS Solutions
Brussels
Belgium

Amel MAMMAR
LOR Telecom SudParis
Evry
France

Jean-Marc MOTA
Thales
Velizy
France

Thierry NAVARRO
RFF
Paris
France

Stanislas PINTE
ERTMS Solutions
Brussels
Belgium

Pascal RAYMOND
Verimag
Gières
France

Omar REZZOUG
Ansaldo STS
Les Ulis
France

Denis SABATIER
Clearsy
Aix-en-Provence
France

Christophe TREMBLIN
Ansaldo STS
Les Ulis
France

Index

I, L, M, O

P, R

S

T

W